TREASURY OF LITERATURE

OUT OF THIS WORLD

SENIOR AUTHORS

ROGER C. FARR
DOROTHY S. STRICKLAND

AUTHORS

RICHARD F. ABRAHAMSON
ELLEN BOOTH CHURCH
BARBARA BOWEN COULTER
BERNICE E. CULLINAN
MARGARET A. GALLEGO
W. DORSEY HAMMOND
JUDITH L. IRVIN
KAREN KUTIPER
DONNA M. OGLE
TIMOTHY SHANAHAN
PATRICIA SMITH
JUNKO YOKOTA
HALLIE KAY YOPP

SENIOR CONSULTANTS

ASA G. HILLIARD III
JUDY M. WALLIS

CONSULTANTS

ALONZO A. CRIM
ROLANDO R. HINOJOSA-SMITH
LEE BENNETT HOPKINS
ROBERT J. STERNBERG

HARCOURT BRACE & COMPANY

Orlando   Atlanta   Austin   Boston   San Francisco   Chicago   Dallas   New York
Toronto   London

Acknowledgments continue on page 622, which constitutes an extension of this copyright page.

Acknowledgments

For permission to reprint copyrighted material, grateful acknowledgment is made to the following sources:

Alurista: "address" from *Floricanto en Aztlán* by Alurista. Copyright © 1971 by Aztlán Publications, UCLA.

Atheneum Publishers, an imprint of Macmillan Publishing Company: From *From the Mixed-up Files of Mrs. Basil E. Frankweiler* by E. L. Konigsburg. Copyright © 1967 by E. L. Konigsburg. From *Beetles, Lightly Toasted* by Phyllis Reynolds Naylor. Text copyright © 1987 by Phyllis Reynolds Naylor.

Avon Books: Cover illustration from *S. O. R. Losers* by Avi. Copyright © 1984 by Avi Wortis.

Bradbury Press, an Affiliate of Macmillan, Inc.: Cover illustration from *Her Seven Brothers* by Paul Goble. Copyright © 1988 by Paul Goble. Cover photograph by Lyn Topinka from *Volcano: The Eruption and Healing of Mount St. Helens* by Patricia Lauber. Cover photograph courtesy of United States Department of the Interior, U. S. Geological Survey, David A. Johnston Cascades Volcano Observatory, Vancouver, Washington. From *Hatchet* by Gary Paulsen. Text copyright © 1987 by Gary Paulsen. Cover illustration by Pat Cummings from *Mariah Loves Rock* by Mildred Pitts Walter. Illustration copyright © 1988 by Pat Cummings.

Brandt & Brandt Literary Agents, Inc.: "Johnny Appleseed" from *A Book of Americans* by Stephen Vincent Benét and Rosemary Carr Benét. Text copyright 1933 by Rosemary and Stephen Vincent Benét; copyright renewed © 1961 by Rosemary Carr Benét.

Carolrhoda Books, Inc., Minneapolis, MN: Cover photograph from *Space Challenger: The Story of Guion Bluford* by Jim Haskins and Kathleen Benson. Cover photograph courtesy of the National Aeronautics and Space Administration. Cover illustration from *Song of the Chirimia* by Jane Anne Volkmer. Copyright © 1990 by Carolrhoda Books, Inc.

Cobblehill Books, an affiliate of Dutton Children's Books, a division of Penguin Books USA Inc.: Cover illustration by Elton C. Fax from *Take a Walk in Their Shoes* by Glennette Tilley Turner. Illustration copyright © 1989 by Elton C. Fax.

Crown Publishers, Inc.: Cover illustration by Mary Rayner from *Babe: The Gallant Pig* by Dick King-Smith. Illustration copyright © 1983 by Mary Rayner.

Delacorte Press, a division of Bantam Doubleday Dell Publishing Group, Inc.: Cover illustration by Richard Lauter from *The War with Grandpa* by Robert Kimmel Smith. Illustration copyright © 1984 by Richard Lauter.

Dell Books, a division of Bantam Doubleday Dell Publishing Group, Inc.: From *Tornado! Poems* by Arnold Adoff, illustrated by Ronald Himler. Text copyright © 1976, 1977 by Arnold Adoff; illustrations copyright © 1977 by Ronald Himler. Cover photograph by Franke Keating from *Walter Warthog* by Betty Leslie-Melville. Copyright © 1989 by Betty Leslie-Melville.

The Dille Family Trust: "Tiger Men of Mars" Buck Rogers® cartoon from *The Collected Works of Buck Rogers in the 25th Century.* © 1929–1967, 1969, 1993 by The Dille Family Trust. Color added to original illustrations with permission.

Dover Publications, Inc.: Text and illustrations from *The American Revolution: A Picture Sourcebook* by John Grafton. Copyright © 1975 by Dover Publications, Inc.

Farrar, Straus & Giroux, Inc.: From *A Wrinkle in Time* by Madeleine L'Engle. Text copyright © 1962 by Madeleine L'Engle Franklin; text copyright renewed © 1990 by Crosswicks, Ltd.; cover illustration copyright © 1979 by Leo and Diane Dillon. From *Whose Side Are You On?* by Emily Moore. Text copyright © 1988 by Emily Moore. Adapted from *The Green Book* by Jill Paton Walsh, cover illustration by Peter Catalanotto. Text copyright © 1982 by Jill Paton Walsh; cover illustration copyright © 1986 by Peter Catalanotto.

Harcourt Brace & Company: From *In for Winter, Out for Spring* by Arnold Adoff, illustrated by Jerry Pinkney. Text copyright © 1991 by Arnold Adoff; illustrations copyright © 1991 by Jerry Pinkney. Cover illustration by Paul Bacon from *Teammates* by Peter Golenbock. Illustration copyright © 1990 by Paul Bacon. From *The Bells of Christmas* by Virginia Hamilton, illustrated by Lambert Davis. Text copyright © 1989 by Virginia Hamilton; illustrations copyright © 1989 by Lambert Davis. From *The Riddle of Penncroft Farm* by Dorothea G. Jensen. Text copyright © 1989 by Dorothea G. Jensen. From *Monarchs* by Kathryn Lasky Knight, photographs by Christopher G. Knight. Text copyright © 1993 by Kathryn Lasky Knight; illustrations copyright © 1993 by Christopher G. Knight. From *Slabs of the Sunburnt West* by Carl Sandburg. Copyright 1922 by Harcourt Brace & Company; copyright renewed 1950 by Carl Sandburg. "La Bamba" from *Baseball in April and Other Stories* by Gary Soto. Text copyright © 1990 by Gary Soto. Originally published in *Fiction Network*. Illustrations from *Many Moons* by James Thurber, illustrated by Marc Simont. Illustrations copyright © 1990 by Marc Simont. Cover illustration by Louis Slobodkin from *Many Moons* by James Thurber. Copyright 1943 by James Thurber, renewed 1971 by Helen Thurber. *New Providence: A Changing Cityscape* by Renata von Tscharner, Ronald Lee Fleming and The Townscape Institute, illustrated by Denis Orloff and The Townscape Institute. Text copyright © 1987 by Renata von Tscharner, Ronald Lee Fleming and The Townscape Institute, Inc.; illustrations copyright © 1987 by The Townscape Institute, Inc. and Denis Orloff. From *Pride of Puerto Rico: The Life of Roberto Clemente* by Paul Robert Walker. Text copyright © 1988 by Harcourt Brace & Company. Pronunciation Key from *HBJ School Dictionary*, Third Edition. Text copyright © 1990 by Harcourt Brace & Company.

continued on page 622

TREASURY OF LITERATURE

Dear Reader,

When you think of your world, what do you see? Your neighborhood? Your school? The planet Earth? What do you think life is like for people beyond your world? The literature in this anthology will take you out of your own world and into the lives of people from all corners of the globe and all corners of the imagination.

Begin by taking a look at the strange world of America as seen through the eyes of Shirley Temple Wong, who has moved to America from China. Then play baseball with young Roberto Clemente in his world of the Barrio San Antón in Puerto Rico. Later, you can run through the fields of the flat, golden land of the Kansas prairie and then join Thomas Small as he explores a house that was once a station on the Underground Railroad.

You may find yourself wiping your brow as you experience—with Bird Wing and her mother—the hottest day on record in the Sonoran Desert. Keep reading, and you'll want to button your coat as you journey to the snowy world of a Vermont farm to help the Lacey family tap sugar maple trees. Finally, in a unit about flights, you will rocket into space with astronaut Sally Ride and have the chance to look back at the "sparkling blue oceans and bright orange deserts" of Earth.

Join us as we travel around the block, around the world, and beyond the solar system. As you visit these exciting places, keep your eyes open for people with experiences and feelings just like your own. Keep your mind open, too, and try to see each world through their eyes. We hope that these literary travels may return you to your world with new insights, interests, and delights.

Sincerely,
The Authors

UNIT ONE
cHALLenges / 16

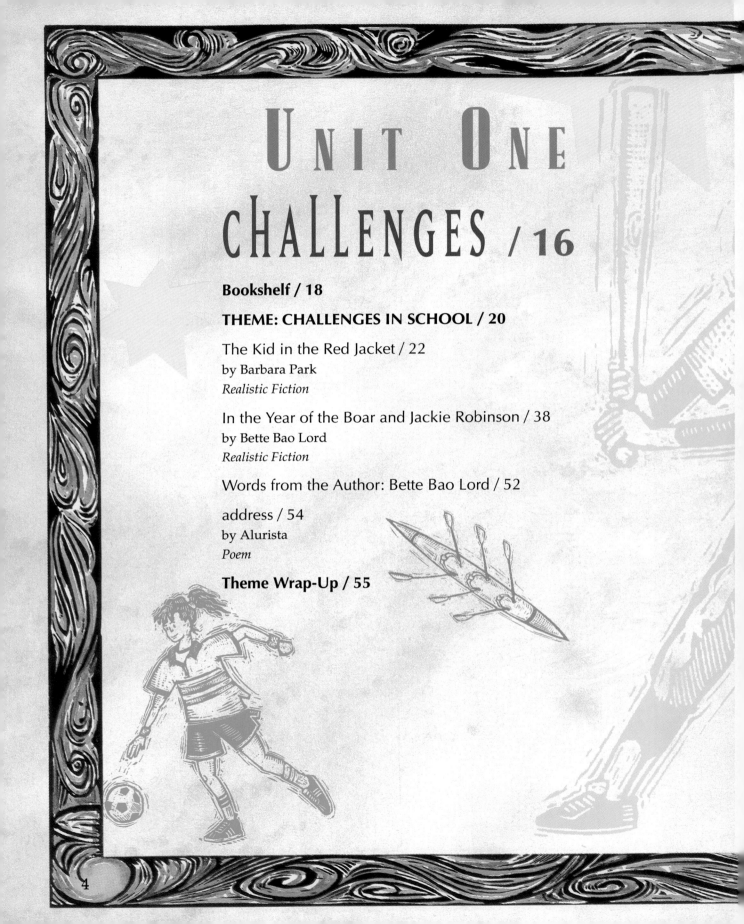

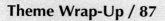

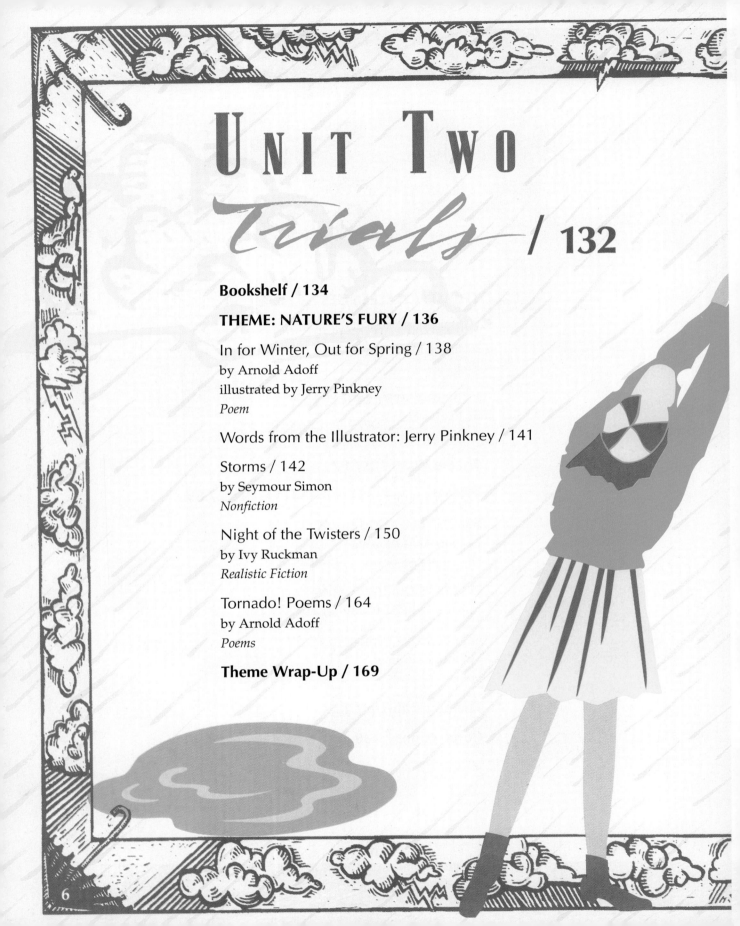

UNIT TWO
Trials / 132

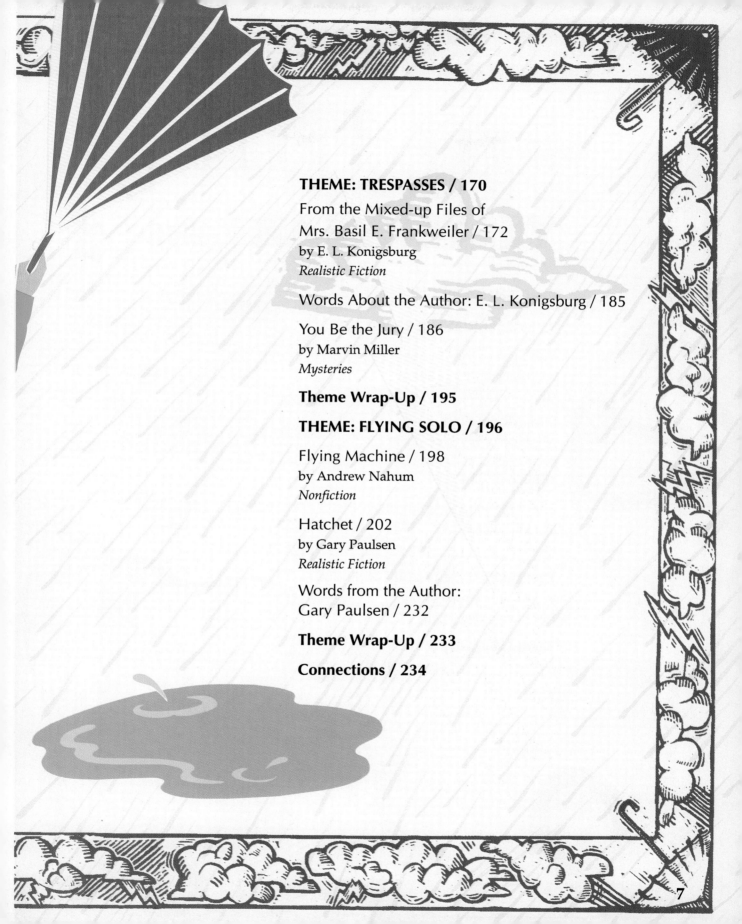

Unit Three

YESTERYEAR / 236

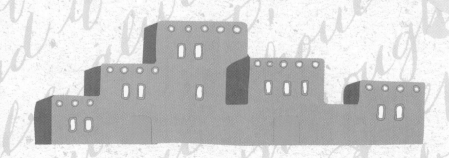

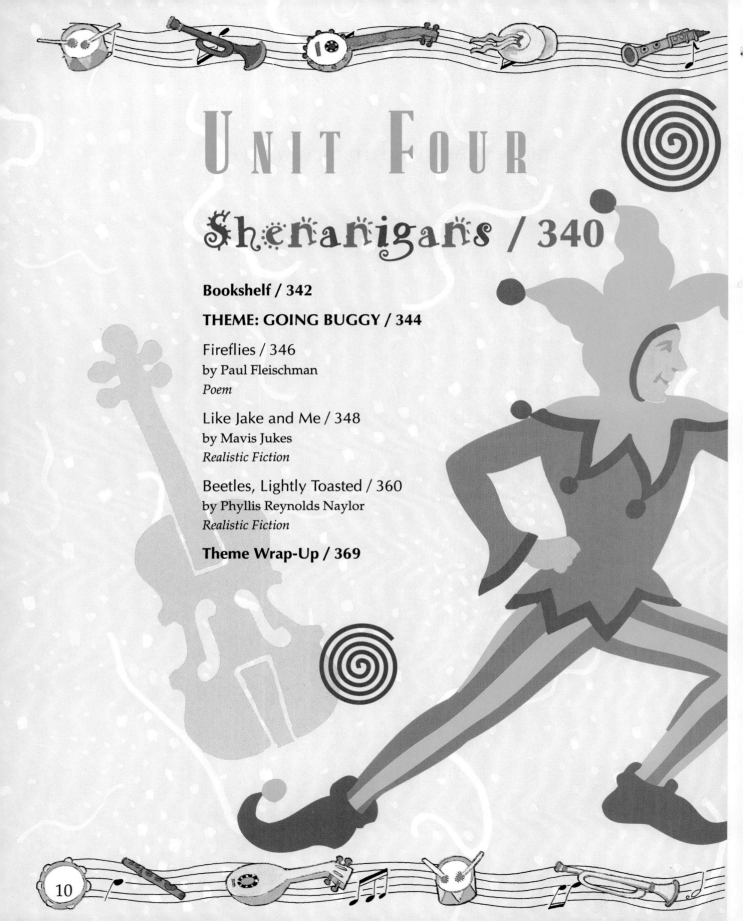

UNIT FOUR

Shenanigans / 340

UNIT FIVE

Lifelines / 424

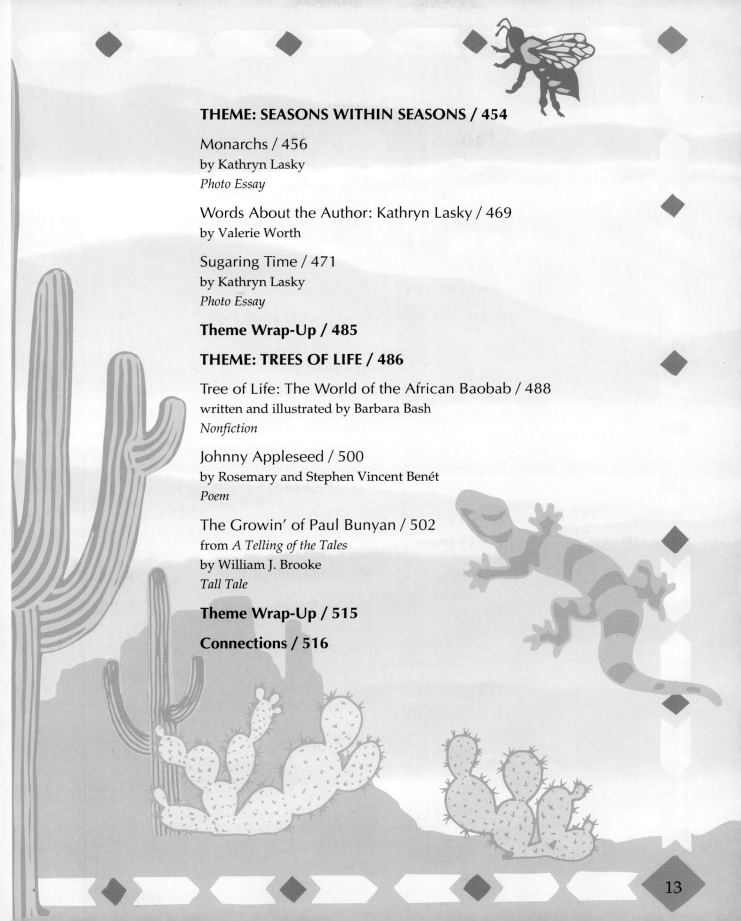

UNIT SIX

Flights / 518

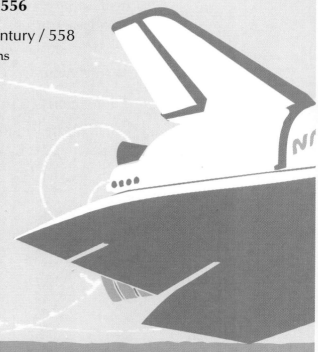

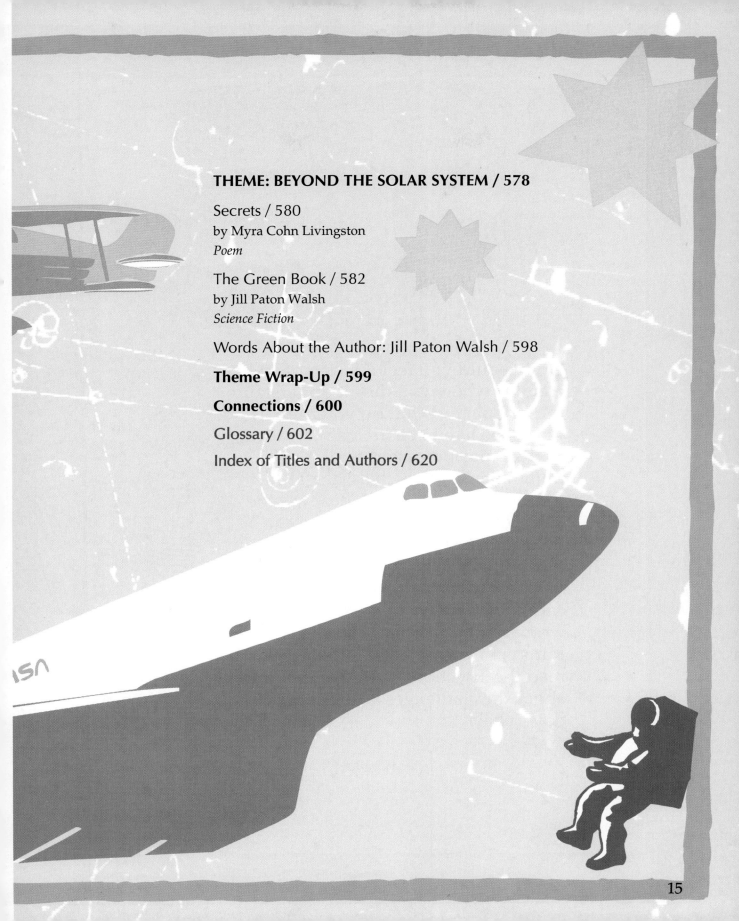

UNIT ONE

CHALLENGES

How would you feel if you moved to a country where you didn't understand the language? What do you think it would be like to be in Spain, Mexico, or the Philippines and to play an unfamiliar sport such as jai alai[hī´lī] for the very first time? These are the kinds of challenges that face some of the characters in this unit. Read about a young girl from China who finds herself in the middle of a strange game called *stickball*. Step into the shoes of a woman from Maine who travels to Kansas to join a new family. As you read the selections in this unit, think about the challenges you face from day to day.

THEMES

BOOKSHELF

THE KID IN THE RED JACKET

by Barbara Park

Howard and his family move to a new home 1,000 miles away, where everything is different and where no one knows his name.

Children's Choice, SLJ Best Books of the Year, Parents' Choice

Harcourt Brace Library Book

TEAMMATES

by Peter Golenbock

In 1947, a great social change came to American sports. Jackie Robinson became the first African American baseball player to be signed by a major league team—the Brooklyn Dodgers.

NCSS Notable Trade Book in the Field of Social Studies

Harcourt Brace Library Book

MARIAH LOVES ROCK

by Mildred Pitts Walter

Mariah loves rock music and is eagerly looking forward to the big concert. But the arrival of her half-sister might ruin everything.

Award-Winning Author

DEAR MR. HENSHAW

by Beverly Cleary

Leigh Botts writes a letter to his favorite author, Mr. Henshaw. When the famous author writes back, Leigh finds himself drawn into sharing more and more about his life.

Newbery Medal, SLJ Best Books of the Year

THE FACTS AND FICTIONS OF MINNA PRATT

by Patricia MacLachlan

As she plays her many roles in life—the daughter, the sister, the friend, the musician—Minna Pratt struggles to sort out the facts from the fictions.

ALA Notable Book

THEME

Challenges in School

➤➤➤

Have you ever been the "new kid" in a school? How did you deal with the many challenges that faced you? The following selections describe new kids who are determined to meet their challenges head-on.

CONTENTS

21

The Kid in the Red Jacket

When Howard's parents decide to move to Rosemont, Massachusetts, Howard is reluctant to go. He doesn't want to be a new kid, on a new block, in a new school.

As the school year begins, Howard is anxious to make friends. Unfortunately, the only person who befriends him is Molly Vera Thompson, his pesky six-year-old neighbor.

———

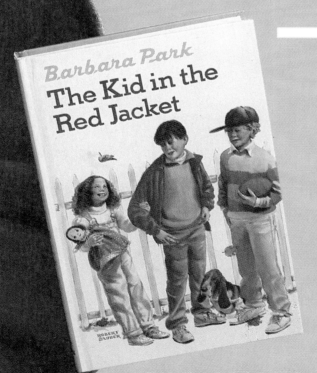

Barbara Park
The Kid in the
Red Jacket

BY BARBARA PARK

ILLUSTRATED BY MICHAEL GARLAND

On my second day at school, believe it or not, I walked there
with Molly Vera Thompson.

I was about halfway down the street when I first heard her.

"Hey! Hey, you! Howard Jeeper! Wait up! It's Molly Vera
Thompson!"

I knew this was going to happen. I just knew it. But even
though I had begged and begged for someone to drive me, both
Mom and Dad had refused.

"One reason we bought this house was so that you could
walk," my father informed me. "The exercise will be good for
you."

"Hey, I said! Hold it!" she shouted again.

Two girls walking on the other side of the street started to laugh.

What was I supposed to do? If I didn't stop, she'd just keep shouting her head off. And if I ran, she'd run after me. Finally, I bent down, pretended to tie my shoe, and waited for her to catch up. The way I figured it, walking to school with a first-grader is bad enough, but being chased by one to school is even worse.

"That was close!" she yelled, running up behind me. "For a minute there I didn't think you heard me or something!"

Why was she still shouting? I was standing right next to her.

"Shhh!" I ordered. "Not so loud."

Molly's voice got quieter as she looked around us. "Why? Is someone listening?"

"Only the whole world."

Molly just shrugged her shoulders and fell into step as I started walking again. We had only gone a couple of yards when she wrinkled up her nose and started to giggle.

"This is fun, isn't it, Howard Jeeper?"

I started walking a little faster.

"Hey! How's the weather up there?" she called, looking up at me. Then she started laughing like it was the funniest thing anyone had ever said.

I didn't answer. What was I supposed to say? Cloudy, with a chance of rain?

"Hey!" she persisted. "What's wrong? Cat got your tongue this morning?" Her legs hurried faster and faster, trying to keep up with me. "That's what my nonny says to me sometimes. 'Cat got your tongue, young lady?' she'll say. It means that you're being quiet."

"Yeah, right," I responded. I wasn't paying attention, of course. All I wanted to do was get to school before anyone saw the two of us together.

"Hey! Why are we walking so fast? Are we in a hurry?"

"Nope," I answered simply. "I always walk this fast. That's why you probably shouldn't walk with me. It's probably not good for a little kid like you."

"No. It's okay," she replied, huffing and puffing beside me. "I like to walk fast. It kind of bobs you up and down, doesn't it? See how fast my legs are going?"

Suddenly I started to run. I just didn't want to be with her anymore, that's all. I knew she couldn't catch me. And since I was getting closer to the playground, I couldn't risk the embarrassment of what she might do when we got there.

This time Molly didn't even try to keep up. As soon as I started to sprint, she stopped to watch me go.

I didn't feel guilty, either. Maybe I should have, but I didn't. Only a few more yards and I would be across the street, heading toward the gate of the playground. Alone. I was just about ready to breathe a sigh of relief when I heard it.

Still on the sidewalk where I left her, Molly had cupped her hands around her mouth like a megaphone and was shouting in the loudest voice I ever heard: *"Hey, Howard Jeeper! Why're you running? Do you have to go to the potty?"*

I wanted to die. I didn't stop running until I got inside the building. I know the whole playground must have heard. I tried not to look at anyone's face as I ran, but I could hear people laughing, so I'm sure they heard. They probably even heard on playgrounds in Russia.

The bell hadn't rung yet when I got to my classroom, but there were already three kids sitting down. One of them was the girl who sits in front of me. She didn't say hi or anything, but as it turned out, she was the first one in my class to talk to me. After I sat down, she turned around and asked if I would mind getting my big feet off the back of her chair.

"They're not big," I answered.

It wasn't much of a conversation, but when you're desperate, you appreciate almost anything.

At lunch, I sat by myself again. Only this time I picked a seat next to the wall so I could sort of blend in with the bricks.

As I started to eat I realized that a lot of the guys in my class were sitting at the next table. And since I was blending in with the wall pretty good, I could watch them without being too obvious. The guy I watched the most was this kid named Pete. I guess I was sort of scouting him out to see what kind of friend he'd make. Scouting is what they do in professional sports. It's a sporty word for spying.

I thought Pete might be someone I could like. I had noticed him on the soccer field. He was pretty athletic, you could tell that. And he wasn't a ball hog. Pete was the kid who had passed me the ball right before I took my big shot.

The good thing about Pete was that when my kick didn't go in, he didn't start swearing or anything. When you get to be my age, swearing comes pretty easily, especially when someone blows a chance for a goal.

The other kid that I couldn't help noticing was this guy named Ollie. You could tell that he was the wise-guy type. He was real loud, and he talked a lot, and practically everything that came out of his mouth was a joke. He seemed like the kind of kid that grownups can't stand but kids sort of admire. The thing is, to be a wise guy in class takes guts. Kids admire guts. Adults don't. It's that simple.

When Ollie sat down, he took one look inside his lunch bag and held his nose. Then, without saying a word, he stood up and threw the whole thing into the garbage can. Back at the table, someone asked him what his mother had packed.

Ollie was still holding his nose. "Something dead and a cookie."

It really cracked me up. Something dead and a cookie. I was sitting all by myself, but I laughed out loud.

After that some kid threw Ollie an orange to eat. Instead of peeling it, he put the whole thing right into his mouth. It must have hurt his mouth to stretch it that far, but that's the great thing about wise guys. When it comes to acting stupid, they know no limit.

Anyway, when Ollie was standing there with that orange in his mouth, even Pete cracked up. You could tell by the expression on his face that he thought Ollie was acting like an idiot, but he still thought it was funny. Even quiet guys like Pete enjoy a good idiot once in a while.

It might sound dumb, but after lunch I felt like I knew the guys in my class a little better. I guess that's why at recess I hung around the group that was getting ready to play soccer. I was sure somebody would pick me. Maybe they'd pick me last, but I'd get picked. It's sort of this unwritten rule every kid knows. If you're standing there to play, somebody's got to pick you, even if you stink.

Just like the day before, Pete and this kid Joe were the captains. Pete picked me before Joe did. I didn't get chosen first or anything; but I wasn't last, either. A kid with his ankle in a cast was last. Still, it felt good when Pete chose me. All of a sudden

he just looked over at me and said, "I'll take the kid in the red jacket."

It's funny. I used to think that being called something like that would really bother me. But the weird thing was, being

called the kid in the red jacket hardly bothered me at all. Let's face it, after a couple of days of not being called anything, almost any name sounds good.

My father gave me some advice. He's tried this kind of thing before, but it's never worked out too well. The trouble is, most of the time his advice is about stuff he doesn't know how to do. Like during basketball season, he'll tell me how to shoot a lay-up. Then he'll shoot a lay-up and miss. It's hard to take advice like that.

"Horn in," he said one night at dinner. I was explaining how much I hated to eat lunch alone, and he looked right up from his pork chop and said, "Horn in."

"Er, horn in?" I repeated, confused. I guess it must be one of those old-time expressions they don't use much anymore.

"Sure. Be a little pushy. Stand up for yourself," he went on. "You can't wait for the whole world to beat a path to your door."

"Beat a path to my door?" I asked again. Another old-time expression, I think.

"That means you can't wait for everyone else to come to you, son," he explained. "Sometimes you've just got to take the bull by the horns."

"Oh geez. Not more horns," I groaned.

"Bull by the horns," repeated Dad. "Haven't you ever heard that before? It means you've got to get right in there and take charge. If you don't want to eat alone, then sit right down at the lunch table with the rest of them. Just walk up there tomorrow, put your lunch on the table, and say, 'Mind if I join you, fellas?' That's all there is to it."

I didn't say anything, but kids just don't go around talking like that. If a kid came up to a bunch of guys eating lunch and said, "Mind if I join you, fellas?" the whole table would fall on the floor laughing.

Still, I knew what Dad was getting at. I think it's something all new kids learn sooner or later. Even if you're the shy type, you have to get a little bold if you want to make any friends. You have to say hi and talk to people, even if it makes you nervous. Sometimes you even have to sit down at a lunch table without being invited. You don't have to say, "Mind if I join you, fellas?" though. I'm almost positive of that.

I have to admit that the "horning in" part worked out pretty well. The next day at lunch I took a deep breath, sat down at the table with the other guys, and started eating. That was that. No one seemed to mind, really. They hardly even stared.

After that it got easier. Once kids have seen you at their table, it's not as hard to accept you the next time. Then pretty soon they figure that you must belong, or you wouldn't be sitting there every day.

I'm not saying that after horning in I automatically started to love Rosemont, Massachusetts. All I mean is, the more days that passed, the less I felt like an outsider. I guess you'd say stuff started feeling more familiar. Like at school, if a stranger had asked me for directions, I could have steered him to all the

water fountains and lavatories. For some reason, knowing your lavatories sort of gives you a feeling of belonging.

I guess moving to a new school is like anything else you hate. Even though you can't stand the thought of it, and you plan to hate it for the rest of your life, after you've been doing it for a while, you start getting used to it. And after you start getting used to it, you forget to hate it as much as you'd planned. I think it's called adjusting. I've given this some thought, and I've decided that adjusting is one of those things that you can't control that much. It's like learning to like girls. It sort of makes you nauseous to think about it, but you know it's going to happen.

Did you feel Howard's day at school was miserable, funny, or both? Explain your answer.

What is Howard's problem in the story?

At what point does Howard begin to feel accepted by his classmates? How do you know?

What do you think is the worst experience Howard has? Explain your choice.

WRITE Do you think Howard goes about making friends in the right way? Write a friendly letter to Howard that gives him your advice on making friends.

BY BETTE BAO LORD
ILLUSTRATED BY AMY HILL

IN THE YEAR OF THE BOAR AND JACKIE ROBINSON

LEAVING YOUR HOMELAND, CHINA, AND
BEGINNING SCHOOL IN THE UNITED STATES
CAN BE A VERY TRYING EXPERIENCE. IN
1947, SHIRLEY TEMPLE WONG MUST FACE
MANY CHALLENGES, INCLUDING A
CONFRONTATION WITH MABEL, THE
STRONGEST GIRL IN THE FIFTH GRADE. BUT
SHIRLEY KEEPS TRYING AND DISCOVERS A
NEW FRIEND, A LOVE OF BASEBALL, AND
THE EXCITEMENT AMERICANS WERE
EXPERIENCING OVER A VERY SPECIAL
TEAM—THE BROOKLYN DODGERS.

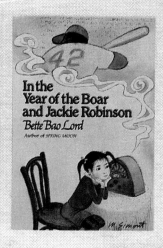

39

MAY

When the sides were chosen, Mabel pointed to a spot by the iron fence. "Shirley, you play right field. If a ball comes your way, catch it and throw it to me. I'll take care of the rest."

"Where you be?"

"I'm the pitcher."

"Picture?"

"Ah, forget it. Look for me, I'll be around."

Resisting the temptation to bow, Shirley headed for her spot.

Mabel's picture was something to see. First, hiding the ball, she gave the stick the evil eye. Then, twisting her torso and jiggling a leg, she whirled her arm around in a most impressive fashion, probably a ritual to shoo away any unfriendly spirits, before speeding the ball furiously into the hands of squatting Joseph.

Once in a great while, the stick got a lucky hit, but the Goddess Kwan Yin was again merciful and sent the ball nowhere near the fence.

After the change of sides, Mabel stood Shirley in place and told her she would be first to hit. Shirley would have preferred to study the problem some more, but was afraid to protest and lose face for her captain. Standing tall, with her feet together, stick on her shoulder, she waited bravely. Dog Breath had a ritual of his own to perform, but then, suddenly, the ball was coming her way. Her eyes squeezed shut.

"Ball one!" shouted the umpire.

"Good eye!" shouted Mabel.

Shirley sighed and started to leave, but was told to stay put.

Again the ball came. Again her eyes shut.

"Ball two!"

"Good eye!" shouted the team. "Two more of those and you're on."

Shirley grinned. How easy it was!

Sure enough, every time she shut her eyes, the ball went astray.

"Take your base," said the umpire.

Mabel came running over. "Stand on that red bookbag until someone hits the ball, then run like mad to touch the blue one. Got it?"

"I got."

Mabel then picked up the stick and with one try sent the ball flying. In no time, Shirley, despite her pigeon toes, had dashed to the blue bookbag. But something was wrong. Mabel was chasing her. "Go. Get going. Run."

Shirley, puzzled over which bookbag to run to next, took a chance and sped off. But Mabel was still chasing her. "Go home! Go home!"

Oh no! She had done the wrong thing. Now even her new friend was angry. "Go home," her teammates shouted. "Go home."

She was starting off the field when she saw Joseph waving. "Here! Over here!" And off she went for the green one. Just before she reached it, she stumbled, knocking over the opponent who stood in her way. He dropped the ball, and Shirley fell on top of the bag like a piece of ripe bean curd.

Her teammates shouted with happiness. Some helped her up. Others patted her back. Then they took up Mabel's chant.

"Hey, hey, you're just great
Jackie Robinson crossed the plate.
Hey, hey, you're a dream
Jackie Robinson's on our team."

Mabel's team won. The score was 10 to 2, and though the Chinese rookie never got on base again or caught even one ball, Shirley was confident that the next time . . . next time, she could. And yes, of course, naturally, stickball was now her favorite game.

On Saturday, Mabel taught her how to throw—overhand. How to catch—with her fingers. How to stand—feet two shoes apart. How to bat—on the level.

On Sunday, Mabel showed her how to propel herself on one skate at a time, then pulled her about on both until Shirley had learned how to go up and down the street without a fall.

Until that day, Shirley had never really understood something Grandfather had told her many times. "Things are not what they seem," he had said. "Good can be bad. Bad can be good. Sadness can be happiness. Joy, sorrow.

"Remember always the tale of Wispy Whiskers, who did not cry when his beautiful stallion ran away. All his neighbors, though, were certain that it was a sign from heaven of his ill fortune.

"Later, when the stallion returned leading a herd of wild horses, he did not boast of his newfound wealth. This time his neighbors were equally certain that it was a sign from heaven of his good fortune.

"Later still when his son broke his leg taming one of the mares, the wise man did not despair. Not even when behind his back all his neighbors spread the terrible rumor that anyone with even one droplet of Wispy Whiskers' blood was forever cursed by the gods.

"And in the end, only his son lived. For the sons of all the inconstant neighbors, being sound of body, were forced into military service and one by one perished in a futile battle for a greedy emperor."

How wise Grandfather was, Shirley thought. Only he could have foreseen how two black eyes would earn her the lasting friendship of the tallest, and the strongest, and the fastest girl in all of the fifth grade.

JUNE

六
月

It was almost summer. An eager sun outshone the neon sign atop the Squibb factory even before the first bell beckoned students to their homerooms. Now alongside the empty milk crates at Mr. P's, brown paper bags with collars neatly rolled boasted plump strawberries, crimson cherries and Chiquita bananas. The cloakroom stood empty. Gone, the sweaters, slickers and galoshes.

At the second bell, the fifth grade, as always, scrambled to their feet. As always, Tommy O'Brien giggled, and each girl checked her seat to see if she was his victim of the day. Susie Spencer, whose tardiness could set clocks, rushed in, her face long with excuses. Popping a last bubble, Maria Gonzales tucked her gum safely behind an ear while Joseph gave an extra stroke to his hair.

Finally Mrs. Rappaport cleared her throat, and the room was still. With hands over hearts, the class performed the ritual that ushered in another day at school.

Shirley's voice was lost in the chorus.

"I pledge a lesson to the frog of the United States of America, and to the wee puppet for witches' hands. One Asian, in the vestibule, with little tea and just rice for all."

"Class, be seated," said Mrs. Rappaport, looking around to see if anyone was absent.

No one was.

"Any questions on the homework?"

All hands remained on or below the desks, etched with initials, new with splinters, brown with age.

"In that case, any questions on any subject at all?"

Irvie's hand shot up. It was quickly pulled down by Maria, who hated even the sound of the word "spider." Spiders were all Irvie ever asked about, talked about, dreamed about. How many eyes do spiders have? Do spiders eat three meals a day? Where are spiders' ears located?

By now, everyone in the fifth grade knew that spiders come with no, six, or eight eyes. That spiders do not have to dine regularly and that some can thrive as long as two years without a bite. That spiders are earless.

Since Irvie was as scared of girls as Maria was of spiders, he sat on his hands, but just in case he changed his mind, Maria's hand went up.

"Yes, Maria?"

"Eh . . . eh, I had a question, but I forgot."

"Was it something we discussed yesterday?"

"Yeah, yeah, that's it."

"Something about air currents or cloud formation, perhaps?"

"Yeah. How come I see lightning before I hear thunder?"

"Does anyone recall the answer?"

Tommy jumped in. "That's easy. 'Cause your eyes are in front, and your ears are off to the side." To prove his point, he wiggled his ears, which framed his disarming smile like the handles of a fancy soup bowl.

Laughter was his reward.

"The correct answer, Maria," said Mrs. Rappaport, trying not to smile too, "is that light waves travel faster than sound waves."

Shirley raised her hand.

"Yes?"

"Who's the girl Jackie Robinson?"

Laughter returned. This time Shirley did not understand the joke. Was the girl very, very bad? So bad that her name should not be uttered in the presence of a grown-up?

Putting a finger to her lips, Mrs. Rappaport quieted the class. "Shirley, you ask an excellent question. A most appropriate one. . . ."

The Chinese blushed, wishing her teacher would stop praising her, or at least not in front of the others. Already, they called her "teacher's dog" or "apple shiner."

"Jackie Robinson," Mrs. Rappaport continued, "is a man, the first Negro to play baseball in the major leagues."

"What is a Negro, Mrs. Rappaport?"

"A Negro is someone who is born with dark skin."

"Like Mabel?"

"Like Mabel and Joey and . . ."

"Maria?"

"No, Maria is not a Negro."

"But Maria is dark. Darker than Joey."

"I see what you mean. Let me try again. A Negro is someone whose ancestors originally came from Africa and who has dark skin."

"Then why I'm called Jackie Robinson?"

Mrs. Rappaport looked mystified. "Who calls you Jackie Robinson?"

"Everybody."

"Then I'll have to ask them. Mabel?"

"'Cause she's pigeon-toed and stole home."

The teacher nodded. "Well, Shirley, it seems you are not only a good student, but a good baseball player."

There, she'd done it again! The kids would surely call her "a shiner of apples for teacher's dog" next. Shirley's unhappiness must have been obvious, because Mrs. Rappaport evidently felt the need to explain further.

"It is a compliment, Shirley. Jackie Robinson is a big hero, especially in Brooklyn, because he plays for the Dodgers."

"Who is dodgers?" Shirley asked.

That question, like a wayward torch in a roomful of firecrackers, sparked answers from everyone.

"De Bums!"

"The best in the history of baseball!"

"Kings of Ebbets Field!"

"They'll kill the Giants!"

"They'll murder the Yankees!"

"The swellest guys in the world!"

"America's favorites!"

"Winners!"

Mrs. Rappaport clapped her hands for order. The girls quieted down first, followed reluctantly by the boys. "That's better. Participation is welcome, but one at a time. Let's do talk about baseball!"

"Yay!" shouted the class.

"And let's combine it with civics too!"

The class did not welcome this proposal as eagerly, but Mrs. Rappaport went ahead anyway.

"Mabel, tell us why baseball is America's favorite pastime."

Pursing her lips in disgust at so ridiculous a question, Mabel answered. "'Cause it's a great game. Everybody plays it, loves it and follows the games on the radio and nabs every chance to go and see it."

"True," said Mrs. Rappaport, nodding. "But what is it about baseball that is ideally suited to Americans?"

Mabel turned around, looking for an answer from someone else, but to no avail. There was nothing to do but throw the question back. "Whatta ya mean by 'suits'?"

"I mean, is there something special about baseball that fits the special kind of people we are and the special kind of country America is?" Mrs. Rappaport tilted her head to one side, inviting a response. When none came, she sighed a sigh so fraught with disappointment that it sounded as if her heart were breaking.

No one wished to be a party to such a sad event, so everybody found some urgent business to attend to like scratching, slumping, sniffing, scribbling, squinting, sucking teeth or removing dirt from underneath a fingernail. Joseph cracked his knuckles.

The ticking of the big clock became so loud that President Washington and President Lincoln, who occupied the wall space to either side of it, exchanged a look of shared displeasure.

But within the frail, birdlike body of Mrs. Rappaport was the spirit of a dragon capable of tackling the heavens and earth. With a quick toss of her red hair, she proceeded to answer her own question with such feeling that no one who heard could be so unkind as to ever forget. Least of all Shirley.

"Baseball is not just another sport. America is not just another country. . . ."

If Shirley did not understand every word, she took its meaning to heart. Unlike Grandfather's stories which quieted the warring spirits within her with the softness of moonlight or the lyric timbre of a lone flute, Mrs. Rappaport's speech thrilled her like sunlight and trumpets.

"In our national pastime, each player is a member of a team, but when he comes to bat, he stands alone. One man. Many opportunities. For no matter how far behind, how late in the game, he, by himself, can make a difference. He can change what has been. He can make it a new ball game.

"In the life of our nation, each man is a citizen of the United States, but he has the right to pursue his own happiness. For no matter what his race, religion or creed, be he pauper or president, he has the right to speak his mind, to live as he wishes within the law, to elect our officials and stand for office, to excel. To make a difference. To change what has been. To make a better America.

"And so can you! And so must you!"

Shirley felt as if the walls of the classroom had vanished. In their stead was a frontier of doors to which she held the keys.

"This year, Jackie Robinson is at bat. He stands for himself, for Americans of every hue, for an America that honors fair play.

"Jackie Robinson is the grandson of a slave, the son of a sharecropper, raised in poverty by a lone mother who took in ironing and washing. But a woman determined to achieve a better life for her son. And she did. For despite hostility and injustice, Jackie Robinson went to college, excelled in all sports, served his country in war. And now, Jackie Robinson is at bat in the big leagues. Jackie Robinson is making a difference. Jackie Robinson has

changed what has been. And Jackie Robinson is making a better America.

"And so can you! And so must you!"

Suddenly Shirley understood why her father had brought her ten thousand miles to live among strangers. Here, she did not have to wait for gray hairs to be considered wise. Here, she could speak up, question even the conduct of the President. Here, Shirley Temple Wong was somebody. She felt as if she had the power of ten tigers, as if she had grown as tall as the Statue of Liberty.

If you were playing baseball, would you like to have Shirley Temple Wong on your team? Why or why not?

Many of our American words and customs seem strange to Shirley Temple Wong. What are some of the things that Shirley does not understand?

Why do you think Shirley is thrilled by Mrs. Rappaport's speech about America, baseball, and Jackie Robinson?

WRITE Imagine that you are about to spend a year in a school in China. Make a list of questions you would ask Shirley Temple Wong about her former country and its schools.

Words from the Author:

Bette Bao Lord

Some of the parts of the story you read are true and others are made up, but the feelings Shirley Temple Wong has were very much my own.

I was eight when I came to America, and I didn't know a word of the language. As I say in *In the Year of the Boar and Jackie Robinson*, the conversation in the classroom sounded "like gargling water" to me. But one of the miracles of childhood is that you can do things that adults cannot. One of them is that you can learn languages easily. I learned English in a surprisingly short time. And I made friends and I learned about baseball. It was a very special year.

At first, I tried writing about that special year of my life as autobiography. But it wasn't right. I sounded like an adult looking back, which of course, I was. I thought the story worked much better when a young girl was telling it.

Another problem in writing the book for an adult audience was that adults don't believe much in the American Dream anymore. But I think children know that the American Dream of success is still possible. I know it. It happened to me. I came from China, and when I grew up, I married the American ambassador to China. And look at Jackie Robinson. He's still a symbol of the American Dream. That's why people remember him.

Jackie ROBINSON
BROOKLYN DODGERS

I've written a number of adult books, but *In the Year of the Boar and Jackie Robinson* is the book I enjoyed writing more than any other. After you write an adult book, you get letters about it for perhaps a year after it comes out. But hardly a week goes by when I do not get a letter about *In the Year of the Boar and Jackie Robinson*. One of the biggest thrills about writing a children's book is getting those letters. It's like a dividend.

AWARD-WINNING
AUTHOR

I get many letters from immigrant children. It's interesting, because I think these children share the same experience I had. They are lonely in a new school, and it's difficult for them to make friends. They like the book because it's funny, but it speaks to them, too. One thing I'd like children to know is that their diversity enriches the group. I couldn't have written this book if I wasn't different! You can be different in any number of ways, but it is important to remember that those differences are what make you special.

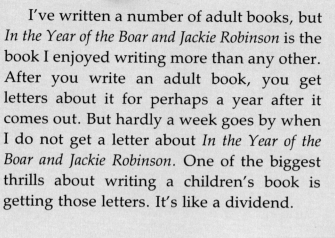

Dodgers

address

from *Floricanto en Aztlán*

by Alurista

illustrated by Buster O'Connor

address _____

occupation _____

age _____

marital status _____

   perdone . . .   *pardon . . .*
     yo me llamo pedro   *my name is pedro*

telephone _____

height _____

hobbies _____

previous employers _____

   perdone . . .   *pardon . . .*
     yo me llamo pedro   *my name is pedro*
     pedro ortega   *pedro ortega*

zip code _____

i.d. number _____

classification _____

rank _____
   perdone . . . mi padre era   *pardon . . . my father was*
     el señor ortega   *señor ortega*
     (a veces don josé)   *(sometimes called don josé)*

race _____

Challenges in School

How are the challenges faced by Howard and Shirley alike? How are Shirley's problems in school different from Howard's?

WRITER'S WORKSHOP

What experiences have you or a schoolmate had that were similar to those described in the selections? Make a list of these experiences. Then choose the one that is the most similar to Howard's or Shirley's, and write a short paragraph about it.

Writer's Choice

Howard and Shirley face similar challenges in school. What other challenges in school might a character face? Choose an idea and write about it. Share your idea in some way with your classmates.

T H E M E

Challenges at Home

Kids everywhere experience disappointments and setbacks. Whether it's a bad report card in New York or a lost baseball game in Puerto Rico, it's not easy to go home afterward.

C O N T E N T S

Whose Side Are You On?

by Emily Moore
illustrated by Thomas Hudson

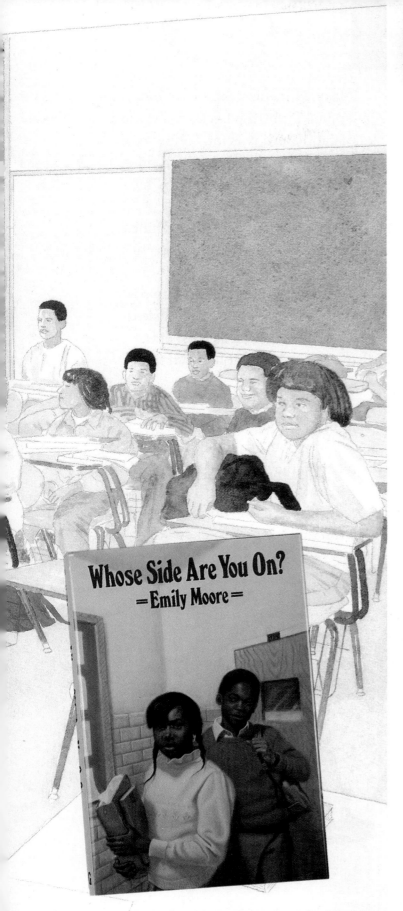

Report-Card Day

THE CLOCK on the teacher's desk ticked away. Just fifteen minutes to go, I thought, as I shifted nervously in my seat. If only it had snowed hard enough for school to be closed, I could be anywhere else but here, sitting at my desk, waiting for my report card. I dreaded getting it because my grades for the first marking period had been lousy compared to last year. It wasn't my fault, though. Everything was so much harder in sixth grade, especially my teacher, Mrs. Stone.

The sound of jangling bracelets brought me back to the chalky smell of the classroom and to the sight of Mrs. Stone standing over my desk.

"Barbra," she said in her metallic voice, "if you're ready to join us, I'll now distribute report cards."

I gulped so loud that the kids around me heard and started giggling. Mrs. Stone shook her head and walked to the front of the room, undoing the rubber band binding the packet of report cards. She began to give them out. I sat on my hands, anxiously waiting for her to get to me. Mrs. Stone had promised that in the second marking period she was going to be even tougher than before. I didn't see how. She was hard enough on me the first time.

Several kids whooped and hollered when they opened their cards. Mrs. Stone smiled at my best friend, Claudia. She patted my other friend, Patricia, on the shoulder and said, "Nice work."

Finally it was my turn. From across the room, Claudia made an A-okay sign at me. I drew in my breath and opened the card.

Tears came to my eyes when I saw my grades. I never dreamed it would be this bad! Not one *Excellent*. In my favorite subject, reading, Mrs. Hernandez only gave me a *Satisfactory*. But that wasn't the worst of it. In math, Mrs. Stone gave me a *U. Unsatisfactory* is the nice word for *failed*. I couldn't believe that Mrs. Stone had actually flunked me! I felt a thump on my back and jerked around.

Nosy Kim was grinning at me. Kids called her Gumdrop because she ate a lot of candy and was fat. "Show me your report card; I'll show you mine." She stuck her report card in my face.

I pushed her hand away.

"What did you get?" she whined.

"Leave me alone, Gumdrop," I snapped.

I stuffed my report card into my schoolbag before anyone else asked to see it, and as soon as Mrs. Stone dismissed us, I took off down the block.

"Barbra, wait up!" Claudia called, walking with Patricia.

"Got to go," I called back, as if I had to get someplace fast.

Since we all lived in the River View Co-ops, I went in the opposite direction. As I ran up the snow-slicked street, my

unzipped boots flapped against my
legs. I didn't stop to zip them or to
swipe at my tear-stained eyes. I kept
running until I passed Harlem Hospital.

Out of breath, I stopped and
opened the report card again. There it
was—a fat, red *U*—the first one of my
life. It made me feel like a real failure.
Nobody in my family had ever failed at
anything before. I couldn't bring this
report card home. What was I going
to do?

Then I saw the solution to my
problem: a trash can on the corner. The
sign tacked on it said *Throw It Here*. So I
did. A feeling of lightness came over
me. I twirled around, holding my
mouth open to catch snowflakes. The
next moment, a snowball splattered
against my back, making me stumble

forward. "Hey!" I said out loud, and
looked around to see who threw it.

The street was empty except for a
woman in a fur coat hurrying along
and two old men talking in the doorway
of Patricia's father's barbershop on
138th Street. I was sure it couldn't have
been any of them. Then I saw the real
culprit peer up from behind a car
and duck down again. I should
have known.

"What's the big idea, T.J.?" I yelled,
marching over to him.

T.J. was tall, with gleaming black
eyes and deep, round dimples. Even
though he was twelve, a year older
than me, he was in Mrs. Stone's class,
too. A long time ago, he told me that
the reason he got left back in first grade
was that his teacher said he wasn't

mature enough to be promoted to second grade. She was probably right.

He opened his mouth wide, pretending to be astonished.

"Don't play innocent," I said. "You hit me."

"You're hallucinating."

"Then why were you trying to hide?"

"I dropped some money." He poked around in the snow. I could tell it was all a big act by the way he kept looking up, grinning that sneaky, crooked grin of his.

"Why weren't you in school today?" I asked.

"Playing hookey," he said sarcastically.

"Seriously."

He took an Oreo cookie from his pocket, waved it in my face, then popped it into his mouth whole. I walked away, disgusted.

"If you must know," he said, tagging after me, "I was getting Pop's asthma medicine and the newspaper." Pop was his grandfather, whom he lived with.

"All day?" Not that I was complaining. In school I sat next to him. It was a relief that he was absent and could not pester me, for a change.

He hitched his old green

knapsack on his shoulders, ignoring my question. "Weren't we supposed to get report cards?" he asked.

"What of it?"

"How did you do?"

"Why does everybody care how I did?"

He made tsk-tsking noises. "That bad, huh?"

"Good as yours, I bet."

He stuck out his pinky and thumb. I knew better than to bet with T.J. He'd always done well in school. He never failed math or anything else. He may have been immature, but he certainly was smart.

Turning up my nose at him, I glanced away and saw a garbage truck stop in front

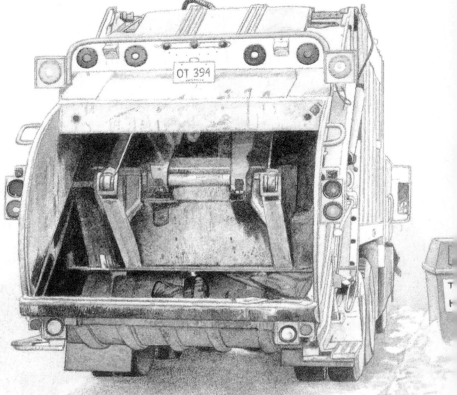

of the trash can. A second later, I realized the terrible thing that was about to happen. I had to get that report card back before it got dumped in the trash for real.

"Stop!" I shouted.

"I'm not doing anything," T.J. said.

I waved him off and ran back to the trash can. "Wait! Stop," I called again, but the sanitation man paid no attention. He picked up the can and shook the contents into the garbage chute in the back of the truck. He climbed inside the cab. The driver put the truck into gear. The truck rumbled away and disappeared around the corner. My report card was on its way to the city dump.

What had I been thinking? My mother was going to be mad enough about my grades, let alone a thrown-away report card. I stamped my foot and kicked over the can. Without a word, T.J. righted it and gave me a strange look.

"Well, I know you're dying to ask me what's wrong," I said.

"Here," he said, offering me a cookie from his pocket.

"No, thanks." I loved Oreos, but I didn't trust T.J. The last time he offered me ice cream, it was a Dixie cup filled with mushed-up peas and mashed potatoes. Besides, I was in no mood to eat now. I sniffed and crossed the street.

He kept walking with me toward my building on Harlem River Drive. The River View Co-ops took up the entire square block from 139th to 140th Streets and from Fifth Avenue to the Drive. The buildings were red and beige brick and were built around an inner courtyard. I lived in building number 4, which faced the Drive and the East River. From halfway down the block, I heard the swishing sound of traffic on the Drive.

"Come on, take it," he said gently. "It will make you feel better."

"Nothing could make me feel better." But the thought of the bittersweet chocolate and sweet, creamy center made my mouth water. "Okay," I finally said. "I'll take one, thanks."

I bit into the cookie and almost broke my tooth. It wasn't a cookie at all, but a wooden disk made to look like one. T.J. bent over, laughing.

I threw the fake cookie at him and pushed through the doors of my building's lobby. "I hate you, Anthony Jordan Brodie!" I'd never fall for one of his tricks again.

"Can't you take a joke?" he called after me.

I turned around, sticking my tongue between my teeth, and gave him a loud, sloppy raspberry.

Wishful Thinking

I DUMPED my books on the kitchen counter and poured myself a glass of ice-cold chocolate milk, hoping it would make the burning in my stomach go away. It only gave me the chills. I stomped upstairs to where our bedrooms were. All the second-floor apartments in our co-op were duplexes.

The door to my brother Billy's room was slightly opened. His baseball and swimming trophies were lined up on his dresser, along with his comb, brush, and cologne bottle in the shape of a steam engine. He loved trains. The Tyco train set he'd received for Christmas took up much of the floor space in his room. Pushing the door open a bit more, I could see the brown report-card envelope leaning up against his mirror like another trophy on display.

"Hey," he said, glancing up from his homework. "What took you so long to get home?"

"I bumped into you-know-who. The pain." I told him about T.J.'s trick and finished by saying, "I felt like smashing his face in the snow."

But Billy only laughed. "He likes you. That's what grownups always say about kids teasing each other."

"They sure don't know anything about me and T.J."

"If you say so," he said and reached into the old, battered briefcase that had belonged to Daddy when he was a reporter. Daddy died in a plane crash when we were four years old. Billy's named after him.

Billy pulled his protractor out of the briefcase. He carefully measured angles and made calculations. While I was still struggling with division and word problems, he was doing geometry. It was hard to believe we were twins. I was ten minutes older; he was ten times smarter—which is why I was in a regular sixth-grade class and he was in the IGC, the class for "intellectually gifted children."

I pushed aside his blue plaid curtains. The snow continued to fall

thick and steady. How I hoped school would be closed tomorrow. Hmmph! Fat chance! I let the curtain fall back in place and went to my own room. After changing into old jeans, I got out my schoolbooks and worked on my homework until it was almost dinnertime.

Passing Billy's room on my way downstairs, I heard his trains chugging around the track. He'd be in for it when Ma saw he hadn't set the table. But as I entered the kitchen, I was surprised to see the yellow dishes on top of the daisy-patterned place mats. Billy had even made a tossed salad. Everything was ready for when Ma came home in a few minutes. Now I would be the only one she'd scold.

When I heard her at the door, I figured it was best to try to be extra nice. I kissed her hello and helped her off with her coat. "Let me take that," I said, putting her briefcase on the lacquered parson's table next to the coat closet.

"My, what did I do to get such treatment?" She pulled off her hat and ran her fingers through her short, curly hair.

"You work hard, and I'm sure you're tired."

She sank down on the sofa. "It's worth it." I put her boots in the bathroom to dry.

She sat with her eyes closed for a while, then got up and stretched. "After I change, I'll warm up the leftover turkey and gravy for sandwiches."

However, instead of going up to her room, she went into Billy's. I tried to hear what they were saying, but the sound of the trains drowned out their voices. All I could do was hope for two things—that Ma did not notice the brown envelope on Billy's dresser and that Billy didn't start blabbing.

In any case, report cards would have to come up during supper, the time when important family discussions took place. Usually, the first thing Ma did once we sat down to eat was to ask us about school. But tonight she started telling us about what happened to her at Citibank, where she is a manager.

"I got a promotion," she said. "It's now official. I'm a vice president."

"Wow!" Billy said. "That's just one step from president."

"It's many steps away, but it's exactly what I've been working toward. It will mean longer hours," she said and then gave us some other details about her new job.

"More money, too?" Billy asked.

She nodded. "Most definitely."

"Oh, Ma, that reminds me," said Billy.

I knew he was going to tell her about his report card. In the excitement of Ma's news, I had almost forgotten about it. My heart began to beat faster.

"Ma," Billy said, "I'm going to need a new baseball uniform. My old one is too small."

"No problem," Ma said, then faced me. "Are you all right? You're awfully quiet."

"I'm okay."

"You sure?" Ma ate a forkful of salad.

"Uh-huh." I pushed my plate to one side. All this suspense took away my appetite.

"Is something wrong with your food?" Ma asked.

"Big lunch," I said, getting up from the table.

"It's almost eight hours since lunch."

"I ate a big snack, too."

Ma told me to sit back down. "You know the rules. We eat as a family."

Rules, rules. Rules made me sick. I propped my elbows on the table, but one look from Ma and I began to eat slowly. Billy was cutting his sandwich into bite-size pieces. Whoever heard of eating a sandwich with a knife and fork, even if it was a sloppy kind of sandwich? Everything about him was so proper and right. He would never even think of throwing away his report card, let alone do it.

"Can I go upstairs now?" I asked after forcing down the last of my turkey sandwich.

Ma put her hand to my forehead. "What's the matter?"

"Nothing."

"You call T.J. nothing?" asked Billy, with a silly grin on his face.

"He's such a pain," I said, grateful to him for changing the subject.

"The way you and T.J. needle each

other," Ma said, shaking her head. "It's . . ."

"It's his fault," I said, cutting her off. "Like when he put that caterpillar down my back."

"That was last summer at the Labor Day picnic," said Billy, as if a few months made a difference. "And the caterpillar was made from a pipe cleaner and yarn."

"It wiggled like it was real. I thought I was going to die."

"Oh, Barbra," Ma said. "You're exaggerating."

"He's always bugging me, Ma."

"You know what they say." Billy was hinting again about T.J. liking me. I kicked at him under the table.

Ma ate some more salad. "Anyway, I've invited his grandfather and him to dinner Friday night," Ma said.

I nearly jumped out of my seat. "Oh, no. You didn't!"

"Since T.J.'s mom is still away, it's probably lonely for him."

"So what," I blurted out.

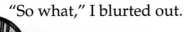

She gave me a look and I knew I had said the wrong thing. So I quickly said, "I don't feel well. May I be excused?"

Ma drew in a long sigh. "Go on."

I ran up the stairs to my room, shut the door, and got ready for bed, even though it was way before my bedtime. Going to sleep was the only way out of my mess. Why, oh, why did I ever do such a stupid thing?

I hugged Brown Bear close until he was all squished up. Ever since I was a little girl, hugging him always comforted me. Just as I was falling asleep, I heard the click of my door.

Ma came into the room. She stood over me a long time before sitting down on the edge of my bed. When she turned on the lamp, my eyelids fluttered, but I kept my eyes squeezed shut.

Brushing down my bangs, she said, "Whatever is bothering you, you can tell me. I'll understand."

I looked up at her. This is silly, I thought. Sooner or later she's going to find out. I should just get it over with. I sat up and finally told her about how Mrs. Stone failed me in math.

"No wonder you're upset. But, honey, I'll see that you get help. And I suspect it's not as bad as you make out."

"It's worse."

"Let me see." She held out her hand.

I looked down. "You can't."
Twisting the blanket around, I said,
"See, there was this trash can, and a
sign. Then T.J. hit me with a snowball
and I forgot all about it. Then a garbage
truck came . . ."

"Talk plainly, Barbra."

"I threw my report card in a trash
can."

She didn't say anything.

"I tried to get it back," I rushed on
to explain, "but I was too late. The
garbage man wouldn't listen."

She sat there, not saying a word.
The change in her expression was like
what happened to that Dr. Jekyll in the
movie. One minute he looked like a
regular person and then the next he
looked real mean and evil.

"How could you do such a thing?"
she said in such a quiet voice I got
goose pimples.

"It was an accident. I never meant
to throw it away. Not really. But that
T.J. . . ."

"Don't blame him," she said.

While my voice was high and
shrieky, Ma stayed quietly angry.

"In a way, it's kind of funny. Don't
you think?" I looked at her hopefully,
but she was not amused.

"It wasn't on purpose!" I said.

"Wasn't it?" she asked. "You never
think. And now look what's
happened."

"I was so upset. I never got a *U*
before, and I was scared of what you
would say."

"I'm disappointed in you." She got
up and left. I threw Brown Bear across
the room. He could stay in that corner
forever.

After a while, Ma came back into

the room with a long, white envelope in her hand. She laid it on the dresser. "Give this to Mrs. Stone. She'll write you another report card, and I'll talk to her tomorrow at the parent-teacher's conference." She saw Brown Bear in the corner, picked him up, and put him on my chair. "You're grounded. You won't have any special privileges."

"Forever?" I asked in a panic.

"Let me finish. No special privileges until your math grades improve."

That may as well be forever, I thought, as she closed the door behind her.

Good News and Bad

FIRST THING the next morning, Mrs. Stone asked for the signed report cards. I pulled Ma's letter halfway out of my schoolbag, but I didn't have the nerve to give it to her in front of the whole class.

"Do I have them all?" Mrs. Stone asked, waving the packet in the air. I wondered if she could feel that one was missing. Sometime later, in private, I would give the letter to her. Until then, I would just act normally. I put my homework on my desk to be collected, then went to sharpen my pencils. On my way back to my seat, I noticed the envelope on the floor. It must have fallen from my schoolbag. Before I could get it, Kim picked it up.

"Give me that," I said, reaching for the envelope.

She hid it behind her back, all the while chomping on something—a gooey gumdrop, no doubt. "Mrs. Stone's name is written on it."

"It's mine."

Kim bit her lip as if thinking it over. Meanwhile, Mrs. Stone noticed, "Kim, bring that up here."

If Mrs. Stone read that letter aloud, I'd be the laughingstock of the whole, entire sixth grade. And all because of Gumdrop. I'd fix her but good. I stuck my foot out into the aisle, but she stepped over it without tripping.

"Thank you, Kim." Mrs. Stone opened the envelope. "And empty your mouth," she added, not even looking at Kim as she spat a wad of gum into the trash can.

Over the rim of her glasses, Mrs. Stone glanced at me as she read the letter. After she finished, she called me to her desk.

"Why do you need another report card?" Mrs. Stone asked in a low voice.

"The letter explains it."

She showed me the letter. Ma requested another report card without any explanation. How could she have done this to me?

"Well, Barbra," Mrs. Stone said. Her head bobbed, showing her impatience.

"I lost it." I swallowed and went on. "I, um, reached into my schoolbag to give it to my mother, you know, um, to sign. And it wasn't there."

She gave me a long, hard look to see if I was really telling the truth. "Why wasn't it in your schoolbag?"

"It was, but . . ." I shifted uneasily, then asked, "Will you give me another one?"

The bell rang for first period and Mrs. Stone said, "Barbra will stay behind. The rest of you may go to your reading classes." She went into the hall to ask her reading group to wait outside.

On her way out with Patricia, Claudia whispered, "We'll wait by the water fountain."

The last person to leave was T.J. At the door, he brushed his two pointer fingers together and said, "Shame, shame."

I threw an ink eraser at him just as Mrs. Stone was coming back. She scolded me, then made me pick it up.

"Do you have a problem, Anthony?" Mrs. Stone asked T.J.

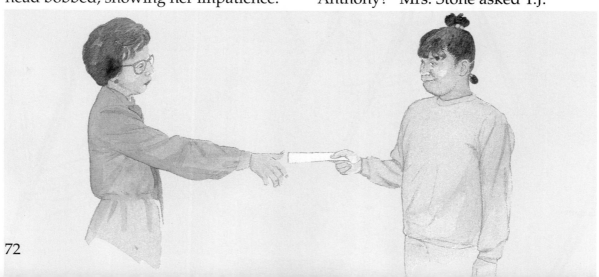

"No, ma'am," he said and hiked out of the room fast.

I knew what Mrs. Stone was going to say—I'd heard it before. "You have to try harder. Don't say you can't." And that's just what she said, adding, "Until you change your attitude, you will continue to do poorly. Losing your report card is an example of your carelessness." With that, she slipped Ma's letter into her roll book and told me to go to reading.

By now, only a few kids were straggling through the hall, but as they promised, Claudia and Patricia were waiting by the water fountain. I hurried to meet them.

Ever since this past summer when Patricia moved into River View, she, Claudia, and I were together every chance we got. Claudia was the lucky one, because she and Patricia both lived in building number 6 and went to the same ballet school. Ma refused to pay for lessons for me on account of what happened last year. She had signed me up and after three lessons I begged her to let me stop. Even though I promised not to drop out this time, she wouldn't let me take them.

"What did Mrs. Stone say?" asked Patricia.

"Gave me a lecture. I lost my report card," I said, trying to sound nonchalant.

"Anybody can lose a report card," said Claudia.

"True," I said and crossed my fingers, hoping they would never find out about the dumb thing I had done.

Would you like to read more about Barbra? Explain why or why not.

Why is what Barbra did with her report card so shocking to her mother?

How does Barbra feel about what she did? What does that tell you about her?

Do the characters in the story seem real to you? Explain why or why not.

WRITE Barbra's mother will be meeting Mrs. Stone at a parent-teacher conference. Write a brief dialogue of their discussion. Include what they think should be done to help Barbra improve her grades.

PRIDE OF PUERTO RICO

by Paul Robert Walker

illustrated by Harvey Chan

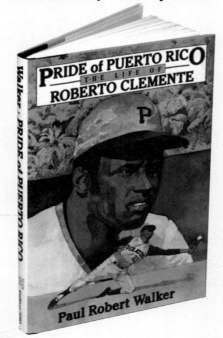

Roberto closed his eyes and imagined himself in the great stadium of San Juan. There were men on first and third with two outs in the bottom of the ninth. His team was losing, 5–3. A double would tie the game. A home run would win it. Everything depended on him.

He stepped confidently into the batter's box and took two level practice swings. Then he cocked his bat and waited for the pitch. The white ball came toward him in slow motion, its seams spinning clearly in the air. His bat was a blur as he whipped it around and smashed the ball over the left-field fence!

75

"Clemente!" cried a voice behind him. "Are you playing or dreaming?"

Roberto opened his eyes and stared seriously at the boy who had spoken. "I am playing," he said.

It was a warm tropical evening in Puerto Rico. Roberto Clemente was playing with a group of boys on a muddy field in Barrio San Antón. It was nothing at all like the great stadium in San Juan. There were bumps and puddles, and the outfield was full of trees. The bat in Roberto's hand was a thick stick cut from the branch of a guava tree. The bases were old coffee sacks. The ball was a tightly-knotted bunch of rags.

The boys on the field were black and white and many shades of brown. They shouted at each other in Spanish, encouraging their teammates, taunting their opponents. This was an important game between the boys of Barrio San Antón and a team from Barrio Martín Gonzalez.

Eight-year-old Roberto Clemente was one of the youngest and smallest boys on the field. As he stepped up to the plate, the thick guava stick felt very heavy in his hands. It was a great honor to represent his neighborhood. Everything depended on him.

Roberto looked over at third base, where his brother Andrés stood waiting to score. He looked at first, where another boy waited impatiently, hoping to score the tying run. Then he took a deep breath, cocked his bat and waited for the pitch.

The big ball of rags arched toward him as if it were in slow motion. Roberto swung with all his strength, but instead of sailing over the left-field fence, the ball rolled weakly back to the mound. The pitcher fielded it easily and threw to first for the final out. The game was over. San Antón had lost by a score of 5–3. Roberto stood alone while the other players left the field. He could feel tears trickling down his cheeks, and he was ashamed to cry in front of the older boys. His brother Andrés called to him from a few feet away. "Momen!" he said. "Are you going to stand there all night? It's time for supper."

"You go ahead," said Roberto. "I promised to meet Papá."

Roberto was the youngest of seven children in the Clemente family. There were six boys and one girl. When he was very little, Roberto's sister Rosa called him "Momen." It didn't mean anything in particular. It was just a made-up word, but to his family Roberto was always Momen.

Roberto's father, Don Melchor Clemente, worked as a foreman in the sugar fields. Sugar was the most important crop for the people of Puerto Rico. At harvest time, the sharp green stalks of sugar cane stood twice as tall as a man.

From sunrise to sunset, the men of Barrio San Antón worked in the fields, cutting the thick stalks of cane with their sharp machetes. It was hard, back-breaking work and the pay was $2.00 per week.

Don Clemente was more fortunate than most. As a foreman, he earned $4.00 a week. He and his wife, Doña Luisa, also ran a small store, selling meat and other goods to the workers on the sugar plantation. There was no money for luxuries like real baseballs and bats, but there was always plenty of rice and beans on the Clemente family table.

As he walked down the dirt road between the tall fields of sugar cane, Roberto thought about the game. He had failed his team. Perhaps he was not good enough to play with the bigger boys. Perhaps he would never be good enough. Once again he could feel the tears in his eyes.

It was late in the evening now, and the sun was setting over the fields like a great orange ball of fire. Roberto reached a high point in the road and looked for his father. Suddenly his tears disappeared. There, above the tall stalks of cane sat Don Melchor Clemente, riding slowly on his paso fino horse.

"Papá! Papá! Wait for me!"

Roberto ran through the cane field to where his father was riding. Don Melchor reached down and helped Roberto climb into the saddle behind him. Don Melchor Clemente was very proud to own such a fine horse. And Roberto was proud to ride behind his father.

"So, Momen," Don Melchor said as they rode home through the fields, "you come at last. I thought you had forgotten."

"Forgive me, Papá," said Roberto. "I was playing baseball."

"Ah, and how was the baseball?"

Roberto was silent for a moment. He thought again of the weak ground ball that ended the game for Barrio San Antón. He did not want to tell his father of his failure, but he knew that Don Melchor Clemente was a man who accepted only the truth. Finally he took a deep breath and spoke. "I lost the game, Papá."

"Hmmm," Don Melchor said. "That is very interesting." Father and son continued to ride in silence. Then Don Melchor spoke again. "I do not know very much about this baseball," he said. "But I know that there are many players on a team. I do not understand how one small boy can lose the game."

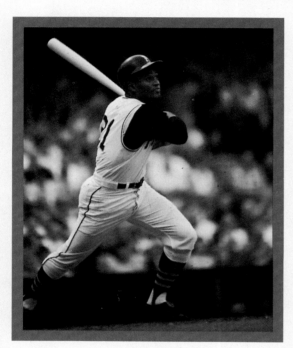

"But, Papá," said Roberto, "I was our only hope. I could have been the hero. Instead I was the last man out. The other boys will never ask me to play again."

They were out of the sugar fields now and riding slowly down the red dirt road that ran through Barrio San Antón. Don Melchor looked straight ahead as he guided his horse toward home. His words were strong and clear in the evening air.

"Momen," he said, "I want you to listen very carefully. Perhaps the other boys will ask you. Perhaps they will not. It does not matter. There are other boys and other teams, but there is only one life. I want you to be a good man. I want you to work hard. And I want you to be a serious person."

Don Melchor stopped his horse in the road. They were only a few hundred yards from home now, and Roberto could clearly see the wood and concrete house set in a grove of banana trees. Barrio San Antón lay on the outskirts of the city of Carolina. To the west was the capital city of San Juan. To the east were the cloud-covered slopes of El Yunque, barely visible in the fading light.

"Remember who you are," Don Melchor said. "Remember where you come from. You are a Jíbaro.[1] Like me. Like my

---

[1]hē′bä·rō′

father and my father's father. We are a proud people. Hundreds of years ago, we went into the mountains because we refused to serve the Spanish noblemen. In the wilderness, we learned to live off the land. Now, even in the sugar fields, we do not forget what we have learned."

"A man must be honest. He must work for what he needs. He must share with his brothers who have less. This is the way of the Jíbaro. This is the way of dignity." Don Melchor paused for a moment. It was dark now, and supper was waiting. "Do you understand, my son?" he asked.

Roberto thought carefully about his father's words. Then he spoke, quietly but firmly. "Yes, Papá," he said, "I understand."

Señora Cáceres stood behind her wooden desk and watched her new students file into the room. "You may choose your own seats," she said. "But remember, that will be your seat for the whole semester."

It was the first day of school at Vizcarrondo High School in the city of Carolina. Señora Cáceres waited until the students were settled into their seats before beginning the lesson.

"Today we will try to speak in English," she said. "I know that will be difficult for many of you, but the only way to improve is to practice. Now, who can tell me something about the history of Puerto Rico?"

Several students eagerly raised their hands. Señora Cáceres pointed to a pretty girl in the front row. The girl stood up and spoke in careful English.

"Puerto Rico was discovered by Christopher Columbus in 1493. He claim the island for Spain. The first governor was Ponce de León."

"Very good," said Señora Cáceres as the girl sat down. "And when did Puerto Rico become part of the United States?"

Again the same students raised their hands. Señora Cáceres looked around the room. Roberto sat in the very last row, his eyes staring at the floor. He had studied English in grammar school, but, like most of his friends, he could not really use it in conversation.

"Come now," said Señora Cáceres. "You'll never learn unless you try it."

Very slowly, Roberto raised his hand. Señora Cáceres smiled and pointed to the back row. As Roberto stood up and began to answer, he kept his eyes cast down toward the floor. His voice was very quiet. "We . . . become . . . United States . . . 1898," he said. "We are American . . . cities."

A few of the students laughed at Roberto's poor pronunciation. Señora Cáceres smiled and gently corrected him. "Citizens," she said. "We are American citizens."

As Roberto took his seat, Señora Cáceres noticed a group of girls giggling and whispering in the corner. "Yes," she thought, "this quiet one is a very handsome boy."

Señora Cáceres soon discovered that her quiet student was not so shy on the playing field. Roberto was the greatest athlete in the history of Vizcarrondo High School. He was not only a star on the baseball diamond; he also excelled in track and field. He could throw the javelin 190 feet, triple-jump 45 feet, and high-jump over 6 feet. Many people hoped that Roberto would represent Puerto Rico in the Olympic Games. But despite his success in track and field, baseball was his greatest love.

Bam! Bam! Bam!

Roberto stood on the muddy field in Barrio San Antón with a broomstick in his hands. Next to the boy on the pitcher's mound was a pile of old tin cans. Roberto and his friends were using the tin cans for batting practice. According to the rules,

Roberto could bat until the pitcher struck him out. The rest of the boys had to wait in the field for their turn at bat.

Frowning in frustration, the pitcher reached down and picked up another tin can. Once again, he leaned back and tried to fire the can past Roberto at the plate. Bam! Once again, Roberto smashed the can into the outfield.

"Hey, Clemente!" yelled a boy at shortstop. "Why don't you give someone else a chance to bat?"

Roberto smiled seriously and shrugged his shoulders. "First you must strike me out," he said.

On the dirt road that ran along the field, Señor Roberto Marín leaned against his car and watched carefully. It was almost sunset, but he could still see the boys clearly in the twilight. Señor Marín was a man who loved baseball, and he was always looking for new talent. As part of his job with the Sello Rojo Rice Company, he was putting together an all-star softball team to represent the company in a big tournament in San Juan.

"*Caramba!*" said Señor Marín. "That boy can really hit those cans." Señor Marín walked across the field to Roberto. "Who are you?" he asked.

"I am Momen," Roberto replied.

"Well, I tell you, Momen. Why don't you come over to Carolina and try out for my softball team? I think we can use you."

The next day, Roberto rode his bicycle into Carolina to try out for the softball team. It was only a couple of miles from Barrio San Antón to the field in Carolina, but it was a big step for Roberto. He was only a freshman in high school. Most of the other players were much older.

"Don't worry," said Señor Marín, "if you can hit a softball like you hit those tin cans, you'll do all right."

Roberto waited patiently at the plate as the softball sailed toward him in the evening air. At the last moment, he whipped his bat around and smashed the ball into right field. Señor Marín smiled with satisfaction. I know a ballplayer when I see one, he thought.

For the next two years, Roberto played for the Sello Rojo softball team. At first he played shortstop, but Señor Marín decided he would be better in the outfield. Soon Roberto was entertaining the softball fans of Carolina and San Juan with his brilliant catches and powerful arm.

Although softball was his favorite game, Roberto also played hardball in the San Juan youth league. When he was sixteen, he played for the Ferdinand Juncos team in the Puerto Rican amateur league. Here the competition was stronger, and the quality of the players was similar to the Class-A minors in the professional leagues of the United States.

One day, Don Melchor came to watch his son. Roberto's father knew very little about baseball. Unfortunately, Roberto's teammates did not hit very well that day. Time after time, they struck out or grounded weakly to the infielders. But when Roberto came to bat, he smashed a long home run and ran at full speed around the bases.

After the game, Roberto approached his father proudly. "Tell me, Papá," he said, "how did you like the baseball?"

"Very interesting," Don Melchor replied. "But no wonder you are always tired! The other players just run to first base and walk back to the dugout. You run all the way around the bases!"

Don Melchor smiled slightly at his own joke. Then his face turned serious. "Momen," he said, "perhaps someday you will run to the major leagues."

What did you like or not like about this story?

What special qualities did people see in young Roberto Clemente?

Roberto was very upset that he had lost the baseball game. Why didn't his father seem to care about that at all?

WRITE Don Melchor gave his son Roberto advice for leading a good life. What other positive qualities and values do you think are important for leading a good life? Write a paragraph describing these qualities and values and providing examples to support your opinion.

Challenges at Home

Think about Barbra's and Roberto's problems. How did talking to their parents help them resolve their problems?

WRITER'S WORKSHOP

Roberto Clemente became a famous baseball player. Imagine that Barbra becomes a famous mathematician and you are asked to write her biography. Write a paragraph or two about the lost report card incident and how it affected Barbra's career.

Writer's Choice

You have seen how the theme Challenges at Home can be expressed through a work of fiction and a work of nonfiction. Think about what this theme means to you. Then think of a way to express your thoughts, and share them with others.

THEME

Understanding Others

America is a huge country, with many types of land and people. Consider the seacoast of Maine and the prairie in Kansas. They are like two different worlds. What might happen when people from these two different worlds meet? Is it possible they could learn from each other?

CONTENTS

Sarah

PLAIN AND TALL

by
Patricia MacLachlan

Illustrations by
Gary Aagaard

Sarah, Plain and Tall
Patricia MacLachlan

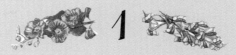

1

"Did Mama sing every day?" asked Caleb. "Every-single-day?" He sat close to the fire, his chin in his hand. It was dusk, and the dogs lay beside him on the warm hearthstones.

"Every-single-day," I told him for the second time this week. For the twentieth time this month. The hundredth time this year? And the past few years?

"And did Papa sing, too?"

"Yes. Papa sang, too. Don't get so close, Caleb. You'll heat up."

He pushed his chair back. It made a hollow scraping sound on the hearthstones, and the dogs stirred. Lottie, small and black, wagged her tail and lifted her head. Nick slept on.

I turned the bread dough over and over on the marble slab on the kitchen table.

"Well, Papa doesn't sing anymore," said Caleb very softly. A log broke apart and crackled in the fireplace. He looked up at me. "What did I look like when I was born?"

"You didn't have any clothes on," I told him.

"I know that," he said.

"You looked like this." I held the bread dough up in a round pale ball.

"I had hair," said Caleb seriously.

"Not enough to talk about," I said.

"And she named me Caleb," he went on, filling in the old familiar story.

"*I* would have named you Troublesome," I said, making Caleb smile.

"And Mama handed me to you in the yellow blanket and said . . ." He waited for me to finish the story. "And said . . .?"

I sighed. "And Mama said, 'Isn't he beautiful, Anna?'"

"And I was," Caleb finished.

Caleb thought the story was over, and I didn't tell him what I had really thought. He was homely and plain, and he had a terrible holler and a horrid smell. But these were not the worst of him. Mama died the next morning. That was the worst thing about Caleb.

"Isn't he beautiful, Anna?" Her last words to me. I had gone to bed thinking how wretched he looked. And I forgot to say good night.

I wiped my hands on my apron and went to the window. Outside, the prairie reached out and touched the places where the sky came down. Though winter was nearly over, there were patches of snow and ice everywhere. I looked at the long dirt road that crawled across the plains, remembering the morning that Mama had died, cruel and sunny. They had come for her in a wagon and taken her away to be buried. And then the cousins and aunts and uncles had come and tried to fill up the house. But they couldn't.

Slowly, one by one, they left. And then the days seemed long and dark like winter days, even though it wasn't winter. And Papa didn't sing.

Isn't he beautiful, Anna?

No, Mama.

It was hard to think of Caleb as beautiful. It took three whole days for me to love him, sitting in the chair by the fire, Papa washing up the supper dishes, Caleb's tiny hand brushing my cheek. And a smile. It was the smile, I know.

"Can you remember her songs?" asked Caleb. "Mama's songs?"

I turned from the window. "No. Only that she sang about flowers and birds. Sometimes about the moon at nighttime."

Caleb reached down and touched Lottie's head.

"Maybe," he said, his voice low, "if you remember the songs, then I might remember her, too."

My eyes widened and tears came. Then the door opened and wind blew in with Papa, and I went to stir the stew. Papa put his arms around me and put his nose in my hair.

"Nice soapy smell, that stew," he said.

I laughed. "That's my hair."

Caleb came over and threw his arms around Papa's neck and hung down as Papa swung him back and forth, and the dogs sat up.

"Cold in town," said Papa. "And Jack was feisty." Jack was Papa's horse that he'd raised from a colt. "Rascal," murmured Papa, smiling, because no matter what Jack did Papa loved him.

I spooned up the stew and lighted the oil lamp and we ate with the dogs crowding under the table, hoping for spills or handouts.

Papa might not have told us about Sarah that night if Caleb hadn't asked him the question. After the dishes were cleared and washed and Papa was filling the tin pail with ashes, Caleb spoke up. It wasn't a question, really.

"You don't sing anymore," he said. He said it harshly. Not because he meant to, but because he had been thinking of it for so long. "Why?" he asked more gently.

Slowly Papa straightened up. There was a long silence, and the dogs looked up, wondering at it.

"I've forgotten the old songs," said Papa quietly. He sat down. "But maybe there's a way to remember them." He looked up at us.

"How?" asked Caleb eagerly.

Papa leaned back in the chair. "I've placed an advertisement in the newspapers. For help."

"You mean a housekeeper?" I asked, surprised.

Caleb and I looked at each other and burst out laughing, remembering Hilly, our old housekeeper. She was round and slow and shuffling. She snored in a high whistle at night, like a teakettle, and let the fire go out.

"No," said Papa slowly. "Not a housekeeper." He paused. "A wife."

Caleb stared at Papa. "A wife? You mean a mother?"

Nick slid his face onto Papa's lap and Papa stroked his ears.

"That, too," said Papa. "Like Maggie."

Matthew, our neighbor to the south, had written to ask for a wife and mother for his children. And Maggie had come from Tennessee. Her hair was the color of turnips and she laughed.

Papa reached into his pocket and unfolded a letter written on white paper. "And I have received an answer." Papa read to us:

"Dear Mr. Jacob Witting,

"I am Sarah Wheaton from Maine as you will see from my letter. I am answering your advertisement. I have never been married, though I have been asked. I have lived with an older brother, William, who is about to be married. His wife-to-be is young and energetic.

"I have always loved to live by the sea, but at this time I feel a move is necessary. And the truth is, the sea is as far east as I can go. My choice, as you can see, is limited. This should not be taken as an insult. I am strong and I work hard and I am willing to travel. But I am not mild mannered. If you should still care to write, I would be interested in your children and about where you live. And you.

"Very truly yours,

"Sarah Elisabeth Wheaton

"P.S. Do you have opinions on cats? I have one."

No one spoke when Papa finished the letter. He kept looking at it in his hands, reading it over to himself. Finally I turned my head a bit to sneak a look at Caleb. He was smiling. I smiled, too.

"One thing," I said in the quiet of the room.

"What's that?" asked Papa, looking up.

I put my arm around Caleb.

"Ask her if she sings," I said.

2

Caleb and Papa and I wrote letters to Sarah, and before the ice and snow had melted from the fields, we all received answers. Mine came first.

Dear Anna,

Yes, I can braid hair and I can make stew and bake bread, though I prefer to build bookshelves and paint.

My favorite colors are the colors of the sea, blue and gray and green, depending on the weather. My brother William is a fisherman, and he tells me that when he is in the middle of a fogbound sea the water is a color for which there is no name. He catches flounder and sea bass and bluefish. Sometimes he sees whales. And birds, too, of course. I am enclosing a book of sea birds so you will see what William and I see every day.

Very truly yours,
Sarah Elisabeth Wheaton

Caleb read and read the letter so many times that the ink began to run and the folds tore. He read the book about sea birds over and over.

"Do you think she'll come?" asked Caleb. "And will she stay? What if she thinks we are loud and pesky?"

"You *are* loud and pesky," I told him. But I was worried, too. Sarah loved the sea, I could tell. Maybe she wouldn't leave there after all to come where there were fields and grass and sky and not much else.

"What if she comes and doesn't like our house?" Caleb asked. "I told her it was small. Maybe I shouldn't have told her it was small."

"Hush, Caleb. Hush."

Caleb's letter came soon after, with a picture of a cat drawn on the envelope.

Dear Caleb,

My cat's name is Seal because she is gray like the seals that swim offshore in Maine. She is glad that Lottie and Nick send their greetings. She likes dogs most of the time. She says their footprints are much larger than hers (which she is enclosing in return).

Your house sounds lovely, even though it is far out in the country with no close neighbors. My house is tall and the shingles are gray because of the salt from the sea. There are roses nearby.

Yes, I do like small rooms sometimes. Yes, I can keep a fire going at night. I do not know if I snore. Seal has never told me.

Very truly yours,
Sarah Elisabeth

"Did you really ask her about fires and snoring?" I asked, amazed.

"I wished to know," Caleb said.

He kept the letter with him, reading it in the barn and in the fields and by the cow pond. And always in bed at night.

One morning, early, Papa and Caleb and I were cleaning out the horse stalls and putting down new bedding. Papa stopped suddenly and leaned on his pitchfork.

"Sarah has said she will come for a month's time if we wish her to," he said, his voice loud in the dark barn. "To see how it is. Just to see."

Caleb stood by the stall door and folded his arms across his chest.

"I think," he began. Then, "I think," he said slowly, "that it would be good—to say yes," he finished in a rush.

Papa looked at me.

"I say yes," I told him, grinning.

"Yes," said Papa. "Then yes it is."

And the three of us, all smiling, went to work again.

The next day Papa went to town to mail his letter to Sarah. It was rainy for days, and the clouds followed. The house was cool and damp and quiet. Once I set four places at the table, then caught myself and put the extra plate away. Three lambs were born, one with a black face. And then Papa's letter came. It was very short.

Dear Jacob,

I will come by train. I will wear a yellow bonnet. I am plain and tall.

Sarah

"What's that?" asked Caleb excitedly, peering over Papa's shoulder. He pointed. "There, written at the bottom of the letter."

Papa read it to himself. Then he smiled, holding up the letter for us to see.

Tell them I sing was all it said.

3

Sarah came in the spring. She came through green grass fields that bloomed with Indian paintbrush, red and orange, and blue-eyed grass.

Papa got up early for the long day's trip to the train and back. He brushed his hair so slick and shiny that Caleb laughed. He wore a clean blue shirt, and a belt instead of suspenders.

He fed and watered the horses, talking to them as he hitched them up to the wagon. Old Bess, calm and kind; Jack, wild-eyed, reaching over to nip Bess on the neck.

"Clear day, Bess," said Papa, rubbing her nose.

"Settle down, Jack." He leaned his head on Jack.

And then Papa drove off along the dirt road to fetch Sarah. Papa's new wife. Maybe. Maybe our new mother.

Gophers ran back and forth across the road, stopping to stand up and watch the wagon. Far off in the field a woodchuck ate and listened. Ate and listened.

Caleb and I did our chores without talking. We shoveled out the stalls and laid down new hay. We fed the sheep. We swept and straightened and carried wood and water. And then our chores were done.

Caleb pulled on my shirt.

"Is my face clean?" he asked. "Can my face be *too* clean?" He looked alarmed.

"No, your face is clean but not too clean," I said.

Caleb slipped his hand into mine as we stood on the porch, watching the road. He was afraid.

"Will she be nice?" he asked. "Like Maggie?"

"Sarah will be nice," I told him.

"How far away is Maine?" he asked.

"You know how far. Far away, by the sea."

"Will Sarah bring some sea?" he asked.

"No, you cannot bring the sea."

The sheep ran in the field, and far off the cows moved slowly to the pond, like turtles.

"Will she like us?" asked Caleb very softly.

I watched a marsh hawk wheel down behind the barn.

He looked up at me.

"Of course she will like us." He answered his own question. "We are nice," he added, making me smile.

We waited and watched. I rocked on the porch and Caleb rolled a marble on the wood floor. Back and forth. Back and forth. The marble was blue.

We saw the dust from the wagon first, rising above the road, about the heads of Jack and Old Bess. Caleb climbed up onto the porch roof and shaded his eyes.

"A bonnet!" he cried. "I see a yellow bonnet!"

The dogs came out from under the porch, ears up, their eyes on the cloud of dust bringing Sarah. The wagon passed the fenced field, and the cows and sheep looked up, too. It rounded the windmill and the barn and the windbreak of Russian olive that Mama had planted long ago. Nick began to bark, then Lottie, and the wagon clattered into the yard and stopped by the steps.

"Hush," said Papa to the dogs.

And it was quiet.

Sarah stepped down from the wagon, a cloth bag in her hand. She reached up and took off her yellow bonnet, smoothing back her brown hair into a bun. She was plain and tall.

"Did you bring some sea?" cried Caleb beside me.

"Something from the sea," said Sarah smiling. "And me." She turned and lifted a black case from the wagon. "And Seal, too."

Carefully she opened the case, and Seal, gray with white feet, stepped out. Lottie lay down, her head on her paws, staring. Nick leaned down to sniff. Then he lay down, too.

"The cat will be good in the barn," said Papa. "For mice."

Sarah smiled. "She will be good in the house, too."

Sarah took Caleb's hand, then mine. Her hands were large and rough. She gave Caleb a shell—a moon snail, she called it—that was curled and smelled of salt.

"The gulls fly high and drop the shells on the rocks below," she told Caleb. "When the shell is broken, they eat what is inside."

"That is very smart," said Caleb.

"For you, Anna," said Sarah, "a sea stone."

And she gave me the smoothest and whitest stone I had ever seen.

"The sea washes over and over and around the stone, rolling it until it is round and perfect."

"That is very smart, too," said Caleb. He looked up at Sarah. "We do not have the sea here."

Sarah turned and looked out over the plains. "No," she said. "There is no sea here. But the land rolls a little like the sea."

My father did not see her look, but I did. And I knew that Caleb had seen it, too. Sarah was not smiling. Sarah was already lonely. In a month's time the preacher might come to marry Sarah and Papa. And a month was a long time. Time enough for her to change her mind and leave us.

Papa took Sarah's bags inside, where her room was ready with a quilt on the bed and blue flax dried in a vase on the night table.

Seal stretched and made a small cat sound. I watched her circle the dogs and sniff the air. Caleb came out and stood beside me.

"When will we sing?" he whispered.

I shook my head, turning the white stone over and over in my hand. I wished everything was as perfect as the stone. I wished that Papa and Caleb and I were perfect for Sarah. I wished we had a sea of our own.

4

The dogs loved Sarah first. Lottie slept beside her bed, curled in a soft circle, and Nick leaned his face on the covers in the morning, watching for the first sign that Sarah was awake.

No one knew where Seal slept. Seal was a roamer.

Sarah's collection of shells sat on the windowsill.

"A scallop," she told us, picking up the shells one by one, "a sea clam, an oyster, a razor clam. And a conch shell. If you put it to your ear you can hear the sea." She put it to Caleb's ear, then mine. Papa listened, too. Then Sarah listened once more, with a look so sad and far away that Caleb leaned against me.

"At least Sarah can hear the sea," he whispered.

Papa was quiet and shy with Sarah, and so was I. But Caleb talked to Sarah from morning until the light left the sky.

"Where are you going?" he asked. "To do what?"

"To pick flowers," said Sarah. "I'll hang some of them upside down and dry them so they'll keep some color. And we can have flowers all winter long."

"I'll come, too!" cried Caleb. "Sarah said winter," he said to me. "That means Sarah will stay."

Together we picked flowers, paintbrush and clover and prairie violets. There were buds on the wild roses that climbed up the paddock fence.

"The roses will bloom in early summer," I told Sarah. I looked to see if she knew what I was thinking. Summer was when the wedding would be. *Might* be. Sarah and Papa's wedding.

We hung the flowers from the ceiling in little bunches. "I've never seen this before," said Sarah. "What is it called?"

"Bride's bonnet," I told her.

Caleb smiled at the name.

"We don't have this by the sea," she said. "We have seaside goldenrod and wild asters and woolly ragwort."

"Woolly ragwort!" Caleb whooped. He made up a song.

"Woolly ragwort all around,
Woolly ragwort on the ground.
Woolly ragwort grows and grows,
Woolly ragwort in your nose."

Sarah and Papa laughed, and the dogs lifted their heads and thumped their tails against the wood floor. Seal sat on a kitchen chair and watched us with yellow eyes.

We ate Sarah's stew, the late light coming through the windows. Papa had baked bread that was still warm from the fire.

"The stew is fine," said Papa.

"Ayuh." Sarah nodded. "The bread, too."

"What does 'ayuh' mean?" asked Caleb.

"In Maine it means yes," said Sarah. "Do you want more stew?"

"Ayuh," said Caleb.

"Ayuh," echoed my father.

After dinner Sarah told us about William. "He has a gray-and-white boat named *Kittiwake*." She looked out the window. "That is a small gull found way off the shore where William

fishes. There are three aunts who live near us. They wear silk dresses and no shoes. You would love them."

"Ayuh," said Caleb.

"Does your brother look like you?" I asked.

"Yes," said Sarah. "He is plain and tall."

At dusk Sarah cut Caleb's hair on the front steps, gathering his curls and scattering them on the fence and ground. Seal batted some hair around the porch as the dogs watched.

"Why?" asked Caleb.

"For the birds," said Sarah. "They will use it for their nests. Later we can look for nests of curls."

"Sarah said 'later,'" Caleb whispered to me as we spread his hair about. "Sarah will stay."

Sarah cut Papa's hair, too. No one else saw, but I found him behind the barn, tossing the pieces of hair into the wind for the birds.

Sarah brushed my hair and tied it up in back with a rose velvet ribbon she had brought from Maine. She brushed hers long and free and tied it back, too, and we stood side by side looking into the mirror. I looked taller, like Sarah, and fair and thin. And with my hair pulled back I looked a little like her daughter. Sarah's daughter.

And then it was time for singing.

Sarah sang us a song we had never heard before as we sat on the porch, insects buzzing in the dark, the rustle of cows in the grasses. It was called "Sumer Is Icumen in," and she taught it to us all, even Papa, who sang as if he had never stopped singing.

"Sumer is icumen in,
Lhude sing cuccu!"

"What is sumer?" asked Caleb. He said it "soomer," the way Sarah had said it.

"Summer," said Papa and Sarah at the same time. Caleb and I looked at each other. Summer was coming.

"Tomorrow," said Sarah, "I want to see the sheep. You know, I've never touched one."

"Never?" Caleb sat up.

"Never," said Sarah. She smiled and leaned back in her chair. "But I've touched seals. Real seals. They are cool and slippery and they slide through the water like fish. They can cry and sing. And sometimes they bark, a little like dogs."

Sarah barked like a seal. And Lottie and Nick came running from the barn to jump up on Sarah and lick her face and make her laugh. Sarah stroked them and scratched their ears and it was quiet again.

"I wish I could touch a seal right now," said Caleb, his voice soft in the night.

"So do I," said Sarah. She sighed, then she began to sing the summer song again. Far off in a field, a meadowlark sang, too.

5

The sheep made Sarah smile. She sank her fingers into their thick, coarse wool. She talked to them, running with the lambs, letting them suck on her fingers. She named them after her favorite aunts, Harriet and Mattie and Lou. She lay down in the field beside them and sang "Sumer Is Icumen in," her voice drifting over the meadow grasses, carried by the wind.

She cried when we found a lamb that had died, and she shouted and shook her fist at the turkey buzzards that came from nowhere to eat it. She would not let Caleb or me come near. And that night, Papa went with a shovel to bury the sheep and a lantern to bring Sarah back. She sat on the porch alone. Nick crept up to lean against her knees.

After dinner, Sarah drew pictures to send home to Maine. She began a charcoal drawing of the fields, rolling like the sea rolled. She drew a sheep whose ears were too big. And she drew a windmill.

"Windmill was my first word," said Caleb. "Papa told me so."

"Mine was flower," I said. "What was yours, Sarah?"

"Dune," said Sarah.

"Dune?" Caleb looked up.

"In Maine," said Sarah, "there are rock cliffs that rise up at the edge of the sea. And there are hills covered with pine and spruce trees, green with needles. But William and I found a sand dune all our own. It was soft and sparkling with bits of mica, and when we were little we would slide down the dune into the water."

Caleb looked out the window.

"We have no dunes here," he said.

Papa stood up.

"Yes we do," he said. He took the lantern and went out the door to the barn.

"We do?" Caleb called after him.

He ran ahead, Sarah and I following, the dogs close behind.

Next to the barn was Papa's mound of hay for bedding, nearly half as tall as the barn, covered with canvas to keep the rain from rotting it. Papa carried the wooden ladder from the barn and leaned it against the hay.

"There." He smiled at Sarah. "Our dune."

Sarah was very quiet. The dogs looked up at her, waiting. Seal brushed against her legs, her tail in the air. Caleb reached over and took her hand.

"It looks high up," he said. "Are you scared, Sarah?"

"Scared? Scared!" exclaimed Sarah. "You bet I'm not scared."

She climbed the ladder, and Nick began to bark.

She climbed to the very top of the hay and sat, looking down at us. Above, the stars were coming out. Papa piled a bed of loose hay below with his pitchfork. The light of the lantern made his eyes shine when he smiled up at Sarah.

"Fine?" called Papa.

"Fine," said Sarah. She lifted her arms over her head and slid down, down, into the soft hay. She lay, laughing, as the dogs rolled beside her.

"Was it a good dune?" called Caleb.

"Yes," said Sarah. "It is a fine dune."

Caleb and I climbed up and slid down. And Sarah did it three more times. At last Papa slid down, too, as the sky grew darker and the stars blinked like fireflies. We were covered with hay and dust, and we sneezed.

In the kitchen, Caleb and I washed in the big wooden tub and Sarah drew more pictures to send to William. One was of Papa, his hair curly and full of hay. She drew Caleb, sliding down the hay, his arms like Sarah's over his head. And she drew a picture of me in the tub, my hair long and straight and wet. She looked at her drawing of the fields for a long time.

"Something is missing," she told Caleb. "Something." And she put it away.

"'Dear William,'" Sarah read to us by lantern light that night. "'Sliding down our dune of hay is almost as fine as sliding down the sand dunes into the sea.'"

Caleb smiled at me across the table. He said nothing, but his mouth formed the words I had heard, too. *Our dune.*

6

The days grew longer. The cows moved close to the pond, where the water was cool and there were trees.

Papa taught Sarah how to plow the fields, guiding the plow behind Jack and Old Bess, the reins around her neck. When the chores were done we sat in the meadow with the sheep, Sarah beside us, watching Papa finish.

"Tell me about winter," said Sarah.

Old Bess nodded her head as she walked, but we could hear Papa speak sharply to Jack.

"Jack doesn't like work," said Caleb. "He wants to be here in the sweet grass with us."

"I don't blame him," said Sarah. She lay back in the grass with her arms under her head. "Tell me about winter," she said again.

"Winter is cold here," said Caleb, and Sarah and I laughed.

"Winter is cold everywhere," I said.

"We go to school in winter," said Caleb. "Sums and writing and books," he sang.

"I am good at sums and writing," said Sarah. "I love books. How do you get to school?"

"Papa drives us in the wagon. Or we walk the three miles when there is not too much snow."

Sarah sat up. "Do you have lots of snow?"

"Lots and lots and lots of snow," chanted Caleb, rolling around in the grass. "Sometimes we have to dig our way out to feed the animals."

"In Maine the barns are attached to the houses sometimes," said Sarah.

Caleb grinned. "So you could have a cow to Sunday supper?"

Sarah and I laughed.

"When there are bad storms, Papa ties a rope from the house to the barn so no one will get lost," said Caleb.

I frowned. I loved winter.

"There is ice on the windows on winter mornings," I told Sarah. "We can draw sparkling pictures and we can see our breath in the air. Papa builds a warm fire, and we bake hot biscuits and put on hundreds of sweaters. And if the snow is too high, we stay home from school and make snow people."

Sarah lay back in the tall grasses again, her face nearly hidden.

"And is there wind?" she asked.

"Do you like wind?" asked Caleb.

"There is wind by the sea," said Sarah.

"There is wind here," said Caleb happily. "It blows the snow and brings tumbleweeds and makes the sheep run. Wind and wind and wind!" Caleb stood up and ran like the wind, and the sheep ran after him. Sarah and I watched him jump over rock and gullies, the sheep behind him, stiff legged and fast. He circled the field, the sun making the top of his hair golden. He collapsed next to Sarah, and the lambs pushed their wet noses into us.

"Hello, Lou," said Sarah smiling. "Hello, Mattie."

The sun rose higher, and Papa stopped to take off his hat and wipe his face with his sleeve.

"I'm hot," said Sarah. "I can't wait for winter wind. Let's swim."

"Swim where?" I asked her.

"I can't swim," said Caleb.

"Can't swim!" exclaimed Sarah. "I'll teach you in the cow pond."

"That's for cows!" I cried.

But Sarah had grabbed our hands and we were running through the fields, ducking under the fence to the far pond.

"Shoo, cows," said Sarah as the cows looked up, startled. She took off her dress and waded into the water in her petticoat. She dived suddenly and disappeared for a moment as Caleb and I watched. She came up, laughing, her hair streaming free. Water beads sat on her shoulders.

She tried to teach us how to float. I sank like a bucket filled with water and came up sputtering. But Caleb lay on his back and learned how to blow streams of water high in the air like a whale. The cows stood on the banks of the pond and stared and stopped their chewing. Water bugs circled us.

"Is this like the sea?" asked Caleb.

Sarah treaded water.

"The sea is salt," said Sarah. "It stretches out as far as you can see. It gleams like the sun on glass. There are waves."

"Like this?" asked Caleb, and he pushed a wave at Sarah, making her cough and laugh.

"Yes," she said. "Like that."

I held my breath and floated at last, looking up into the sky, afraid to speak. Crows flew over, three in a row. And I could hear a killdeer in the field.

We climbed the bank and dried ourselves and lay in the grass again. The cows watched, their eyes sad in their dinner-plate faces. And I slept, dreaming a perfect dream. The fields had turned to a sea that gleamed like sun on glass. And Sarah was happy.

7

The dandelions in the fields had gone by, their heads soft as feathers. The summer roses were opening.

Our neighbors, Matthew and Maggie, came to help Papa plow up a new field for corn. Sarah stood with us on the porch, watching their wagon wind up the road, two horses pulling it and one tied in back. I remembered the last time we had stood here alone, Caleb and I, waiting for Sarah.

Sarah's hair was in thick braids that circled her head, wild daisies tucked here and there. Papa had picked them for her.

Old Bess and Jack ran along the inside of the fence, whickering at the new horses.

"Papa needs five horses for the big gang plow," Caleb told Sarah. "Prairie grass is hard."

Matthew and Maggie came with their two children and a sackful of chickens. Maggie emptied the sack into the yard and three red banty chickens clucked and scattered.

"They are for you," she told Sarah. "For eating."

Sarah loved the chickens. She clucked back to them and fed them grain. They followed her, shuffling and scratching primly in the dirt. I knew they would not be for eating.

The children were young and named Rose and Violet, after flowers. They hooted and laughed and chased the chickens, who flew up to the porch roof, then the dogs, who crept quietly under the porch. Seal had long ago fled to the barn to sleep in cool hay.

Sarah and Maggie helped hitch the horses to the plow, then they set up a big table in the shade of the barn, covering it with a quilt and a kettle of flowers in the middle. They sat on the porch while Caleb and Matthew and Papa began their morning of plowing. I mixed biscuit dough just inside the door, watching.

"You are lonely, yes?" asked Maggie in her soft voice.

Sarah's eyes filled with tears. Slowly I stirred the dough.
Maggie reached over and took Sarah's hand.

"I miss the hills of Tennessee sometimes," she said.

Do not miss the hills, Maggie, I thought.

"I miss the sea," said Sarah.

Do not miss the hills. Do not miss the sea.

I stirred and stirred the dough.

"I miss my brother William," said Sarah. "But he is
married. The house is hers now. Not mine any longer. There
are three old aunts who all squawk together like crows at
dawn. I miss them, too."

"There are always things to miss," said Maggie. "No
matter where you are."

I looked out and saw Papa and Matthew and Caleb
working. Rose and Violet ran in the fields. I felt something
brush my legs and looked down at Nick, wagging his tail.

"I would miss you, Nick," I whispered. "I would." I knelt down and scratched his ears. "I miss Mama."

"I nearly forgot," said Maggie on the porch. "I have something more for you."

I carried the bowl outside and watched Maggie lift a low wooden box out of the wagon.

"Plants," she said to Sarah. "For your garden."

"My garden?" Sarah bent down to touch the plants.

"Zinnias and marigolds and wild feverfew," said Maggie. "You must have a garden. Wherever you are."

Sarah smiled. "I had a garden in Maine with dahlias and columbine. And nasturtiums the color of the sun when it sets. I don't know if nasturtiums would grow here."

"Try," said Maggie. "You must have a garden."

We planted the flowers by the porch, turning over the soil and patting it around them, and watering. Lottie and Nick came to sniff, and the chickens walked in the dirt, leaving prints. In the fields, the horses pulled the plow up and down under the hot summer sun.

Maggie wiped her face, leaving a streak of dirt.

"Soon you can drive your wagon over to my house and I will give you more. I have tansy."

Sarah frowned. "I have never driven a wagon."

"I can teach you," said Maggie. "And so can Anna and Caleb. And Jacob."

Sarah turned to me.

"Can you?" she asked. "Can you drive a wagon?"

I nodded.

"And Caleb?"

"Yes."

"In Maine," said Sarah, "I would walk to town."

"Here it is different," said Maggie. "Here you will drive."

Way off in the sky, clouds gathered. Matthew and Papa and Caleb came in from the fields, their work done. We all ate in the shade.

"We are glad you are here," said Matthew to Sarah. "A new friend. Maggie misses her friends sometimes."

Sarah nodded. "There is always something to miss, no matter where you are," she said, smiling at Maggie.

Rose and Violet fell asleep in the grass, their bellies full of meat and greens and biscuits. And when it was time to go, Papa and Matthew lifted them into the wagon to sleep on blankets.

Sarah walked slowly behind the wagon for a long time, waving, watching it disappear. Caleb and I ran to bring her back, the chickens running wildly behind us.

"What shall we name them?" asked Sarah, laughing as the chickens followed us into the house.

I smiled. I was right. The chickens would not be for eating.

And then Papa came, just before the rain, bringing Sarah the first roses of summer.

 **8**

The rain came and passed, but strange clouds hung in the northwest, low and black and green. And the air grew still.

In the morning, Sarah dressed in a pair of overalls and went to the barn to have an argument with Papa. She took apples for Old Bess and Jack.

"Women don't wear overalls," said Caleb, running along behind her like one of Sarah's chickens.

"This woman does," said Sarah crisply.

Papa stood by the fence.

"I want to learn how to ride a horse," Sarah told him. "And then I want to learn how to drive the wagon. By myself."

Jack leaned over and nipped at Sarah's overalls. She fed him an apple. Caleb and I stood behind Sarah.

"I can ride a horse, I know," said Sarah. "I rode once when I was twelve. I will ride Jack." Jack was Sarah's favorite.

Papa shook his head. "Not Jack," he said. "Jack is sly."

"I am sly, too," said Sarah stubbornly.

Papa smiled. "Ayuh," he said, nodding. "But not Jack."

"Yes, Jack!" Sarah's voice was very loud.

"I can teach you how to drive a wagon. I have already taught you how to plow."

"And then I can go to town. By myself."

"Say no, Papa," Caleb whispered beside me.

"That's a fair thing, Sarah," said Papa. "We'll practice."

A soft rumble of thunder sounded. Papa looked up at the clouds.

"Today? Can we begin today?" asked Sarah.

"Tomorrow is best," said Papa, looking worried. "I have to fix the house roof. A portion of it is loose. And there's a storm coming."

"We," said Sarah.

"What?" Papa turned.

"*We* will fix the roof," said Sarah. "I've done it before. I know about roofs. I am a good carpenter. Remember, I told you?"

There was thunder again, and Papa went to get the ladder.

"Are you fast?" he asked Sarah.

"I am fast and I am good," said Sarah. And they climbed the ladder to the roof, Sarah with wisps of hair around her face, her mouth full of nails, overalls like Papa's. Overalls that *were* Papa's.

Caleb and I went inside to close the windows. We could hear the steady sound of hammers pounding the roof overhead.

"Why does she want to go to town by herself?" asked Caleb. "To leave us?"

I shook my head, weary with Caleb's questions. Tears gathered at the corners of my eyes. But there was no time to cry, for suddenly Papa called out.

"Caleb! Anna!"

We ran outside and saw a huge cloud, horribly black, moving toward us over the north fields. Papa slid down the roof, helping Sarah after him.

"A squall!" he yelled to us. He held up his arms and Sarah jumped off the porch roof.

"Get the horses inside," he ordered Caleb. "Get the sheep, Anna. And the cows. The barn is safest."

The grasses flattened. There was a hiss of wind, a sudden pungent smell. Our faces looked yellow in the strange light. Caleb and I jumped over the fence and found the animals huddled by the barn. I counted the sheep to make sure they were all there, and herded them into a large stall. A few raindrops came, gentle at first, then stronger and louder, so that Caleb and I covered our ears and stared at each other without speaking. Caleb looked frightened and I tried to smile at him. Sarah carried a sack into the barn, her hair wet and streaming down her neck. Papa came behind, Lottie and Nick with him, their ears flat against their heads.

"Wait!" cried Sarah. "My chickens!"

"No, Sarah!" Papa called after her. But Sarah had already run from the barn into a sheet of rain. My father followed her. The sheep nosed open their stall door and milled around the barn, bleating. Nick crept under my arm, and a lamb, Mattie with the black face, stood close to me, trembling. There was a soft paw on my lap, then a gray body. Seal. And then, as the thunder pounded and the wind rose and there was the terrible crackling of lightning close by, Sarah and Papa stood in the barn doorway, wet to the skin. Papa carried Sarah's chickens. Sarah came with an armful of summer roses.

Sarah's chickens were not afraid, and they settled like small red bundles in the hay. Papa closed the door at last, shutting out some of the sounds of the storm. The barn was eerie and half lighted, like dusk without a lantern. Papa spread blankets around our shoulders and Sarah unpacked a bag of cheese and bread and jam. At the very bottom of the bag were Sarah's shells.

Caleb got up and went over to the small barn window.

"What color is the sea when it storms?" he asked Sarah.

"Blue," said Sarah, brushing her wet hair back with her fingers. "And gray and green."

Caleb nodded and smiled.

"Look," he said to her. "Look what is missing from your drawing."

Sarah went to stand between Caleb and Papa by the window. She looked a long time without speaking. Finally, she touched Papa's shoulder.

"We have squalls in Maine, too," she said. "Just like this. It will be all right, Jacob."

Papa said nothing. But he put his arm around her, and leaned over to rest his chin in her hair. I closed my eyes, suddenly remembering Mama and Papa standing that way, Mama smaller than Sarah, her hair fair against Papa's shoulder. When I opened my eyes again, it was Sarah standing there. Caleb looked at me and smiled and smiled until he could smile no more.

We slept in the hay all night, waking when the wind was wild, sleeping again when it was quiet. And at dawn there was the sudden sound of hail, like stones tossed against the barn. We stared out the window, watching the ice marbles bounce on the ground. And when it was over we opened the barn door and walked out into the early-morning light. The hail crunched and melted beneath our feet. It was white and gleaming for as far as we looked, like sun on glass. Like the sea.

9

It was very quiet. The dogs leaned down to eat the hailstones. Seal stepped around them and leaped up on the fence to groom herself. A tree had blown over near the cow pond. And the wild roses were scattered on the ground, as if a wedding had come and gone there. "I'm glad I saved an armful" was all that Sarah said.

Only one field was badly damaged, and Sarah and Papa hitched up the horses and plowed and replanted during the next two days. The roof had held.

"I told you I know about roofs," Sarah told Papa, making him smile.

Papa kept his promise to Sarah. When the work was done, he took her out into the fields, Papa riding Jack who was sly, and Sarah riding Old Bess. Sarah was quick to learn.

"Too quick," Caleb complained to me as we watched from the fence. He thought a moment. "Maybe she'll fall off and have to stay here. Why?" he asked, turning to me. "Why does she have to go away alone?"

"Hush up, Caleb," I said crossly. "Hush up."

"I could get sick and make her stay here," said Caleb.

"No."

"We could tie her up."

"No."

And Caleb began to cry, and I took him inside the barn where we could both cry.

Papa and Sarah came to hitch the horses to the wagon, so Sarah could practice driving. Papa didn't see Caleb's tears, and he sent him with an ax to begin chopping up the tree by the pond for firewood. I stood and watched Sarah, the reins in her hands, Papa next to her in the wagon. I could see Caleb standing by the pond, one hand shading his eyes, watching, too. I went into the safe darkness of the barn then, Sarah's chickens scuttling along behind me.

"Why?" I asked out loud, echoing Caleb's question.

The chickens watched me, their eyes small and bright.

The next morning Sarah got up early and put on her blue dress. She took apples to the barn. She loaded a bundle of hay on the wagon for Old Bess and Jack. She put on her yellow bonnet.

"Remember Jack," said Papa. "A strong hand."

"Yes, Jacob."

"Best to be home before dark," said Papa. "Driving a wagon is hard if there's no full moon."

"Yes, Jacob."

Sarah kissed us all, even my father, who looked surprised.

"Take care of Seal," she said to Caleb and me. And with a whisper to Old Bess and a stern word to Jack, Sarah climbed up in the wagon and drove away.

"Very good," murmured Papa as he watched. And after a while he turned and went out into the fields.

Caleb and I watched Sarah from the porch. Caleb took my hand, and the dogs lay down beside us. It was sunny, and I remembered another time when a wagon had taken Mama away. It had been a day just like this day. And Mama had never come back.

Seal jumped up to the porch, her feet making a small thump. Caleb leaned down and picked her up and walked inside. I took the broom and slowly swept the porch. Then I watered Sarah's plants. Caleb cleaned out the wood stove and carried the ashes to the barn, spilling them so that I had to sweep the porch again.

"I *am* loud and pesky," Caleb cried suddenly. "You said so! And she has gone to buy a train ticket to go away!"

"No, Caleb. She would tell us."

"The house is too small," said Caleb. "That's what it is."

"The house is not too small," I said.

I looked at Sarah's drawing of the fields pinned up on the wall next to the window.

"What is missing?" I asked Caleb. "You said you knew what was missing."

"Colors," said Caleb wearily. "The colors of the sea."

Outside, clouds moved into the sky and went away again. We took lunch to Papa, cheese and bread and lemonade. Caleb nudged me.

"Ask him. Ask Papa."

"What has Sarah gone to do?" I asked.

"I don't know," said Papa. He squinted at me. Then he sighed and put one hand on Caleb's head, one on mine. "Sarah is Sarah. She does things her way, you know."

"I know," said Caleb very softly.

Papa picked up his shovel and put on his hat.

"Ask if she's coming back," whispered Caleb.

"Of course she's coming back," I said. "Seal is here." But I would not ask the question. I was afraid to hear the answer.

We fed the sheep, and I set the table for dinner. Four plates. The sun dropped low over the west fields. Lottie and Nick stood at the door, wagging their tails, asking for supper. Papa came to light the stove. And then it was dusk. Soon it would be dark. Caleb sat on the porch steps, turning his moon snail shell over and over in his hand. Seal brushed back and forth against him.

Suddenly Lottie began to bark, and Nick jumped off the porch and ran down the road.

"Dust!" cried Caleb. He climbed the porch and stood on the roof. "Dust, and a yellow bonnet!"

Slowly the wagon came around the windmill and the barn and the windbreak and into the yard, the dogs jumping happily beside it.

"Hush, dogs," said Sarah. And Nick leaped up into the wagon to sit by Sarah.

Papa took the reins and Sarah climbed down from the wagon.

Caleb burst into tears.

"Seal was very worried!" he cried.

Sarah put her arms around him, and he wailed into her dress. "And the house is too small, we thought! And I am loud and pesky!"

Sarah looked at Papa and me over Caleb's head.

"We thought you might be thinking of leaving us," I told her. "Because you miss the sea."

Sarah smiled.

"No," she said. "I will always miss my old home, but the truth of it is I would miss you more."

Papa smiled at Sarah, then he bent quickly to unhitch the horses from the wagon. He led them to the barn for water.

Sarah handed me a package.

"For Anna," she said. "And Caleb. For all of us."

The package was small, wrapped in brown paper with a rubber band around it. Very carefully I unwrapped it, Caleb peering closely. Inside were three colored pencils.

"Blue," said Caleb slowly, "and gray. And green."

Sarah nodded.

Suddenly Caleb grinned.

"Papa," he called. "Papa, come quickly! Sarah has brought the sea!"

We eat our night meal by candlelight, the four of us. Sarah has brought candles from town. And nasturtium seeds for her garden, and a book of songs to teach us. It is late, and Caleb is nearly sleeping by

his plate and Sarah is smiling at my father. Soon there will be a wedding. Papa says that when the preacher asks if he will have Sarah for his wife, he will answer, "Ayuh."

Autumn will come, then winter, cold with a wind that blows like the wind off the sea in Maine. There will be nests of curls to look for, and dried flowers all winter long. When there are storms, Papa will stretch a rope from the door to the barn so we will not be lost when we feed the sheep and the cows and Jack and Old Bess. And Sarah's chickens, if they aren't living in the house. There will be Sarah's sea, blue and gray and green, hanging on the wall. And songs, old ones and new. And Seal with yellow eyes. And there will be Sarah, plain and tall.

Do you think Sarah is brave? Explain why or why not.

How does Sarah help the Witting family? How do the Wittings help Sarah?

What is the importance of singing in this story?

Would you enjoy living in Anna and Caleb's time and place? Explain why or why not.

WRITE   Sarah first writes to Jacob to ask about his children and about the place where they live. Write a list that describes the place where you live. Note the appearance, the weather, and the plants and animals.

Patricia MacLachlan

Descriptions of the prairie in *Sarah, Plain and Tall* are vivid, vibrant, and true because the author, Patricia MacLachlan, knows the prairie well. MacLachlan, who was born in Cheyenne, Wyoming, says that for her "the western landscape has always been a powerful force . . . fueling mind and imagination."

That lively imagination began in childhood when MacLachlan—an only child—invented characters she wished to be. She was encouraged to read by her parents, who were teachers, so she filled her world with characters from books as well as from her imagination. With such a vivid imagination and strong love of reading, writing stories should have followed naturally.

Yet the only story the author remembers writing as a child was a school assignment at age eight. The story was to be about a pet and had to have "a beginning, a middle, and an ending." Her teacher was not impressed with the story she turned in on a three-by-five card: *My cats have names and seem happy. Often they play. The end.* The young author was discouraged enough to write in her diary: "I shall try not to be a writer."

MacLachlan did indeed "try not to be a writer." Following in her parents' footsteps, she became an English teacher. But her powerful imagination and her love for books proved too strong a combination to resist. In her thirties, Patricia MacLachlan began to write novels with proper beginnings, middles, and endings. Now she shares her talent and experience in creative writing workshops that she conducts for adults and children.

Much of the action in *Sarah, Plain and Tall* comes from MacLachlan's imagination, but the basic story idea is factual. When Patricia was a child, her mother told her about "the real Sarah, who came from the coast of Maine to the prairie to become a wife and mother." Building on that fact, MacLachlan crafted a simple but fine story that expresses the importance of family—a theme that runs through many of her books. She has received several awards for *Sarah, Plain and Tall*, among them the 1986 Newbery Medal. The little girl who tried not to be a writer grew up to distinguish herself in that profession.

Kansas Boy

Illustrations by Davy Liu

This Kansas boy who never saw the sea
Walks through the young corn rippling at his knee
As sailors walk; and when the grain grows higher
Watches the dark waves leap with greener fire
Than ever oceans hold. He follows ships,
Tasting the bitter spray upon his lips,
For in his blood up-stirs the salty ghost
Of one who sailed a storm-bound English coast.
Across wide fields he hears the sea winds crying,
Shouts at the crows — and dreams of white gulls flying.

Ruth Lechlitner

Understanding Others

What character traits might the boy in "Kansas Boy" and Sarah Wheaton have in common?

WRITER'S WORKSHOP

Imagine that you, like Caleb or Anna, want a certain person to visit you. Think about who it is, where he or she lives, and why you want the person to visit you. Then write a letter to persuade that person to come.

Writer's Choice
What can we do to understand people who are different from us? Perhaps you could give some advice. Perhaps you could tell what you have done to understand such a person. Write your response and share it in some way.

CONNECTIONS

MULTICULTURAL CONNECTION

Imported Ball Games

A ballplayer sprints across a walled court similar to a handball court. He leaps forward and catches a ball in a scoop called a *cesta* and flings the ball back at the wall at a speed well over 100 miles per hour.

He's playing *jai alai* (pronounced hī´lī), named by the Basque people of Spain and France. This name has been used in the Americas since jai alai came to Cuba in 1900. In Spain the game is called *pelota* (pronounced pā·lō´ta), meaning "ball."

Although the Basques may have improved jai alai, they may not have been its inventors. Some historians believe that the game was first played by the Aztecs in Mexico and that Spanish explorer Hernando Cortés carried it back to Spain more than 400 years ago.

Like jai alai, many of the games enjoyed in the Americas have come from other countries. With your classmates, list some games you enjoy. Then, on your own, research one or more of them. Write a report that describes the origin and rules of each game. You and your classmates can publish your reports in a games encyclopedia.

SOCIAL STUDIES CONNECTION

Guard the Chief!

Games and sports have always helped young people prepare for life. Find out what games Native American children played to develop important survival skills. Teach one to your classmates. Then, with a group, create a bulletin board on Native American games.

Southern Ute schoolchildren play *Nia-Kup,* "The Hand Game"

HEALTH CONNECTION

Fit for Living

Playing sports and games can make people healthier. Research how activity affects such physical functions as digestion, muscle tone, and circulation. Find out which physical activities are most beneficial and which are least beneficial. Share what you learn in a health newsletter.

UNIT TWO

Trials

Trials can mean different things to different people. Trials can happen in front of hundreds of spectators or, as in trials held in many Native American nations, in front of only two participants and a judge. Maybe the most challenging trials are those that involve only one—a person standing alone while being tested by nature. As you read the selections in this unit, compare the many types of trials that people face. Which experiences have you shared? Which can you learn from?

THEMES

BOOKSHELF

STORMS

by Seymour Simon

Spectacular photographs illustrate some of nature's most extreme moments–including hurricanes, lightning strikes, and tornadoes.

Award-Winning Author

Harcourt Brace Library Book

ANNO'S HAT TRICKS

by Akihiro Nozaki and Mitsumasa Anno

If you like brainteasers, then hold on to your hat! Enter the world of the hatter. To solve his puzzles, you must learn how to think like a computer.

Outstanding Science Trade Book for Children

Harcourt Brace Library Book

BOAT GIRL

by Bernard Ashley

How will Kim cope with being the only refugee and
the only Vietnamese in her London school?

BORIS

by Jaap ter Haar

Boris and Nadia struggle to survive as their home
city of Leningrad is bombed during World War II.
Award-Winning Author

SONG OF THE CHIRIMIA

by Jane Anne Volkmer

Illustrations based on Mayan stone carvings
accompany this colorful folktale from Guatemala,
told in both Spanish and English.

T H E M E

Nature's Fury

Have you ever been frightened by lightning, pounded by hailstones, or snowed in by high drifts? If so, then you, like the people in these selections, know what it is like to face nature's fury.

C O N T E N T S

137

In for Winter, Out for Spring

by Arnold Adoff
illustrated by Jerry Pinkney

My Brother Aaron Runs Outside To Tell Us There Is A Severe
                                        Thunder
                                        Storm
                                        Warning

Just Announced On The Radio While We Were Out
                              U n d e r

A Perfectly Blue Sky
We Know How Fast The   Weather Can Change   How
                        Fast Those Storms   Can
                        Blow Across These   Corn
                        Fields   Every   Spring

We Bring   Our   Books
And Toys Inside And
Listen To The Noon
                 News
Between   The   Soup
And   Sandwiches
And
Try   To Only   Think
        A b o u t
        Our Lunch

AWARD-WINNING
AUTHOR

139

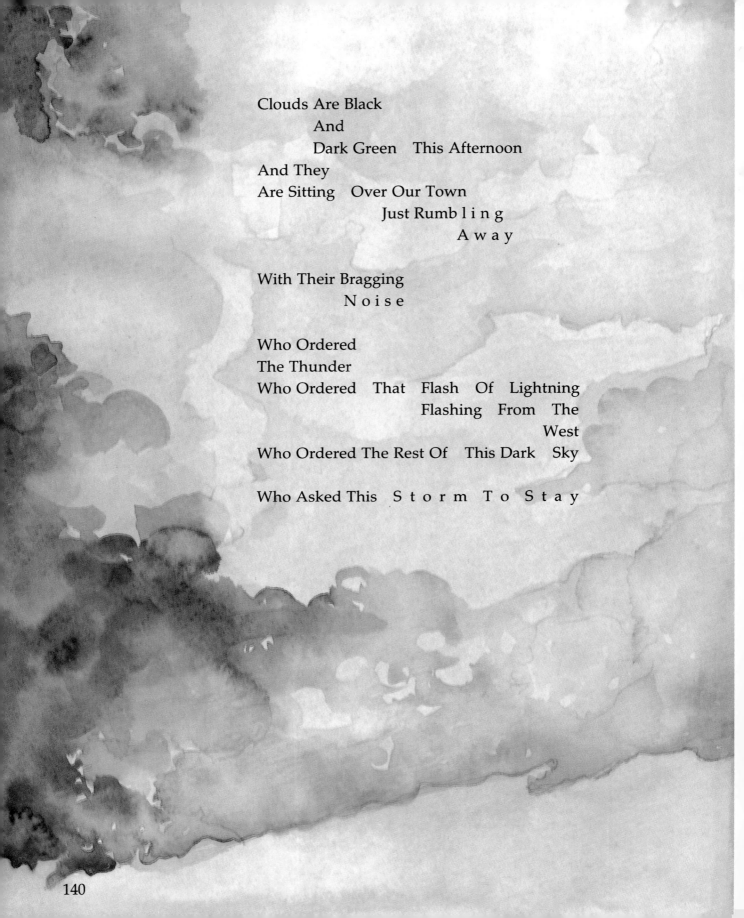

Clouds Are Black
        And
            Dark Green   This Afternoon
And They
Are Sitting   Over Our Town
                    Just Rumb l i n g
                        A w a y

With Their Bragging
            N o i s e

Who Ordered
The Thunder
Who Ordered   That   Flash   Of   Lightning
                    Flashing   From   The
                                    West
Who Ordered The Rest Of   This Dark   Sky

Who Asked This   S t o r m   To   S t a y

Words from the Illustrator: Jerry Pinkney

People often think that an author and an illustrator work together on a book, but this is rarely the case. Usually, the author writes the book, and then the illustrator takes over. The situation with *In for Winter, Out for Spring* was a little different, though. I often run into Arnold Adoff, so for the first time I was working with an author I knew. While there was no discussion of how I would illustrate the book, Arnold did send me a tape of him reading the poems. That added a great deal to my interpretation.

After reading a manuscript, I draw small sketches called thumbnails. In these I sketch the situations that I think are the most interesting. Then I put together a dummy. This is a mock copy of the book showing the characters I plan to use. I send the dummy to the publisher, and if everyone agrees, I go ahead and hire the models for the characters.

With Arnold's poetry, I had a lot of images I could have chosen to illustrate. In the excerpt you read, for instance, I could have drawn more of the storm. But I had been looking for an opportunity to put the mother, the daughter, and the son in the same picture, and this seemed like a good place to do it. More than anything else, I wanted to emphasize the family aspect of this book.

141

AWARD-WINNING
AUTHOR

STORMS

SEYMOUR SIMON

MORROW

We live at the bottom of a blanket of air called the atmosphere. The atmosphere is always moving, sometimes slowly, other times quickly and violently. These changes in the atmosphere are called the weather. We call the violent changes storms.

Thunderstorms are the most powerful electrical storms in the atmosphere. In twenty minutes, a single thunderstorm can drop 125 million gallons of water and give off more electrical energy than is used in a large city during an entire week.

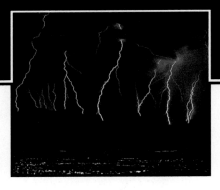

Lightning is an electrical discharge within a thunderstorm. As a thunderstorm develops, the clouds become charged with electricity. Scientists are still not sure exactly what causes this to happen. But they do know that as much as 100 million volts build up in the lower part of a thunderhead, and the temperature of a single bolt of lightning reaches 50,000 degrees F. within a few millionths of a second. That's almost five times greater than the temperature at the sun's surface.

Lightning flashes when the voltage becomes high enough for electricity to leap across the air from one place to another. Lightning can spark within the cloud, from one cloud to another, from ground to cloud, or from cloud to ground.

Thunder is the sound given off by the explosive expansion of air heated by a lightning stroke. When lightning is close, thunder sounds like a single, sharp crack. From farther away, thunder sounds like a growling or rumbling noise. Thunder usually can be heard easily from six or seven miles away, and even from twenty miles away on a quiet day.

Light is about a million times faster than sound, so you see a lightning bolt almost instantly, but the sound of thunder takes about five seconds to travel one mile. This makes it possible for you to judge the distance of a lightning stroke by timing how long it takes you to hear the thunder.

Count the number of seconds between the flash and the thunder. (You can count seconds by counting slowly in this way: and a one and a two and a three and a four and a five, and so on.) Divide the number of seconds by five. The number you get is the number of miles away the lightning struck.

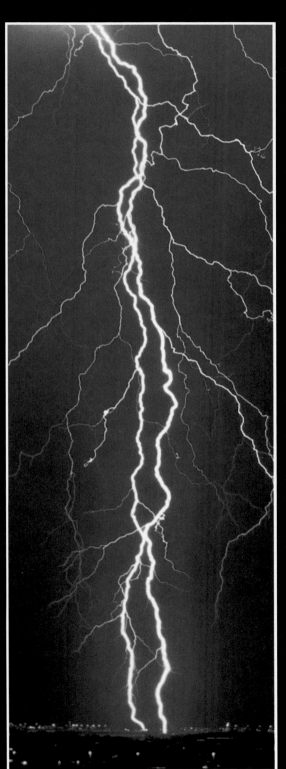

Sometimes a thunderstorm gives birth to a tornado. The wind blows hard and trees bend. Heavy rains or hailstones fall. Lightning and thunder rip the dark sky, and a howling roar like hundreds of jet planes fills the air.

Spinning winds inside the thunderstorm begin forming a funnel-shaped cloud that reaches downward to the ground. When it contacts the earth, an explosion of flying dirt turns the tornado dark.

This remarkable series of photos shows the life of a tornado in hours, minutes, and seconds.

As the spinning winds pick up speed, the tornado grows larger and larger. The funnel skips across the ground, sometimes setting down, sometimes bouncing upward, and then touching down again, leaving semicircular marks on the ground like the hoofprints of giant horses. The funnel moves forward at speeds averaging thirty miles per hour, but some tornadoes travel at more than sixty miles per hour.

Like the hose of an enormous vacuum cleaner, the tornado picks up loose materials and whirls them aloft. In less than fifteen minutes, the funnel cloud becomes clogged with dirt and air and can no longer suck up any more. The cloud becomes lighter in color as less dirt is swept aloft. As the tornado begins to lag behind the parent thunder-head, it narrows and finally vanishes altogether.

The twisting winds of a tornado whirl around the funnel at speeds of 200 miles an hour or more. Houses may be knocked down and blown apart by the wind. Then the tornado picks up the pieces, along with chairs, tables, and beds, and carries them away.

If you know a tornado is coming, go indoors, but stay away from windows. In a house, the safest place is in the cellar. Get under a table or under the stairs. If there is no cellar, go to a closet or a small room in the middle of the house. Cover yourself with a blanket or heavy towels to protect against flying glass.

Tornadoes sometimes do strange things. Once a car with two people inside was lifted to a height of 100 feet, then deposited right side up without injuring the passengers. Another tornado lifted a train locomotive from one track, spun it around in midair, and then set it down on another track facing the opposite direction.

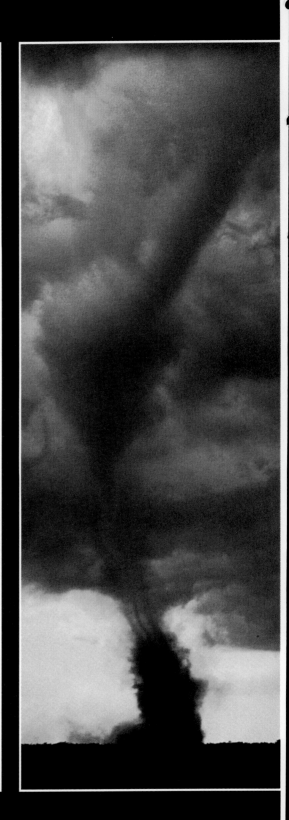

HURRICANE ALICIA
7PM CDT AUG 17 1983

There are many ancient myths about storms. The early Norsemen believed that Thor was the god of thunderstorms. They thought that lightning struck when Thor threw his mighty hammer and thunder rumbled when his chariot struck storm clouds.

Nowadays, radar, satellites, and computers keep track of storms and help scientists forecast their behavior. But the more scientists learn about storms, the more complicated they find them to be. Storms still arouse our sense of awe and wonder.

Do you agree with Seymour Simon that storms "arouse our sense of awe and wonder"? Why or why not?

What are some of the dangerous things that can happen during a thunderstorm?

According to the selection, what is one thing that ancient myths and modern technology have in common?

WRITE   What would you do if you knew a tornado was coming? Write a set of directions telling what to do and what not to do during a tornado.

Night

of

the

Twisters

by Ivy Ruckman
illustrated by Jeffrey Terreson

CHILDREN'S CHOICE

The night of June 4, 1980, is a dark and stormy one in Grand Island, Nebraska. Some people are even predicting a tornado. Dan is at home with his mother and his baby brother Ryan. Unafraid of the gathering storm, Dan's friend Arthur has come over to watch a comedy on TV.

Mom's forehead puckered as she walked away. I knew what was on her mind. We were both wishing Dad was home.

We watched TV another few minutes, but I couldn't get into it like before. Not that I was scared, exactly. I'd been through dozens of tornado watches in my life and nothing ever happened, though a barn roof got rearranged over in Clay Center one year. Every spring, practically, we have to "hit for the cellar," as Grandpa puts it. But when a tornado watch changes to a warning, and when the siren starts . . . well . . . that's when things aren't so mellow anymore.

"Shouldn't you call your mother, Arthur?" Mom said to him after trying the phone again. "I'm not sure she'd want you to stay here tonight."

"Oh, Mom!" I groaned. (There I was, thinking the sun rose and set on me.)

"Wait, I'd better call Goldie first," she said. "Someone should run over and check on Mrs. Smiley. When she turns that hearing aid down . . ."

After a while she hung up again. "Doesn't anybody stay home?" she muttered.

By then I was standing in the kitchen doorway, trying to tell her Aunt Goldie had probably gone bowling.

"Who you calling now?" I asked instead. Her attacks on the phone were suddenly more interesting than what was happening in living color on the nineteen-inch screen.

"Mrs. Smiley. Sssssh . . ."

"She's trying to finish a needlepoint cushion for the Presbyterians," Arthur piped up from the sofa.

"Yeah," I whispered in Mom's face, remembering, "and I'm supposed to tell you not to forget she's coming Friday for you to fix her hair."

All the while Mom was waving her hand for us to be quiet, so I backed away.

Next thing I knew she was at the hall closet, putting her red Windbreaker on over her jeans and Hastings College T-shirt.

"She doesn't answer," she said. "I'm driving over there to make sure she has her TV on. I won't be long. Now listen, both of you."

We listened. She was using a very firm voice.

"I want you to take this flashlight"—she got it off the shelf and handed it to me—"and a blanket and put them in the downstairs bathroom. I want you to do it *this minute!*" I nodded, trying the flashlight to make sure it worked.

"If the siren starts, get Ryan and go downstairs. Don't wake him up if you can help it, all right?"

Arthur's eyes got big listening to Mom. He told me once they never go to the basement during windstorms. That figures. They moved here from California, what do they know? Ever hear of a tornado in good old CA?

Mom went to get a blanket.

"I'll be right back," she told us, hooking her purse on her shoulder. "I'm sure nothing's going to happen, but we have to be prepared, right? Your father would have a fit if we ignored the siren."

She smiled and waved her car keys at us as she left, barely squeezing out before the door slammed shut again.

"Whooeeeee!" Arthur exclaimed. "Sounds like my bull-roarer outside!"

I hurried downstairs with the emergency stuff and set it on the bathroom counter. Minerva went with me, scurrying across my feet on the steps, acting the way she does when she wants attention.

I picked her up by the middle, smoothed down her stripes, and balanced her on the glass door of the shower. Usually

she'll do a tightrope act for me, but she only yowled and jumped off. After giving me her mean jungle look, she sat down to dig at her ear.

"You got a flea in there?" I asked, bending to give her a good scratching.

She didn't like that, either.

Upstairs, Arthur was hooting and hollering again. I decided I was missing all the good parts, so I hurried up the two short flights of steps, with Minerva dashing ahead of me.

Sometime in there, in the middle of all that comedy on the screen, the siren began. Now, *that* is a very sobering sound. It's unlike anything else, having its own built-in chill factor.

I thought of Mom first. She'd hear it and come back, I told myself.

Then I thought of Dad and how far the farm was from town. They wouldn't even hear the siren out there.

In half a second, I was at the phone, dialing 555-2379.

Four rings. Then I heard Grandma's voice.

"Grandma!" I shouted into the phone. "Where have you been? There's a tornado just north of G.I. The siren's going, can you hear it?"

A voice said something, but it sounded so far away.

"Talk louder, Grandma! I can't hear you."

The voice faded away entirely. I wasn't even sure it was Grandma's now.

"There's a tornado coming! Can you hear me?"

Finally, there wasn't anything on the line but the sound of another phone ringing very faintly, as if it were in New York or someplace far away. I couldn't figure it out.

By then, Arthur was standing next to me. I was just about to hand him the phone when, abruptly, the siren stopped. It didn't taper off, it just quit, as if someone snipped it with scissors. Except for the TV, everything around us suddenly seemed very still.

"Hey," he said, raising his eyebrows, "they changed their minds."

I hung up the phone. I didn't know what was happening.

"Maybe they got their weather signals crossed," he suggested happily. "They could, you know. I read a book once about that happening, where this whole fleet of fishing boats put out to sea . . ." he rattled on.

I ran to the door, thinking I might see Mom pulling into the driveway, but no luck.

"It's quit blowing," I called over my shoulder to Arthur.

Sure enough, the wind had died down. Maybe the storm wouldn't amount to anything after all.

That nice comforting thought had hardly entered my mind when the siren blared forth again. With a jolt, I remembered what Mom had told us to do.

"We always turn on the radio," Arthur said, already on his way to the kitchen. "You want me to? I'll get the weather station."

I was hardly listening. I hurried down the bedroom hallway to Ryan's room at the end. I hated like everything to get him up. He'd cry. I knew he'd wake up and cry. Without Mom, Arthur and I would have him screaming in our ears the whole time.

When I saw him in his crib, peacefully sleeping on the side of his face, his rear end in the air, I just didn't have the heart to wake him up. I'd wait a minute or two. Mom would be back. Anyway, it's blowing over, I told myself, it won't last.

Quietly, I closed the door behind me.

That's when the lights started flickering.

In the hallway, I practically had a head-on with Arthur, who was coming at me real fast. The look on his face scared me.

"There's no . . . there's no . . ."

"What?"

"There's no radio reception anymore. It just went dead! This guy . . . He kept saying, 'Tornado alert, tornado alert!' Then it went dead."

We rushed back to the living room. The TV was flashing these big letters that filled the entire screen: CD . . . CD . . . CD . . .

"What's it mean?" Arthur cried.

"Civil Defense Emergency!" I whirled around. "I'm getting Ryan!"

The lights flickered again.

At the same time we heard these really strange sounds that stopped us in our tracks. They were coming from the bathroom and the kitchen. Sucking sounds. The drains were sucking! I felt this awful pulling in my ears, too, as if there were vacuums on both sides of my head.

"I've got to go home!" Arthur cried all of a sudden, bolting for the door.

I ran after him. "You're not—you can't!" I grabbed the back of his T-shirt, hauled him around, and pushed him toward the stairs. "Get *down* there. I have to get Ryan! Now *go!*"

I don't know what I'd have done if he hadn't minded me. We were catching the fear from each other, and even though the siren was screaming on and off again, so I didn't know what it was telling us, I knew we had to take cover fast.

The lights went out for good just before I reached Ryan's room. I smashed face first into Ryan's butterfly mobile. That's how I knew I was at the crib. I felt for him, got my hands under his nightshirt and diaper, rolled him over. I lifted him, but we didn't get far. He was caught in the mobile, his arm or his head . . . I couldn't see . . . I couldn't get him loose. . . .

"Mom!" I yelled, though I knew she wasn't there.

I tried to lay him down again, but he was so tangled, part of him was still up in the air. He started to cry.

"Wait, Ryan, I'll get you out!" But I couldn't.

Finally, holding him with my left arm, I climbed onto the side of the crib. My right hand followed the string up the mobile, way up to the hook. I yanked it loose. The whole thing came crashing down on top of us as I jumped backward off the crib.

The plastic butterfly poking me was poking Ryan, too, but I didn't care. The tornado was close, and I knew it. Both my ears had popped, and I had this crazy fear that those drains, sucking like monsters now, would get us if the storm didn't.

Arthur was at the bottom of the stairs, waiting. Thank God he'd found the flashlight! I jumped the last half-flight to the floor.

"Hurry!" I screamed. I swung into the doorway of the bathroom, with Arthur right behind me. We crouched under the towel rack.

"Shine it here, on Ryan," I gasped. "He's caught in this thing." By now Ryan was kicking and screaming, and his eyes were big in the light.

Once we got the mess of strings free of Ryan's sweaty nightshirt, Arthur kicked the mobile against the wall by the toilet.

"I have to go home!" he cried. "They won't go to the basement. Mama never does."

The beam of light bounced around the blackness of the bathroom as Arthur scrambled to his feet, but I grabbed and held on to him.

"You can't go! It's here! Can't you feel it?"

The siren quit again as I pulled him back down and threw my leg over him. The flashlight clattered to the floor and rolled away from us.

We heard it next. The lull. The deadliest quiet ever, one that makes you think you might explode. The heat in that room built until I couldn't get my breath.

Then I began to hear noises. A chair scraping across the kitchen floor upstairs.

"Your mom's back!" Arthur said, pushing at my leg.

I knew it wasn't my mother moving the chair.

The noises got worse. It seemed as if every piece of furniture was moving around up there . . . big, heavy things, smashing into each other.

A window popped.

Crash! Another.

Glass, shattering—everywhere—right next to us in the laundry room.

I pulled a towel down over Ryan and held him tight. If he was still crying, I didn't know it because I was *feeling* the sucking this time. It was like something trying to lift my body right up off the floor.

Arthur felt it, too. "Mother of God!" He crossed himself. "We're going to die!"

Ten seconds more and that howling, shrieking tornado was upon us.

"The blanket!" I screamed at Arthur's ear.

He pulled it down from the countertop and we covered ourselves, our hands shaking wildly. I wasn't worrying about my mom then or my dad or Mrs. Smiley. Just us. Ryan and Arthur and me, huddled together there on the floor.

The roaring had started somewhere to the east, then came bearing down on us like a hundred freight trains. Only that twister didn't move on. It stationed itself right overhead, making the loudest noise I'd ever heard, whining worse than any jet. There was a tremendous crack, and I felt the wall shudder behind us. I knew then our house was being ripped apart. Suddenly chunks of ceiling were falling on our heads.

We'll be buried! was all I could think.

At that moment, as plain as anything above that deafening roar, I heard my dad's voice: *The shower's the safest place.*

I didn't question hearing it. Holding Ryan against me with one arm, I began crawling toward the shower stall. I reached back and yanked at Arthur's shirt. Somehow we got inside with the blanket. Another explosion, and the glass shower door shattered all over the bathroom floor.

We pulled the blanket over our heads and I began to pray. Out loud, though I couldn't hear my own voice: "God help us, God help us." I said it over and over, into Ryan's damp hair, my lips moving against his head. I knew Arthur was praying, too, jammed there into my side. I could feel Ryan's heart beating through his undershirt against mine. *My* heart was thanking God for making me go back for him, but not in words. Outside those places where our bodies touched, there was nothing but terror as the roar of that tornado went on and

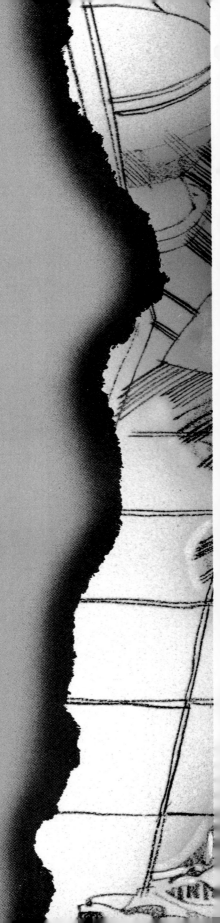

161

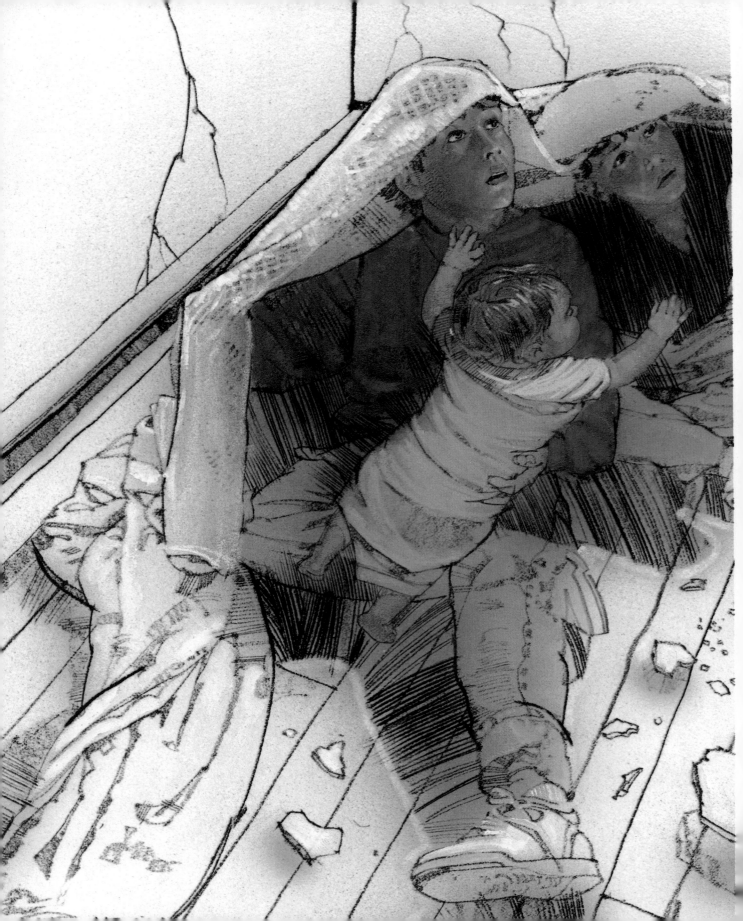

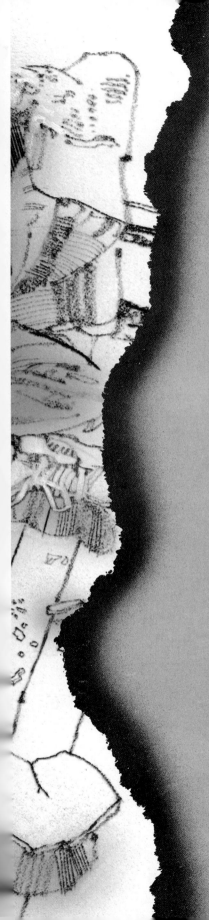

on. I thought the world was coming to an end, *had* come to an end, and so would we, any minute.

Then I felt Ryan's fat fingers close around one of mine. He pulled my hand to his mouth and started sucking on my finger. It made me cry. The tears ran down my cheeks and onto his head. With the whole world blowing to pieces around us, Ryan took my hand and made me feel better.

Afterward, neither Arthur nor I was able to say how long we huddled there in the basement shower.

"A tornado's forward speed is generally thirty to fifty miles an hour," the meteorologist had told us.

Our tornado's forward speed was zero. It parked right there on Sand Crane Drive. Five minutes or ten, we couldn't tell, but it seemed like an hour. Roaring and humming and shrieking, that twister was right on top of us. I'll never be that scared again as long as I live. Neither will Arthur.

How did you feel while you read the story?

What problems does Dan face in the story?

At the beginning of the selection, Dan and Arthur are not very worried about the approaching storm. What events lead them to realize that they are in great danger?

The story does not say that the boys are cold during the tornado. Why do they cover themselves with a blanket?

WRITE   Think about Dan's behavior throughout the selection. How would you react in the same situation? Write a report that praises some of Dan's actions and criticizes others.

FROM
TORNADO!
POEMS
BY ARNOLD ADOFF
ILLUSTRATED BY RONALD HIMLER

Poet Arnold Adoff lived through the fury of a tornado strike in his home near Xenia, Ohio. In these poems, he describes how the people rose up on the day after and went on with their lives.

CHILDREN'S CHOICE

in the morning

the sky is blue
and it is school
again

hungry
hungry hurry
up

at our school

the skylights have big holes
through their glass panes
there is glass all over
all the floors

it is a day for wearing shoes
even on the mats

the firemen start yelling

get away from there
these
buildings
can fall
at any time

will have to be
knocked
down as soon as the people
move their things away

one girl is carrying
her winter coat
her boots
out to a truck

one boy is playing
where
his
house had been
is not

you can see

a broken house
a street of broken
houses
a broken baby doll
in the boards

dogs and cats
are
sniffing
hungry
and
cows are strolling
down the
street

the woman

is telling about the wind

it was not just the wind
and the pressure
on your back
on your head
you couldn't get up
you couldn't
move

but the wind was full of dirt
and sand and filth and rocks
so many bits of
glass
and heavy things

heavy things
in the
air

momma says

that's why
the funnel
cloud
is
black

not the
color
of
the
wind

but dirt and boards
and trees
and stone

daddy says

there will be
storms for many springs
for many summers

momma says
we can be tougher
than some thunder
noise
some flash

grandma
says
the last time one came
through here was fifty
years ago and i can
wait another fifty
for the next

brother says

it never seems to rain
in a quiet way out here
just water
for the garden
and the corn fields
when they get dry

just wet
no
wind
it never seems to rain
in a quiet
way

i say
that's right
good
night

and anyway

no
old
tornado

i don't care
how
bad

is stronger
than the
people on the land

Nature's Fury

According to the selections and poems, what impact can a tornado have on people's lives?

WRITER'S WORKSHOP

Not all parts of the country experience tornadoes, but people everywhere know nature's fury firsthand. For example, people who live in some coastal states are familiar with hurricanes, while people living in northern states are prepared for ice storms. What sorts of weather emergencies have you experienced? Write a descriptive paragraph about a severe storm or other weather condition you have lived through.

Writer's Choice

Storms are a part of nature. What are your feelings about nature's fury now that you have read these selections? Respond in your own way. Share your feelings with your classmates.

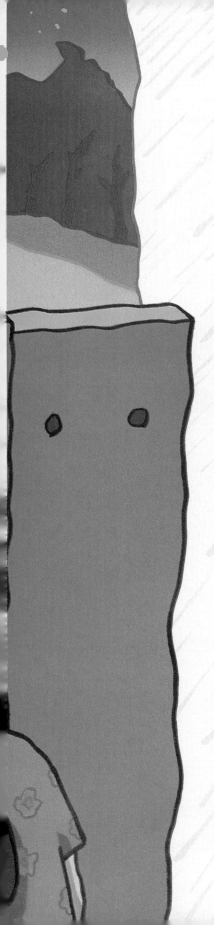

T H E M E

Trespasses

There are boundaries that can be seen—such as locked doors—and boundaries that cannot be seen—such as laws. When the characters in these selections cross those boundaries, they trespass.

C O N T E N T S

171

From the Mixed-up Files of Mrs. Basil E. Frankweiler

NEWBERY MEDAL
LEWIS CARROLL
SHELF AWARD

FROM THE MIXED-UP FILES OF
MRS. BASIL E. FRANKWEILER
WRITTEN AND ILLUSTRATED BY
E. L. KONIGSBURG

**Written and illustrated
by
E. L.
Konigsburg**

Claudia has a goal—to make her family appreciate her more. She also has a plan—to run away, temporarily, so that they'll all have a chance to miss her.

Problem 1: Where can she go that is nearby, safe, and interesting?
Solution: The Metropolitan Museum of Art in New York City

Problem 2: How can she finance such an adventure?
Solution: Bring along her penny-wise younger brother Jamie as treasurer

In the following account, written by Mrs. Basil E. Frankweiler to a lawyer named Saxonberg, Claudia sets her plan in motion.

AS SOON AS THEY REACHED THE SIDEWALK, JAMIE made his first decision as treasurer. "We'll walk from here to the museum."

"Walk?" Claudia asked. "Do you realize that it is over forty blocks from here?"

"Well, how much does the bus cost?"

"The bus!" Claudia exclaimed. "Who said anything about taking a bus? I want to take a taxi."

"Claudia," Jamie said, "you are quietly out of your mind. How can you even think of a taxi? We have no more allowance. No more income. You can't be extravagant any longer. It's not my money we're spending. It's *our* money. We're in this together, remember?"

"You're right," Claudia answered. "A taxi is expensive. The bus is cheaper. It's only twenty cents each. We'll take the bus."

"*Only* twenty cents each. That's forty cents total. No bus. We'll walk."

"We'll wear out forty cents worth of shoe leather," Claudia mumbled. "You're sure we have to walk?"

"Positive," Jamie answered. "Which way do we go?"

"Sure you won't change your mind?" The look on Jamie's face gave her the answer. She sighed. No wonder Jamie had more than twenty-four dollars; he was a gambler and a cheapskate. If that's the way he wants to be, she thought, I'll never again ask him for bus fare; I'll suffer and never, never let him know about it. But he'll regret it when I simply collapse from exhaustion. I'll collapse quietly.

"We'd better walk up Madison Avenue," she told her brother. "I'll see too many ways to spend *our* precious money if we walk on Fifth Avenue. All those gorgeous stores."

She and Jamie did not walk exactly side by side. Her violin case kept bumping him, and he began to walk a few steps ahead of her. As Claudia's pace slowed down from what she was sure was an accumulation of carbon dioxide in her system (she had not yet learned about muscle fatigue in science class even though she was in the sixth grade honors class), Jamie's pace quickened. Soon he was walking a block and a half ahead of her. They would meet when a red light held him up. At one of these mutual stops Claudia instructed Jamie to wait for her on the corner of Madison Avenue and 80th Street, for there they would turn left to Fifth Avenue.

She found Jamie standing on that corner, probably one of the most civilized street corners in the whole world, consulting a compass and announcing that when they turned left, they would be heading "due northwest." Claudia was tired and cold at the tips; her fingers, her toes, her nose were all cold while the rest of her was perspiring under the weight of her winter clothes. She never liked feeling either very hot or very cold, and she hated feeling both at the same time. "Head due northwest. Head due northwest," she mimicked. "Can't you simply say turn right or turn left as everyone else does? Who do you think you are? Daniel Boone? I'll bet no one's used a compass in Manhattan since Henry Hudson."

Jamie didn't answer. He briskly rounded the corner of 80th Street and made his hand into a sun visor as he peered down the street. Claudia needed an argument. Her internal heat, the heat of anger, was cooking that accumulated carbon dioxide. It would soon explode out of her if she didn't give it some vent. "Don't you realize that we must try to be inconspicuous?" she demanded of her brother.

"What's inconspicuous?"

"Un-noticeable."

Jamie looked all around. "I think you're brilliant, Claude. New York is a great place to hide out. No one notices no one."

"Anyone," Claudia corrected. She looked at Jamie and found him smiling. She softened. She had to agree with her brother. She was brilliant. New York was a great place, and being called brilliant had cooled her down. The bubbles dissolved. By the time they reached the museum, she no longer needed an argument.

As they entered the main door on Fifth Avenue, the guard clicked off two numbers on his people counter. Guards always

count the people going into the museum, but they don't count
them going out. (My chauffeur, Sheldon, has a friend named
Morris who is a guard at the Metropolitan. I've kept Sheldon
busy getting information from Morris. It's not hard to do since
Morris loves to talk about his work. He'll tell about anything
except security. Ask him a question he won't or can't answer,
and he says, "I'm not at liberty to tell. Security.")

By the time Claudia and Jamie reached their destination, it
was one o'clock, and the museum was busy. On any ordinary
Wednesday over 26,000 people come. They spread out over the
twenty acres of floor space; they roam from room to room to
room to room to room. On Wednesday come the gentle old

ladies who are using the time before the Broadway matinee begins. They walk around in pairs. You can tell they are a set because they wear matching pairs of orthopedic shoes, the kind that lace on the side. Tourists visit the museum on Wednesdays. You can tell them because the men carry cameras, and the women look as if their feet hurt; they wear high heeled shoes. (I always say that those who wear 'em deserve 'em.) And there are art students. Any day of the week. They also walk around in pairs. You can tell that they are a set because they carry matching black sketchbooks.

(You've missed all this, Saxonberg. Shame on you! You've never set your well-polished shoe inside that museum. More than a quarter of a million people come to that museum every week. They come from Mankato, Kansas, where they have no museums and from Paris, France, where they have lots. And they all enter free of charge because that's what the museum is: great and large and wonderful and free to all. And complicated. Complicated enough even for Jamie Kincaid.)

No one thought it strange that a boy and a girl, each carrying a book bag and an instrument case and who would normally be in school, were visiting a museum. After all, about a thousand school children visit the museum every day. The guard at the entrance merely stopped them and told them to check their cases and book bags. A museum rule: no bags, food, or umbrellas. None that the guards can see. Rule or no rule, Claudia decided it was a good idea. A big sign in the checking room said NO TIPPING, so she knew that Jamie couldn't object. Jamie did object, however; he pulled his sister aside and asked her how she expected him to change into his pajamas. His pajamas, he explained, were rolled into a tiny ball in his trumpet case.

Claudia told him that she fully expected to check out at 4:30. They would then leave the museum by the front door and within five minutes would re-enter from the back, through the door that leads from the parking lot to the Children's Museum. After all, didn't that solve all their problems? (1) They would be seen leaving the museum. (2) They would be free of their baggage while they scouted around for a place to spend the night. And (3) it was free.

Claudia checked her coat as well as her packages. Jamie was condemned to walking around in his ski jacket. When the jacket was on and zippered, it covered up that exposed strip of skin. Besides, the orlon plush lining did a great deal to muffle his twenty-four-dollar rattle. Claudia would never have permitted herself to become so overheated, but Jamie liked perspiration, a little bit of dirt, and complications.

Right now, however, he wanted lunch. Claudia wished to eat in the restaurant on the main floor, but Jamie wished to eat in the snack bar downstairs; he thought it would be less glamorous, but cheaper, and as chancellor of the exchequer, as holder of the veto power, and as tightwad of the year, he got his wish. Claudia didn't really mind too much when she saw the snack bar. It was plain but clean.

James was dismayed at the prices. They had $28.61 when they went into the cafeteria, and only $27.11 when they came out still feeling hungry. "Claudia," he demanded, "did you know food would cost so much? Now, aren't you glad that we didn't take a bus?"

Claudia was no such thing. She was not glad that they hadn't taken a bus. She was merely furious that her parents, and Jamie's too, had been so stingy that she had been away from home for less than one whole day and was already worried about survival money. She chose not to answer Jamie. Jamie didn't notice; he was completely wrapped up in problems of finance.

"Do you think I could get one of the guards to play me a game of war?" he asked.

"That's ridiculous," Claudia said.

"Why? I brought my cards along. A whole deck."

Claudia said, "*Inconspicuous* is exactly the opposite of that. Even a guard at the Metropolitan who sees thousands of people every day would remember a boy who played him a game of cards."

Jamie's pride was involved. "I cheated Bruce through all second grade and through all third grade so far, and he still isn't wise."

"Jamie! Is that how you knew you'd win?"

Jamie bowed his head and answered, "Well, yeah. Besides, Brucie has trouble keeping straight the jacks, queens, and kings. He gets mixed up."

"Why do you cheat your best friend?"

"I sure don't know. I guess I like complications."

"Well, quit worrying about money now. Worry about where we're going to hide while they're locking up this place."

They took a map from the information stand, for free. Claudia selected where they would hide during that dangerous time immediately after the museum was closed to the public and before all the guards and helpers left. She decided that she would go to the ladies' room, and Jamie would go to the men's room just before the museum closed. "Go to the one near the restaurant on the main floor," she told Jamie.

"I'm not spending a night in a men's room. All that tile. It's cold. And, besides, men's rooms make noises sound louder. And I rattle enough now."

Claudia explained to Jamie that he was to enter a booth in the men's room. "And then stand on it," she continued.

"Stand on it? Stand on what?" Jamie demanded.

"You know," Claudia insisted. "Stand on it!"

"You mean stand on the toilet?" Jamie needed everything spelled out.

"Well, what else would I mean? What else is there in a booth in the men's room? And keep your head down. And keep the door to the booth very slightly open," Claudia finished.

"Feet up. Head down. Door open. Why?"

"Because I'm certain that when they check the ladies' room and the men's room, they peek under the door and check only to see if there are feet. We must stay there until we're sure all the people and guards have gone home."

"How about the night watchman?" Jamie asked.

Claudia displayed a lot more confidence than she really felt. "Oh! there'll be a night watchman, I'm sure. But he mostly walks around the roof trying to keep people from breaking in. We'll already be in. They call what he walks, a cat walk. We'll learn his habits soon enough. They must mostly use burglar alarms in the inside. We'll just never touch a window, a door, or a valuable painting. Now, let's find a place to spend the night."

They wandered back to the rooms of fine French and English furniture. It was here Claudia knew for sure that she had chosen the most elegant place in the world to hide. She wanted to sit on the lounge chair that had been made for Marie Antoinette or at least sit at her writing table. But signs everywhere said not to step on the platform. And some of the chairs had silken ropes strung across the arms to keep you from even trying to sit down. She would have to wait until after lights out to be Marie Antoinette.

At last she found a bed that she considered perfectly wonderful, and she told Jamie that they would spend the night there. The bed had a tall canopy, supported by an ornately carved headboard at one end and by two gigantic posts at the other. (I'm familiar with that bed, Saxonberg. It is as enormous and fussy as mine. And it dates from the sixteenth century like mine. I once considered donating my bed to the museum, but Mr. Untermyer gave them this one first. I was somewhat relieved when he did. Now I can enjoy my bed without feeling guilty because the museum doesn't have one. Besides, I'm not that fond of donating things.)

Claudia had always known that she was meant for such fine things. Jamie, on the other hand, thought that running away from home to sleep in just another bed was really no challenge at all. He, James, would rather sleep on the bathroom floor, after all. Claudia then pulled him around to the foot of the bed and told him to read what the card said.

Jamie read, "Please do not step on the platform."

Claudia knew that he was being difficult on purpose; therefore, she read for him, "State bed—scene of the alleged murder of Amy Robsart, first wife of Lord Robert Dudley, later Earl of . . ."

Jamie couldn't control his smile. He said, "You know, Claude, for a sister and a fussbudget, you're not too bad."

Claudia replied, "You know, Jamie, for a brother and a cheapskate, you're not too bad."

Something happened at precisely that moment. Both Claudia and Jamie tried to explain to me about it, but they couldn't quite. I know what happened, though I never told

them. Having words and explanations for everything is too modern. I especially wouldn't tell Claudia. She has too many explanations already.

What happened was: they became a team, a family of two. There had been times before they ran away when they had acted like a team, but those were very different from *feeling* like a team. Becoming a team didn't mean the end of their arguments. But it did mean that the arguments became a part of the adventure, became discussions not threats. To an outsider the arguments would appear to be the same because feeling like part of a team is something that happens invisibly. You might call it *caring*. You could even call it *love*. And it is very rarely, indeed, that it happens to two people at the same time— especially a brother and a sister who had always spent more time with activities than they had with each other.

They followed their plan: checked out of the museum and re-entered through a back door. When the guard at that entrance told them to check their instrument cases, Claudia told him that they were just passing through on their way to meet their mother. The guard let them go, knowing that if they went very far, some other guard would stop them again. However, they managed to avoid other guards for the remaining minutes until the bell rang. The bell meant that the museum was closing in five minutes. They then entered the booths of the rest rooms.

They waited in the booths until five-thirty, when they felt certain that everyone had gone. Then they came out and met. Five-thirty in winter is dark, but nowhere seems as dark as the Metropolitan Museum of Art. The ceilings are so high that they fill up with a lot of darkness. It seemed to Jamie and Claudia that they walked through miles of corridors. Fortunately, the corridors were wide, and they were spared bumping into things.

At last they came to the hall of the English Renaissance. Jamie quickly threw himself upon the bed forgetting that it was only about six o'clock and thinking that he would be so exhausted that he would immediately fall asleep. He didn't.

He was hungry. That was one reason he didn't fall asleep immediately. He was uncomfortable, too. So he got up from bed, changed into his pajamas and got back into bed. He felt a little better. Claudia had already changed into her pajamas. She, too, was hungry, and she, too, was uncomfortable. How could so elegant and romantic a bed smell so musty? She would have liked to wash everything in a good, strong, sweet-smelling detergent.

As Jamie got into bed, he still felt uneasy, and it wasn't because he was worried about being caught. Claudia had planned everything so well that he didn't concern himself about that. The strange way he felt had little to do with the strange place in which they were sleeping. Claudia felt it, too. Jamie lay there thinking. Finally, realization came.

"You know, Claude," he whispered, "I didn't brush my teeth."

Claudia answered, "Well, Jamie, you can't always brush after every meal." They both laughed very quietly. "Tomorrow," Claudia reassured him, "we'll be even better organized."

It was much earlier than her bedtime at home, but still Claudia felt tired. She thought she might have an iron deficiency anemia: tired blood. Perhaps, the pressures of everyday stress and strain had gotten her down. Maybe she was light-headed from hunger; her brain cells were being robbed of vitally needed oxygen for good growth and, and . . . yawn.

She shouldn't have worried. It had been an unusually busy day. A busy and unusual day. So she lay there in the great quiet of the museum next to the warm quiet of her brother and allowed the soft stillness to settle around them: a comforter of quiet. The silence seeped from their heads to their soles and into their souls. They stretched out and relaxed. Instead of oxygen and stress, Claudia thought now of hushed and quiet words: glide, fur, banana, peace. Even the footsteps of the night watchman added only an accented quarter-note to the silence that had become a hum, a lullaby.

They lay perfectly still even long after he passed. Then they whispered good night to each other and fell asleep. They were quiet sleepers and hidden by the heaviness of the dark, they were easily not discovered.

(Of course, Saxonberg, the draperies of that bed helped, too.)

Would you have stayed with Claudia in the museum? Why or why not?

How do you know that Claudia is familiar with the museum?

Describe Claudia's personality. Describe Jamie's personality. Why do they make a good team for their adventure?

Why do Claudia and Jamie visit the French and English furniture section of the museum?

WRITE   What do you think will happen in the morning? Write a short description of what you think will happen next. Include some dialogue between Claudia and Jamie.

Author E. L. (Elaine) Konigsburg got the idea for *From the Mixed-up Files of Mrs. Basil E. Frankweiler* from three experiences. Two of them were reading experiences. "I read in the *New York Times* that the Metropolitan Museum of Art in New York City had bought a statue for $225. At the time of the purchase they did not know who had sculpted it, but they suspected it had been done by someone famous."

"Shortly after that article appeared in the paper, I read a book about the adventures of some children, who, upon being sent by ship from their island home to England, were captured by pirates. In the company of the pirates, the children became piratical themselves."

The third thing that happened was a picnic that Mrs. Konigsburg went on with her husband and three children in Yellowstone Park. There were no outdoor tables or chairs, so the family had to eat their salami and bread and chips and chocolate milk crouching slightly above the ground. "Then," she says, "the complaints began: the milk was getting warm, and there were ants over everything, and the sun was melting the icing on the cupcakes. I thought to myself, that if my children ever left home they would never become barbarians even if they were captured by pirates. They would want at least all the comforts of home plus a few extra dashes of elegance." She began thinking of places where they might go and decided the only place they would possibly run away to would be the Metropolitan Museum of Art.

185

You Be the Jury

by **Marvin Miller**

illustrated by **Harvey Chan**

◆

Ladies and Gentlemen of the Jury:

This court is now in session. My name is Judge John Denenberg. You are the jury, and the trials are set to begin.

You have a serious responsibility. Will the innocent be sent to jail and the guilty go free? Let's hope not. Your job is to make sure that justice is served.

Read each case carefully. Study the evidence presented and then decide:

Innocent or Guilty?

Both sides of the case will be presented to you. The person who has the complaint is called the *plaintiff*. He has brought the case to court.

The person being accused is called the *defendant*. He is pleading his innocence and presents a much different version of what happened.

IN EACH CASE, THREE PIECES OF EVIDENCE WILL BE PRESENTED AS EXHIBITS A, B, AND C. EXAMINE THE EXHIBITS VERY CAREFULLY. A *CLUE* TO THE SOLUTION OF EACH CASE WILL BE FOUND THERE. IT WILL DIRECTLY POINT TO THE INNOCENCE OR GUILT OF THE ACCUSED.

Remember, each side will try to convince you that his version is what actually happened. BUT YOU MUST MAKE THE FINAL DECISION.

◆———◆———◆

◆ The Case of the Wrong Bag ◆

LADIES AND GENTLEMEN OF THE JURY:

A person who is found with stolen property is not necessarily a thief.

Keep this in mind as you go over the facts in this case. Since we are in criminal court today, the State is the accuser. In this case, the State, represented by the district attorney, has accused John Summers of robbing Kay's Jewelry Store. John Summers, the defendant, has pleaded innocent and claims that his arrest is a mistake.

The State called the owner of Kay's Jewelry Store as its first witness. She has testified as follows:

"My name is Wendy Kay, and I own Kay's Jewelry Store in Martinville. I was working alone in the store on Wednesday afternoon, December 2, when a man walked in. It was exactly 3:30. I noticed the time because I had just put a new collection of diamond watches from Switzerland on display. I noticed the man because he had a handkerchief over his face. I thought that was odd until I also noticed the outline of a gun projecting from his pocket. That's when I got scared."

The man ordered Wendy Kay to empty a case of jewels and all the store's cash into a black bag. The robbery took only minutes, and the thief escaped on foot.

At four o'clock the next afternoon, John Summers entered the lobby of the Bristol Hotel and walked over to the luggage checkroom. He pointed to a black bag, which the bellman gave him. As he handed the bellman a tip, a hotel detective noticed that Summers's bag matched the description of the bag used in the jewelry store robbery. He arrested Summers and called the police.

When the police opened the bag and emptied its contents, a look of shock and surprise spread over Summers's face. Inside was the stolen jewelry.

John Summers was dumbfounded. He claimed he had pointed to the wrong bag in the hotel checkroom. This bag was not his, he said, but an identical twin belonging to someone else. His own bag contained a blue toothbrush and underwear, and it was locked.

The police returned to the luggage checkroom and questioned the bellman. The man thought there might have been two bags in the checkroom, although a second black bag was nowhere to be found.

EXHIBIT A is a picture of the bag and jewelry. John Summers claims that he checked an identical bag and that he mistakenly picked up this bag from the luggage room.

The State has drawn your attention to the shape of this bag, its handle, and lock. The State submits that this is an unusual-looking bag, and that it is very unlikely, if not impossible, that another bag looking just like it would be checked into the same hotel on the same day.

The State also presented EXHIBIT B, a list of the contents of John Summers's pockets at the time he was arrested. His wallet contained $710 in cash, a sizable sum for a person spending only one night in town. The State alleges that the $710 in Summers's wallet is the money stolen from the jewelry store.

No gun was found in Summers's pocket. The State claims a simple explanation. John Summers robbed Kay's Jewelry Store by pretending the object in his pocket was a gun. In reality, it was only his pointed finger.

On the basis of all this evidence, John Summers was accused of the jewelry store robbery.

John Summers has given the following testimony:

"My visit to Martinville was supposed to be a simple overnight trip. Every year around this time, the Martinville Museum has its annual art sale, and I wanted to buy a painting. I just started collecting art last year. I may not know a lot about art, but I know what I like. I've already got two of those pictures of the sad-looking kids with the big eyes. But this time I wanted something really stupendous to go over the sofa in the living room. Maybe something with some purple in it to match the drapes. I saved up more than eight hundred bucks to buy a painting this trip."

Summers's schedule was easy to reconstruct. He arrived by bus on Wednesday morning and checked into the Bristol Hotel. The Museum opened at noon. Mr. Summers was one of the first persons to enter the Museum. He spent the entire afternoon there. But to his disappointment, he could not find any artwork he liked.

EXHIBIT C is a torn Museum ticket stub for the day in question. The Museum hours were noon to four o'clock. The robbery of Kay's Jewelry Store took place at 3:30. While there was no witness who can testify he saw John Summers in the museum the entire time, the stub shows he indeed visited the Museum.

When the Museum closed, John Summers went back to his hotel, disappointed his trip was in vain. The following day, he checked out of the hotel at noon. Since his bus did not leave until later that day, Summers locked his black bag, checked it in the hotel's luggage checkroom, and went sightseeing. Later he returned to pick up his bag, and he was promptly arrested.

John Summers claims that he is the victim of an unfortunate coincidence.

LADIES AND GENTLEMEN OF THE JURY: You have just heard the Case of the Wrong Bag. You must decide the merit of the State's accusation. Be sure to carefully examine the evidence in EXHIBITS A, B, and C.

Did John Summers rob Kay's Jewelry Store? Or had he indeed picked up the wrong bag?

(The jury's verdict appears on page 194.)

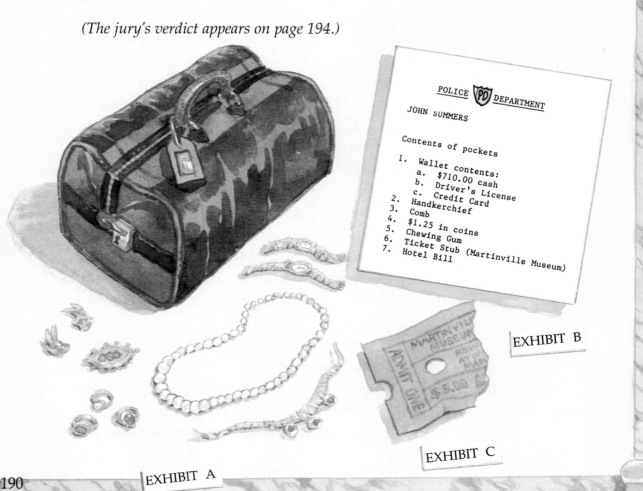

POLICE ⬡PD⬡ DEPARTMENT

JOHN SUMMERS

Contents of pockets

1. Wallet contents:
   a. $710.00 cash
   b. Driver's License
   c. Credit Card
2. Handkerchief
3. Comb
4. $1.25 in coins
5. Chewing Gum
6. Ticket Stub (Martinville Museum)
7. Hotel Bill

EXHIBIT B

EXHIBIT C

EXHIBIT A

◆ The Case of the Power Blackout ◆

LADIES AND GENTLEMEN OF THE JURY:

A company that provides a public service, such as a power company, has special responsibilities. When the service fails, the company is responsible for any damages that may happen.

Keep this in mind as you decide the case before you today. Mel Mudd, the plaintiff and owner of Mudd's Diner, claims that a power failure lasted sixteen hours and he was unable to serve his customers. Mr. Mudd wants to be paid for this lost business. Allied Utilities, the defendant, is a power company that provides electricity and gas to the people in Fairchester County. Allied Utilities admits to the power failure. But it claims to have repaired it three hours after it was reported.

Mel Mudd has given the following testimony:

"My name is Mudd. I'm the owner of Mudd's Diner. On Thursday, February 16 at 9:30 P.M., just as I was about to close up for the night, the lights went out. Do you know that old joke: Where was Thomas Edison when the lights went out? Well, the answer is: In the dark. And that's exactly where I was, too. I immediately called the power company and was assured the power would be restored promptly."

Mr. Mudd returned to his diner the following morning, opened the back door and flipped on the light switch. The room was totally dark.

He telephoned the power company several times, and each time the line was busy. After posting a "closed" sign on the front of the diner, Mudd returned to the back room and tried to telephone the company again. The line was still busy.

Mr. Mudd kept phoning the utility company and after two hours finally got through. The company told him they had fixed the problem the night before, but they promised they would send a repairman right away.

It took two hours for the repairman to arrive. By that time, Mr. Mudd had turned away the noon lunch crowd.

The repairman again checked the outside cable. He tightened the couplings but found nothing to indicate further repairs were needed. When the repairman went back to the diner to report his findings, the lights were on in the back room.

Mr. Mudd insisted the second visit was necessary to repair the lost power because the work had not been done properly the night before. He telephoned Allied Utilities and told them he planned to sue the company for lost business. A supervisor arrived at the diner in five minutes.

EXHIBIT A shows the lost business at Mudd's Diner during the time Mudd claims he had no power. You will note on that day he had only $146.35 in business. Entries for other days show he usually had up to $450.00 worth of business. This is the amount Mudd seeks from the utility company—$450.00.

Mel Mudd was extremely angry when the supervisor arrived at the back room of the diner. The man assured Mudd the power failure had been fixed the night before. Mudd strongly disagreed.

Allied Utilities enters as EXHIBIT B the repair work-order for the diner. This is a record kept for each customer complaint. You will note that the first call came in at 9:35 P.M. The repair order shows that the power failure lasted only three hours during the time the diner was closed. Power was claimed to have been restored by 12:36 A.M.

The company also enters EXHIBIT C, a photograph of the back room that was taken shortly after the supervisor arrived. You will note that the supervisor is holding up a light bulb. He had found it in a wastebasket in the diner's back room. Tests have shown this bulb is burned out and no longer in working order.

The company contends that while its repairman was outside checking the power the second time, Mudd somehow realized he may have been mistaken about the power failure.

The light in the back room had failed to go on because of a burned-out bulb. Mr. Mudd then replaced the bulb with a new one but said nothing to the company so he could sue them for lost business. Allied Utilities refuses to pay the money Mel Mudd has requested.

LADIES AND GENTLEMEN OF THE JURY: You have just heard the Case of the Power Blackout. You must decide the merit of Mel Mudd's claim. Be sure to carefully examine the evidence in EXHIBITS A, B, and C.

Should Allied Utilities pay Mr. Mudd for the income he lost during the power failure? Or did Mudd know that the power had been restored?

(The jury's verdict appears on page 194.)

EXHIBIT A

GROSS RECEIPTS
WEEK OF FEB. 12

DATE	BREAKFAST 6-11	LUNCH 11-5	DINNER 5-9	TOTAL
2/12	93.25	116.42	170.52	380.15
2/13	123.60	88.35	225.80	437.45
2/14	85.25	116.45	248.20	450.20
2/15	47.55	93.85	286.45	427.95
2/16	48.10	106.75	254.05	408.20
2/17		20.22	126.35	146.35
2/18	94.45	123.22	204.20	421.45

WEEKLY TOTAL - $2,673.25

ALLIED ⚡ UTILITIES
TELEPHONE LOG

DATE	TIME	NAME	ADDRESS	REPAIR MAN	DIS. TIME	COMP. TIME
2/16	7:12p	B. ROPER	186 CHEW ST.	8	7:30p	7:50p
2/16	7:26p	G. MORRISON	S. POINT ST.	17	8:10p	8:55p
2/16	8:17p	K. SPENCER	294 8th ST.	15	8:30p	9:58p
2/16	8:42p	B. SEATED	26 BLAIR AVE.	8	9:30p	10:15p
2/16	9:35p	M. MUDD	15 SOUTH ST.	17	10:43p	12:36p
2/16	9:55p	R. LEMON	7 W. POINT	9	10:55p	11:30p
2/16	10:30p	H. RUBIN	19 2nd AVE.	8	11:15p	11:35p
2/16	10:40p	D. CLARK	40 TONS. RD.	15	12:00p	12:20p

EXHIBIT B

EXHIBIT C

◆ The Case of the Wrong Bag ◆

John Summers claimed that the bag he stored in the check-room was *locked*. But the contents of his pockets in EXHIBIT B showed he had no key. Summers was lying. He had indeed robbed Kay's Jewelry Store, and the bag with the jewelry was his.

◆ The Case of the Power Blackout ◆

EXHIBIT C shows the back room of Mudd's Diner after the supervisor arrived. An empty glass with ice cubes is on a table. If the electricity was out until shortly before the supervisor got there, it would have been impossible for Mudd to have used ice cubes in the drink. When Mudd realized he had ice, he knew the power had been restored the night before. This was confirmed when he replaced the burned-out light bulb. However, he had already turned away his lunchtime customers, so he said nothing to the supervisor so he could illegally sue the power company.

When you were acting as the jury, did you guess the right verdicts? Explain why or why not.

What are the similarities and the differences in the cases of John Summers and Mel Mudd?

Why was it important to note that John Summers did not have a key in his pocket?

No light came on when Mel Mudd flipped the switch, so he closed his restaurant. If you had been Mel, what would you have done?

WRITE What would you do to find out whether someone was innocent or guilty of a crime? Write a list of steps you might follow.

Trespasses

To trespass can mean "to go beyond a boundary."
How are Claudia, John Summers, and Mel Mudd all
guilty of trespassing?

WRITER'S WORKSHOP

Do you think you could have persuaded one of the
characters in these selections not to do what he or
she did? Write a persuasive paragraph giving strong
reasons that could change one character's mind. Use
facts from the story to bolster your case.

Writer's Choice   In these selections,
people commit different types of trespasses.
What do you think about their actions? Write down
your thoughts, and think of a way to present them.

T H E M E

Flying Solo

Imagine that you are left alone in a small airplane. You don't know how to fly, but the plane seems to be able to fly itself. The problem is that it doesn't know how to land, and neither do you.

C O N T E N T S

197

FLYING MACHINE

WRITTEN BY ANDREW NAHUM

ENCLOSED COCKPITS had to await the development of safety glass in the late 1920s. Until then, pilots sat in the open, exposed to howling winds, freezing cold, and damp—with nothing more to protect them than a tiny windshield and warm clothes. Naturally, comfort was a low priority in these open cockpits, and they were very basic and functional in appearance. There were few instruments, and engine gauges were just as often on the engine itself as in the cockpit. The layout of the main flight controls became established fairly early on, with a rudder bar at the pilot's feet for turning and a control column, or "joy stick," between the knees for diving, climbing, and banking. Some early planes had a wheel rather than a joy stick, but it served the same purpose. This basic layout is still used in light planes today.

By the 1930s, the joy stick had become the standard form of control, and even the simplest planes, like this De Havilland Tiger Moth, had a range of basic instruments. The whole cockpit was functional and basic, with none of the comforts light planes usually have today, such as carpets, molded seats, and heaters.

Turn indicator

Small windshield

Notice saying that aerobatic maneuvers may be performed

Engine rev counter

Compass

Airspeed indicator

Altimeter

Joy stick

Notice reminding the pilot that the plane can cruise at 94 mph (150 kmh) but will stall if flown slower than 45 mph (72 kmh)

Lever to close landing/takeoff slats on the wing during aerobatic maneuvers

Engine oil pressure gauge

Rudder bar

Throttle

Landing and
taxi light
switches

Engine starting
controls

Engine data such
as fuel flow, torque
(the force turning
the turbines), and
turbine
temperature

Battery-powered,
stand-by main
flight instruments,
enabling the pilot
to land safely in
case of complete
electrical failure

Navigation
computer
equipment

Engine
speed
control
(throttle)

Indicators for brakes and
hydraulic systems

THE FLIGHT DECK of a modern jetliner looks dauntingly complicated, with its array of switches, dials, and displays for such
things as engine condition, hydraulics, navigational aids, and
so on, not to mention the basic flight controls. Increasingly,

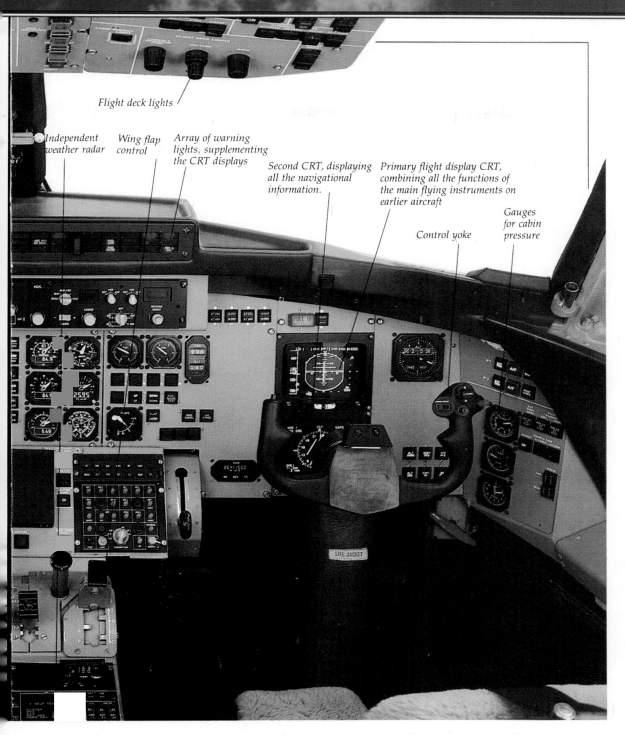

Flight deck lights

Independent weather radar

Wing flap control

Array of warning lights, supplementing the CRT displays

Second CRT, displaying all the navigational information.

Primary flight display CRT, combining all the functions of the main flying instruments on earlier aircraft

Control yoke

Gauges for cabin pressure

however, computers are taking over certain functions, and the mass of dials is being replaced by neat screens called CRTs (for "cathode ray tube"), on which the pilot can change the information displayed at the flick of a button.

HATCHET

WRITTEN BY GARY PAULSEN
ILLUSTRATED BY MARK REIDY

Brian is flying 7,000 feet above the Canadian wilderness on the way to visit his father. Brian is enjoying his first flight in a small plane, until the unthinkable happens.

The pilot sat large, his hands lightly on the wheel, feet on the rudder pedals. He seemed more a machine than a man, an extension of the plane. On the dashboard in front of him Brian saw dials, switches, meters, knobs, levers, cranks, lights, handles that were wiggling and flickering, all indicating nothing that he understood and the pilot seemed the same way. Part of the plane, not human.

When he saw Brian look at him, the pilot seemed to open up a bit and he smiled. "Ever fly in the copilot's seat before?" He leaned over and lifted the headset off his right ear and put it on his temple, yelling to overcome the sound of the engine.

Brian shook his head. He had never been in any kind of plane, never seen the cockpit of a plane except in films or on television. It was loud and confusing. "First time."

"It's not as complicated as it looks. Good plane like this almost flies itself." The pilot shrugged. "Makes my job easy."

He took Brian's left arm. "Here, put your hands on the controls, your feet on the rudder pedals, and I'll show you what I mean."

Brian shook his head. "I'd better not."

"Sure. Try it . . ."

Brian reached out and took the wheel in a grip so tight his knuckles were white. He pushed his feet down on the pedals. The plane slewed suddenly to the right.

"Not so hard. Take her light, take her light."

Brian eased off, relaxed his grip. The burning in his eyes was forgotten momentarily as the vibration of the plane came through the wheel and the pedals. It seemed almost alive.

"See?" The pilot let go of his wheel, raised his hands in the air and took his feet off the pedals to show Brian he was actually flying the plane alone. "Simple. Now turn the wheel a little to the right and push on the right rudder pedal a small amount."

Brian turned the wheel slightly and the plane immediately banked to the right, and when he pressed on the right rudder pedal the nose slid across the horizon to the right. He left off on the pressure and straightened the wheel and the plane righted itself.

"Now you can turn. Bring her back to the left a little."

Brian turned the wheel left, pushed on the left pedal, and the plane came back around. "It's easy." He smiled. "At least this part."

The pilot nodded. "All of flying is easy. Just takes learning. Like everything else. Like everything else." He took the controls back, then reached up and rubbed his left shoulder. "Aches and pains—must be getting old."

Brian let go of the controls and moved his feet away from the pedals as the pilot put his hands on the wheel. "Thank you . . ."

But the pilot had put his headset back on and the gratitude was lost in the engine noise and things went back to Brian looking out the window at the ocean of trees and lakes. The burning eyes did not come back, but memories did, came flooding in. The words. Always the words.

Divorce.

The Secret.

Fights.

Split.

The big split. Brian's father did not understand as Brian did, knew only that Brian's mother wanted to break the marriage apart. The split had come and then the divorce, all so fast, and the court had left him with his mother except for the summers and what the judge called "visitation rights." So formal. Brian hated judges as he hated lawyers. Judges that leaned over the bench and asked Brian if he understood where he was to live and why. Judges who did not know what had really happened. Judges with the caring look that meant nothing as lawyers said legal phrases that meant nothing.

In the summer Brian would live with his father. In the school year, with his mother. That's what the judge said after looking at papers on his desk and listening to the lawyers talk. Talk. Words.

Now the plane lurched slightly to the right and Brian looked at the pilot. He was rubbing his shoulder again and there was the sudden smell of body gas in the plane. Brian turned back to avoid embarrassing the pilot, who was obviously in some discomfort. Must have stomach troubles.

So this summer, this first summer when he was allowed to have "visitation rights" with his father, with the divorce only one month old, Brian was heading north. His father was a mechanical engineer who had designed or invented a new drill bit for oil drilling, a self-cleaning, self-sharpening bit. He was working in the oil fields of Canada, up on the tree line where the tundra started and the forests ended. Brian was riding up from New York with some drilling equipment—it was lashed down in the rear of the plane next to a fabric bag the pilot had called a survival pack, which had emergency supplies in case they had to make an emergency landing—that had to be specially made in the city, riding in a bushplane with the pilot named Jim or Jake or something who had turned out to be an all right guy, letting him fly and all.

Except for the smell. Now there was a constant odor, and Brian took another look at the pilot, found him rubbing the shoulder and down the arm now, the left arm, letting go more gas and wincing. Probably something he ate, Brian thought.

His mother had driven him from the city to meet the plane at Hampton where it came to pick up the drilling equipment. A drive in silence, a long drive in silence. Two and a half hours of sitting in the car, staring out the window just as he was now staring out the window of the plane. Once, after an hour, when they were out of the city she turned to him.

"Look, can't we talk this over? Can't we talk this out? Can't you tell me what's bothering you?"

And there were the words again. Divorce. Split. The Secret. How could he tell her what he knew? So he had remained silent, shook his head and continued to stare unseeing at the countryside, and his mother had gone back to driving only to speak to him one more time when they were close to Hampton.

She reached over the back of the seat and brought up a paper sack. "I got something for you, for the trip."

Brian took the sack and opened the top. Inside there was a hatchet, the kind with a steel handle and a rubber handgrip. The head was in a stout leather case that had a brass-riveted belt loop.

"It goes on your belt." His mother spoke now without looking at him. There were some farm trucks on the road now and she had to weave through them and watch traffic. "The man at the store said you could use it. You know. In the woods with your father."

Dad, he thought. Not "my father." My dad. "Thanks. It's really nice." But the words sounded hollow, even to Brian.

"Try it on. See how it looks on your belt."

And he would normally have said no, would normally have said no that it looked too hokey to have a hatchet on your belt. Those were the normal things he would say. But her voice was thin, had a sound like something thin that would break if you touched it, and he felt bad for not speaking to her. Knowing what he knew, even with the anger, the hot white hate of his anger at her, he still felt bad for not speaking to her, and so to humor her he loosened his belt and pulled the right side out and put the hatchet on and rethreaded the belt.

"Scootch around so I can see."

He moved around in the seat, feeling only slightly ridiculous.

She nodded. "Just like a scout. My little scout." And there was the tenderness in her voice that she had when he was small, the tenderness that she had when he was small and sick, with a cold, and she put her hand on his forehead, and the burning came into his eyes again and he had turned away from her and looked out the window, forgotten the hatchet on his belt and so arrived at the plane with the hatchet still on his belt.

Because it was a bush flight from a small airport there had been no security and the plane had been waiting, with the engine running when he arrived and he had grabbed his suitcase and pack bag and run for the plane without stopping to remove the hatchet.

So it was still on his belt. At first he had been embarrassed but the pilot had said nothing about it and Brian forgot it as they took off and began flying.

More smell now. Bad. Brian turned again to glance at the pilot, who had both hands on his stomach and was grimacing in pain, reaching for the left shoulder again as Brian watched.

"Don't know, kid . . ." The pilot's words were a hiss, barely audible. "Bad aches here. Bad aches. Thought it was something I ate but . . ."

He stopped as a fresh spasm of pain hit him. Even Brian could see how bad it was—the pain drove the pilot back into the seat, back and down.

"I've never had anything like this . . ."

The pilot reached for the switch on his mike cord, his hand coming up in a small arc from his stomach, and he flipped the switch and said, "This is flight four six . . ."

And now a jolt took him like a hammerblow, so forcefully that he seemed to crush back into the seat, and Brian reached for him, could not understand at first what it was, could not know.

And then knew.

Brian knew. The pilot's mouth went rigid, he swore and jerked a short series of slams into the seat, holding his shoulder now. Swore and hissed, "Chest! Oh God, my chest is coming apart!"

Brian knew now.

The pilot was having a heart attack. Brian had been in the shopping mall with his mother when a man in front of Paisley's store had suffered a heart attack. He had gone down and screamed about his chest. An old man. Much older than the pilot.

Brian knew.

The pilot was having a heart attack and even as the knowledge came to Brian he saw the pilot slam into the seat one more time, one more awful time he slammed back into the seat and his right leg jerked, pulling the plane to the side in a sudden twist and his head fell forward and spit came. Spit came from the corners of his mouth and his legs contracted up, up into the seat, and his eyes rolled back in his head until there was only white.

Only white for his eyes and the smell became worse, filled the cockpit, and all of it so fast, so incredibly fast that Brian's mind could not take it in at first. Could only see it in stages.

The pilot had been talking, just a moment ago, complaining of the pain. He had been talking.

Then the jolts had come.

The jolts that took the pilot back had come, and now Brian sat and there was a strange feeling of silence in the thrumming roar of the engine—a strange feeling of silence and being alone. Brian was stopped.

He was stopped. Inside he was stopped. He could not think past what he saw, what he felt. All was stopped. The very core of him, the very center of Brian Robeson was stopped and stricken with a white-flash of horror, a terror so intense that his breathing, his thinking, and nearly his heart had stopped.

Stopped.

Seconds passed, seconds that became all of his life, and he began to know what he was seeing, began to understand what he saw and that was worse, so much worse that he wanted to make his mind freeze again.

He was sitting in a bushplane roaring seven thousand feet above the northern wilderness with a pilot who had suffered a massive heart attack and who was either dead or in something close to a coma.

He was alone.

In the roaring plane with no pilot he was alone.

Alone.

For a time that he could not understand Brian could do nothing. Even after his mind began working and he could see what had happened he could do nothing. It was as if his hands and arms were lead.

Then he looked for ways for it not to have happened. Be asleep, his mind screamed at the pilot. Just be asleep and your eyes will open now and your hands will take the controls and your feet will move to the pedals—but it did not happen.

The pilot did not move except that his head rolled on a neck impossibly loose as the plane hit a small bit of turbulence.

The plane.

Somehow the plane was still flying. Seconds had passed, nearly a minute, and the plane flew on as if nothing had happened and he had to do something, had to do something but did not know what.

Help.

He had to help.

He stretched one hand toward the pilot, saw that his fingers were trembling, and touched the pilot on the chest. He did not know what to do. He knew there were procedures, that you could do mouth-to-mouth on victims of heart attacks and push their chests—C.P.R.—but he did not know how to do it and in any case could not do it with the pilot, who was sitting up in the seat and still strapped in with his seatbelt. So he touched the pilot with the tips of his fingers, touched him on the chest and could feel nothing, no heartbeat, no rise and fall of breathing. Which meant that the pilot was almost certainly dead.

"Please," Brian said. But did not know what or who to ask. "Please . . ."

The plane lurched again, hit more turbulence, and Brian felt the nose drop. It did not dive, but the nose went down slightly and the down-angle increased the speed, and he knew that at this angle, this slight angle down, he would ultimately fly into the trees. He could see them ahead on the horizon where before he could see only sky.

He had to fly it somehow. Had to fly the plane. He had to help himself. The pilot was gone, beyond anything he could do. He had to try and fly the plane.

He turned back in the seat, facing the front, and put his hands—still trembling—on the control wheel, his feet gently on the rudder pedals. You pulled back on the stick to raise the plane, he knew that from reading. You always pulled back on the wheel. He gave it a tug and it slid back toward him easily.

Too easily. The plane, with the increased speed from the tilt down, swooped eagerly up and drove Brian's stomach down. He pushed the wheel back in, went too far this time, and the plane's nose went below the horizon and the engine speed increased with the shallow dive.

Too much.

He pulled back again, more gently this time, and the nose floated up again, too far but not as violently as before, then down a bit too much, and up again, very easily, and the front of the engine cowling settled. When he had it aimed at the horizon and it seemed to be steady, he held the wheel where it was, let out his breath—which he had been holding all this time—and tried to think what to do next.

It was a clear, blue-sky day with fluffy bits of clouds here and there and he looked out the window for a moment, hoping to see something, a town or village, but there was nothing. Just the green of the trees, endless green, and lakes scattered more and more thickly as the plane flew—where?

He was flying but did not know where, had no idea where he was going. He looked at the dashboard of the plane, studied the dials and hoped to get some help, hoped to find a compass, but it was all so confusing, a jumble of numbers and lights. One lighted display in the top center of the dashboard said the number 342, another next to it said 22. Down beneath that were dials with lines that seemed to indicate what the wings were doing, tipping or moving, and one dial with a needle pointing to the number 70, which he thought—only thought—might be the altimeter. The device that told him his height above the ground. Or above sea level. Somewhere he had read something about altimeters but he couldn't remember what, or where, or anything about them.

Slightly to the left and below the altimeter he saw a small rectangular panel with a lighted dial and two knobs. His eyes had passed over it two or three times before he saw what was written in tiny letters on top of the panel. TRANSMITTER 221 was stamped in the metal and it hit him, finally, that this was the radio.

The radio. Of course. He had to use the radio. When the pilot had—had been hit that way (he couldn't bring himself to say that the pilot was dead, couldn't think it), he had been trying to use the radio.

Brian looked to the pilot. The headset was still on his head, turned sideways a bit from his jamming back into the seat, and the microphone switch was clipped into his belt.

Brian had to get the headset from the pilot. Had to reach over and get the headset from the pilot or he would not be able to use the radio to call for help. He had to reach over . . .

His hands began trembling again. He did not want to touch the pilot, did not want to reach for him. But he had to. Had to get the radio. He lifted his hands from the wheel, just slightly, and held them waiting to see what would happen. The plane flew on normally, smoothly.

All right, he thought. Now. Now to do this thing. He turned and reached for the headset, slid it from the pilot's head, one eye on the plane, waiting for it to dive. The headset came easily, but the microphone switch at the pilot's belt was jammed in and he had to pull to get it loose. When he pulled, his elbow bumped the wheel and pushed it in and the plane started down in a shallow dive. Brian grabbed the wheel and pulled it back, too hard again, and the plane went through another series of stomach-wrenching swoops up and down before he could get it under control.

When things had settled again he pulled at the mike cord once more and at last jerked the cord free. It took him another second or two to place the headset on his own head and position the small microphone tube in front of his mouth. He had seen the pilot use it, had seen him depress the switch at his belt, so Brian pushed the switch in and blew into the mike.

He heard the sound of his breath in the headset. "Hello! Is there anybody listening on this? Hello . . ."

He repeated it two or three times and then waited but heard nothing except his own breathing.

Panic came then. He had been afraid, had been stopped with the terror of what was happening, but now panic came and he began to scream into the microphone, scream over and over.

"Help! Somebody help me! I'm in this plane and don't know . . . don't know . . . don't know . . ."

And he started crying with the screams, crying and slamming his hands against the wheel of the plane, causing it to jerk down, then back up. But again, he heard nothing but the sound of his own sobs in the microphone, his own screams mocking him, coming back into his ears.

The microphone. Awareness cut into him. He had used a CB radio in his uncle's pickup once. You had to turn the mike switch off to hear anybody else. He reached to his belt and released the switch.

For a second all he heard was the *whusssh* of the empty air waves. Then, through the noise and static he heard a voice.

"Whoever is calling on this radio net, I repeat, release your mike switch—you are covering me. You are covering me. Over."

It stopped and Brian hit his mike switch. "I hear you! I hear you. This is me . . . !" He released the switch.

"Roger, I have you now." The voice was very faint and breaking up. "Please state your difficulty and location. And say *over* to signal end of transmission. Over."

Please state my difficulty, Brian thought. God. My difficulty. "I am in a plane with a pilot who is—who has had a heart attack or something. He is—he can't fly. And I don't know how to fly. Help me. Help . . ." He turned his mike off without ending transmission properly.

There was a moment's hesitation before the answer. "Your signal is breaking up and I lost most of it. Understand . . . pilot . . . you can't fly. Correct? Over."

Brian could barely hear him now, heard mostly noise and static. "That's right. I can't fly. The plane is flying now but I don't know how much longer. Over."

". . . lost signal. Your location please. Flight number . . . location . . . ver."

"I don't know my flight number or location. I don't know anything. I told you that, over."

He waited now, waited but there was nothing. Once, for a second, he thought he heard a break in the noise, some part of a word, but it could have been static. Two, three minutes, ten minutes, the plane roared and Brian listened but heard no one. Then he hit the switch again.

"I do not know the flight number. My name is Brian Robeson and we left Hampton, New York headed for the Canadian oil fields to visit my father and I do not know how to fly an airplane and the pilot . . ."

He let go of the mike. His voice was starting to rattle and he felt as if he might start screaming at any second. He took a deep breath. "If there is anybody listening who can help me fly a plane, please answer."

Again he released the mike but heard nothing but the hissing of noise in the headset. After half an hour of listening and repeating the cry for help he tore the headset off in frustration and threw it to the floor. It all seemed so hopeless. Even if he did get somebody, what could anybody do? Tell him to be careful?

All so hopeless.

He tried to figure out the dials again. He thought he might know which was speed—it was a lighted number that read 160—but he didn't know if that was actual miles an hour, or kilometers, or if it just meant how fast the plane was moving through the air and not over the ground. He knew airspeed was different from groundspeed but not by how much.

Parts of books he'd read about flying came to him. How wings worked, how the propellor pulled the plane through the sky. Simple things that wouldn't help him now.

Nothing could help him now.

An hour passed. He picked up the headset and tried again—it was, he knew, in the end all he had—but there was no answer. He felt like a prisoner, kept in a small cell that was hurtling through the sky at what he thought to be 160 miles an hour, headed—he didn't know where—just headed somewhere until . . .

There it was. Until what? Until he ran out of fuel. When the plane ran out of fuel it would go down.

Period.

Or he could pull the throttle out and make it go down now. He had seen the pilot push the throttle in to increase speed. If he pulled the throttle back out, the engine would slow down and the plane would go down.

Those were his choices. He could wait for the plane to run out of gas and fall or he could push the throttle in and make it happen sooner. If he waited for the plane to run out of fuel he would go farther—but he did not know which way he was moving. When the pilot had jerked he had moved the plane, but Brian could not remember how much or if it had come back to its original course. Since he did not know the original course anyway and could only guess at which display might be the compass—the one reading 342—he did not know where he had been or where he was going, so it didn't make much difference if he went down now or waited.

Everything in him rebelled against stopping the engine and falling now. He had a vague feeling that he was wrong to keep heading as the plane was heading, a feeling that he might be going off in the wrong direction, but he could not bring himself to stop the engine and fall. Now he was safe, or safer than if he went down—the plane was flying, he was still breathing. When the engine stopped he would go down.

So he left the plane running, holding altitude, and kept trying the radio. He worked out a system. Every ten minutes by the small clock built into the dashboard he tried the radio with a simple message: "I need help. Is there anybody listening to me?"

In the times between transmissions he tried to prepare himself for what he knew was coming. When he ran out of fuel the plane would start down. He guessed that without the propellor pulling he would have to push the nose down to keep the plane flying—he thought he may have read that somewhere, or it just came to him. Either way it made sense. He would have to push the nose down to keep flying speed and then, just before he hit, he would have to pull the nose back up to slow the plane as much as possible.

It all made sense. Glide down, then slow the plane and hit. Hit.

He would have to find a clearing as he went down. The problem with that was he hadn't seen one clearing since they'd started flying over the forest. Some swamps, but they had trees scattered through them. No roads, no trails, no clearings.

Just the lakes, and it came to him that he would have to use a lake for landing. If he went down in the trees he was certain to die. The trees would tear the plane to pieces as it went into them.

He would have to come down in a lake. No. On the edge of a lake. He would have to come down near the edge of a lake and try to slow the plane as much as possible just before he hit the water.

Easy to say, he thought, hard to do.

Easy say, hard do. Easy say, hard do. It became a chant that beat with the engine. Easy say, hard do.

Impossible to do.

He repeated the radio call seventeen times at the ten-minute intervals, working on what he would do between transmissions. Once more he reached over to the pilot and touched him on the face, but the skin was cold, hard cold, death cold, and Brian turned back to the dashboard. He did what he could, tightened his seatbelt, positioned himself, rehearsed mentally again and again what his procedure should be.

When the plane ran out of gas he should hold the nose down and head for the nearest lake and try to fly the plane kind of onto the water. That's how he thought of it. Kind of fly the plane onto the water. And just before it hit he should pull back on the wheel and slow the plane down to reduce the impact.

Over and over his mind ran the picture of how it would go. The plane running out of gas, flying the plane onto the water, the crash—from pictures he'd seen on television. He tried to visualize it. He tried to be ready.

But between the seventeenth and eighteenth radio transmissions, without a warning, the engine coughed, roared violently for a second and died. There was sudden silence, cut only by the sound of the windmilling propellor and the wind past the cockpit.

Brian pushed the nose of the plane down and threw up.

Going to die, Brian thought. Going to die, gonna die, gonna die—his whole brain screamed it in the sudden silence.

Gonna die.

He wiped his mouth with the back of his arm and held the nose down. The plane went into a glide, a very fast glide that ate altitude, and suddenly there weren't any lakes. All he'd seen since they started flying over the forest was lakes and now they were gone. Gone. Out in front, far away at the horizon, he could see lots of them, off to the right and left more of them, glittering blue in the late afternoon sun.

But he needed one right in front. He desperately needed a lake right in front of the plane and all he saw through the windshield were trees, green death trees. If he had to turn—if he had to turn he didn't think he could keep the plane flying. His stomach tightened into a series of rolling knots and his breath came in short bursts . . .

There!

Not quite in front but slightly to the right he saw a lake. L-shaped, with rounded corners, and the plane was nearly aimed at the long part of the L, coming from the bottom and heading to the top. Just a tiny bit to the right. He pushed the right rudder pedal gently and the nose moved over.

But the turn cost him speed and now the lake was above the nose. He pulled back on the wheel slightly and the nose came up. This caused the plane to slow dramatically and almost seem to stop and wallow in the air. The controls became very loose-feeling and frightened Brian, making him push the wheel back in. This increased the speed a bit but filled the windshield once more with nothing but trees, and put the lake well above the nose and out of reach.

For a space of three or four seconds things seemed to hang, almost to stop. The plane was flying, but so slowly, so slowly . . . it would never reach the lake. Brian looked out to the side and saw a small pond and at the edge of the pond some large animal—he thought a moose—standing out in the water. All so still looking, so stopped, the pond and the moose and the trees, as he slid over them now only three or four hundred feet off the ground—all like a picture.

Then everything happened at once. Trees suddenly took on detail, filled his whole field of vision with green, and he knew he would hit and die, would die, but his luck held and just as he was to hit he came into an open lane, a channel of fallen trees, a wide place leading to the lake.

The plane, committed now to landing, to crashing, fell into the wide place like a stone, and Brian eased back on the wheel and braced himself for the crash. But there was a tiny bit of speed left and when he pulled on the wheel the nose came up and he saw in front the blue of the lake and at that instant the plane hit the trees.

There was a great wrenching as the wings caught the pines at the side of the clearing and broke back, ripping back just

outside the main braces. Dust and dirt blew off the floor into his face so hard he thought there must have been some kind of explosion. He was momentarily blinded and slammed forward in the seat, smashing his head on the wheel.

Then a wild crashing sound, ripping of metal, and the plane rolled to the right and blew through the trees, out over the water and down, down to slam into the lake, skip once on water as hard as concrete, water that tore the windshield out and shattered the side windows, water that drove him back into the seat. Somebody was screaming, screaming as the plane drove down into the water. Someone screamed tight animal screams of fear and pain and he did not know that it was his sound, that he roared against the water that took him and the plane still deeper, down in the water. He saw nothing but sensed blue, cold blue-green, and he raked at the seatbelt catch, tore his nails loose on one hand. He ripped at it until it released and somehow—the water trying to kill him, to end him—somehow he pulled himself out of the shattered front window and clawed up into the blue, felt something hold him back, felt his windbreaker tear and he was free. Tearing free. Ripping free.

But so far! So far to the surface and his lungs could not do this thing, could not hold and were through, and he sucked water, took a great pull of water that would—finally—win, finally take him, and his head broke into light and he vomited and swam, pulling without knowing what he was, what he was doing. Without knowing anything. Pulling until his hands caught at weeds and muck, pulling and screaming until his hands caught at last in grass and brush and he felt his chest on land, felt his face in the coarse blades of grass and he stopped, everything stopped. A color came that he had never seen before, a color that exploded in his mind with the pain and he was gone, gone from it all, spiraling out into the world, spiraling out into nothing.

Nothing.

Brian opened his eyes and screamed.

For seconds he did not know where he was, only that the crash was still happening and he was going to die, and he screamed until his breath was gone.

Then silence, filled with sobs as he pulled in air, half crying. How could it be so quiet? Moments ago there was nothing but noise, crashing and tearing, screaming, now quiet.

Some birds were singing.

How could birds be singing?

His legs felt wet and he raised up on his hands and looked back down at them. They were in the lake. Strange. They went down into the water. He tried to move, but pain hammered into him and made his breath shorten into gasps and he stopped, his legs still in the water.

Pain.

Memory.

He turned again and sun came across the water, late sun, cut into his eyes and made him turn away.

It was over then. The crash.

He was alive.

The crash is over and I am alive, he thought. Then his eyes closed and he lowered his head for minutes that seemed longer. When he opened them again it was evening and some of the sharp pain had abated—there were many dull aches—and the crash came back to him fully.

Into the trees and out onto the lake. The plane had crashed and sunk in the lake and he had somehow pulled free.

He raised himself and crawled out of the water, grunting with the pain of movement. His legs were on fire, and his forehead felt as if somebody had been pounding on it with a hammer, but he could move. He pulled his legs out of the lake and crawled on his hands and knees until he was away from the wet-soft shore and near a small stand of brush of some kind.

Then he went down, only this time to rest, to save something of himself. He lay on his side and put his head on his arm and closed his eyes because that was all he could do now, all he could think of being able to do. He closed his eyes and slept, dreamless, deep and down.

There was almost no light when he opened his eyes again. The darkness of night was thick and for a moment he began to panic again. To see, he thought. To see is everything. And he could not see. But he turned his head without moving his body and saw that across the lake the sky was a light gray, that the sun was starting to come up, and he remembered that it had been evening when he went to sleep.

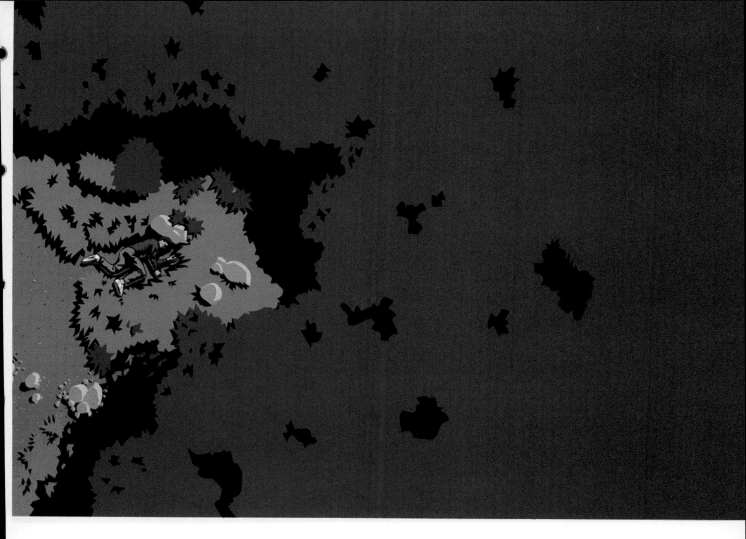

"Must be morning now . . ." He mumbled it, almost in a hoarse whisper. As the thickness of sleep left him the world came back.

He was still in pain, all-over pain. His legs were cramped and drawn up, tight and aching, and his back hurt when he tried to move. Worst was a keening throb in his head that pulsed with every beat of his heart. It seemed that the whole crash had happened to his head.

He rolled on his back and felt his sides and his legs, moving things slowly. He rubbed his arms; nothing seemed to be shattered or even sprained all that badly. When he was nine he had plowed his small dirt bike into a parked car and broken his

ankle, had to wear a cast for eight weeks, and there was nothing now like that. Nothing broken. Just battered around a bit.

His forehead felt massively swollen to the touch, almost like a mound out over his eyes, and it was so tender that when his fingers grazed it he nearly cried. But there was nothing he could do about it and, like the rest of him, it seemed to be bruised more than broken.

I'm alive, he thought. I'm alive.

Do you think that a teenager like Brian could actually do what he does in this story? Why or why not?

What are the problems that Brian Robeson faces in this story?

Why wouldn't air traffic controllers or any other authorities know the real path of Brian's flight?

What personal qualities does Brian exhibit in the selection? How do these qualities help him to survive?

WRITE   Imagine that it is your job to contact Brian's father about the accident. Write down the message that you would leave for him.

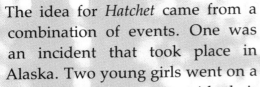

The idea for *Hatchet* came from a combination of events. One was an incident that took place in Alaska. Two young girls went on a boating trip with their father. The boat began to leak, so he put the girls off on an island, telling them he'd come back as soon as he could. But he took ill, and he couldn't get right back. The girls didn't even have a hatchet! He expected they would be dead by the time he got back. Living on seaweed, and using an old piece of tarp for shelter, the girls somehow survived. I was very interested in that story because I've lived off the land, too. There was a time in my life when I got by with gardening, trapping, and hunting.

Most of the things that happen in the book have happened to me, too. I've been in a forced landing of a small plane, so I know about that kind of fear. I also know what it means to depend on yourself to survive. I wanted to write a book about young people being self-sufficient, on all levels—emotional, intellectual, physical. I decided to take a basically urban boy, put him in a hostile environment, and then see what happened.

When you're writing, there's no substitute for personal experience. When I realized that writing isn't just something I do, but is what I am, things changed for me. Like the storytellers of long ago, I'm the person who puts an animal skin on his back, dances around the fire, and tells what the hunt was like.

AWARD-WINNING
AUTHOR

Flying Solo

What feelings and ideas about life might Brian share with the author who created him, Gary Paulsen?

WRITER'S WORKSHOP

Imagine what it would be like to fly a plane, drive a bus, or ride a wild horse without really knowing how. Think of a character who must do something he or she has never done before. Write a short story about the adventure. Tell the story in the first person, using words such as *I*, *me*, and *mine*.

Writer's Choice

What do you think about the theme Flying Solo? Write down your ideas, and think of a way to share them with friends.

CONNECTIONS

Multicultural Connection

Courts of a Different Order

Every society has written or unwritten laws and a system for enforcing those laws. The early Native Americans had a very efficient and just system. Wrongdoers were brought before tribal leaders, who were usually a council of elders, warriors, or religious heads. The council's goal was not to hand out punishments but to settle the case in a way that satisfied both sides.

This idea of justice lives on in modern tribal courts on Indian reservations. Such courts deal mostly with disputes between people.

The Oglala Sioux Court is a good example. It has one chief judge and three other judges, all elected by the tribal council, and one "special judge" who must have legal training. Lawyers seldom appear. The judges' good sense and their knowledge of tribal law enable them to hand down fair decisions.

Imagine a problem that might come before a tribal court. With a group, create a dramatic skit in which you try a case and settle it in a way that satisfies both parties.

Social Studies Connection

Tracking Down Facts About Different Ways of Life

Indian reservations are governed much as states are. With a group, find out about some of the differences between life on and off Indian reservations. Share your findings in an oral report.

Science/Literature Connection

Ancient Mysteries

There were some natural mysteries the Indians of ancient times couldn't solve. So they made up "why" stories, similar to the myths of the Greeks and Romans, to explain nature's riddles. Read and summarize an Indian "why" story. Then write a scientific explanation of the condition or event the story is about.

UNIT THREE

YESTERYEAR

*A people without history
is like the wind on the buffalo grass.*
— *a Sioux saying*

How did General George Washington command his troops in battle? Why did free African-American men and women risk their lives for others in the Underground Railroad? Who were the Chinese pioneers of the American West? Historians such as Ruthanne Lum McCunn seek answers to such questions. You too can find out about America's history by being curious and asking your own questions. As you read the selections in this unit, see how many of your questions are answered.

THEMES

BOOKSHELF

THE HOUSE OF DIES DREAR

by Virginia Hamilton

Thomas and his family move into a house with a long history of danger as a stop on the Underground Railroad. Thomas soon begins to wonder if the "danger" part is over.

Edgar Allan Poe Award

Harcourt Brace Library Book

A GATHERING OF DAYS

by Joan W. Blos

What was it like to live in the United States 160 years ago? Share the daily life and struggles of thirteen-year-old Catherine Hall of New Hampshire in the 1830s.

Newbery Medal

Harcourt Brace Library Book

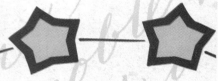

TAKE A WALK IN THEIR SHOES

by Glennette Tilley Turner

The stories of fourteen great African Americans are told, first in short biographies and then in dramatic skits that allow you to "walk in their shoes."

Notable Trade Book in the Field of Social Studies

LINCOLN: A PHOTOBIOGRAPHY

by Russell Freedman

Photographs and drawings depict the life of Abraham Lincoln and the many faces of the American Civil War.

Newbery Medal, Notable Trade Book in the Field of Social Studies

HER SEVEN BROTHERS

by Paul Goble

This Cheyenne legend explains the origin of the constellation that we call "The Big Dipper."

Children's Choice, Teachers' Choice

THEME

EARLY AMERICA

When you think about the early days of the United States of America, what pictures come to mind? The following selections may provide you with new pictures, including some seen through the eyes of children who were there when it all began.

CONTENTS

The Sign of the Beaver

Elizabeth George Speare

Winner of the Newbery Award for both *The Witch of Blackbird Pond*
and *The Bronze Bow*

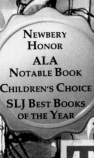

The Sign of the Beaver

by Elizabeth George Speare

Illustrations by Tom Ricks

Father has gone back to Massachusetts to fetch the rest of the family, leaving Matt alone to guard their cabin. When Matt stumbles into a swarm of bees, he is rescued by an Indian chief and his grandson. The chief will accept no reward, but he will allow Matt to teach his grandson, Attean, how to read English. Attean hates the idea of learning from Matt and quickly reverses their roles of student and teacher.

When they came upon a row of short tree stumps, birch and aspen cut off close to the ground, Matt's heart gave a leap. Were there settlers nearby? Or Indians? There was no proper clearing. Then he noticed that whoever had cut the trees had left jagged points on each one. No axe would cut a tree in that way. He could see marks where the trees had been dragged along the ground.

In a few steps the boys came out on the bank of an unfamiliar creek. There Matt saw what had happened to those trees. They had been piled in a mound right over the water, from one bank to the other. Water trickled through them in tiny cascades. Behind the piled-up branches, a small pond stretched smooth and still.

"It's a beaver dam!" he exclaimed. "The first one I've ever seen."

"*Qwa bit*," said Attean. "Have red tail. There beaver wigwam." He pointed to a heap of branches at one side, some of them new with green leaves still clinging. Matt stepped closer to look. Instantly there was the crack of a rifle. A ring of water rippled the surface of the pond. Near its edge a black head appeared for just a flash and vanished again in a splutter of bubbles.

Attean laughed at the way Matt had started. "Beaver make big noise with tail," he explained.

"I thought someone had shot a gun," Matt said. "I wish I had my rifle now."

Attean scowled. "Not shoot," he warned. "Not white man, not Indian. Young beaver not ready."

He pointed to a tree nearby. "Sign of beaver," he said. "Belong to family."

Carved on the bark, Matt could make out the crude figure of an animal that could, with some imagination, be a beaver.

"Sign show beaver house belong to people of beaver," Attean explained. "By and by, when young beaver all grown, people of beaver hunt here. No one hunt but people of beaver."

"You mean, just from that mark on the tree, another hunter would not shoot here?"

"That our way," Attean said gravely. "All Indian understand."

Would a white man understand? Matt wondered. He thought of Ben with his stolen rifle. It wasn't likely Ben would respect an Indian sign. But he must remember to warn his father.

When it seemed the beaver did not intend to show itself again, the two boys climbed back up the bank. At the row of stumps, Attean halted and signaled for Matt to go ahead.

"Show way to cabin," he ordered.

All Matt's suspicions came rushing back. Did Attean intend to sneak off behind his back and leave him to find his own way home?

"Is this some kind of trick?" he demanded hotly.

Attean looked stern. "Not trick," he said. "Matt need learn."

To Matt's relief, he took the lead again. After a short distance he stopped and pointed to a broken stick leaning in the direction of the creek. A little farther on there was a small stone set against a larger one. Not far away a tuft of dried grass dangled from a branch of a small tree.

"Indian make sign," Attean said. "Always make sign to tell way. Matt must same. Not get lost in forest."

Now Matt remembered how Attean had paused every so often, sometimes to break off a branch that hung in their path, once to nudge aside a stone with the toe of his moccasin. He had done these things so quickly that Matt had paid no mind. He saw now that Attean had carefully been leaving markers.

"Of course," he exclaimed. "But my father always made blazes on the trees with his knife."

Attean nodded. "That white man's way. Indians maybe not want to show where he go. Not want hunters to find beaver house."

So there were secret signs. Nothing anyone following them would notice. It would take sharp eyes to find them, even if you knew they were there.

"Matt do same," Attean repeated. "Always make sign to show way back."

Matt was ashamed of his suspicions. Attean had only meant to help him. If only he didn't have to be so superior about it.

As though Attean sensed that Matt was disgruntled, he stopped, whipped out his knife, and neatly sliced off two shining gobs of dried sap from a nearby spruce. He grinned and held out one of them like a peace offering. "Chaw," he ordered. He popped the other piece into his mouth and began to chew with evident pleasure.

Gingerly, Matt copied him. The gob fell to pieces between his teeth, filling his mouth with a bitter juice. He wanted to spit it out in disgust, but Attean was plainly enjoying the stuff, so he stubbornly forced his jaws to keep moving. In a moment the bits came together in a rubbery gum, and the first bitterness gave way to a fresh piney taste. To his surprise, it was very good. The two boys tramped on, chewing companionably. Once more, Matt acknowledged to himself, Attean had taught him another secret of the forest.

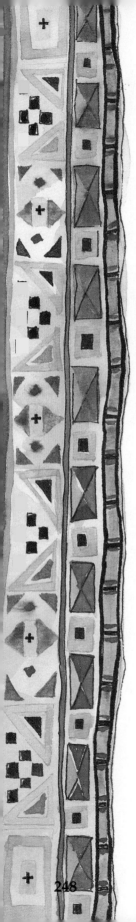

I MUST HAVE A BOW, MATT DECIDED ONE MORNING.
He was envious of the bow Attean often carried behind his
shoulder, and of the blunt arrows he tucked into his belt. Only
the day before, Matt had watched him swing it suddenly into
position and bring down a flying duck. Attean had picked up
the dead bird carefully and carried it away with him. No doubt
the Indians would find some use for every scrap of bone and
feather. Matt knew by now that Attean never shot anything
just for the fun of it. With a bow and a little practice, Matt
thought now, he might get a duck for himself. It would be a
fine change from his usual fish.

He had no doubt he could shoot with a bow. In fact he had
made them years ago back in Quincy. He and his friends had
played at Indians, stalking each other through the woods and
whooping out from behind trees. They had even practiced half-
earnestly at shooting at a target. How could he have known
that someday he would have need of such a skill?

He cut a straight branch, notched it at either end, and
stretched tight a bit of string his father had left. Arrows he
whittled out of slender twigs. But something was definitely
wrong. His arrows wobbled off in odd directions or flopped on
the ground a few feet away. He was chagrined when next
morning Attean came walking out of the woods and surprised
him at his practice.

Attean looked at the bow. "Not good wood," he said at
once. "I get better."

He was very exacting about the wood he chose. He
searched along the edge of the clearing, testing saplings,
bending slender branches, discarding one after another, till
he found a dead branch of ash about the thickness of his three
fingers. He cut a rod almost his own height and handed it
to Matt.

"Take off bark," he directed, and squatted down to watch
while Matt scraped the branch clean. Then, taking it in his
hands again, he marked off several inches in the center where

248

Matt's hand would grip the bow. "Cut off wood here," he said, running his hand from center to ends. "Make small like this." He held up one slim finger.

Matt set to work too hastily. "Slow," Attean warned him. "Knife take off wood too fast. Indian use stone."

Under the Indian's critical eye, Matt shaved down the branch, paring off the thinnest possible shavings. The slow work took all his patience. Twice he considered the task finished, but Attean, running his hand along the curve of the bow, was not satisfied till it was smooth as an animal bone.

"Need fat now," he said. "Bear fat best."

"Will this do?" Matt asked, bringing out a bowl of fish stew he had left cooling on the table. Carefully, with a bit of bark, Attean skimmed off the drops of oil that had risen to the surface. He rubbed the oil from one end of the bow to the other

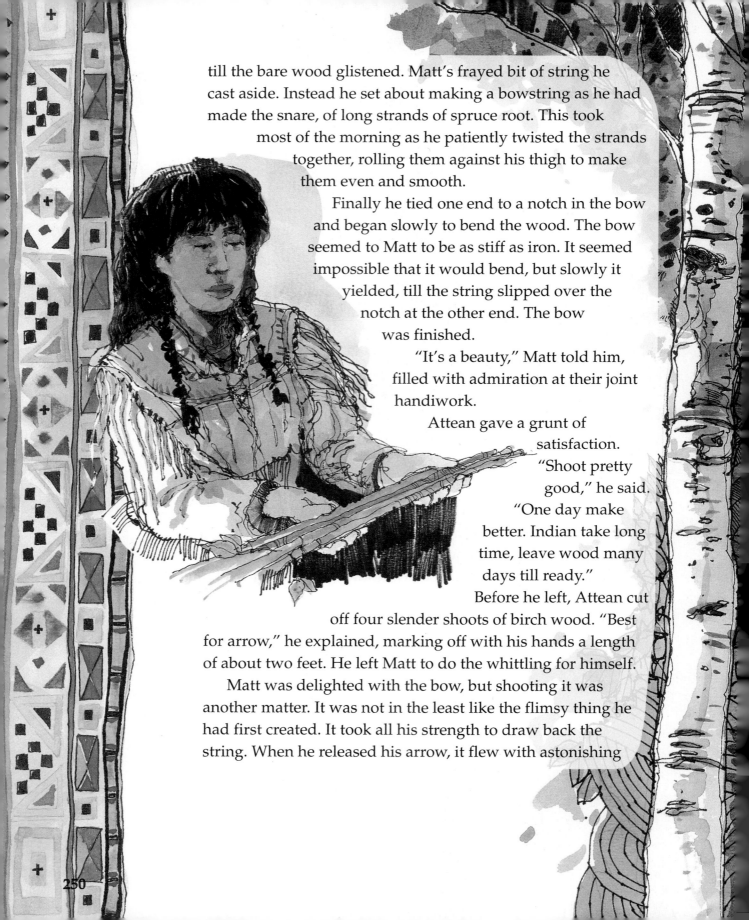

till the bare wood glistened. Matt's frayed bit of string he cast aside. Instead he set about making a bowstring as he had made the snare, of long strands of spruce root. This took most of the morning as he patiently twisted the strands together, rolling them against his thigh to make them even and smooth.

Finally he tied one end to a notch in the bow and began slowly to bend the wood. The bow seemed to Matt to be as stiff as iron. It seemed impossible that it would bend, but slowly it yielded, till the string slipped over the notch at the other end. The bow was finished.

"It's a beauty," Matt told him, filled with admiration at their joint handiwork.

Attean gave a grunt of satisfaction.

"Shoot pretty good," he said. "One day make better. Indian take long time, leave wood many days till ready."

Before he left, Attean cut off four slender shoots of birch wood. "Best for arrow," he explained, marking off with his hands a length of about two feet. He left Matt to do the whittling for himself.

Matt was delighted with the bow, but shooting it was another matter. It was not in the least like the flimsy thing he had first created. It took all his strength to draw back the string. When he released his arrow, it flew with astonishing

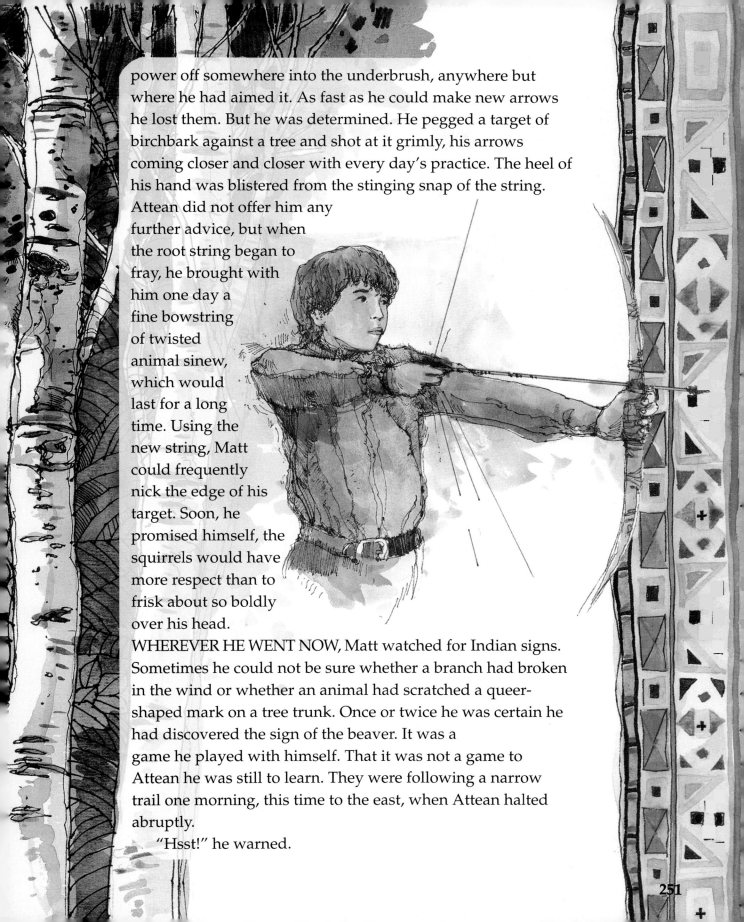

power off somewhere into the underbrush, anywhere but where he had aimed it. As fast as he could make new arrows he lost them. But he was determined. He pegged a target of birchbark against a tree and shot at it grimly, his arrows coming closer and closer with every day's practice. The heel of his hand was blistered from the stinging snap of the string. Attean did not offer him any further advice, but when the root string began to fray, he brought with him one day a fine bowstring of twisted animal sinew, which would last for a long time. Using the new string, Matt could frequently nick the edge of his target. Soon, he promised himself, the squirrels would have more respect than to frisk about so boldly over his head.

WHEREVER HE WENT NOW, Matt watched for Indian signs. Sometimes he could not be sure whether a branch had broken in the wind or whether an animal had scratched a queer-shaped mark on a tree trunk. Once or twice he was certain he had discovered the sign of the beaver. It was a game he played with himself. That it was not a game to Attean he was still to learn. They were following a narrow trail one morning, this time to the east, when Attean halted abruptly.

"Hsst!" he warned.

Off in the brush Matt heard a low, rasping breathing and a
frantic scratching in the leaves. The noise stopped the moment
they stood still. Moving warily, the boys came upon a fox
crouched low on the ground. It did not run, but lay snarling at
them, and as he came nearer, Matt saw that its foreleg was
caught fast. With a long stick Attean pushed aside the leaves
and Matt caught the glint of metal.

"White man's trap," said Attean.

"How do you know?" Matt demanded.

"Indians not use iron trap. Iron trap bad."

"You mean a white man set this trap?" Matt thought of Ben.

"No. Some white man pay for bad Indian to hunt for him.
White man not know how to hide trap so good." Attean

showed Matt how cleverly the trap had been hidden, the leaves and earth mounded up like an animal burrow with two half-eaten fish heads concealed inside.

The fox watched them, its teeth bared. The angry eyes made Matt uncomfortable. "We're in luck to find it first," he said, to cover his uneasiness.

Attean shook his head. "Not beaver hunting ground," he said. "Turtle clan hunt here." He pointed to a nearby tree. On the bark Matt could just make out a crude scar that had a shape somewhat like a turtle. He was indignant.

"We found it," he said. "You mean you're just going to leave it here because of a mark on a tree?"

"Beaver people not take animal on turtle land," Attean repeated.

"We can't just let it suffer," Matt protested. "Suppose no one comes here for days?"

"Then fox get away."

"How can he get away?"

"Bite off foot."

Indeed, Matt could see now that the creature had already gnawed its own flesh down to the bone.

"Leg mend soon," Attean added, noting Matt's troubled face. "Fox have three leg beside."

"I don't like it," Matt insisted. He wondered why he minded so much. He had long ago got used to clubbing the small animals caught in his own snares. There was something about this fox that was different. Those defiant eyes showed no trace of fear. He was struck by the bravery that could inflict such pain on itself to gain freedom. Reluctantly he followed Attean back to the trail, leaving the miserable animal behind.

"It's a cruel way to trap an animal," he muttered. "Worse than our snares."

"*Ehe*," Attean agreed. "My grandfather not allow beaver people to buy iron trap. Some Indian hunt like white man now. One time many moose and beaver. Plenty for all Indians and

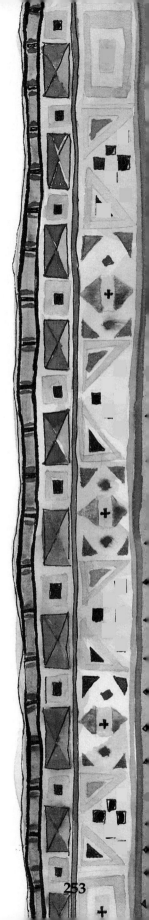

for white man too. But white man not hunt to eat, only for skin. Him pay Indian to get skin. So Indian use white man's trap."

Matt could not find an answer. Tramping beside Attean he was confused and angry as well. He couldn't understand the Indian code that left an animal to suffer just because of a mark on a tree. And he was fed up with Attean's scorn for white men. It was ridiculous to think that he and Attean could ever really be friends. Sometimes he wished he could never see Attean again.

Even at the same moment, he realized that this was really not true. Even though Attean annoyed him, Matt was constantly goaded to keep trying to win this strange boy's respect. He would lie awake in the night, staring up at the chinks of starlight in the cabin roof, and make up stories in which he himself, not Attean, was the hero. Sometimes he imagined how Attean would be in some terrible danger, and he, Matt, would be brave and calm and come swiftly to the rescue. He would kill a bear unaided, or a panther, or fend off a rattlesnake about to strike. Or he would learn about an enemy band of Indians sneaking through the forest to attack the place where Attean was sleeping, and he would run through the woods and give the alarm in time.

In the morning he laughed at himself for this childish daydreaming. There was little chance he would ever be a hero, and little chance too that Attean would ever need his help. Matt knew that the Indian boy came day after day only because his grandfather sent him. For some reason the old man had taken pity on this helpless white boy, and at the same time

he had shrewdly grasped at the chance for his grandson to learn to read. If he suspected that Attean had become the teacher instead, he would doubtless put a stop to the visits altogether.

Matt knew he ought to feel grateful for Attean's teaching. Every day Attean taught him some new thing—a plant like an onion that he could drop into his cooking pot to make his stew more tasty—a weed with a small orange flower and a milky juice in its stem that took away the sting of insect bites or poison ivy—a plant with brownish flowers and roots bearing a string of nutlike bulbs that thickened his stew and made it more nourishing. He had pointed out plants that Matt must never eat, no matter how hungry he might be. He had even shown Matt how to improvise a rain cape in a sudden rain by quickly punching a hole through the center of a wide strip of birchbark and making a cone of bark for his head.

The only thing that Matt could teach him, Attean was set against learning. For Attean the white man's signs on paper were *piz wat*—good for nothing. Nevertheless, Matt noticed that in spite of himself Attean had learned something from the white boy. He was speaking the English tongue with greater ease. Perhaps he was not aware himself how differently he spoke. He picked up new words readily. Sometimes he used them with that odd humor that Matt was beginning to recognize. Matt knew that Attean was mocking when some of his own favorite expressions came solemnly out of the Indian's mouth.

"Reckon so," Attean would say. "Rain come soon, by golly." Sometimes he even took a fancy to a word out of *Robinson Crusoe*. He especially liked the sound of *verily*.

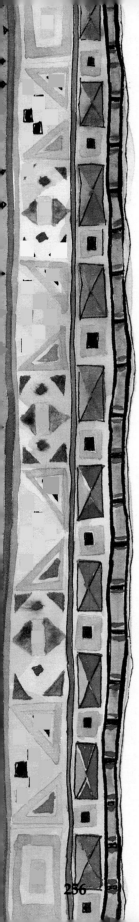

In return, Matt liked to try out Indian words. They were not hard to understand but impossible to get his tongue around. He didn't think he could ever quite get them right, but he could see that though it amused Attean when he tried, it also pleased him.

"*Cha kwa*—this morning," Matt might say, "I chased a *kogw* out of the corn patch." He wouldn't add that he had wasted an arrow and watched the porcupine waddle off unharmed.

Perhaps, after all, those lessons hadn't been entirely wasted.

Which character do you like better, Matt or Attean? Explain your answer.

What does Matt learn from Attean? How does it help him?

What about Attean annoys Matt?

What character traits help Matt succeed in living in the forest? Find events in the story that show these traits.

WRITE   Everyone needs some help adapting to new situations. What would you tell a new person in your neighborhood that would make life easier for him or her? Write a list of neighborhood survival skills that you think are important.

POEMS SELECTED BY

VIRGINIA DRIVING HAWK SNEVE

To American Indians, the spoken word was sacred. Children listened to their grandparents tell stories, recite ceremonial prayers and chants, and sing lullabies and other tribal songs. The children grew up remembering the music and knew that the act of speaking words gave life to Native American stories, songs, and prayers. Words were chosen carefully and rarely wasted.

Sun, Moon, Stars

Sun, moon, stars,
You that move in the heavens,
Hear this mother!
A new life has come among you.
Make its life smooth.

(from an Omaha ceremony for the
newborn)

My Horse, Fly Like a Bird

My horse, fly like a bird
To carry me far
From the arrows of my enemies,
And I will tie red ribbons
To your streaming hair.

(adapted from a Lakota warrior's
song to his horse)

257

AN AMERICAN
SOLDIER

The American Revolution: A Picture Sourcebook

by John Grafton

A BRITISH GRENADIER

JOIN, or DIE.

This cartoon of a rattlesnake cut in segments representing parts of America with the legend "Join, or Die" was designed by Benjamin Franklin at the time of the Albany Congress of 1754. (The issue then was joint action with regard to the Indians, not the British.)

INDIANS AND THE FRONTIER:
MOHAWK CHIEF JOSEPH BRANT
The main area of Indian activity during the Revolutionary period was western New York and Pennsylvania, where the Six Nations of the Iroquois and their British allies battled American settlers and villages.

GEORGE WASHINGTON

THE HESSIANS IN THE REVOLUTION

During the period from 1776 to 1783 as many as 17,000 German mercenary soldiers—primarily from the state of Hesse-Cassel, thus the name Hessians—fought for the British in America.

A HESSIAN GRENADIER

THE BATTLE OF THE BRANDYWINE

American forces at the battle of Brandywine Creek. In the late summer of 1777, the British Commander Howe landed with his army from New York at the northern tip of Chesapeake Bay, fifty miles from his objective, Philadelphia. Washington met Howe at the Brandywine on September 11 and suffered a tactical defeat largely through insufficient knowledge of the terrain. Later that month the British army occupied Philadelphia, driving the American Congress first to Lancaster and then to York. Washington attacked the British at their main base, Germantown, on October 4 and nearly won a major victory before being forced back.

THE BOSTON MASSACRE

A contemporary broadside gives evidence of popular reaction to the Boston Massacre. The list of victims, of course, includes the last name of Crispus Attucks, a black man killed by the British.

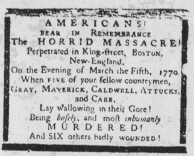

AMERICANS!
BEAR IN REMEMBRANCE
The HORRID MASSACRE!
Perpetrated in King-ftreet, Boston,
New-England,
On the Evening of March the Fifth, 1770.
When FIVE of your fellow countrymen,
GRAY, MAVERICK, CALDWELL, ATTUCKS,
and CARR,
Lay wallowing in their Gore!
Being bafely, and moft inhumanly
MURDERED!
And SIX others badly WOUNDED!

The Riddle of Penncroft Farm

by Dorothea Jensen

In the fall of 1777, in the midst of the American Revolution, Philadelphia has been taken over by George Washington's patriot forces. Many farmers in that area are Tories, colonists who side with the British.

Geordie's father, a stout Tory, is outraged when his oldest son, Will, leaves to fight for the patriot cause. He is angered further when the Continental Congress decrees that apples cannot be exported to England. In response, he sends Geordie to Philadelphia to try to peddle their farm goods.

illustrated by Gary Lippincott
map by Michelle Nidenoff

West Branch

Brandywine Creek

Buck Run

Big Elk Creek

Red Clay Creek

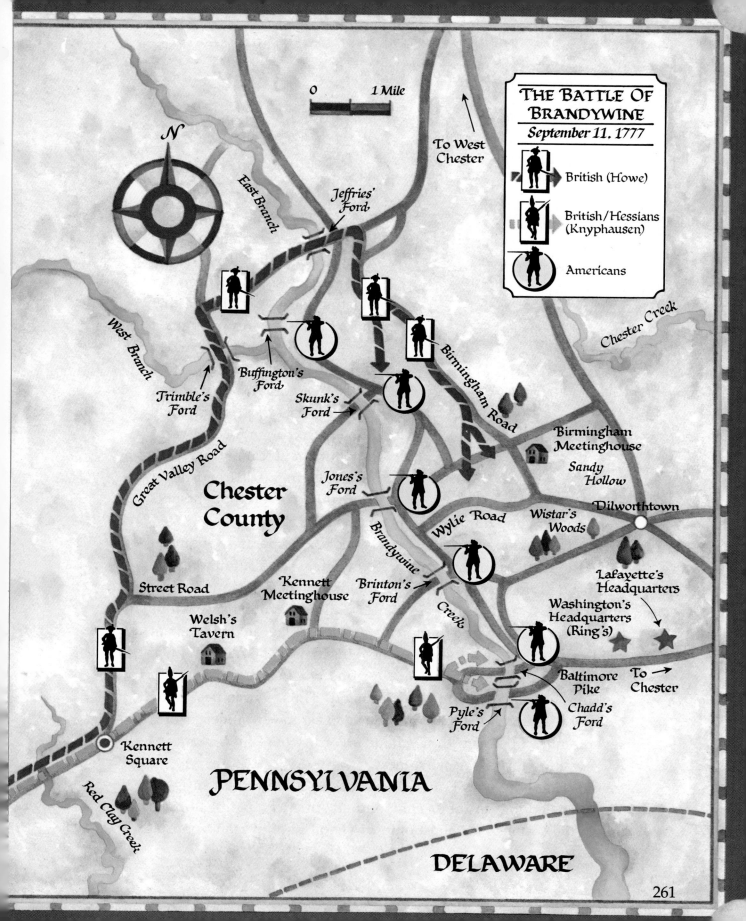

$\mathcal{S}$ ince the British columns blocked the road going west, I was forced to turn east, toward Chadd's Ford. Soon I came in sight of Kennett Meetinghouse. I could see that the Friends were assembled for midweek meeting, and I stopped to warn them that the British were not far behind me. What a waste of precious time! They thanked me for the warning but went calmly on with their meeting as if I had never interrupted, even though shots were now ringing out behind me on the road.

I hunkered down on the seat and looked desperately about for a place to turn off the main road. To my great relief, I found a lane that headed north. It was barely more than wheel ruts in the dirt, but at least 'twas clear of trees—and soldiers. Seemingly oblivious to my fears, Daisy and Buttercup ambled along at their regular snail's pace, despite my shaking the reins to urge them faster. Such efforts only delayed me further, for one of the reins snapped. It took the better part of an hour to mend. Thus, it was past noon before I reached Street Road and turned east toward Jones's Ford, several miles upstream from Chadd's Ford, where the Americans were waiting for the British attack.

Crossing at Jones's Ford was not easy—I had to pick my way around felled logs in the stream, and an American patrol stopped me on the east side for questioning. When I said I'd seen troops at

Welsh's but none since, the captain nodded. "Just what Major Spear reported. I don't know what that blind fool Colonel Bland saw going up to the fork, but it surely wasn't redcoats[1]! Now you'd best get along, boy," he said.

Mystified, I got along. Then, toiling up a steep slope, I heard rolling, distant thunder. I looked at the sky. It was cloudless—even the morning fog had burned away under the bright, hot sun. Again the rumbling rent the air, and this time I knew 'twas no thunderclap but the firing of guns, louder than I'd ever heard. I stopped the wagon to listen closely, trying to decide where the ominous sound was coming from. Panic rose in my chest until I could scarcely catch my breath. Instinctively, I reached into my pocket and brought out my lucky piece. The small, lead grenadier[2] in the red-painted tunic stood on my palm, aiming down his long musket. Clutching the toy, I made a childish wish that it could tell me what to do.

But a much larger and less silent figure decided my course of action. I heard a peculiar muttering in the woods nearby—a string of oaths. Without stopping to think, I raised up my lead soldier to throw at the mutterer. Then I saw his face: it belonged to Squire Thomas Cheyney, a swarthy, thickset man who had been a friend of my father's before the war had set them at odds. As the squire thrashed his way through the bushes with his riding crop, he scowled and swore like a madman. When he spotted me, his mouth opened into a perfect O of astonishment.

"Why, Geordie, what are you doing here?" he gasped.

"Been delivering perry[3] at Welsh's."

"Then your horses are fresh?" he inquired eagerly.

"If you want to call them that. Slowest nags in creation."

---

[1]British soldiers
[2]soldier
[3]pear cider

"At least they're not lame," he said with disgust. "I had to leave *my* infernal mount tied to a stile and was nearly caught by the redcoats! Give me a hand up, lad. We must hurry."

"What do you mean?" I asked, helping him up beside me.

"Why, we must warn Washington about this flanking action!"

"Flanking action?" I echoed, still not understanding.

"Aye. Ten thousand British are crossing the two branches of the Brandywine north of the fork, guided by the Tory Galloway. I saw them myself! They'll come down Birmingham Road behind the American line and fall upon the Continentals[4] from the rear. And by the cannon fire coming from the south, I judge Howe has sent some troops to make Washington believe that *that* is where the main attack will come."

"Aye, troops under Knyphausen[5] are moving against Chadd's."

Cheyney pounded his fist down on the seat. "I thought so! 'Tis the same trick Howe used to win at Long Island! I tried to warn General Sullivan of this, but he thought I was exaggerating! Well, at least the fool gave me a pass to Washington's headquarters. I'll need your wagon."

My expression must have resembled one of the idiots the Hessian[6] thought me to be, for the squire said, more kindly, "If you're too feared to come, wait here for me. I'll be back as soon as I can."

"Father will flay me if I help the Continentals, but . . ." Suddenly I thought of my brother, Will. I couldn't let him be taken by surprise. "Aye, I'm going with you!" I blurted out.

"That's a brave lad!" the squire cried. He seized the reins and whipped up the horses until they ran as if wolves were nipping at their hooves.

* * * * *

---

[4]American soldiers

[5]British/Hessian officer who had questioned Geordie earlier and thought him an "idiot"

[6]German soldier fighting for the British

As it turned out, Squire Cheyney and I didn't get far before the road along the creek grew too crowded with American troops for our wagon to pass. Nothing daunted, Cheyney said we must leave the wagon on Wylie Road and ride the three miles overland to Ring's house, Washington's headquarters near Chadd's Ford. With growing misgivings, I helped unhitch the team and conceal the wagon in the woods, and soon we were up on Daisy and Buttercup's bare backs, trotting over the rough ground. I clutched Buttercup's reins and mane for dear life as I followed Squire Cheyney up and down the steep wooded hills, more than once nearly sliding backwards off Buttercup's rump or forward over his head. Cheyney, all unheeding, allowed branches to whip behind him into my face; they stung like the very devil.

As we came out of the trees on the hill behind Ring's house and paused to get our bearings, I quickly forgot my stinging face, for I could hear the sharp staccato of musketry coming from Brandywine Creek below. The thought that Will might be the target made me sick with fear.

Cheyney glanced at me. "Never heard muskets before, boy?" he asked brusquely, gathering up his reins.

I shuddered. "Not trained on men. And not when one of those men might be my brother, and he could be shot from the back."

"We'll prevent that if we get through in time! And Ring's is just below!" the squire cried, goading the winded Daisy into a gallop down the hill. As we reached the stone wall behind Washington's headquarters, a line of Continentals blocked our way. One grabbed Daisy's bridle and barked, "Don't you know there's a battle brewing? This is no place for farmers!"

"Don't be daft, sir!" Cheyney roared. "We've a pass from Sullivan to deliver urgent information to General Washington."

He held out a piece of paper. After the guard read it, he quickly motioned us on. Cheyney chirruped his horse down the hill, with mine wheezing along behind. We stopped beside the well. Dismounting, the squire sprinted around the side of the house and I scuttled behind him to the wide front door.

Two brawny sentries brought us both to a halt. Squire Cheyney, glaring at them, simply hallooed through the doorway in a voice Knyphausen likely could hear above the booming cannon beyond the Brandywine. I caught my breath, not only because my brother's life hung in the balance, but also because I was to see the man many revered as a god—and my father reviled as the devil.

My suspense lasted but a trice.[7] A dignified figure in a buff-and-blue uniform appeared before us—General Washington.

Broad-shouldered, taller than anyone I'd ever seen, he regarded us through icy blue eyes. "There had better be an excellent reason for this interruption, sir," he exclaimed.

After all his sprinting and bellowing, Cheyney had little breath for speech. He panted like a landed fish for several long moments. Then, finally, he gasped out, " 'Tis the British, ten thousand strong, crossing upstream to attack from behind."

Washington narrowed his eyes, looked us over as if we stank of barn muck, and motioned us into the house.

---

[7] an instant

"I heard some such nonsense from Colonel Bland, but later reports proved this false," he said, frowning. "Local sources have assured me there is no ford above the fork that's close enough to offer a serious threat. No, it's here at Chadd's Ford that the British attack will come, and here at the Brandywine is where we'll hold them!" In an undertone, he added, "Indeed we must: no other obstacles lie 'twixt Howe and Philadelphia save the Schuylkill River—at the very doors of the city!"

The squire could barely contain his outrage. "Local sources!" he spluttered. "I *am* a local source. And a local source most loyal to your efforts! Don't you know that most of the farmers who've stayed nearby, in Howe's path, are neutrals or Tories who want to throw dust in your eyes?" His voice squeaked with fury, and with despair I perceived that he sounded too much like a bedlamite[8] to be taken seriously.

Washington dismissed Cheyney's words with a wave of his hand. "And why should I not think *you* are doing the same? Nay, I choose to believe the word of an innocent youth before that of a man puffed full of Tory guile!"

"Tory guile?!" Cheyney squawked, as ruffled as a fighting cock.

"Yes, an innocent such as this lad here."

Suddenly I felt pride and glory swelling within me. As puffed up as any guileful man, I stepped forward and gazed up expectantly at that lofty, grave countenance.

"Aye, this lad," repeated Washington. "Now confound the boy, where'd he get to? . . . Ned—Ned Owens?"

"Here, Excellency." As we stood in the corridor, I could see a pudgy boy standing at a sideboard in the room to the right. In one hand he held a meat pasty; in the other, a pewter tankard. Juice from one or the other was dribbling down his cheeks. Crestfallen, I watched him wipe his mouth on his sleeve.

"Have you heard what this man says, Owens?"

---

[8]insane person

"Aye, sir. And it be lies. I've been up and down the Brandy-wine—all the way north to the fork—and there's nary a ford you've not covered with patrols." He leveled a look at me that was brimming over with self-importance. 'Twas this barefaced conceit that gave me back my tongue.

"But the British crossed *above* the fork, at *Jeffries'* Ford!" I exclaimed. "The squire saw them, and I *know* him to be true to the patriot cause. Redcoats in the *thousands* will be coming south down Birmingham Road, behind you to the east! Don't let them flank your troops, sir. My brother, Will, is a Continental, and I couldn't bear . . ."

I shall never know why—'twas probably a storm of nerves after all I'd been through and my fears for Will—but then and there I burst into tears. No man would have done so, but 'tis likely my sobs did more than any man's vows (and surely more than Cheyney's dismayed howls) to convince Washington of the truth.

For a long moment those cool blue eyes took my measure. Just then an aide dashed into the room and thrust some papers into Washington's hand. From what he said, it appeared they were reports verifying all that Squire Cheyney and I had told the general. Washington immediately ordered word sent to Sullivan to meet the column advancing on his rear. After the aide's departure, the general buckled on his sword. As he did so, he asked, "What's your name, lad?"

"Geordie."

"We need drummer boys, Geordie. Join us, as Owens here has done." He threw these words over his shoulder as he strode from the room. Jealously, I glanced at Owens. How much I wanted to take up the drum—and how impossible that I do so!

Squire Cheyney cleared his throat. "Well done, Geordie." He mopped his brow with a handkerchief. "We'd best head back north to Wylie Road. 'Twill be safe enough—the main battle will surely be to the east, where the redcoats are."

We hurried outside, but before we could mount, one of Washington's aides sped up the path and stopped the squire.

"Go along with the courier and show Sullivan the way to Birmingham Road!" He cast a disparaging look at Daisy. "That nag will not be quick enough. Come, I'll find another for you."

Squire Cheyney handed me Daisy's reins with a warning to waste no time, then rushed away with the aide. By this time the gunfire was quickening, making Buttercup as skittish as an unbroken filly. I was still trying to get up on her when General Washington himself emerged from the house, calling for a guide to lead him to Birmingham Road.

I half hoped and half feared that I would be that guide, but instead his aides brought up an elderly man from the neighborhood, Mr. Joseph Brown. Old Mr. Brown made every possible excuse not to go, but in the end was convinced at swordpoint where his duty lay. When he protested his lack of a horse, one of Washington's aides dismounted from his own fine charger.

As Brown reluctantly climbed into the saddle, Washington sat impatiently on his own beautiful white horse. The instant the frightened farmer was in place, Washington snapped a whip at the rump of the reluctant guide's horse, which leapt into a gallop. The general followed, spurring his own mount until its nose pushed into the leader's flank like a colt suckling its mother. Even this didn't satisfy Washington, who cracked his whip and shouted, "Push along, old man, push along!" Spellbound, I watched the two race up the hill across the golden fields, jumping the fences as they came to them. I had never seen such horsemanship—superb on the part of the general, dreadful on the part of Mr. Brown. Behind them ran a ragged line of soldiers, rucksacks[9] bobbing as they sped over the uneven ground.

After the two mismatched leaders disappeared over the brow of the hill, I managed to get on Buttercup and take hold of Daisy's bri-

---

[9]backpacks

dle. It took very little urging to hasten the two frightened horses north, away from the sound of gunfire. By the time I got back to my wagon, my hands were too shaky for my fingers to work properly, and it took ages to harness the team. At the very moment I climbed to the seat and took up the reins, the valley behind me exploded with artillery fire. Terrified, Daisy and Buttercup reared in their traces. Up and up they went, pawing the smoke-filled air. Then they plunged back to the ground, landing at a dead run. For a few breathless moments I simply clung to the reins, pulling for all I was worth, but the horses were too panic-stricken to feel the bits sawing at their mouths. My arms ached from the effort, and I eased off to recover some strength for another try. *Perhaps my horses bolting might be a blessing in disguise,* I thought. It would surely get me away from the Brandywine much faster than their usual pace. Then I realized where we were headed: due east toward Birmingham Road, where the British and Americans were about to clash in battle.

With strength born of fear, I reached for the brake, only to have the lever break off in my hand. Clutching the reins, I shut my eyes and prayed. At the sound of gunfire, my eyes flew open once more. Up the hill to my left were two lines of soldiers. At the top of the ridge, one line raised their muskets in unconscious mimicry of the toy soldier in my pocket. Their tall caps were as pointed as my little grenadier's; their tunics as scarlet. But my toy had never spat forth puffs of smoke or blazes of fire as did the muzzles glinting in the sun. My eyes shifted down to the target below: the second line of soldiers, whose black cockaded hats proclaimed them Continentals. Under my horrified gaze, this American line wavered and broke, some few soldiers staying to return fire, but most wheeling in confusion toward the road down which my team was bolting.

As the wagon careened down the dusty lane, I glimpsed still, crumpled figures, their coats turning red with blood, lying in the field where the American line had stood. The thought that Will might be bleeding to death under the hot September sun made me steer my winded team into a thick copse of beech trees to consider what to do. 'Twas lucky I did, else I'd never have heard it—the faint but unmistakable sound of Will's whistle. I shook my head, thinking I must be imagining things. Then it came again more clearly from the thicket ahead.

I shot off the wagon seat and hurtled into the woods, crashing through underbrush in the manner of an animal fleeing a forest fire. My lips puckered soundlessly in the vain effort to whistle back. "Will! Where are you?" I finally called hoarsely.

Through the leaves, a gleam of pallid skin told me I'd found him. Will lay at the base of a beech tree looking much as he did napping in our orchard after a dip in our pond on a hot summer day. But the dark red daubs on his leg came from no pond.

"Geordie! I thought my eyes were playing tricks on me, seeing you pull up in our wagon. But when I whistled and you looked startled as a deer, I knew 'twas really you. Trust you to be in Wistar's Woods just when things got hot." Managing a feeble grin, he tried to sit up. Then, his face contorted with pain, and he fell back with a groan that tore at my heart.

"Don't you worry, Will," I said with a confidence I was far from feeling. "I'm taking you home."

"Nay," Will said weakly. "If the lobsterbacks[10] catch you . . ."

"Hush, you great booby. I still have some perry in the wagon; I can bribe my way through the whole British army with you safely hidden under the hay. You look as if you could use a cupful." I ran to the wagon and fetched a tin cup full of perry for him. Will's hands shook so much I had to help him hold the cup, but the strong cider appeared to strengthen him a little.

With every moment, the sounds of battle crept closer. In my distraction, I noticed that golden leaves were sifting down upon us, but it was early for the trees to be shedding so much of their foliage. An odd buzzing sound drew my attention. I looked up and

---

[10]British soldiers

saw the cause of the early autumn: deadly grapeshot whizzing back and forth through the trees cutting down the leaves as it had cut down the young men in the field.

Frantically, I ripped off my shirt and tore it in two. As gently as I could, I wrapped one half around Will's wounded leg. It was agony for both of us, but I had to staunch the bleeding, else he'd die before I even got him into the wagon. If I could get him that far. He was at least a foot taller than I, and heavier by several stone.[11] Without daring to think of the impossibility of my task, I knotted the other piece of shirt round Will's wrists, slipped them over my head, and started to crawl for the wagon, dragging my brother beneath me. He cried out so piteously that I froze, but a burst of artillery fire shook the earth beneath me and I lunged forward convulsively. I don't know if Will struck his head or fainted, but suddenly he went slack, his dead weight bringing me down on top of him so abruptly that my face hit the ground. Everything swirled in a dizzy spiral.

It was the blood streaming down my own face that spurred me back into action. I clawed wildly to lift myself enough to give Will air. Then, slowly we inched forward to the wagon, stopped behind it, and I gently eased my head out from Will's hands. Leaving him below, I jumped up on the wagon and fixed the slats down at their loading angle. Grabbing the rope of the loading pulley, I tied it to Will's wrist and grasped the other end. Though I strained and heaved with every ounce of strength I possessed, I couldn't budge him.

Will's eyes flickered open and he moaned.

"Will," I cried. "Can you crawl any? I can't pull you. . . ."

But Will fell back senseless once more.

I was in such despair that I didn't hear anyone approaching until I saw him standing next to me—a man in a scarlet jacket with little wings on the shoulders and a tall helmet of black fur. Even without it, he was the tallest man I'd ever seen, that British grenadier.

---

[11]British unit of weight equal to 14 pounds

Without a word, we stared at each other. Then he drew one arm over his face to wipe the sweat out of his eyes. I didn't move, though I could feel the blood dripping down my own face and the sting of the sweat running into the cuts on my cheek.

His eyes flicked over me and then down to Will and the telltale cockade on his hat.

"My brother," I said, and opened my palms to him in appeal.

Still silent, the grenadier set down his musket and swung the pack off his back to the ground with a loud thud that showed how very heavy it was. Then he gathered Will up in his arms and carefully laid him down upon the wagon bed.

"Be that drink?" he asked, jutting his chin toward the barrel of perry.

I nodded my head, speechless.

"I could use a bit o' drink. Seventeen miles I've marched since dawn. Seventeen miles in all this heat. 'Tis enough to kill a man, even without the efforts of this lot." He jerked his thumb at Will.

I swarmed up the slats, filled a cup, and thrust it at him. The soldier drained it in one gulp and held the cup out for more. I hastily obliged. After downing the second cupful, he picked up his pack and musket.

"Thankee, lad," he growled, and plunged back into the woods before I could thank him in return.

I had no time to ponder what had happened. The sounds of muskets were all around me in the woods, and the next redcoat to come upon us might not be so helpful. Quickly, I replaced the slats across the wagon and flung myself back on the seat. Even in my hurry, I felt an uncomfortable lump under my breeches.

It was my lead soldier. I took him up in my hand and gazed at it. After the flesh-and-blood grenadiers I'd seen in the field and in the forest, the toy seemed different. With all the force that remained to me, I threw it down to the ground and left it behind me on the Brandywine battlefield.

I turned southeast past Sandy Hollow, joining a trickle of Continentals fleeing toward Dilworthtown. I slaked their thirst with the perry, while it lasted. The poor fellows deserved it.

It was midnight by the time we came up our lane. By great good fortune my father, exhausted by his harvest work, was sleeping too soundly to hear us arrive, but my mother's ear was sharpened with worry. She soon rushed out of the house, lantern in hand. As she stood there, the wind swirled her long white shift about her ankles and sent her long brown hair, loosened for bed, flying about her head.

"Geordie, I thought thee'd never get home!" she cried when she saw me.

"There was a battle at Brandywine, Mother. I found . . . "

"Geordie, thee knows I don't believe in bloodshed . . . no matter what the cause," she cut in. "It's bad enough to have thy brother run away and break thy father's heart, but now thee, too. . . ." Her voice faltered as she followed my mute gesture toward the wagon bed. "It's Will! Oh, Geordie, he isn't dead?"

"No, but grievously wounded."

Mother felt Will's forehead, then quickly looked over his wounds, murmuring under her breath all the while. "Ever since Will ran away, thy father has said he would treat him like the traitor he is should he return. I must think what's best to do." She pressed her hands to her head as if that would untangle her thoughts. Then, with an air of decision, she told me we would hide Will in Grampa's Folly.

This was a secret room my grandfather had insisted Father build into the barn foundation. Grampa had a fear of Indian raids and wanted a refuge handy in case of attack. Of course, there had never been any Indian raids—in fact, the only raids I heard about were the other way around. The Indians in our part of the colony had always been peaceful farmers. Indeed, they had taught the settlers the best ways to till the soil.

Now, however, we were heartily glad of Grandfather's stubbornness. The two of us managed to get Will to the barn, open the hidden door, and put him down on a pile of straw.

Will's eyes fluttered open. "Water," he murmured, then his eyelids closed once more.

Mother and I looked at each other, jubilant at this proof that he still lived. I ran for the spring, she for the herb garden to gather lamb's ear leaves to bandage and soothe his wounds.

It was not easy over the next few weeks to care for Will and keep Father ignorant of his presence in the barn. During that time I confided to my gentle Quaker mother the tale of how I had come to find Will in the beech grove. Though horror-struck by the dangers I had run and the sights I had seen, she conceded that my action had surely saved my brother's life.

Reports sifted in about the outcome of the Brandywine battle that had engulfed me and wounded Will. I heard that the American divisions, lacking the training to wheel and face the redcoats coming up behind them, had ended up dangerously separated from each other. Attempts to close the gap resulted in even more confusion—so much so that some Continentals had even fired on their own advance lines. As for the men pelting across the fields behind Washington and Mr. Brown, they had fought valiantly, but finally had had to retreat in disarray.

Still, 'twas said that Washington's men were not downcast by their defeat, especially since the British were too exhausted by their long day's march to pursue them. For a fortnight after Brandywine, the Continentals had done their best to keep Howe from crossing the Schuylkill, but to no avail. By late September, the British occupied Philadelphia.

Father was delighted, but Mother and I scarcely cared about the capture of the capital (if it could be called such after Congress had fled), for Will was safe at home again.

Would you like to have lived in Geordie's time? Explain why or why not.

What does Geordie learn about himself and his feelings about war?

Why does Geordie throw away his toy grenadier when he drives from the battlefield?

WRITE   Imagine that you are Geordie and that Father discovers you have hidden Will in the barn. What would you say? Write a note to Father to explain your actions.

EARLY AMERICA

Do you think Matt could do what Geordie does? Do you think Geordie could live in the forest as Matt does? Explain why you think as you do.

WRITER'S WORKSHOP

Attean teaches Matt valuable skills for living in the forest. Geordie uses skills such as hitching up a team and driving a wagon to go to Philadelphia. What skills could you teach someone? Write a paragraph that teaches someone your skill.

Writer's Choice
In early America, young people were often left on their own to do important jobs. What do you think about life in early America? Respond in your own way. Share your writing with your classmates.

THEME

WOMEN WHO LED THE WAY

Throughout American history, men and women have had to fight to win their freedoms. Names of leaders such as George Washington and Abraham Lincoln are well known to us, but what are the names of some of the women who led the way? The following selections may help you find out.

CONTENTS

ELIZABETH BLACKWELL

from INDEPENDENT VOICES ▪ by EVE MERRIAM

What will you do when you grow up,
nineteenth-century-young-lady?
Will you sew a fine seam and spoon dappled cream
under an apple tree shady?

Or will you be a teacher
in a dames' school
and train the little dears
by the scientific rule
that mental activity
may strain
the delicate female brain;
therefore let
the curriculum stress music, French, and especially
etiquette:
teach how to set
a truly refined banquet.
Question One:
What kind of sauce
for the fish dish,
and pickle or lemon fork?
Quickly, students,
which should it be?

Now Elizabeth Blackwell, how about you?
Seamstress or teacher, which of the two?
You know there's not much else that a girl can do.
Don't mumble, Elizabeth. Learn to raise your head.

"I'm not very nimble with a needle and thread.
"I could teach music—if I had to," she said,
"But I think I'd rather be a doctor instead."

"Is this some kind of joke?"
asked the proper menfolk.
"A woman be a doctor?
Not in our respectable day!
A doctor? An M.D.! Did you hear what she said?
She's clearly and indubitably out of her head!"

"Indeed, indeed, we are thoroughly agreed,"
hissed the ladies of society all laced in and prim,
"it's a scientific fact a doctor has to be a him.
"Yes, sir,
"'twould be against nature
"if a doctor were a her."

Hibble hobble bibble bobble
widdle waddle wag
tsk tsk
    twit twit
        flip flap flutter
            mitter matter mutter
moan groan wail and rail
    Indecorous!
            Revolting!!
                A scandal
                    A SIN

their voices pierced the air like a jabbing hat-pin.
But little miss Elizabeth wouldn't give in.

To medical schools she applied.
In vain.
And applied again
and again
and again
and one rejection offered this plan:
why not disguise herself as a man?
If she pulled back her hair, put on boots and pants,
she might attend medical lectures in France.
Although she wouldn't earn a degree,
they'd let her study anatomy.

Elizabeth refused to hide
her feminine pride.
She drew herself up tall
(all five feet one of her!)
and tried again.
And denied again.
The letters answering no
mounted like winter snow.

Until the day
when her ramrod will
finally had its way.
After the twenty-ninth try,
there came from Geneva, New York
the reply
of a blessed
Yes!
Geneva,
Geneva,
how sweet the sound;
Geneva,
Geneva,
sweet sanctuary found. . . .

. . . . and the ladies of Geneva
passing by her in the street
drew back their hoopskirts
so they wouldn't have to meet.

>   Psst, psst,
>   hiss, hiss
>   this sinister scarlet miss.
>   Avoid her, the hoyden, the hussy,
>   lest we all be contaminated!
>   If your glove so much as touch her, my dear,
>   best go get it fumigated!

When Elizabeth came to table,
their talking all would halt;
wouldn't so much as ask her
please to pass the salt.

In between classes
without a kind word,
Elizabeth dwelt
like a pale gray bird.

In a bare attic room
cold as a stone,
far from her family,
huddled alone

studying, studying
throughout the night
warming herself
with an inner light:

don't let it darken,
the spark of fire;
keep it aglow,
that heart's desire:

the will to serve,
to help those in pain—
flickered and flared
and flickered again—

until
like a fairy tale
(except it was true!)
Elizabeth received
her honored due.

The perfect happy ending
came to pass:
Elizabeth graduated . . .
. . . at the head of her class.

And the ladies of Geneva
all rushed forward now to greet
that clever, dear Elizabeth,
so talented, so sweet!

Wasn't it glorious
she'd won first prize?

Elizabeth smiled
with cool gray eyes

and she wrapped her shawl
against the praise:

how soon there might come
more chilling days.

Turned to leave
without hesitating.

She was ready now,
and the world was waiting.

Women in Washington

by Angela de Hoyos

First there was a teacher, then a lawyer, then a doctor . . . and the career fields for women in America continued to grow. Today, women's opportunities are unlimited, due to the leadership of people such as Elizabeth Blackwell. The following portraits show six women who were and are leaders in their fields in our nation's capital, Washington, D.C.

FRANCES PERKINS   (April 10, 1880–May 14, 1965)

Secretary of Labor

In 1933, Frances Perkins was appointed the first female member of the Cabinet, the group of official advisers to the president. As Secretary of Labor during the hard times of the Great Depression, Perkins helped to pass laws such as the Federal Emergency Relief Act and the Social Security Act. These laws led to programs that are still in effect and helping people today.

JEANNETTE RANKIN   (June 11, 1880–May 18, 1973)

Congresswoman

In 1917, Jeannette Rankin from Montana became the first woman ever elected to the House of Representatives. Jeannette Rankin firmly believed in world peace. She was the only member of Congress to vote against the entry of the United States into both World War I and World War II. Of her first antiwar vote she said, "It was the most significant thing I ever did."

HELEN THOMAS   (August 4, 1920–)

White House Bureau Chief

In 1974, Helen Thomas became the first woman to serve as the White House Bureau Chief for a major news service, the United Press International. This honor came after working for more than thirty years as a reporter. Thirteen of those years had been spent in the White House, which she calls "the most exciting place in the world." In 1976, the *World Almanac* named Helen Thomas as one of the most influential women in America.

SANDRA DAY O'CONNOR   (March 26, 1930–)

Supreme Court Justice

In 1981, Sandra Day O'Connor was nominated to fill a vacant position on the Supreme Court of the United States. Sandra Day O'Connor was a successful lawyer, state senator, and judge from Arizona. Her appointment was approved unanimously, making one of her fondest dreams come true: to be "remembered as the first woman who served on the Supreme Court."

DR. ANTONIA NOVELLO   (August 23, 1944–)

Surgeon General of the United States

In 1990, Dr. Antonia Novello became the first female Surgeon General, the highest-ranking officer in the United States Public Health Service. Dr. Antonia Novello, who was born in Puerto Rico, suffered from a serious birth defect throughout her childhood. This condition required frequent surgery and was not corrected until she was eighteen years old. She decided to become a doctor then, saying " . . . no other person is going to wait eighteen years."

SHARON PRATT KELLY   (January 30, 1944–)

Mayor of Washington, D.C.

In January of 1991, Sharon Pratt Kelly was sworn in as the first woman mayor of Washington, D.C. During her campaign, she wore a pin in the shape of a shovel, the symbol of her promise to clean up the city. Sharon Pratt Kelly began her career as a successful lawyer. She is also the first woman and the first African American to serve as national treasurer of the Democratic Party.

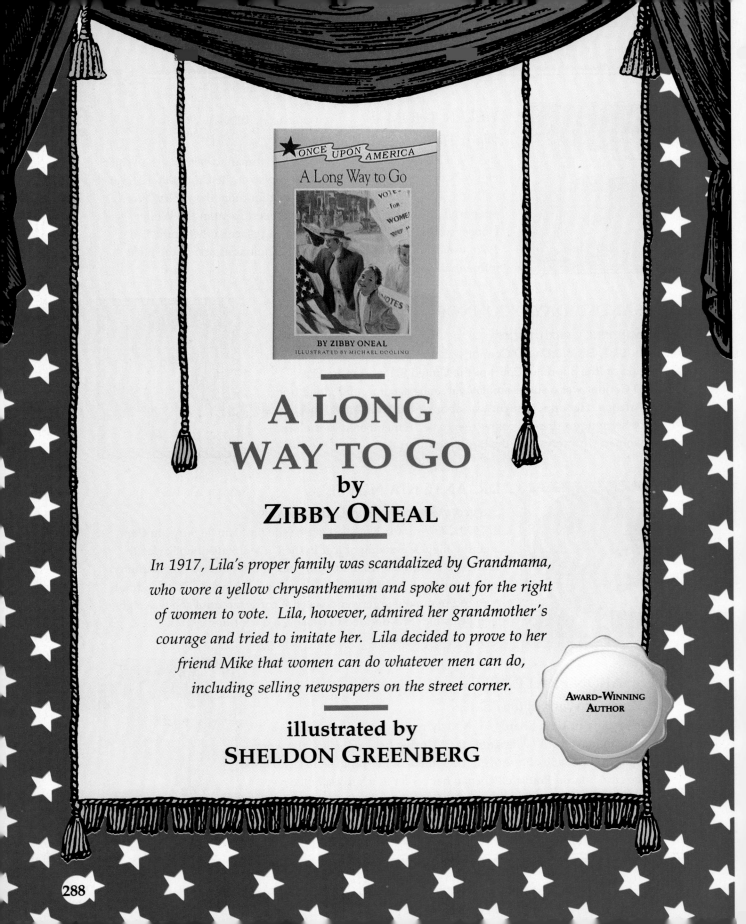

ONCE UPON AMERICA

A Long Way to Go

VOTE FOR WOMEN

VOTES

BY ZIBBY ONEAL
ILLUSTRATED BY MICHAEL DOOLING

A LONG
WAY TO GO
by
ZIBBY ONEAL

*In 1917, Lila's proper family was scandalized by Grandmama,
who wore a yellow chrysanthemum and spoke out for the right
of women to vote. Lila, however, admired her grandmother's
courage and tried to imitate her. Lila decided to prove to her
friend Mike that women can do whatever men can do,
including selling newspapers on the street corner.*

illustrated by
SHELDON GREENBERG

AWARD-WINNING
AUTHOR

"Now let's see you sell," Mike said, but he didn't wait to watch. Instead he began running after customers, waving papers, shouting, "Read all about the big fire in Brooklyn! Read about the flames forty feet high!"

Lila pulled a paper from the bag and looked at it. She couldn't see where he was getting all that. The paper didn't say a thing about flames. It didn't really say much about the fire. That was what he meant by imagination, she guessed, but it didn't seem quite fair to fool people that way.

She ran her eyes down the front page. The bond speech. The fire. But then she saw, down at the bottom of the page, not taking much space, a small article headed, SUFFRAGISTS REFUSE TO EAT. Lila read as fast as she could. There were suffragists in jail in Washington who wouldn't eat a bite. They said they'd rather starve than do without the vote. The paper called it a hunger strike.

Lila's eyes widened. This was news. This was something interesting. And, besides, it was true. She pulled a few more papers from her bag and stood herself right in the middle of the sidewalk. "Suffragists starving to death!" she yelled. "Read all about it!"

To her amazement, someone stopped to buy a paper. She tried again. "Read all about the ladies starving to death in Washington!" And, again, someone stopped.

"Crazy women," the man said, but he paid her and didn't seem to think it was strange at all to see a girl selling papers.

Lila felt encouraged. Over and over she waved her papers at people walking past. She shouted her headline until she was hoarse, but it felt good to be hoarse, to be shouting and running.

"President making women starve!" she cried. "They won't eat till they get to vote!" Anything she said seemed to work. People bought papers. Maybe they would have bought them anyway, thought Lila. She didn't know, but she didn't care. She was too busy selling. In no time, her bag was empty.

She hadn't had time to think about Mike, but now, bag empty, she turned around to look for him. He was leaning against a lamppost, watching her. "I sold them all," she said breathlessly.

"I noticed."

"Here's the money." She fished the change and a few bills from her pocket.

"You keep it."

"No. Why?"

"You earned it."

"But I didn't do it for that. You take the money. I just did it to show you I could."

"Yeah. Well." Mike kicked the lamppost with the toe of his shoe. "I guess you showed me."

There were things that Lila felt like saying, but she decided not to say them. Instead she picked up the empty canvas bag and slung it over her shoulder. Together they started back the way they had come.

* * * * *

"Lila, you've told me all about it three times."

She had. She couldn't help it. Saturday afternoon was like a story she didn't want to finish, like a book of beautiful colored pictures that she couldn't bear to close.

"Oh, I liked it all so much, but I'm not going to tell anyone else about it. Just you." Lila looked out the window at the sunlight on the fence around the park. "I wish girls could sell papers," she said a little sadly. "I mean all the time."

"There are more and more things that girls can do. Think of all the jobs women have now that there's a war on. When I was your age we didn't dream of working in offices and factories."

"That's women. I mean girls." And then, "Do you think that if women could vote, they'd let girls sell papers?"

Grandmama laughed. "I don't know. I suppose there'd be a better chance of that happening."

"Then I'm a suffragist," Lila said. "I *thought* I was, but now I'm sure."

"That's fine."

Lila frowned. "But what can I do?"

"Believe that women have rights the same as men."

That wasn't what Lila had in mind. She wanted action. She wanted to shout headlines, run around yelling. "I could give speeches," she said. She imagined herself standing on a wooden box speaking to crowds in the street. It would be a lot like selling papers.

But Grandmama only laughed again. "You're still too young to make speeches."

"But I want to do *something*. It's no use just sitting around believing things."

Grandmama looked thoughtful. "Well, there's a suffragist parade a week or so before the state election. We're going to march up Fifth Avenue all the way from Washington Square to Fifty-ninth Street."

"With signs?" said Lila. "And banners?"

"Oh, yes, and music, too. We're going to make people notice us."

"Would you take me?"

"Well, I was thinking—"

Lila sat up straight. "I'm coming."

"But not without permission you aren't. Not unless your mama and papa agree."

"I'll make them agree," said Lila, though she had no idea how she'd do that.

"Well, I'll try to help you," Grandmama said. "At least I'll mention the parade."

Lila sat quietly in church with her hands in her lap. She played nicely with George until lunchtime, rolling his ball to him over and over though this was the most boring game in the world. She sat straight at the table and ate all of her lunch, though that included beets. Really, Lila thought, she was being so perfect it was hard to see how Mama and Papa could say no.

But that was what Papa said. While they were waiting for dessert, Grandmama brought up the parade. She did it in a kind of offhanded way, as if it were something she'd only just remembered. "And I think Lila would like to march, too," she said. Lila looked down at her napkin and crossed her fingers. But Papa said no.

It was such a small word, no, but it seemed to Lila that it was the biggest word in her life. So many nos. She felt tears of disappointment prickling in her eyes. She couldn't look up.

When, after lunch, Papa said, "Come on, Lila, it's time for our Sunday walk," Lila felt like saying, "No!" She didn't want to go for a walk with her father. She felt too mad and disappointed. All the same, she went to get her coat, because a little girl didn't say no to her father.

"Which way shall we walk?" he asked her when they were standing on the pavement.

"I don't care." And she didn't. She didn't care at all.

"What about Fifth Avenue then?"

Lila had known he'd choose that. Papa liked walking along Fifth Avenue, looking at the new motorcars pass by. One day, he said, he thought he might buy one.

And so they walked over to Fifth Avenue. Lila was wearing her best coat again and clean white gloves because Papa liked her to look like a lady when they went walking. But her hands felt crowded in the gloves and her shoulders felt crowded in her coat. She felt crowded all over.

At the corner of Fifth Avenue, they turned and walked north, past banks and office buildings, past shops and department stores. Usually Lila liked looking into the department store windows, but today they didn't seem exciting. Fifth Avenue was dull.

"Has the cat got your tongue?" Papa said.

"No. I'm thinking."

"About important things?"

"I was thinking about the parade. It's going to come right up this street."

"Lila, you must forget the parade."

But how could she? She couldn't stop thinking about it, even though the thinking made her sad.

They waited to cross the street while a car passed. "That's a Pierce Arrow," Papa said. "It's really something, isn't it?"

Lila nodded. She supposed so.

"Maybe when George is older we'll buy one like that. He can learn to drive it."

"What about me?"

"Oh, you'll be a beautiful grown lady by then. You can ride in the back and tell George where to take you. You'll have all kinds of pretty clothes to wear. We'll go shopping for things like the dress in that window."

Lila glanced at the dress in the shop window. She had to admit it was pretty. She wondered why she didn't like it more, and then she knew. It looked like the kind of dress that was for sitting around doing nothing.

"I'd rather learn how to drive a motorcar," she said. "I'd rather be *doing* something."

Papa didn't understand. "There'll be plenty for you to do. Tea dances and parties and all that sort of thing."

"Those aren't the things I want to do."

"No? What then?"

"Oh!" Lists of things came tumbling into Lila's head. She wanted to march in the parade, turn cartwheels, walk on her hands, roll her stockings down. She wanted to run and yell, sell papers—but that was not what Papa meant. He meant later, when she was grown-up. What did she want to do *then*? Lila closed her eyes and squeezed them tight. "I want to vote," she said.

The words were out before she knew she was going to say them, but suddenly they seemed just right. "I want to be able to vote same as George."

When she opened her eyes, Papa was looking at her. "That's what you want more than anything?"

Lila nodded. She dug her fists into her pockets and looked up at Papa bravely. "It's what Grandmama says. Girls are people, too. They have rights. It isn't fair the way it is. Billy Ash says he's smarter than me just because he's a boy. But I'm the one who gets all *A*'s, not him. So why should he be allowed to vote and not me? Why should George if I can't? It's not fair, Papa. It's not fair to girls."

Lila paused for breath, but she couldn't stop talking. "When I grow up, I want to be just like Grandmama. I want to make things fair for everyone. That's why I want to march in the parade—to show people that's what I think. And if they put me in jail for marching, then I just won't eat, like the ladies in Washington."

Then Lila stopped. She didn't have anything else to say.

"Well," said Papa, "that was quite a speech."

Lila couldn't tell what he was thinking. His face was very serious. She wondered if he would stop loving her now because of all she'd said. She wondered if he'd already stopped. She waited for him to say something more, but he said nothing at all. He took her hand and they kept on walking.

Lila's feet slapped along beside him. It was too late now to take it back, and, anyway, she couldn't take it back without lying. She'd said what she meant. But Papa wasn't saying anything at all. He was looking straight ahead as if he had forgotten all about her, as if he didn't know she was there any more.

Lila felt hollow in the middle. She bit the insides of her cheeks to keep from crying. On the way home, she counted cracks in the sidewalk.

When they reached the corner of Twenty-first Street and were almost home, Papa said, "How did you happen to know about those women in Washington, the ones who aren't eating? Did Grandmama tell you?"

Lila shook her head, still counting cracks. "No," she said. "I read it in the paper."

"Did you really? For heaven's sake." Lila could have sworn, if she hadn't known better, that he sounded proud of her.

After supper, she had her bath and watched Katie Rose laying out her clothes for school the next day. The same old stockings. The same old dress. Lila sighed. Everything was the same old thing again, except that now it would be different with Papa. She climbed out of the tub and wrapped herself in a towel. She went into her room to put on her nightgown.

And that was when Grandmama came in. She had a funny, puzzled sort of expression. "It looks as if we'll be going to the parade together," she said.

Lila paused. The damp ends of her hair swung against her shoulders. "What?"

"Your father says you may go."

"With you? To the parade?" Lila felt as if she couldn't take it all in so fast.

"That's what he says."

"But why?"

Grandmama shrugged. "I don't know what you said to him on that walk, but you must have said something."

Lila swallowed. He had called it a speech. She had made a speech and he'd listened! A bubble of happiness began to rise inside her. He had listened and it was all right. She grinned at Grandmama. She dropped her towel. And then right there, in the middle of her bedroom, stark naked, she turned a cartwheel.

Do you think Lila is right to question her father's decision? Why or why not?

What is Lila's problem in this story? How does she solve it?

As they walk along Fifth Avenue, Lila tells Papa about the things she wants to do in her life. What are some of these things?

The author says Lila feels crowded in her gloves and coat. Why do you think she feels that way?

WRITE   Imagine that you are a newspaper headline writer. Write headlines that describe what might happen to Mike, to Lila, to Grandmama, and to Papa.

WOMEN WHO LED THE WAY

What do the selections reveal about obstacles in the paths of women who wanted to do something different? What qualities helped the women overcome these obstacles?

WRITER'S WORKSHOP

Eve Merriam chose Elizabeth Blackwell as the subject of her poem. Choose a woman whom you admire, and write a poem about her. The woman may be from the past or may be alive today. Tell what she has done that makes you admire her. Use words that will make other people feel as you do.

Writer's Choice
What do you think of the women in these selections? Plan a way to respond to the theme Women Who Led the Way. Then carry out your plan.

THEME

INTERPRETING THE PAST

Do you ever think about the vast amount of history that has gone before you? Every event that has ever happened is a part of history, but not every event is worth writing about. Think about how authors such as Virginia Hamilton decide what is important to write about when they interpret the past.

CONTENTS

AN INTERVIEW

with the

AUTHOR:
Virginia Hamilton

AWARD-WINNING AUTHOR

Writer Ilene Cooper had the opportunity to talk with Virginia Hamilton about two of her novels: *The House of Dies Drear* and *The Bells of Christmas*. This is what Virginia Hamilton had to say about interpreting the past for her readers.

COOPER: You write about history from both historical and personal points of view. In your work they often blend together, don't they?

HAMILTON: My personal history does enhance my fiction. In *The House of Dies Drear*, I started with the town history as well as the stories that I heard growing up. For one thing, my grandfather, a fugitive from slavery, had come north to Ohio. The area where I live in Ohio had been a station on the Underground Railroad. Because of that there were many houses in my town that had hidden rooms and secret passages. In fact, here in Yellow Springs is the Octagon House, one of the few buildings left that was designed specifically to hide slaves. The eight corners of the house were made into little cubbyholes that could be used as hiding places. I knew all this and found it fascinating. Enough so that when I started writing *The House of Dies Drear*, I called on what I knew. In the first chapter, when the family is traveling north, they are using one of the same routes that the fugitives had used a century before. Though you don't know that from reading the book, I called on that information to make it historically correct.

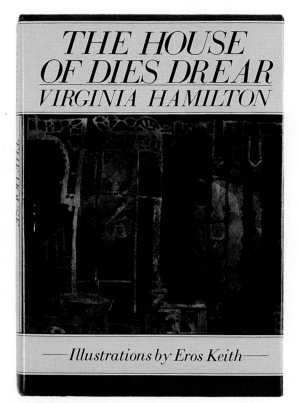

THE HOUSE OF DIES DREAR

VIRGINIA HAMILTON

—Illustrations by Eros Keith—

COOPER: Where did you get the idea for *The Bells of Christmas*?

HAMILTON: One of my editors said to me, "You've never done a Christmas book." The idea appealed to me greatly because of the stories I had heard growing up about the way my mother's family spent the holiday. There were sleighs and sleigh bells, big snows, and lots of family around.

COOPER: So that was personal history. Did you research facts for the story as well?

HAMILTON: Oh, yes. I'm lucky enough to live near the National Road. I've often used aspects of the National Road in books. The Midwest was opened up by people using that road, and so that became a part of the story. I also wanted a big snow in my book. I began researching the newspapers from one hundred years or so back to see what year there was a huge snowfall at Christmas. I couldn't find one! I was dying. Finally, I found one; you see, it is very important to me that details be historically correct. I would never say in a book that there was a snow during a particular year if there wasn't one.

COOPER: Can we say that when the story is historical, you still inject some of your personal history, and when the story is personal, you still make sure the facts are correct?

HAMILTON: Yes, I'm lucky enough to have a personal history to draw on *and* an area to draw on that is important to our country's history. I used to say it was serendipity that helped me find material. Now I believe that all of the things a writer needs are out there waiting; you just have to be able to recognize them.

The House of Dies Drear

by Virginia Hamilton

Illustrations by Scott Scheidly

Thomas Small and his family have just moved into a fascinating old house—a house that was once a stopover for runaway slaves along the Underground Railroad.

Thomas is eager to explore the old house. He quickly discovers a wood button hidden in the design of the front door. When he presses the button, it reveals a tunnel under the front porch. Thomas's further exploration is interrupted, however, by two children and a big black horse.

"I think you children just better get off my father's land," said Thomas. He stepped off the porch. "Part of the Underground Railroad must be under these steps. I've got work to do."

"There's no train tracks down there," said Pesty. "There never was none that I ever seen."

But Thomas was not stopping for them. The boy stood up, eyeing Thomas seriously now. Pesty backed the horse off so Thomas could kneel down by the hole.

"You fixing to go down under there? You want some company?" asked the boy.

"You'd just better get out of here," said Thomas, not looking at him. "I don't need any of your help."

"Well, I reckon that's true as far as it goes," said the boy. "But I suspect you'll be needing me later."

"We'll come back after a while to see how you come out," said the child on the horse. And then she and the boy fell into more laughter.

"Naw," said the boy laughing. "Naw, Pesty, you can't come back today. You are all ready for bed in your pajamas, and after supper I'm going to lock you up so you can't bother this here new boy. How you like Pesty's pretty night clothes, new boy? She likes to wear red because Mr. Pluto told her red was the best color. Mr. Pluto likes red because it is the color of fire, and he is the keeper of fire. Pesty is the keeper's helper!" The boy laughed and laughed.

Thomas was excited at having met such odd children. But he hid his feelings from them by turning calmly away. "You get out of here," he said, "before I call my father!"

"Oh, we're going," said the boy. "And I'm M. C. Darrow, the youngest."

"I don't really care who you are," said Thomas right back at him. "I am Thomas Small, the oldest son of my father."

"But you can just call me Mac," said M. C. Darrow. "Everybody calls me Mac, even Mr. Pluto, when I let him get close enough."

Thomas didn't say anything. Lying flat on his stomach, he looked into the hole; his head and shoulders disappeared inside. It was then he lost his grip and fell head first into thin, black air. He landed some five feet down, on damp sod that smelled like a mixture of yellow grass and mildew. All the breath was knocked out of him. He lay there unable to move or think for at least ten seconds, until air seeped back into his lungs. Otherwise he seemed not to have hurt himself. He could hear Pesty and M. C. Darrow going away. Mac was talking quietly to the child. Then Thomas couldn't hear them anymore.

There was gray light filtering down from the opening of the steps to where Thomas lay, and he could see that he was at the edge of a steep stairway cut out of rock. The stairs were wet; he could hear water dripping down on them from somewhere.

"I could have rolled down those steps," he whispered. Mac Darrow and Pesty must have known there was a drop down to where Thomas now lay. But they hadn't told him. "They are not friends then," said Thomas softly. He cautioned himself to be more careful.

I was showing off, he thought. I hurried and I fell. That was just what they'd wanted.

"Move slowly. Think fast," Thomas whispered. "Keep in mind what's behind and look closely at what's in front."

Thomas always carried a pencil-thin flashlight, which he sometimes used for reading in the car. He sat up suddenly and pulled out the flashlight. It wasn't broken from the fall, and he flicked it on. He sat in a kind of circle enclosed by brick walls. In some places, the brick had crumbled into powder, which was slowly filling up the circle of sod.

That will take a long time, thought Thomas. He looked up at the underside of the veranda steps.

Thomas got to his feet and made his way down the rock stairway into

darkness. At the foot of the stairs was a path with walls of dirt and rock on either side of it. The walls were so close, Thomas could touch them by extending his arms a few inches. Above his head was a low ceiling carved out of rock. Such cramped space made him uneasy. The foundation of the house had to be somewhere above the natural rock. The idea of the whole three-story house of Dies Drear pressing down on him caused him to stop a moment on the path. Since he had fallen, he hadn't had time to be afraid. He wasn't now, but he did begin to worry a little about where the path led. He thought of ghosts, and yet he did not seriously believe in them. "No," he told himself, "not with the flashlight. Not when I can turn back . . . when I can run."

And besides, he thought, I'm strong. I can take care of myself.

Thomas continued along the path, flickering his tiny beam of light this way and that. Pools of water stood in some places. He felt a coldness, like the stream of air that came from around the button on the oak door-frame. His shoes were soon soaked. His socks grew cold and wet, and he thought about taking them off. He could hear water running a long way off. He stopped again to listen, but he couldn't tell from what direction the sound came.

"It's just one of the springs," he said. His voice bounced off the walls strangely.

Better not speak. There could be tunnels leading off this one. You can't tell what might hear you in a place like this.

Thomas was scaring himself. He decided not to think again about other tunnels or ghosts. He did think for the first time of how he would get out of this tunnel. He had fallen five feet, and he wasn't sure he would be able to climb back up the crumbling brick walls. Still, the path he walked had to lead somewhere. There had to be another way out.

Thomas felt his feet begin to climb; the path was slanting up. He walked slowly on the slippery rock; then suddenly the path was very wide. The walls were four feet away on either side, and there were long stone slabs against each wall. Thomas sat down on one of the slabs. It was wet, but he didn't even notice.

"Why these slabs?" he asked himself. "For the slaves, hiding and running?"

He opened and closed a moist hand around the flashlight. The light beam could not keep back the dark. Thomas had a lonely feeling, the kind of feeling running slaves must have had.

And they dared not use light, he thought. How long would they have to hide down here? How could they stand it?

Thomas got up and went on. He placed one foot carefully in front of the other on the path, which had narrowed again. He heard the faint sound of movement somewhere. Maybe it was a voice he heard, he couldn't be sure. He swirled the light around over the damp walls, and fumbled it. The flashlight slid out of his hand. For a long moment, he caught and held it between his knees before finally dropping it. He bent quickly to pick it up and stepped down on it. Then he accidentally kicked it with his heel, and it went rattling somewhere over the path. It hit the wall, but it had gone out before then. Now all was very dark.

"It's not far," Thomas said. "All I have to do is feel around."

He felt around with his hands over smooth, moist rock; his hands grew cold. He felt water, and it was icy, slimy. His hands

trembled, they ached, feeling in the dark, but he could not find the flashlight.

"I couldn't have kicked it far because I wasn't moving." His voice bounced in a whisper off the walls. He tried crawling backward, hoping to hit the flashlight with his heels.

"It's got to be here . . . Papa?" Thomas stood, turning toward the way he had come, the way he had been, crawling backward. He didn't at all like walking in the pitch blackness of the tunnel.

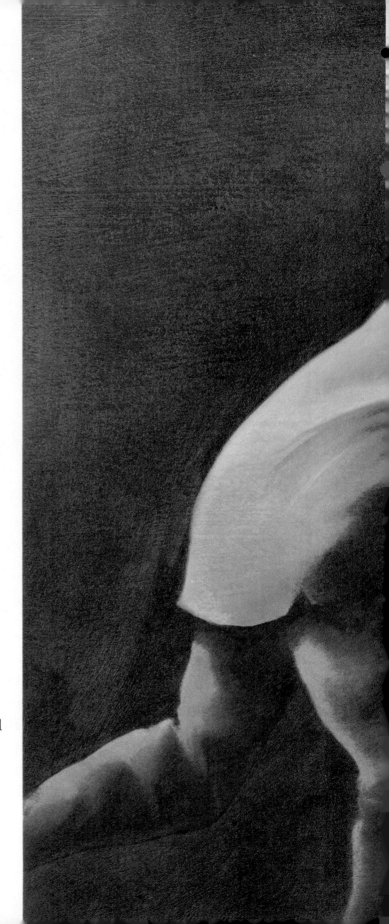

"I'll go on back," he said. "I'll just walk back as quick as I can. There'll be light coming from the veranda steps. I'll climb up that wall and then I'll be out of this. I'll get Papa and we'll do it together."

He went quickly now, with his hands extended to keep himself from hitting the close walls. But then something happened that caused him to stop in his tracks. He stood still, with his whole body tense and alert, the way he could be when he sensed a storm before there was any sign of it in the air or sky.

Thomas had the queerest notion that he was not alone. In front of him, between him and the steps of the veranda, something waited.

"Papa?" he said. He heard something.

The sound went, "Ahhh, ahhh, ahhh." It was not moaning, nor crying. It wasn't laughter, but something forlorn and lost and old.

Thomas backed away. "No," he said. "Oh please!"

"Ahhh, ahhh," something said. It was closer to him now. Thomas could hear no footsteps on the path. He could see nothing in the darkness.

He opened his mouth to yell, but his voice wouldn't come. Fear rose in him; he was cold, freezing, as though he had rolled in snow.

"Papa!" he managed to say. His voice was a whisper. "Papa, come get me . . . Papa!"

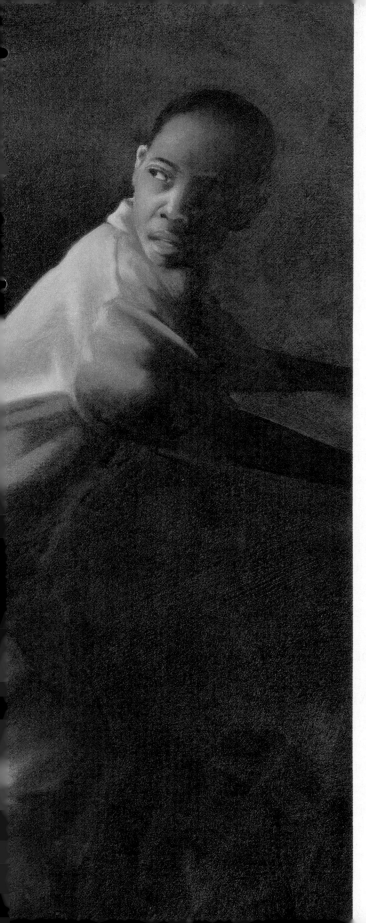

"Ahhhh." Whatever it was, was quite close now. Thomas still backed away from it, then he turned around, away from the direction of the veranda. He started running up the path, with his arms outstretched in front of him. He ran and ran, his eyes wide in the darkness. At any moment, the thing would grab him and smother his face. At any time, the thing would paralyze him with cold. It would take him away. It would tie him in one of the tunnels, and no one would ever find him.

"Don't let it touch me! Don't let it catch me!"

Thomas ran smack into a wall. His arms and hands hit first; then, his head and chest. The impact jarred him from head to foot. He thought his wrists were broken, but ever so slowly, painful feeling flowed back into his hands. The ache moved dully up to the sockets of his shoulders. He opened and closed his hands. They hurt so much, his eyes began to tear, but he didn't seem to have broken anything.

Thomas felt frantically along the wall. The wall was wood. He knew the feel of it right away. It was heavy wood, perhaps oak, and it was man made, man hewn. Thomas pounded on it, hurting himself more, causing his head to spin. He kept on, because he knew he was about to be taken from behind by something ghostly and cold.

"Help me! It's going to get me!" he called. "Help me!"

Thomas heard a high, clear scream on the other side of the wall. Next came the sound of feet scurrying, and then the wall slid silently up.

"Thomas Small!" his mother said. "What in heaven's name do you think you are doing inside that wall!"

"I see you've found yourself a secret passage," said Mr. Small. "I hadn't thought you'd find that button by the front door so soon."

Mr. Small, with Billy and Buster, was seated at the kitchen table. They were finishing supper. Mr. Small smiled at Thomas, while the twins stared at him with solemn eyes.

Mrs. Small stood directly in front of Thomas and then stepped aside so that he could take a few steps into the kitchen. Thomas glanced behind him at the tunnel, a gaping space carved out of the comfortable kitchen. He saw nothing at all on the path.

He sat down beside his father. There was the good smell of food hanging in the air. The twins seemed full and content.

"You knew about that tunnel, Papa?" Thomas said. He felt discouraged, as though he'd been tricked.

"If anyone came unexpectedly to the front door," said Mr. Small, "the slaves could hide in the tunnel until whoever it was had gone. Or, if and when the callers began a search, the slaves could escape through the kitchen or by way of the veranda steps."

It's not any fun, Thomas thought. Not if he already knows about it.

"Thomas, you frightened me!" Mrs. Small said. She had recovered enough to take her eyes from the tunnel and sit down beside Thomas at the table.

"Goodness, yelling like that all of a sudden," she said. "I didn't know what it was." She jumped up, remembering Thomas hadn't eaten, and quickly fixed his plate. Then she seated herself as before.

"Yes, why were you calling for help, Thomas?" asked Mr. Small. "You really made your mama scream."

Thomas bent down to take off his shoes and socks. A pool of water stood dark and brackish on the linoleum. "There was something there," he said.

Mrs. Small looked at him hard. Without a word, she got up and disappeared down the long hall from the kitchen toward the front of the house. When she returned, she carried a pair of Mr. Small's socks and Thomas's old tennis shoes.

"This is all I could find," she said to Thomas. She fairly flung the shoes and socks into his lap. Then she cleaned up the pool of water.

"There was something on that path," Thomas said. "It was coming after me as sure as I'm sitting here."

"You shouldn't make up stories like that," his mother said, "not even as a joke."

"There was something there." His voice quivered slightly, and the sound of that was enough to tell Mr. Small that Thomas wasn't joking.

"Then what was it?" asked Mr. Small. He watched Thomas closely.

"I don't know," Thomas said. "I didn't see anything."

His father smiled. "It was probably no more than your fear of the dark and strange surroundings getting the best of you."

"I heard something though," Thomas said. "It went 'ahhh, ahhh' at me and it came closer and closer."

Mrs. Small sucked in her breath. She looked all around the kitchen, at the gaping hole and quickly away from it. The kitchen was large, with a single lamp of varicolored glass

hanging from the ceiling on a heavy, black chain. Her shadow, along with Thomas's, loomed long and thin on a far wall.

"Thomas, don't make up things!" his father said sternly.

"I'm not, Papa!" There was a lump in Thomas's throat. He gripped the table and swallowed a few times. He had to find just the right words if ever his father was to believe him.

His hands rose in the air. They began to shape the air, to carve it, as though it were a pretty piece of pine. "It was like no other voice," he began. "It wasn't a high voice or a low voice, or even a man's voice. It didn't have anything bad in it or anything. I was just in its way, that's all. It had to get by me and it would have done anything to get around me along that path."

"I forbid you to go into that tunnel again!" whispered Mrs. Small. She was afraid now, and even Mr. Small stared at Thomas.

Mr. Small seemed to be thinking beyond what Thomas had told them. "You say you saw nothing?" he asked.

"I thought I heard somebody moving around," Thomas said, "but that could have been you all in here. Or maybe it was the kids, come back to scare me."

"Kids?" said Mr. Small.

"The Darrow children," Thomas said. "I mean that youngest Darrow boy and that little girl he calls Pesty that lives with them although she doesn't really belong to them. She came riding around the house in her pajamas on this big horse, and M. C. Darrow was hanging on the horse's tail. He was trying to get the horse to stop, but it wouldn't. Only Pesty could stop that big horse, and she was so little, too."

"What in the world . . ." said his father.

"Thomas, if you don't stop it!" warned Mrs. Small.

"Mama, it's the truth!" said Thomas. "There were these children, I'm not making it up! I can't help it if this is the craziest place we've ever lived in!"

"All right now," said Mr. Small. "Start over and take it slowly. You say there were children here?"

"Yes, they came from around the house just after I found the button and moved the steps." Then Thomas told all about Pesty, the horse and Mac Darrow. He even managed to make his father and mother understand that the children had been playing with him, toying with him, as if he were the object of a game.

"They were not friends," Thomas said finally. "They let me fall under those steps."

"No, they weren't, if they did let you fall," said his mother, "but maybe they didn't know about that drop down."

"No," said Mr. Small, "they probably knew, but I would guess they had no real intention of causing Thomas harm. It was their joke on the 'new boy.' It wasn't a very nice joke and it was a joke that might have not worked at all. They were playing with you, Thomas, to find out what you knew. They must have thought you knew more than they did. After all, you came from far away to live in a house that no child in his right mind in these parts would dare enter. I would think that by now you are pretty famous all over town."

"I see," said Thomas. "Because I dared go into 'Mr. Pluto's tunnel'!"

"Yes," his father said.

"It wasn't a human voice I heard," Thomas said. "It wasn't alive."

They all fell silent for a moment. Then Mr. Small asked, "And you're sure you heard nothing more than that sighing?"

"That's all," Thomas said. "It just kept coming at me, getting closer."

Mr. Small got up and stood at the tunnel opening. He went into the long hall after a few seconds and came back with a flashlight. "I'll go with you," Thomas said.

"I'd rather you stayed here. I'll only be a minute," said his father.

Mr. Small was gone less than a minute. Thomas and his mother waited, staring into the tunnel opening, flooded with

the light from the kitchen. A few feet beyond the opening, the kitchen light ended in a wall of blackness. They could see the light from Mr. Small's flashlight darting here and there along the ceiling of the tunnel until the path descended.

Mr. Small returned by way of the veranda steps. His white shirt was soiled from scaling the brick wall. As he came into the kitchen, muddying the floor as Thomas had, he was thoughtful, but not at all afraid.

He walked over to a high cabinet on the opposite wall from the tunnel. Beneath it, a small panel in the wall slid open at his touch. The panel had been invisible to the eye, but now revealed what seemed to be a jumble of miniature machinery. Mr. Small released a lever. The tunnel door slid silently down, and the patterned wallpaper of the kitchen showed no trace of what lay hidden behind it. Lastly, Mr. Small removed a mechanism of some kind from the panel and put it in his pocket.

"Did you see anything?" Thomas asked him. "Did you find my flashlight?"

"I didn't see anything," Mr. Small said, "and I didn't hear any sighing."

"Well, that's a relief," said Mrs. Small. "Goodness, if you'd found somebody . . . I'm sure my nerves would just give way."

"Your flashlight must have fallen in a crack," said Mr. Small. "I couldn't find it. Oh, yes, I removed the control from the panel. Without it, a giant couldn't raise that tunnel door."

"But you said there wasn't anything in the tunnel," said Thomas.

"That's so, but I don't want you wandering around in there," his father said. "The walls and ceiling are dirt and rock. There hasn't been a cave-in that I know of in a century, yet I think it best we don't take chances. I also removed the gears that control the front steps."

All he had to do was tell me not to go into the tunnel, Thomas thought. Give me a good reason and I wouldn't go . . . he knows that's all he has to do. He saw something or he heard something, and he's not going to tell anybody!

Undaunted, Thomas will continue to investigate the mysteries of his historic new house—mysteries from days long ago and mysteries in the present day—in The House of Dies Drear *and its sequel,* The Mystery of Drear House.

Would you like to read more about the house of Dies Drear? Why or why not?

How do Thomas's feelings change as he explores the tunnel? What causes the change?

What kind of person is Thomas? Give examples from the story to support your answer.

What does Thomas think was in the tunnel? What do you think was in the tunnel? Explain your answer.

WRITE Thomas is fascinated by the history of the old house he lives in. Think of a place that fascinates you. Write a paragraph or two to explain what attracts you to this place.

VIRGINIA HAMILTON

THE BELLS OF CHRISTMAS

ILLUSTRATED BY LAMBERT DAVIS

The Bells of CHRISTMAS

ALA NOTABLE
BOOK

by Virginia Hamilton

illustrated by Lambert Davis

It is Christmastime in 1890. Jason Bell, his
sister Lissy, and his brother Bob are waiting
for their relatives, who are traveling down
the National Road in Ohio.

The National Road, a part of American
history, is the way west for the pioneers.
It is also a part of the Bells' family history
because it is the place where Papa lost his leg
in an accident.

issy smiled and looked happy as she could be. Well, it was Christmas, and to me it felt like she was less of a bother as the day wore on.

We broke out of the trees, away from the patches of cattails, and stood a few feet off the Road.

"Ah, me!" I exclaimed.

"Ah, me!" said copy-cat Lissy.

"That makes the three of us—ah, me!" said Bob.

All was a sight to see on this Great Day. On the National Road!

And bells. Bells! No, not my relative Bells, not yet!

But bells, sets of three or five attached to the collars around horses' necks. Sometimes there was a whole string of bells tied to horses' harnesses. As the horses of a team moved, guided by the driver holding the reins, the bells sounded *jing-jing, jing-a-ling!* up and down the Road. And *ching, ching-aling*.

"Never in my life!" said I.

"Never in my life!" said Lissy.

Bob laughed. "Then feast your eyes!" said he. "This is the best part of a deep-snow day."

The snow kept on snowing, all over us and everything. Horses, teams of two and four, pulled sleighs! And the sleighs were full of laughing, talking, shouting Christmas folks. Whole families sometimes, if a sleigh was large enough. Whole families out for a sleigh ride before the favorite, Great Day supper.

The sky emptied its heart out. I knew I would hear the scudding sound of sleigh runners gliding through snow even in my dreams. And the muffley clip-clop of teams as snow deepened on the Road.

"Bob, will our sleigh work—can we sleigh ride?" I asked.

"Yes! Yes!" shouted Melissy. "Let's go before the snow stops!"

"This snow won't stop, Lissy, not for a good while," Bob said. "We'll sleigh ride when the relatives get here."

The snowfall and the sleigh bells must have heard him. For all at once there was a shout down the Road. We all turned as a four-horse team pulling a large, covered sleigh swung into view. The riders had spied me and Bob and Lissy before we spied them.

"Ho-ho!" shouted Bob.

"Ho-ho-ho-o-o!" came the return call.

"Bells!" I shouted. "It's Uncle Levi!"

"They're here!" shouted Lissy.

We jumped up and down for joy.

The horses came on, decorated with harness bells. They trotted briskly and snorted loudly at the driver's directions.

The covered sleigh top was homemade and fashioned to look like an old Conestoga wagon top.

Oh, it was a sight, that sleigh of merry Bells. "Tisha! Tisha!" we called out.

"You look like pioneers!" I hollered.

And they all waved and laughed and shouted, "Merry Christmas, Bells!"

"Same to you!" I called.

"Jason! Lissy! Bob! Jason! Jason! Merry Christmas!" called Tisha.

Then they were with us. Tisha was just the prettiest girl! She wore a hooded cloak of dark wool and a skirt with back drapery.

"You look all new!" I told her, gaping. "Haven't seen you in *so* long!"

"And you!" she said, eyes big and wide. "Jason, you look thirteen!"

Uncle Levi and Aunt Etta Bell gave hugs all around. The older brothers, Anthony and Chester, and cousin Sebella, took in Christmas packages.

The best gifts for the younger relatives had been exchanged. But there were some few gifts, such as Jason's from Tisha, and goods for the best meal, that had come with the Bells on this Great Day.

My present for Tisha was waiting for her under the tree.

"My pa has brought his grand surprise for Uncle James," whispered Tisha. "Remember, I said it was a secret, and I can't tell."

"Yes," I said. And I wondered all over again what it could be.

"You'll be surprised," she said.

Then brother Bob and Chester, my oldest Bell cousin, took Lissy, me, and Tisha for a sleigh ride. Just a short one. For the team was tired and needed tending to.

"Oh, now!" I said to Tisha. We were settled under the blanket, and we were a grand sight through the snow on our lane by the National Road. "How are you—shall we stop for Matthew?"

We did stop for him. We talked excitedly about everything as we neared his house. Tisha called from the sleigh: "Here, Matthew. I've come to get you!"

The door of Matthew's house flew open. Matthew sprang out so quickly he fairly slid halfway to us.

"Ah, gee! A fine sleigh this is, is it new?" he asked, climbing in next to Tisha. I was on her other side. Lissy sat in the front seat between Bob and Chester, listening to their eager talk.

"Poor Matthew! I suppose you've forgotten me as well as this sleigh. Now then, shall we ride, or shall we take you back before you forget where you came from?" she asked.

Matthew sat grinning from ear to ear. But his tongue was tied. Speechless.

"We ride! We glide!" I said. Matthew stole glances at Tisha. She looked just perfect, I thought. I was proud she was my relative and here for the Great Day.

"Aunt Lou Rhetta made this wonderful cloak," Tisha was telling Matthew, about Mama. "There's no other like it," said Tisha.

"It looks so nice on you, too," said Matthew, shyly.

I smothered a laugh so as not to disturb their talk.

"And this muff my ma found for me. I put it to my face when my nose gets cold," said Tisha. "I declare, I no longer can feel my feet!"

Matthew looked ready to wrap her feet in the blanket and run to the fire with them.

I grinned and looked away. I knew Bob and Chester smiled as Lissy chattered about the snow making her a white cloak with a hood, like Tisha's.

Soon we headed back, and in no time we were home. The house was a supper house, full of smells of good food—a mixture of sauces and meats and desserts. The spicy-sweet scent of pumpkin pie rode high above everything. My big brothers Ken and Samuel were here now with their families. The house was just full to bursting with relatives. Tisha and I circled the tree. I gave her the present I had picked out for her.

"Oh!" she exclaimed. "I did hope for a toilet set!" It had a brush, a comb, and a mirror. "It's so pretty, thank you, Jason."

She gave me a pocketknife of quality, and I praised it highly and showed Matthew.

"That's the finest I've seen," he said. Shyly, he handed Tisha his gift for her.

"I adore presents at Christmas," she said, and opened it. It was a bracelet with charms upon it. Quite pretty, too, and Tisha was delighted.

"Matthew, you weren't to spend a great lot of money, don't you know," she told him. But I could tell Tisha was pleased. Matthew had saved for months.

Then he went home for his supper. I thought he might refuse altogether to leave Tisha's side. "You can come back for pie," she said.

"I will," said Matthew.

Oh, but Christmas lasted long on its Great Day! I was filling up with it, and each sweet morsel of it was the best yet.

Mama received wonderful bead necklaces from Aunt Etta. She presented Aunt Etta with a silk umbrella. Aunt Etta loved it. She and Tisha and I went outside to open it. We three got under the umbrella.

Large flakes of snow came streaming down upon it as we stood there, shivering.

Papa gave his brother, Uncle Levi, a spokeshave, a cutting tool with a blade set between two handles. Uncle Levi was pleased.

We all waited eagerly to see what Uncle Levi would give to Papa. But they took Papa's present and went into the sitting room. They were gone a short while. And in that time, we children helped out. We moved tables, spread tablecloths, and arranged chairs for supper. Tisha and I placed the plates and silverware.

* * * * *

When Papa and Uncle Levi made their appearance, we were all back in the parlor. Mama had herded us there to sing carols. We had finished a sweet "Silent Night" when in came Papa, empty-handed. I couldn't see the present. It had been wrapped in a big box, too. Uncle Levi didn't have it either. What had happened to it?

Everybody stared at the two of them. Papa cut quite a figure in his Christmas suit. As he walked toward all of us and the tree, he held onto Uncle Levi's shoulder.

"Well, I declare," said Aunt Etta Bell. "Lou Rhetta, it sure is a wonder!" And she smiled brightly at Mama and all around. Mama looked Papa up and down and then, she, too, broke into a smile. "It's a wonder, indeed!" she said.

"And takes some getting use to, I'll wager," said cousin Chester Bell.

My brother Bob nodded agreement. "Papa will get used to it as quick as you please, if I know him," he said.

Well, I wondered! I gazed at my papa and he looked just like my papa, which he was. It was Christmas, with everybody and Tisha and oh, so many new things and goings on. That was the wonder, that I could see anything atall.

"What in the world is everybody talking about?" I asked.

"Yes, what are you all talking . . ." Lissy began.

I cut her off. "Hush up!" I said. I did not like being left out of things.

Papa smiled at me and said, "Calm down, son." He took his hand from Uncle Levi's shoulder.

"Now," said Papa, "come see what your Uncle Levi made me."

There was silence as I came up close to Papa. Lissy was right behind me with her walking doll. Everybody else crowded around. To my surprise, Papa raised his pant leg.

"Just look," said Papa. "Two true feet!"

I bent near with my hands on my knees. Well, it was a shock! Sure enough, where once there had been only the tip of a peg leg, there was now a shoe. And I hadn't noticed atall. And in Papa's stocking in the shoe was a foot. It matched the foot he'd always had. Attached to the foot was an ankle and then a leg. Not a peg leg atall. It was a wonder, all right.

"Knock on it, Jason," said Papa. And I did. I knocked on the leg, and it was wood. Very gently, I touched it with my fingers, and it was smooth oak, turned and made perfect by a master carver. It looked true, like the one that was real.

I shook my head, it was so hard to believe. "Is it a mechanical thing?" I asked Uncle Levi, for I knew he had made it.

"In some ways it is," said he. "There are wonders going on in mechanics."

"The foot moves up and down, like any foot," said Papa, "and it walks comfortable. For now, I will wear Levi's fine 'mechanical thing' on special occasions, such as this Great Day."

We all applauded wildly.

"You should both take a bow," said brother Bob. And they did. Uncle Levi and Papa bowed, holding onto each other for support. Each swept his free arm back in a grand gesture. They gave us a swell stage bow.

"It's a great wonder," I said, "to have a mechanical leg and foot. Papa, you look just like everybody!"

The grown-ups laughed at that. I was not too embarrassed. Tisha knew what I meant. So did Papa. It was a good son that wanted his papa to be just like folks. Oh, I liked him fine in his wheel-a-chair or on his peg leg. He was only different to me because he was such a fine carpenter and woodworker. But his two true feet did look the marvel. And then I just swelled up with pride at my papa and Uncle Levi.

"I'm glad of you both!" I couldn't help saying. "What true brothers you are!" And then Papa put his arm around me. And it was me and Uncle Levi who helped him to the dining room, and then into his wheel-a-chair, off his new leg for a while.

Well, it was a wonderful Christmas, 1890. A Great Day.

What feeling did you get from this story as you read it?

What are some of the things that make the Christmas of 1890 so memorable for Jason?

What do the Bells think of family celebrations? How can you tell?

WRITE   Think of a past holiday that is as memorable to you as this holiday is to Jason. Write a narrative paragraph telling about this holiday.

INTERPRETING THE PAST

What do "The House of Dies Drear" and "The Bells of Christmas" have in common? How do these stories reflect the interests and beliefs of Virginia Hamilton?

WRITER'S WORKSHOP

There are many places around the country that were important in our history. Picture a place, such as the Drear house or the National Road, that might call up memories of the past. As you imagine the place, make notes on what you see in your mind. Try to recall the history connected to the place. Then use your notes to write a short story involving the place's past. Write a story about the people who lived at that time. A drawing might help your audience visualize the place as they read your story.

Writer's Choice
What do you think about explaining history through a fictional story? Write down your ideas on the subject. Then think of a way to share your ideas.

Connections

Multicultural Connection

Keeping Our Yesteryears Alive

What picture comes to your mind when you hear the word *pioneers*? You should have a vision of men, women, and children of every age and race.

Years ago, one San Francisco teacher decided that not enough people were aware of the contributions of Chinese American pioneers. Ruthanne Lum McCunn also felt that she could understand how the pioneers felt living in a new country because she had spent her own childhood in Hong Kong.

To share the fascinating stories of Chinese Americans, McCunn wrote a book for young readers called *An Illustrated History of the Chinese in America*. Since that book was published, she has become a full-time writer and historian. Besides a folktale called *Pie Biter*, she has written three more books about America's Chinese heritage.

Use research books and other materials to make a classroom display that highlights the contributions of Chinese pioneers and their descendants.

March Fong Eu,
California
Secretary of State

子英孝情友愛美

Social Studies/Art Connection

Our Past Is Many People

From what parts of the world did the people who settled in your community come? How did they contribute to the history of your region? Find the answers to these questions, and then work with classmates to create a mural that reflects your community heritage.

Music Connection

Songs That Save the Past

In addition to books, songs keep our history and heritage alive. With a group, find two songs about political or social events that took place between 1750 and 1950. If the songs are in another language, you should provide a translation. Before singing the songs, tell your classmates why these songs were popular.

Judge Thomas Tang,
State Bar of Arizona

339

Unit Four 4

Shenanigans

O once upon a time in Arkansas,
An old man sat in his little cabin door,
And fiddled a tune that he lik'd to hear,
A jolly old tune that he'd play by ear.
                    —an American folk song

Entertainers seem to speak in a universal language, a language to which people all over the world can respond. How might a television newscaster such as Ed Bradley go about sharing world events with an audience of millions? Do you ever wonder how writers such as Gary Soto and Kazue Mizumura consistently dream up images and adventures that entertain readers? Think about what entertains and enlightens you as you read the selections in this unit.

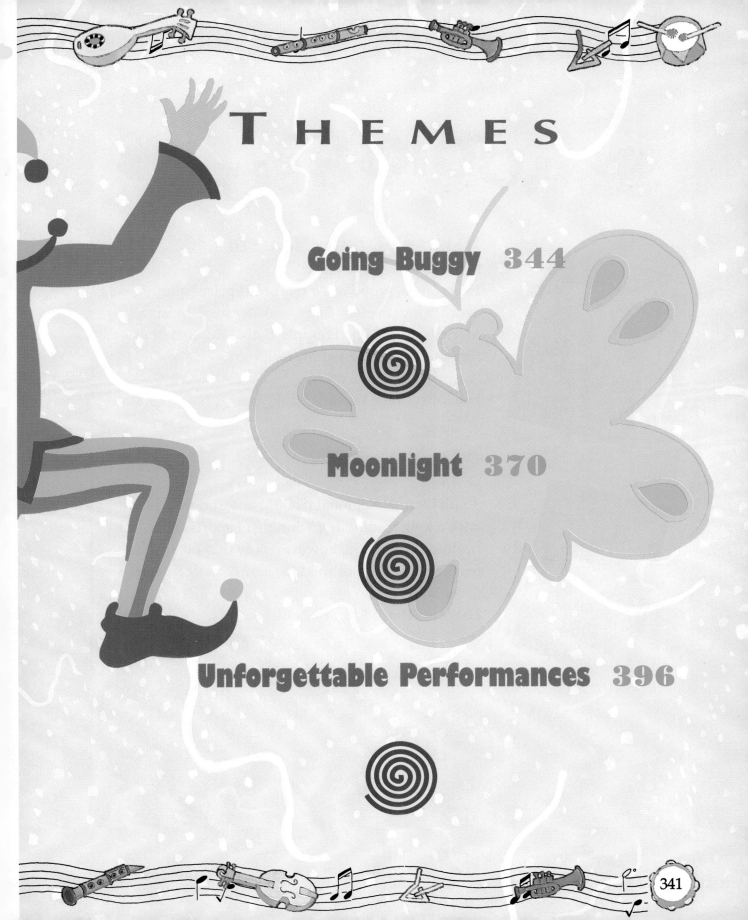

THEMES

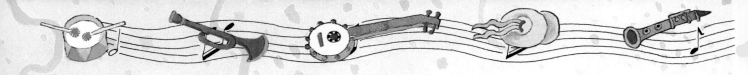

BOOKSHELF

BEETLES, LIGHTLY TOASTED

by Phyllis Reynolds Naylor

Everyone is proud of Andy for his prize-winning essay "How Beetles, Bugs, and Worms Can Save Money and the Food Supply Both." But then they find out how he tested his recipes.

Award-Winning Author

Harcourt Brace Library Book

S.O.R. LOSERS

by Avi

South Orange Regional (S.O.R.) is a middle school with a long tradition of winning at sports. That tradition could end, however, now that Ed and his friends have been drafted for a misfit soccer team.

Parents' Choice

Harcourt Brace Library Book

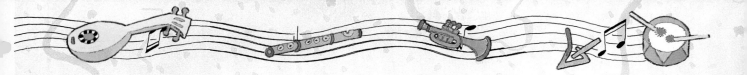

BABE: THE GALLANT PIG

by Dick King-Smith

Babe, the new pig at Farmer Hogget's, finds ways to help out on the farm and to avoid becoming a meal.

ALA Notable Book,

Boston Globe-Horn Book Honor Book

THE WAR WITH GRANDPA

by Robert Kimmell Smith

When Peter is forced to give up his room to his grandfather, he decides to declare war. It is a decision that Peter soon comes to regret.

Award-Winning Author

FERRET IN THE BEDROOM, LIZARDS IN THE FRIDGE

by Bill Wallace

All Liz wants to do is lead a normal life. But Liz's dad works with some strange and unusual animals, and he keeps bringing his work home.

Children's Choice

Going Buggy

How do you feel about bugs? They share the planet with us, yet we usually try to avoid them. The following selections are based upon some encounters between people and insects.

CONTENTS

·F·I·R·E·F·L·I·E·S·

from Joyful Noise: Poems for Two Voices

by Paul Fleischman

illustrated by Eric Beddows

Light	Light
	is the ink we use
Night	Night
is our parchment	
	We're
	fireflies
fireflies	flickering
flitting	
	flashing
fireflies	
glimmering	fireflies
	gleaming
glowing	
Insect calligraphers	Insect calligraphers
practicing penmanship	
	copying sentences
Six-legged scribblers	Six-legged scribblers
of vanishing messages,	
	fleeting graffiti
Fine artists in flight	Fine artists in flight
adding dabs of light	
	bright brush strokes
Signing the June nights	Signing the June nights
as if they were paintings	as if they were paintings
	We're
flickering	fireflies
fireflies	flickering
fireflies.	fireflies.

LIKE JAKE AND ME

by Mavis Jukes · pictures by Lloyd Bloom

THE RAIN HAD STOPPED. The sun was
setting. There were clouds in the sky the color of
smoke. Alex was watching his stepfather, Jake, split
wood at the edge of the cypress grove. Somewhere a
toad was grunting.

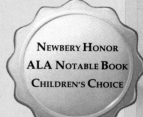

"Jake!" called Alex.

Jake swung the axe, and wood flew into the air.

"Jake!" Alex called again. "Need me?" Alex had a loose tooth
in front. He moved it in and out with his tongue.

Jake rested the axe head in the grass and leaned on the handle. "What?" he said. He took off his Stetson hat and wiped his
forehead on his jacket sleeve.

Alex cupped his hands around his mouth. "Do . . . you . . .
need . . . me . . . to . . . help?" he hollered. Then he tripped
over a pumpkin, fell on it, and broke it. A toad flopped away.

Jake adjusted the raven feather behind his hatband. "Better
stay there!" he called. He put his hat back on. With powerful
arms, he sunk the axe blade into a log. It fell in half.

"Wow," thought Alex. "I'll never be able to do that."

Alex's mother was standing close by, under the pear tree.
She was wearing fuzzy woolen leg warmers, a huge knitted coat
with pictures of reindeer on the back, and a red scarf with the
name *Virginia* on it. "I need you," she said.

Alex stood up, dumped the pumpkin over the fence for the
sheep, and went to Virginia.

"I dropped two quarters and a dime in the grass. If I bend
down, I may never be able to get up again," she said. Virginia
was enormous. She was pregnant with twins, and her belly
blocked her view to the ground. "I can't even see where
they fell."

"Here!" said Alex. He gave her two quarters. Then he
found the dime. He tied her shoe while he was down there.

"Thanks," said Virginia. "I also need you for some advice."
She pointed up. "Think it's ready?"

One of the branches of the pear tree had a glass bottle over the end of it. Inside were some twigs and leaves *and* two pears. In the spring, Virginia had pushed the bottle onto the branch, over the blossoms. During the summer, the pears had grown and sweetened inside the bottle. Now they were fat and crowding each other.

The plan was that when the pears were ripe, Virginia would pull the bottle from the tree, leaving the fruit inside. Then she'd fill the bottle with pear nectar and trick her sister, Caroline. Caroline would never guess how Virginia got the pears into the bottle!

"Shall we pick it?" asked Virginia.

"Up to you!" said Alex.

Months ago, Virginia had told him that the pears, and the babies, would be ready in the fall. Alex looked away at the hills. They were dusky gray. There were smudges of yellow poplars on the land. Autumn was here.

Alex fiddled with his tooth. "Mom," he asked, "do you think the twins are brothers or sisters?"

"Maybe both," said Virginia.

"If there's a boy, do you think he'll be like Jake or like me?"

"Maybe like Jake *and* you," said Virginia.

"Like Jake *and* me?" Alex wondered how that could be possible.

"Right," said Virginia.

"Well, anyway," said Alex, "would you like to see something I can do?"

"Of course," she said.

Alex straightened. Gracefully he lifted his arms and rose up on his toes. He looked like a bird about to take off. Then he lowered his arms and crouched. Suddenly he sprang up. He spun once around in midair and landed lightly.

Virginia clapped. "Great!"

Alex did it again, faster. Then again, and again. He whirled and danced around the tree for Virginia. He spun until he was pooped. Jake had put down the axe and was watching.

"Ballet class!" gasped Alex. "Dad signed me up for lessons, remember?"

"Of course I remember," said Virginia. "Go show Jake!"

"No," panted Alex. "Jake isn't the ballet type."

"He might like it," said Virginia. "Go see!"

"Maybe another time," said Alex. He raced across the field to where Jake was loading his arms with logs. "Jake, I'll carry the axe."

"Carry the axe?" Jake shook his head. "I just sharpened that axe."

Alex moved his tooth with his tongue and squinted up at Jake. "I'm careful," he said.

Jake looked over at the sheep nosing the pumpkin. "Maybe another time," he told Alex.

Alex walked beside him as they headed toward the house. The air was so cold Jake was breathing steam. The logs were stacked to his chin.

Virginia stood under the pear tree, watching the sunset. Alex ran past her to open the door.

Jake thundered up the stairs and onto the porch. His boots were covered with moss and dirt. Alex stood in the doorway.

"Watch it!" said Jake. He shoved the door open farther with his shoulder, and Alex backed up against the wall. Jake moved sideways through the door.

"Here, I'll help you stack the wood!" said Alex.

"Watch it!" Jake came down on one knee and set the wood by the side of the woodstove. Then he said kindly, "You've really got to watch it, Alex. I can't see where I'm going with so big a load."

Alex wiggled his tooth with his tongue. "I just wanted to help you," he said. He went to Jake and put his hand on Jake's shoulder. Then he leaned around and looked under his Stetson hat. There was bark in Jake's beard. "You look like a cowboy in the movies."

"I have news for you," said Jake. "I *am* a cowboy. A real one." He unsnapped his jacket. On his belt buckle was a silver longhorn steer. "Or was one." He looked over at Alex.

Alex shoved his tooth forward with his tongue.

"Why don't you just pull out that tooth?" Jake asked him.

"Too chicken," said Alex. He closed his mouth.

"Well, everybody's chicken of something," said Jake. He opened his jacket pocket and took out a wooden match. He chewed on the end of it and looked out the windows behind the stove. He could see Virginia, still standing beneath the tree. Her hands were folded under her belly.

Jake balled up newspaper and broke some sticks. He had giant hands. He filled the woodstove with the wadded paper and the sticks and pushed in a couple of logs.

"Can I light the fire?" Alex asked.

"Maybe another time," said Jake. He struck the match on his rodeo belt buckle. He lit the paper and threw the match into the fire.

Just then Alex noticed that there was a wolf spider on the back of Jake's neck. There were fuzzy babies holding on to her body. "Did you know wolf spiders carry their babies around?" said Alex.

"Says who?" asked Jake.

"My dad," said Alex. He moved his tooth out as far as it would go. "He's an entomologist, remember?"

"I remember," said Jake.

"Dad says they only bite you if you bother them, or if you're squashing them," said Alex. "But still, I never mess with wolf spiders." He pulled his tooth back in with his tongue.

"Is that what he says, huh," said Jake. He jammed another log into the stove, then looked out again at Virginia. She was gazing at the landscape. The hills were fading. The farms were fading. The cypress trees were turning black.

"I think she's pretty," said Alex, looking at the spider.

"I do, too," said Jake, looking at Virginia.

"It's a nice design on her back," said Alex, examining the spider.

"Yep!" said Jake. He admired the reindeer coat, which he'd loaned to Virginia.

"Her belly sure is big!" said Alex.

"It has to be big, to carry the babies," said Jake.

"She's got an awful lot of babies there," said Alex.

Jake laughed. Virginia was shaped something like a pear.

"And boy! Are her legs woolly!" said Alex.

Jake looked at Virginia's leg warmers. "Itchy," said Jake. He rubbed his neck. The spider crawled over his collar.

"She's in your coat!" said Alex. He backed away a step.

"We can share it," said Jake. He liked to see Virginia bundled up. "It's big enough for both of us. She's got to stay warm." Jake stood up.

"You sure are brave," said Alex. "I like wolf spiders, but I wouldn't have let that one into my coat. That's the biggest, hairiest wolf spider I've ever seen."

Jake froze. "Wolf spider! Where?"

"In your coat getting warm," said Alex.

Jake stared at Alex. "What wolf spider?"

"The one we were talking about, with the babies!" said Alex. "And the furry legs."

"Wolf spider!" Jake moaned. "I thought we were talking about Virginia!" He was holding his shoulders up around his ears.

"You never told me you were scared of spiders," said Alex.

"You never asked me," said Jake in a high voice. "Help!"

"How?" asked Alex.

"Get my jacket off!"

Alex took hold of Jake's jacket sleeve as Jake eased his arm out. Cautiously, Alex took the jacket from Jake's shoulders. Alex looked in the coat.

"No spider, Jake," said Alex. "I think she went into your shirt."

"My shirt?" asked Jake. "You think?"

"Maybe," said Alex.

Jake gasped. "Inside? I hope not!"

"Feel anything *furry* crawling on you?" asked Alex.

"Anything *furry* crawling on me?" Jake shuddered. "No!"

"Try to get your shirt off without squashing her," said Alex. "Remember, we don't want to hurt her. She's a mama."

"With babies," added Jake. *"Eek!"*

"And," said Alex, "she'll bite!"

"Bite? Yes, I know!" said Jake. "Come out on the porch and help me! I don't want her to get loose in the house!"

Jake walked stiffly to the door. Alex opened it. They walked out onto the porch. The sky was thick gray and salmon colored, with blue windows through the clouds.

"Feel anything?" asked Alex.

"Something . . ." said Jake. He unsnapped the snaps on his sleeves, then the ones down the front. He opened his shirt. On his chest was a tattoo of an eagle that was either taking off or landing. He let the shirt drop to the floor.

"No spider, back or front," reported Alex.

They shook out the shirt.

"Maybe your jeans," said Alex. "Maybe she got into your jeans!"

"Not my *jeans!*" said Jake. He quickly undid his rodeo belt.

"Your boots!" said Alex. "First you have to take off your boots!"

"Right!" said Jake. He sat down on the boards. Each boot had a yellow rose and the name *Jake* stitched on the side. "Could you help?" he asked.

"Okay," said Alex. He grappled with one boot and got it off. He checked it. He pulled off and checked the sock. No spider. He tugged on the other boot.

"You've got to pull harder," said Jake, as Alex pulled and struggled. "Harder!"

The boot came off and smacked Alex in the mouth. "Ouch!" Alex put his tongue in the gap. "Knocked my tooth out!" He looked in the boot. "It's in the boot!"

"Yikes!" said Jake.

"Not the spider," said Alex. "My tooth." He rolled it out of the boot and into his hand to examine it.

"Dang," said Jake. "Then hurry up." Alex dropped the tooth back into the boot. Jake climbed out of his jeans and looked down each leg. He hopped on one foot to get the other sock off.

"She won't be in your sock," said Alex. "But maybe—"

"Don't tell me," said Jake. "Not my shorts!"

Alex stared at Jake's shorts. There were pictures of mallard ducks on them. "Your shorts," said Alex.

"I'm afraid to look," said Jake. He thought he felt something creeping just below his belly button.

"Someone's coming!" said Alex. "Quick! Give me your hat! I'll hold it up and you can stand behind it."

"Help!" said Jake in a small voice. He gave Alex the hat and quickly stepped out of his shorts. He brushed himself off in the front.

"Okay in the back," said Alex, peering over the brim of the hat.

Jake turned his shorts inside out, then right side in again. No spider. When he bent over to put them on, he backed into his hat, and the raven feather poked him. Jake howled and jumped up and spun around in midair.

"I didn't know you could do ballet!" said Alex. "You dance like me!"

"I thought I felt the spider!" said Jake. He put on his shorts.

"What on *earth* are you doing?" huffed Virginia. She was standing at the top of the stairs, holding the bottle with the pears inside.

"We're hunting for a spider," said Jake.

"Well!" said Virginia. "I like your hunting outfit. But aren't those *duck*-hunting shorts, and aren't you cold?"

"We're not hunting spiders," explained Jake. "We're hunting *for* a spider."

"A big and hairy one that *bites!*" added Alex.

"A wolf spider!" said Jake, shivering. He had goose bumps.

"Really!" said Virginia. She set the bottle down beside Jake's boot. "Aha!" she cried, spying Alex's tooth inside. "Here's one of the spider's teeth!"

Alex grinned at his mother. He put his tongue where his tooth wasn't.

Jake took his hat from Alex and put it on.

"Hey!" said Virginia.

"What?" said Jake.

"The spider!" she said. "It's on your hat!"

"Help!" said Jake. "Somebody help me!"

Alex sprang up into the air and snatched the hat from Jake's head.

"Look!" said Alex.

"Holy smoke!" said Jake.

There, hiding behind the black feather, was the spider.

Alex tapped the hat brim. The spider dropped to the floor. Then off she swaggered with her fuzzy babies, across the porch and into a crack.

Jake went over to Alex. He knelt down. "Thanks, Alex," said Jake. It was the closest Alex had ever been to the eagle. Jake pressed Alex against its wings. "May I have this dance?" Jake asked.

Ravens were lifting from the blackening fields and calling. The last light had settled in the clouds like pink dust.

Jake stood up holding Alex, and together they looked at Virginia. She was rubbing her belly. "Something is happening here," she told them. "It feels like the twins are beginning to dance."

"Like Jake and me," said Alex. And Jake whirled around the porch with Alex in his arms.

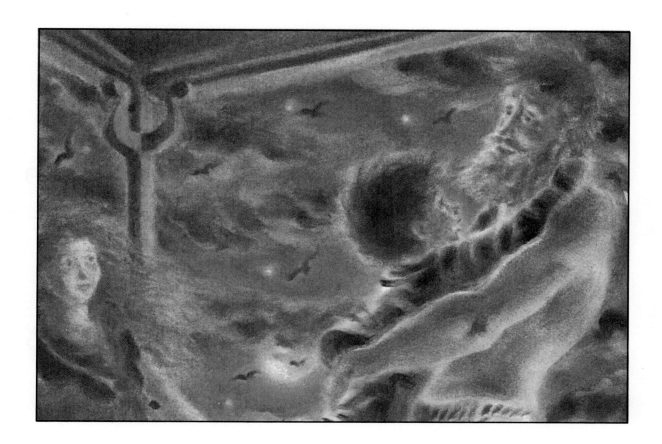

Do you think Jake should have allowed Alex to
help with the chores? Why or why not?

How does Jake change from the beginning to the
end of the story?

Why doesn't Alex want to show Jake what he
learned at his ballet class?

WRITE   The incident with the wolf spider
brings Jake and Alex closer together. Write a
journal entry telling about a meaningful or funny
experience you shared with a family member or
a friend.

BEETLES, LIGHTLY TOASTED

by Phyllis Reynolds Naylor

After weeks of preparing and testing his bug recipes, Andy entered the Roger B. Sudermann Contest. Andy felt confident that his essay about using beetles, bugs, and worms as food was good enough to win first prize.

illustrated by Katy Farmer

AWARD-WINNING AUTHOR

On JUNE 4, TWO DAYS BEFORE SCHOOL WAS OUT, Mrs. Haynes' class sat waiting as Luther Sudermann's car pulled up outside the window. As they watched him shake hands with the principal, the teacher said, "No matter who wins the contest, I want you to know that I read all the essays myself before I sent them to Mr. Sudermann, and I think that every one of them was good. *All* of you who entered the contest deserve to feel proud of what you've done."

There were footsteps in the hall, then the principal came in, followed by a gray-haired man in a blue suit. His eyes seemed to take in the whole room at once, and he smiled as the principal introduced him. Then he sat down on the edge of Mrs. Haynes' desk and looked the students over.

"I was disappointed," he said, "that only nine of you decided to enter my contest this year, but I'm delighted with those who did. It just goes to show that imagination is alive and well in these United States, and if the future of our country depends on people like you, then we're in good hands."

The principal beamed.

Mr. Sudermann went on to talk about his son Roger when he was alive, and how Roger was always building something or taking it apart.

"If something broke around the house, Roger would say, 'Maybe I can fix it, Dad,' and when he saw something new, he'd say, 'Show me how it works.' He was intellectually curious—always tried to improve things, make them a little better." Mr. Sudermann bowed his head for a moment and stared at the floor. "Needless to say, I miss him," he told the class, "but through this contest, I can keep the idea of him alive—I can keep his imagination going, and reward others who show the same inventiveness as Roger."

Andy had never known anything about Roger Sudermann before, and could almost see the boy that Mr. Sudermann was talking about. He was wondering, too, if *he* ever died young, what his dad would say about *him*. That Andy was imaginative? Helpful? Open to new ideas?

"To the nine of you who entered my contest," Mr. Sudermann went on, "I want you to know that I have read your essays carefully—some of them several times. I narrowed my choice down to five, then four, then three, and I had a very hard time narrowing it down to two. But once I had eliminated all but two, I simply could go no further, and so—for the first time in the history of the Roger B. Sudermann Contest—I am declaring two winners this year, and each will receive a check for fifty dollars. The two winning essays were: 'Saving Energy When You Cook,' by Jack Barth, and 'How Beetles, Bugs, and Worms Can Save Money and the Food Supply Both,' by Andy Moller. Would you two boys come up here, please?"

The class began to clap as Andy, swallowing, stood up and moved numbly to the front of the classroom beside Jack. The teacher and principal were clapping too.

Mr. Sudermann shook both boys' hands. "I saw a little of my son in what each of you boys wrote," he said, "and I know that if Roger were alive, he'd want to be your friend. You have both shown the spirit of initiative and creativity that Mrs. Sudermann and I so admire, and on June 10, I am going to feel very honored to shake your hands again on the steps of the library."

"Thank you," said Jack.

"Thank you," said Andy, barely audible.

The principal walked Mr. Sudermann back out to his car again, and Mrs. Haynes beamed at Jack and Andy.

"Read their essays out loud!" someone said.

"Yes!" said the others.

"Isn't it lucky that I made copies?" Mrs. Haynes smiled, and took them out of her drawer. Andy stared down at his feet.

Mrs. Haynes read Jack's essay first. Everybody laughed when she read the part about the hamburgers almost catching fire under the hood of the car. The class clapped when the essay was over, and Mrs. Haynes said she was looking forward to cooking fish in her dishwasher. Then she picked up Andy's essay.

When it was clear that Andy was talking about *eating* beetles, bugs, and worms, there were gasps.

"Oh, gross!" someone giggled.

"Eeeyuuk!" said somebody else.

Andy saw Sam look over at him nervously and smile. He tried to smile back but his face felt frozen. When Mrs. Haynes read about using little bits of beetles, lightly toasted, in brownies, the room suddenly got very quiet. And when at last she finished reading, nobody clapped. Sam started to, then stopped. Mrs. Haynes looked around, puzzled.

"Wasn't that a good essay, class?" she said. "I suppose it might take some getting used to, but there is really no reason why we can't use insects as a source of protein."

Dora Kray raised her hand. "What if somebody gives you a brownie with beetles in it and doesn't tell you?"

The teacher thought about it. "Well, I think everyone has the right, certainly, to know what he's eating, but . . ." She looked around, puzzled. "Andy wouldn't do . . ." She stopped.

The room was embarrassingly quiet, and Mrs. Haynes didn't quite know what to do. Finally she asked everyone to take out his arithmetic book, and she started the morning's lesson.

"Listen, they had to find out sooner or later," Sam said to Andy at recess when the others walked by without talking to him. "Heck, they'll get over it. They'll forget."

"Go on and play kickball with them," Andy said. "I don't want them mad at you, too."

It was one of the most horrible days Andy had ever spent. Whenever the other students walked by his desk, they either looked the other way or glared at him. Jack, strangely, spoke to him on the bus going home, but no one else did. Andy didn't know just how he was going to tell his family. He was relieved, when he reached the house, that Mother had forgotten what day it was, and she and Aunt Wanda were busily putting up pints of strawberry jam.

In a matter of minutes, however, the phone rang and it was Aunt Bernie, telling Mother that both Jack and Andy had won the contest together, and Mother said she would call her back later, that the preserves were boiling.

"For heaven's sake, Andy, you didn't even tell us," Mother said, turning back to the stove. "How wonderful!"

Andy faked a smile.

"You're going to have to tell us all about it at supper," she went on. "Won't your dad be pleased, though?"

"What did you write about?" Aunt Wanda asked, pouring a pitcherful of sugar into the pot of boiling berries.

"Oh, saving money on groceries," Andy said.

"Well, I'll be glad to hear how to do that!" Mother told him.

Andy went out in the barn and began shoveling out the stalls. The whole fifth-grade class was mad at him, and he couldn't much blame them. In another hour or so, the entire family would be angry, too. He didn't see how saying that he was sorry would help. What was done was done, and no one would ever forget it.

At supper that evening, Dad had no sooner asked the blessing than Mother said, "Andy has some good news tonight. Tell them, Andy."

Andy swallowed. His cheeks felt as though they would crack if he tried to make them smile once more. "I was one of the winners of the Roger B. Sudermann Contest," he said. "There were two winners this year, and Jack was the other one."

"Isn't that marvelous?" said Mother. "Did Mr. Sudermann come to school and announce the winners himself?"

Andy told them about the little speech Mr. Sudermann had given the class, glad to turn the attention away from himself. He said how Luther Sudermann had told them that Roger was always inventing things, trying to find out how something worked.

"He *was* the boy who came to school as a TV set!" Lois said suddenly. "I remember now! He was wearing this box with knobs, and his face was where the screen would be. When you turned one knob, he gave you a dog food commercial, and when you turned the other one, he shut up."

"Well!" said Andy's father. "We'll have to read that essay you wrote. What was it about?"

"Saving money on groceries," said Aunt Wanda. "I'd certainly like to know how Andy knows anything about that."

"What did you call your essay?" Wendell asked, reaching for another slice of beef.

Andy took a deep breath and put down his fork. " 'How Beetles, Bugs, and Worms Can Save Money and the Food Supply Both,' " he said.

The family stared at him.

"How can they do *that?* " asked Mother.

Andy's face felt flushed. His tongue seemed to be swelling. "You eat them," he said.

"*Eat* them?" cried Lois.

Andy continued staring down at his hands. "I wrote to a man at the University and he told me how to fix them."

"*Safely?* " said Mother.

Andy nodded.

"Did you *try* it?" she asked.

"I cooked them," Andy said, not quite answering.

Suddenly no one was eating.

"What . . . did . . . you . . . cook?" came Aunt Wanda's voice, slow and steady.

Andy closed his eyes. "Brownies . . .," he said.

He heard Wendell cough.

"Deep-fried worms . . ."

The family seemed to have stopped breathing.

"And . . . grubs in egg salad."

"Egg salad!" Lois leaped up, tipping over her chair. "Not *my* egg salad!"

Andy didn't answer.

A long, piercing shriek filled the kitchen, rattling the walls. "Arrrrgggggh!" Lois lunged for the sink, stuck her mouth under the faucet and turned the water on full force. "Yauuugghh!" she screamed again, gargling and screeching, both at the same time.

"Andy," said Aunt Wanda, and her voice was like lead weights. "Did you touch my Okra Surprise?"

Andy couldn't answer that either, and continued staring down at his lap. And at that very moment, the phone rang.

Andy got up from the table and answered the phone because he needed an excuse to leave. If he could have sailed out the window and over the treetops, he would have done so gladly. A ringing telephone was the next best thing. It saved him from simply getting up from the table and going upstairs to his room, which was what he was about to do anyway.

"Could I speak to Andy Moller, please?" said a man's voice at the other end.

"I'm Andy."

"Good! This is Frank Harris, a photographer from the *Bucksville Gazette.* Mr. Sudermann told me about you winning the essay contest—you and another boy—and we'd like to get a photo of the winners."

It was what Andy had been waiting for for two years—the reason he had entered the contest. Now, the last thing in the world he wanted was his picture in the *Bucksville Gazette,* but there was no way he could get out of it.

"You're the one who wrote about beetles and bugs, aren't you?" the photographer asked.

"Yes . . ."

"Well, what Mr. Sudermann has in mind, see, is a photo of you right there on the steps of the library eating one of those meals you wrote about."

Should Andy have told his classmates and his family about the ingredients he used before they ate his dishes?

What is Andy's problem in the story?

Why doesn't anyone in the classroom applaud after Mrs. Haynes reads Andy's essay?

How would you react if you were in Andy's class and realized you had eaten one of his brownies?

WRITE Put yourself in Andy's place. Decide whether Andy should accept or back down from the challenge of eating one of his dishes on the steps of the library. Write a statement from Andy explaining why he will accept or decline.

Going Buggy

Insects play a big part in the outcomes of both "Like Jake and Me" and "Beetles, Lightly Toasted." How do insects make life better for Alex and worse for Andy?

WRITER'S WORKSHOP

Andy wrote a letter to a university, asking for information on the food value of insects. Think of a topic for which you need some expert information. Decide who could give you that information, and write a business letter making your request.

Writer's Choice   What do you think of the theme Going Buggy now that you have read these selections? Respond to the theme in your own way, and write about your response to it. Share your feelings with your classmates.

Moonlight

The same moon shines down upon us all with the same light. Yet each person looks back at the moon with different thoughts and different feelings.

C O N T E N T S

MOON

from *Flower Moon Snow: A Book of Haiku*
written and illustrated by Kazue Mizumura

Following me all along the road,
The moon came home
With me tonight.

Coming home late,
Only my moonlit shadow
Dances on the street.

Again and again,
The wind wipes away the clouds
And shines up the moon.

Clink!
An iced branch falls.
I see the shattered moonlight
Scatter at my feet.

The party is over.
The moon in the swimming pool
Is all alone.

Many Moons

by JAMES THURBER

Illustrated by MARC SIMONT

ONCE UPON A TIME, in a kingdom by the sea, there lived a little Princess named Lenore. She was ten years old, going on eleven. One day Lenore fell ill of a surfeit of raspberry tarts and took to her bed.

The Royal Physician came to see her and took her temperature and felt her pulse and made her stick out her tongue. The Royal Physician was worried. He sent for the King, Lenore's father, and the King came to see her.

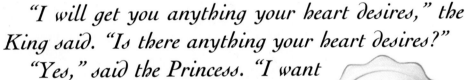

"I will get you anything your heart desires," the King said. "Is there anything your heart desires?"

"Yes," said the Princess. "I want the moon. If I can have the moon, I will be well again."

AWARD-WINNING
AUTHOR

Now the King had a great many wise men who always got for him anything he wanted, so he told his daughter that she could have the moon. Then he went to the throne room and pulled a bell cord, three long pulls and a short pull, and presently the Lord High Chamberlain came into the room.

The Lord High Chamberlain was a large, fat man who wore thick glasses which made his eyes seem twice as big as they really were. This made the Lord High Chamberlain seem twice as wise as he really was.

"I want you to get the moon," said the King. "The Princess Lenore wants the moon. If she can have the moon, she will get well again."

"The moon?" exclaimed the Lord High Chamberlain, his eyes widening. This made him look four times as wise as he really was.

"Yes, the moon," said the King. "M-o-o-n, moon. Get it tonight, tomorrow at the latest."

The Lord High Chamberlain wiped his forehead with a handkerchief and then blew his nose loudly. "I have got a great many things for you in my time, your Majesty," he said. "It just happens that I have with me a list of the things I have got for you in my time." He pulled a long scroll of parchment out of his pocket.

"Let me see, now." He glanced at the list, frowning. "I have got ivory, apes, and peacocks, rubies, opals, and emeralds, black orchids, pink elephants, and blue poodles, gold bugs, scarabs, and flies in amber, hummingbirds' tongues, angels' feathers, and unicorns' horns, giants, midgets, and mermaids, frankincense, ambergris, and myrrh, troubadours, minstrels, and dancing women, a pound of butter, two dozen eggs, and a sack of sugar—sorry, my wife wrote that in there."

"I don't remember any blue poodles," said the King.

"It says blue poodles right here on the list, and they are checked off with a little check mark," said the Lord High Chamberlain. "So there must have been blue poodles. You just forget."

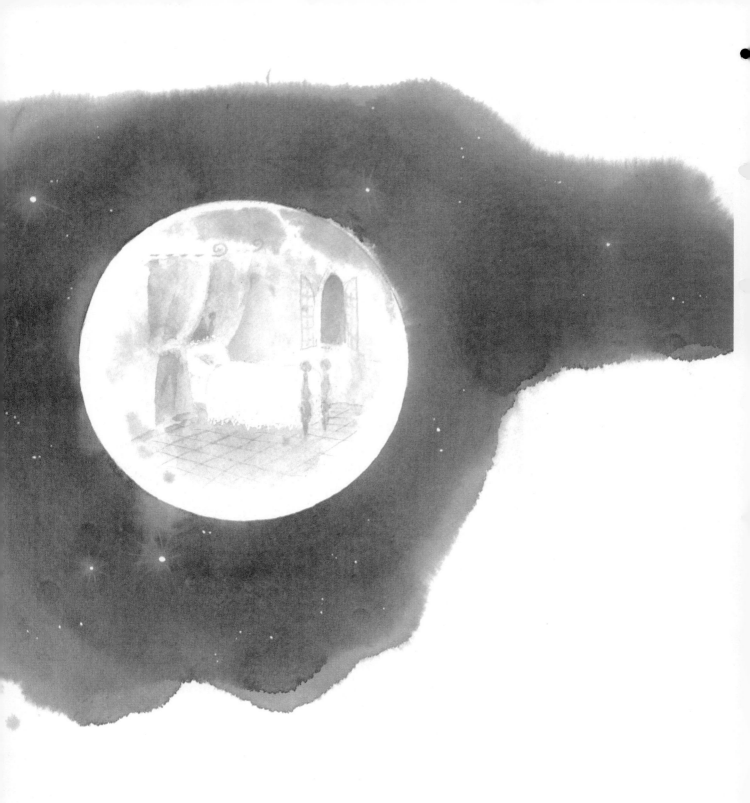

"Never mind the blue poodles," said the King. "What I want now is the moon."

"I have sent as far as Samarkand and Araby and Zanzibar to get things for you, your Majesty," said the Lord High Chamberlain. "But the moon is out of the question. It is 35,000 miles away and it is bigger than the room the Princess lies in. Furthermore, it is made of molten copper. I cannot get the moon for you. Blue poodles, yes; the moon, no."

The King flew into a rage and told the Lord High Chamberlain to leave the room and to send the Royal Wizard to the throne room.

The Royal Wizard was a little, thin man with a long face. He wore a high red peaked hat covered with silver stars, and a long blue robe covered with golden owls. His face grew very pale when the King told him that he wanted the moon for his little daughter, and that he expected the Royal Wizard to get it.

"I have worked a great deal of magic for you in my time, your Majesty," said the Royal Wizard. "As a matter of fact, I just happen to have in my pocket a list of the wizardries I have performed for you." He drew a paper from a deep pocket of his robe. "It begins: 'Dear Royal Wizard: I am returning herewith the so-called philosopher's stone which you claimed—' no, that isn't it." The Royal Wizard brought a long scroll of parchment from another pocket of his robe. "Here it is," he said. "Now, let's see. I have squeezed blood out of turnips for you, and turnips out of blood. I have produced rabbits out of silk hats, and silk hats out of rabbits. I have conjured up flowers, tambourines, and doves out of nowhere, and nowhere out of flowers, tambourines, and doves. I have brought you divining rods, magic wands, and crystal spheres in which to behold the future. I have compounded philters, unguents, and potions, to cure heartbreak, surfeit, and ringing in the ears. I have made you my own special mixture of wolfbane, nightshade, and eagles' tears, to ward off witches, demons, and things that go bump in the night. I have given you seven-league boots, the golden touch, and a cloak of invisibility—"

"It didn't work," said the King. "The cloak of invisibility didn't work."

"Yes, it did," said the Royal Wizard.

"No, it didn't," said the King. "I kept bumping into things, the same as ever."

"The cloak is supposed to make you invisible," said the Royal Wizard. "It is not supposed to keep you from bumping into things."

"All I know is, I kept bumping into things," said the King.

The Royal Wizard looked at his list again. "I got you," he said, "horns from Elfland, sand from the Sandman, and gold from the rainbow. Also a spool of thread, a paper of needles, and a lump of beeswax—sorry, those are things my wife wrote down for me to get her."

"What I want you to do now," said the King, "is to get me the moon. The Princess Lenore wants the moon, and when she gets it, she will be well again."

"Nobody can get the moon," said the Royal Wizard. "It is 150,000 miles away, and it is made of green cheese, and it is twice as big as this palace."

The King flew into another rage and sent the Royal Wizard back to his cave. Then he rang a gong and summoned the Royal Mathematician.

The Royal Mathematician was a bald-headed, nearsighted man, with a skullcap on his head and a pencil behind each ear. He wore a black suit with white numbers on it.

"I don't want to hear a long list of all the things you have figured out for me since 1907," the King said to him. "I want you to figure out right now how to get the moon for the Princess Lenore. When she gets the moon, she will be well again."

"I am glad you mentioned all the things I have figured out for you since 1907," said the Royal Mathematician. "It so happens that I have a list of them with me."

He pulled a long scroll of parchment out of a pocket and looked at it. "Now, let me see. I have figured out for you the distance between the horns of a dilemma, night and day, and A and Z. I have computed how far is Up, how long it takes to get to Away, and what becomes of Gone. I have discovered the length of the sea serpent, the price of the priceless, and the square of the hippopotamus. I know where you are when you are at Sixes and Sevens, how much Is you have to have to make an Are, and how many birds you can catch with the salt in the ocean—187,796,132, if it would interest you to know."

"There aren't that many birds," said the King.

"I didn't say there were," said the Royal Mathematician. "I said if there were."

"I don't want to hear about seven hundred million imaginary birds," said the King. "I want you to get the moon for the Princess Lenore."

"The moon is 300,000 miles away," said the Royal Mathematician. "It is round and flat like a coin, only it is made of asbestos, and it is half the size of this kingdom. Furthermore, it is pasted on the sky. Nobody can get the moon."

The King flew into still another rage and sent the Royal Mathematician away. Then he rang for the Court Jester.

The Jester came bounding into the throne room in his motley and his cap and bells, and sat at the foot of the throne.

"What can I do for you, your Majesty?" asked the Court Jester.

"Nobody can do anything for me," said the King mournfully. "The Princess Lenore wants the moon, and she cannot be well till she gets it, but nobody can get it for her. Every time I ask anybody for the moon, it gets larger and farther away. There is nothing you can do for me except play on your lute. Something sad."

"How big do they say the moon is," asked the Court Jester, "and how far away?"

"The Lord High Chamberlain says it is 35,000 miles away, and bigger than the Princess Lenore's room," said the King. "The Royal Wizard says it is 150,000 miles away, and twice as big as this palace. The Royal Mathematician says it is 300,000 miles away, and half the size of this kingdom."

The Court Jester strummed on his lute for a little while. "They are all wise men," he said, "and so they must all be right. If they are all right, then the moon must be just as large and as far away as each person thinks it is. The thing to do is find out how big the Princess Lenore thinks it is, and how far away."

"I never thought of that," said the King.

"I will go and ask her, your Majesty," said the Court Jester. And he crept softly into the little girl's room.

The Princess Lenore was awake, and she was glad to see the Court Jester, but her face was very pale and her voice very weak.

"Have you brought the moon to me?" she asked.

"Not yet," said the Court Jester, "but I will get it for you right away. How big do you think it is?"

"It is just a little smaller than my thumbnail," she said, "for when I hold my thumbnail up at the moon, it just covers it."

"And how far away is it?" asked the Court Jester.

"It is not as high as the big tree outside my window," said the Princess, "for sometimes it gets caught in the top branches."

"It will be very easy to get the moon for you," said the Court Jester. "I will climb the tree tonight when it gets caught in the top branches and bring it to you."

Then he thought of something else. "What is the moon made of, Princess?" he asked.

"Oh," she said, "it's made of gold, of course, silly."

The Court Jester left the Princess Lenore's room and went to see the Royal Goldsmith. He had the Royal Goldsmith make a tiny round golden moon just a little smaller than the thumbnail of the Princess Lenore. Then he had him string it on a golden chain so the Princess could wear it around her neck.

"What is this thing I have made?" asked the Royal Goldsmith when he had finished it.

"You have made the moon," said the Court Jester. "That is the moon."

"But the moon," said the Royal Goldsmith, "is 500,000 miles away and is made of bronze and is round like a marble."

"That's what you think," said the Court Jester as he went away with the moon.

The Court Jester took the moon to the Princess Lenore, and she was overjoyed. The next day she was well again and could get up and go out in the gardens to play.

But the King's worries were not yet over. He knew that the moon would shine in the sky again that night, and he did not want the Princess Lenore to see it. If she did, she would know that the moon she wore on a chain around her neck was not the real moon.

So the King sent for the Lord High Chamberlain and said, "We must keep the Princess Lenore from seeing the moon when it shines in the sky tonight. Think of something."

The Lord High Chamberlain tapped his forehead with his fingers thoughtfully and said, "I know just the thing. We can make some dark glasses for the Princess Lenore. We can make them so dark that she will not be able to see anything at all through them. Then she will not be able to see the moon when it shines in the sky."

This made the King very angry, and he shook his head from side to side. "If she wore dark glasses, she would bump into things," he said, "and then she would be ill again." So he sent the Lord High Chamberlain away and called the Royal Wizard.

"We must hide the moon," said the King, "so that the Princess Lenore will not see it when it shines in the sky tonight. How are we going to do that?"

The Royal Wizard stood on his hands and then he stood on his head and then he stood on his feet again.

"I know what we can do," he said. "We can stretch some black velvet curtains on poles. The curtains will cover all the palace gardens like a circus tent, and the Princess Lenore will not be able to see through them, so she will not see the moon in the sky."

The King was so angry at this that he waved his arms around. "Black velvet curtains would keep out the air," he said. "The Princess Lenore would not be able to breathe, and she would be ill again." So he sent the Royal Wizard away and summoned the Royal Mathematician.

"We must do something," said the King, "so that the Princess Lenore will not see the moon when it shines in the sky tonight. If you know so much, figure out a way to do that."

The Royal Mathematician walked around in a circle, and then he walked around in a square, and then he stood still. "I have it!" he said.

"We can set off fireworks in the gardens every night. We will make a lot of silver fountains and golden cascades, and when they go off, they will fill the sky with so many sparks that it will be as light as day and the Princess Lenore will not be able to see the moon."

The King flew into such a rage that he began jumping up and down. "Fireworks would keep the Princess Lenore awake," he said. "She would not get any sleep at all and she would be ill again." So the King sent the Royal Mathematician away.

When he looked up again, it was dark outside and he saw the bright rim of the moon just peeping over the horizon. He jumped up in a great fright and rang for the Court Jester. The Court Jester came bounding into the room and sat down at the foot of the throne.

"What can I do for you, your Majesty?" he asked.

"Nobody can do anything for me," said the King mournfully. "The moon is coming up again. It will shine into the Princess Lenore's bedroom, and she will know it is still in the sky and that she does not wear it on a golden chain around her neck. Play me something on your lute, something very sad, for when the Princess sees the moon, she will be ill again."

The Court Jester strummed on his lute. "What do your wise men say?" he asked.

"They can think of no way to hide the moon that will not make the Princess Lenore ill," said the King.

The Court Jester played another song, very softly. "Your wise men know everything," he said, "and if they cannot hide the moon, then it cannot be hidden."

The King put his head in his hands again and sighed.

Suddenly he jumped up from his throne and pointed to the windows. "Look!" he cried. "The moon is already shining into the Princess Lenore's bedroom. Who can explain how the moon can be shining in the sky when it is hanging on a golden chain around her neck?"

The Court Jester stopped playing on his lute. "Who could explain how to get the moon when your wise men said it was too large and too far away? It was the Princess Lenore. Therefore the Princess Lenore is wiser than your wise men and knows more about the moon than they do. So I will ask *her*." And before the King could stop him, the Court Jester slipped quietly out of the throne room and up the wide marble staircase to the Princess Lenore's bedroom.

The Princess was lying in bed, but she was wide awake and she was looking out the window at the moon shining in the sky. Shining in her hand was the moon the Court Jester had got for her. He looked very sad, and there seemed to be tears in his eyes.

"Tell me, Princess Lenore," he said mournfully, "how can the moon be shining in the sky when it is hanging on a golden chain around your neck?"

The Princess looked at him and laughed. "That is easy, silly," she said. "When I lose a tooth, a new one grows in its place, doesn't it?"

"Of course," said the Court Jester. "And when the unicorn loses his horn in the forest, a new one grows in the middle of his forehead."

"That is right," said the Princess. "And when the Royal Gardener cuts the flowers in the garden, other flowers come to take their place."

"I should have thought of that," said the Court Jester, "for it is the same way with the daylight."

"And it is the same way with the moon," said the Princess Lenore. "I guess it is the same way with everything." Her voice became very low and faded away, and the Court Jester saw that she was asleep. Gently he tucked the covers in around the sleeping Princess.

But before he left the room, he went over to the window and winked at the moon, for it seemed to the Court Jester that the moon had winked at him.

Who is your favorite character in the story? What qualities make this character likable?

Why are the King and his advisers in such an uproar?

How does Princess Lenore's opinion about the moon differ from the opinions of the King's advisers?

Why is the King still worried on the day after the Princess gets the moon?

WRITE The Lord High Chamberlain, the Royal Wizard, the Royal Mathematician, and the Royal Goldsmith all provide information about the moon. Compile a list of your own imaginary "facts" about the moon.

Words from the ILLUSTRATOR:
MARC SIMONT

I first met James Thurber and his family when they moved to Cornwall, Connecticut, during the late 1940s. *Many Moons* had already been written. It was illustrated by Louis Slobodkin and had won the Caldecott Medal.

A few years ago, when Mrs. Thurber was asked about doing a newly illustrated edition, she had qualms. But she and her family finally decided to do it. Since I had illustrated other James Thurber books, *The Wonderful O* and *The Thirteen Clocks,* she asked me to do this one.

Usually, I don't like to meet the authors of the books I'm illustrating. They have their own ideas, and it creates conflicts. But James Thurber was my friend before he was my collaborator. We had talked about various things in *Many Moons* before I ever knew that I would one day illustrate it.

Some people have asked me how I felt about reillustrating a book that is so famous. To tell you the truth, when I illustrate a book, I decide to make it all my own, my personal interpretation of the story. Yes, I was interested in seeing how Louis Slobodkin had done it, but in no way did his work affect my vision, which was quite different. There are some things I like about Slobodkin's version, but his *Many Moons* had no impact on my own. When it comes to an artist's vision, every artist is in a different world.

Moonlight

Think about the descriptions of the moon in the story and in the poetry. Explain how they are alike and how they are different.

WRITER'S WORKSHOP

The Court Jester finds a way to give the Princess the moon. If the Princess's ideas about the moon had been impossible to fulfill, however, he would have had to persuade her not to desire the moon. What reasons might he have given her? Write a paragraph giving reasons the Court Jester could use to convince the Princess that she does not need the moon.

Writer's Choice   Moonlight affects people in different ways. How does moonlight affect you? Respond in your own way. Plan a way to share your writing.

THEME

Unforgettable Performances

Have you ever performed before a large audience? Or even before an audience of one? If so, you probably learned what the characters in these selections learned: You just never know what might happen!

CONTENTS

397

Oliver Hyde's DISHCLOTH CONCERT

from

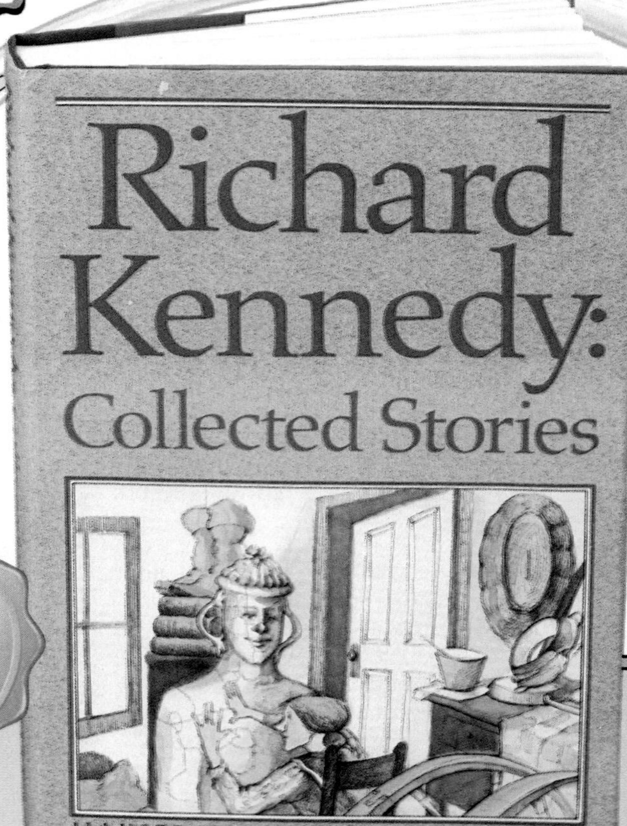

Richard Kennedy:
Collected Stories

ILLUSTRATIONS BY MARCIA SEWALL

CHILDREN'S CHOICE

Now maybe it's sad and maybe it's spooky, but there was a man who lived just out of town on a scrubby farm and no one had seen his face for years. If he was outside working, he kept his hat pulled down and his collar turned up, and if anyone approached him he ran up the hill to his house and shut himself inside. He left notes pinned to his door for a brave errand boy who brought him supplies from town. The people asked the boy what he heard up there in that tomblike house when he collected the notes and delivered the supplies. "Darkness and quietness," said the boy. "I hear darkness and quietness." The people nodded and looked at the boy. "Aren't you afraid?" The boy bit his lip. "A fellow has to make a living," he said.

Sometimes the children would come out of town and sing a little song up at the house and then run away. They sang:

"The beautiful bride of Oliver Hyde,
Fell down dead on the mountainside."

Yes, it was true. The man was full of grief and bitterness. He was Oliver Hyde, and his young bride's wagon had been washed into a canyon by a mudslide and it killed her, horse and all. But that was years ago. The children sang some more:

"Oliver Hyde is a strange old man,
He sticks his head in a coffee can,
And hides his face when there's folks about,
He's outside in, and he's inside out."

It was too bad. Oliver used to have many friends, and he played the fastest and sweetest fiddle in the county. And for the few short weeks he was married his playing was sweeter than ever. But on the day his wife was buried he busted his fiddle across a porch post, and now he sat cold, dark, and quiet on his little hill. No one had visited him for years. There was a reason. You shall see.

One day a man came from the town and walked up the hill toward Oliver's house. He was carrying a fiddle case. Two or three times he stopped and looked up at the house and shook his head, as if trying to free himself from a ghost, and continued on. He arrived at the porch steps. All the window shades were pulled down and it was dead quiet inside. The three porch steps creaked like cats moaning in their dreams, and the man knocked on the door. For a little bit it was quiet, then there was the sound of a chair being scooted across the floor. A voice said, "Come in."

The man opened the door a crack and peeked inside.

"Oliver?" he said. "It's me, Jim." No answer. Jim opened the door farther and put a foot inside. It was dark, and smelled stale. Jim opened the door all the way.

Off in a corner where the light didn't touch sat a figure in a chair, perfectly upright, with his hands on his knees like a stone god, as still and silent as a thousand years ago. The head was draped completely with a dishcloth. Not a breath ruffled the ghost head.

Jim swallowed and spoke. "Haven't seen you around lately, Oliver." No answer.

People used to visit Oliver for a while after his beautiful bride fell down dead on the mountainside, but this is how it was—Oliver sitting in the dark with a dishcloth over his head, and he never spoke to them. It was too strange. His friends stopped visiting.

All Jim wanted was a single word from Oliver—yes or no.

He had a favor to ask. He was Oliver's oldest friend. He moved inside.

"Sue's getting married, Oliver," he said. No answer. "You remember my little girl, Sue? She's all growed up now, Oliver, and mighty pretty, too." For all the notice he got, Jim might just as well have been talking to a stove. He cleared his voice and went on. "The reason I came, Oliver, was to ask you to come and play the fiddle for us at the dance. We was the best friends, and I don't see how I can marry off Sue without you being there to fiddle for us. You can just say yes or no, Oliver."

Now Oliver wasn't dead himself yet, so he still had feelings, and Jim had been his best friend. They had played and fought together, fished and hunted, and grown up together. So Oliver hated to say "No" just flat out like that, so he said instead, "No fiddle." Jim was prepared for that, and he laid the fiddle case down on the floor and flipped it open.

"Here, I brought a fiddle, Oliver. Porky Fellows was happy to make a lend of it."

Oliver felt trapped now. He was silent for a long time, then finally he said, "Tell you what. I can't wear this dishcloth on my head and fiddle, but if everyone else wears a dishcloth I'll come."

Jim was quiet for a long time, but at last he said, "All right, Oliver, I'll ask if they'll do it. The dance is tomorrow night at Edward's barn. I'll leave the fiddle here, and if I don't come back to pick it up, then you got to come to the dance and fiddle for us. I got your promise."

Oliver smiled under his dishcloth. They'd be fools to agree to that. You can't have any fun with a dishcloth over your head.

"So long, Oliver," Jim said. Oliver didn't answer. Jim went back on down the hill.

Oliver took the dishcloth off. The fiddle was laying in the light of the open door. He sucked a whisker and looked at it. Oliver knew the fiddle, and it was a good fiddle. He wondered if it was in tune and wanted to pick it up, but he let it lay there. His foot was tapping, and he slapped his knee to make it stop. He laughed to himself and muttered, "Them donkeys—what do they know?" Then he got up and moved around the little house on his dreary business.

The sun went down and the shadow of the fiddle case stretched across the floor. Oliver's eyes kept landing on the

fiddle, and he stepped over the shadow when he crossed that way. It looked to him like the bow had new horsehair on it. But it didn't make any difference to him. He figured he'd never be playing on that fiddle, and he never touched it.

Next morning Oliver watched down the hill for Jim to come and tell him the deal was off and to get the fiddle. Noon came. Oliver ate some beans. Afternoon came on. Jim didn't show. Oliver began to get mad. He was mad that he had ever made the promise. It started to get dark. "Those cluckheads!" Oliver said, pulling the window shut. "They can't dance with dish-cloths on their heads, or drink punch, either. They'll have a rotten time."

But a promise is a promise.

Finally he decided it was time to put his hat and coat on. "They tricked me," Oliver grumbled, "but I got a trick for them, too. They'll be sorry I came to their party." It wasn't a great trick Oliver had in mind, but just a miserable little one to make sure nobody could have any fun while he was there. He figured they'd ask him to leave shortly. He wouldn't even bother to take off his hat and coat.

He headed down the hill with the fiddle and into the little town. He entered Edward's barn with his hat pulled down and his collar turned up. It was dark except for two bare, hanging light bulbs, one over the center of the barn and one at the end where a sort of stage was built up. Oliver had played at shindigs there many times. He kept his head down, and only from the corners of his eyes could he see all the people sitting around the walls. "Lord, it's awfully dark," Oliver thought to himself, "and quiet. I figure they know that's the way I like it." He got under the light bulb that hung over the stage and took out the fiddle.

He tuned down to a fretful and lonesome sound, and then he played.

Of course he knew they were all looking for happy dancing tunes, so first off he played a slow and sad tune about a man who was walking down a long road that had no ending and was gray all about, and the man was looking forward to being dead because it might be more cheerful. Nobody danced, naturally, and didn't clap either when Oliver finished it. "That's just right," Oliver thought. "I'll give them a wretched time." And he started on another.

The second tune he played was even slower and sadder, about a man who thought his heart was a pincushion and it seemed to him that everyone was sticking pins and needles into it, and it was hurtful even to listen to it. Nobody danced, and nobody even moved to the punch bowl to get their spirits up. "Now they're sorry I came," Oliver thought. Still, he had played that last tune especially sweet, and he expected that someone might have clapped a little just for that, even if it was sad.

Oliver looked out a little under his hat as he retuned a bit. He tried to see Jim. He ought to come up and say hello at least, not just let him stand there completely alone. And he wondered where the other musicians were. Four people were sitting down off to the right of the stage. That would be them. Oliver considered it would be nice to have a little slide guitar on these slow ones, sort of mournful played, and a mouth harp and mandolin would fit in nice. "Naw! This is just the way I want it. One more gloomy song and they'll ask me to leave."

So then he played another, this one about a man who had a wife that just recently moved to heaven, and how roses grew all over her tombstone even in the winter. Oliver was halfway through that before he remembered that he'd played that tune at his own wedding party. He pulled up short a bit then, but kept on playing it out, and a tear rolled down his cheek. Well, nobody could see. He wiped his eyes when he was finished.

Nobody clapped and nobody moved, just sat against the dark walls perfectly still. Among the dark figures was a lighter shape. Probably the bride in her white gown. Oliver remembered how lovely and happy his bride had been, and he felt a little mean when he thought about that, giving out such sad tunes.

He spoke out loud, the first words that were spoken since he came in. "Well, I guess you're all ready for me to leave now, and I will. But first I want to play just one happy tune for the bride, and so you can dance, and then I'll go." Then he did play a happy one, a fast one, carrying on with fiddling lively enough to scramble eggs. But nobody got up to dance, and when he was finished nobody moved or made a sound.

"Look here," Oliver said. "I reckon you can't dance with those dishcloths over your heads, I forgot about that. So take 'em off. I'll give you another dancing tune, then I'll go." And then he went into another, as sweet and light and fast as any-

one ever could, something to get even a rock up and dancing, but nobody moved. And when he was finished they all sat silent with the dishcloths still on their heads.

"Come on," Oliver said. "Take those things off your heads. You other fellows get up here with your music and help me out. Let's have some dancing, drink some punch, let's get alive now." He stomped his foot three times and threw into a tune that would churn butter all by itself. But the other four musicians sat perfectly still, and so did everybody else, and Oliver was standing there under the light bulb in silence when he finished the tune.

He stood there with his head down, understanding things, and how it felt to be on the other side of the darkness and silence when all you wanted was some sign of life to help out. Then he leaned over and put the fiddle in the case and closed it. He said one last thing, then walked out from under the light toward the door. "Okay," he said. "That's a hard lesson, but I got it."

When he opened the door he bumped into someone sitting next to it against the wall, and the fellow fell off his chair. Oliver put a hand down to help him up. But the fellow just lay there. Oliver touched him. "What's this?" He felt around, then shoved back his hat for a look. It was a sack of grain he'd knocked over. And the next person sitting there was a sack of grain, too. And the next was a bale of hay.

Oliver walked completely around the barn. All the people were sacks of grain and bales of hay sitting against the dark walls, and the bride was a white sack of flour. The four musicians sitting off to the right of the stage were four old saddles setting on a rail.

When Oliver came around to the door again he heard music. He stepped outside and looked down the street. A barn down near the end was all lit up, and lots of people were moving about. He went back up on the stage, got the fiddle, and headed down the street.

Jim was standing by the door. "Waiting for you, Oliver," he said. "We're just getting under way—come on in." When he led Oliver inside everyone became quiet, first one little group of people, then another, until at last everyone was silent and looking at Oliver. The bride and groom were holding hands. Jim made a motion and everyone headed for a chair against the walls. They all took out dishcloths to put over their heads.

"Edward's got himself a new barn, huh?" Oliver said.

"Yeah," said Jim. "I guess you didn't know that. Uses the old one to store stuff. I shoulda told you."

"It's all right," Oliver said. He looked up on the stage. Four musicians were sitting there with dishcloths over their heads. Then Jim took out a large dishcloth. Oliver touched him on the arm.

"Never mind that. And everyone else, too. Just be regular and dance. I'll fiddle for you."

Jim slapped him on the back and shouted out the good news. Oliver went up on the stage. Someone got him a mug of punch. The musicians tuned up. Oliver took off his hat and dropped it, and tossed his coat on a chair. They lit into a fast, happy tune. They danced and played and sang half the night.

Ah, they had a wonderful time. Oliver included.

If Oliver Hyde were your friend, would you have asked him to play at a wedding? Explain your answer.

Oliver Hyde intends to play only sad songs when he gets to Edward's barn. Why does he change his mind while he is performing?

Do you think Oliver Hyde has the right to behave as he does? Explain why you feel as you do.

Why, in the end, does Oliver Hyde tell the wedding guests to take off the dishcloths?

WRITE If this story were a fable, it would have a moral, or lesson. Write your own moral for this story.

LA BAMBA

from Baseball in April and Other Stories

Best Books for Young Adults

by Gary Soto

illustrated by David Diaz

anuel was the fourth of seven children and looked like a lot of kids in his neighborhood: black hair, brown face, and skinny legs scuffed from summer play. But summer was giving way to fall: the trees were turning red, the lawns brown, and the pomegranate trees were heavy with fruit. Manuel walked to school in the frosty morning, kicking leaves and thinking of tomorrow's talent show. He was still amazed that he had volunteered. He was going to pretend to sing Ritchie Valens's "La Bamba" before the entire school.

Why did I raise my hand? he asked himself, but in his heart he knew the answer. He yearned for the limelight. He wanted applause as loud as a thunderstorm, and to hear his friends say, "Man, that was bad!" And he wanted to impress the girls, especially Petra Lopez, the second-prettiest girl in his class. The prettiest was already taken by his friend Ernie. Manuel knew he should be reasonable, since he himself was not great-looking, just average.

Manuel kicked through the fresh-fallen leaves. When he got to school he realized he had forgotten his math workbook. If the teacher found out, he would have to stay after school and miss practice for the talent show. But fortunately for him, they did drills that morning.

During lunch Manuel hung around with Benny, who was also in the talent show. Benny was going to play the trumpet in spite of the fat lip he had gotten playing football.

"How do I look?" Manuel asked. He cleared his throat and started moving his lips in pantomime. No words came out, just a hiss that sounded like a snake. Manuel tried to look emotional, flailing his arms on the high notes and opening his eyes and mouth as wide as he could when he came to *"Para bailar la baaaaammmba."*

After Manuel finished, Benny said it looked all right, but suggested Manuel dance while he sang. Manuel thought for a moment and decided it was a good idea.

"Yeah, just think you're like Michael Jackson or someone like that," Benny suggested. "But don't get carried away."

During rehearsal, Mr. Roybal, nervous about his debut as the school's talent coordinator, cursed under his breath when the lever that controlled the speed on the record player jammed.

"Darn," he growled, trying to force the lever. "What's wrong with you?"

"Is it broken?" Manuel asked, bending over for a closer look. It looked all right to him.

Mr. Roybal assured Manuel that he would have a good record player at the talent show, even if it meant bringing his own stereo from home.

Manuel sat in a folding chair, twirling his record on his thumb. He watched a skit about personal hygiene, a mother-and-daughter violin duo, five first-grade girls jumping rope, a karate kid breaking boards, three girls singing, and a skit about the pilgrims. If the record player hadn't been broken, he would have gone after the karate kid, an easy act to follow, he told himself.

As he twirled his forty-five record, Manuel thought they had a great talent show. The entire school would be amazed. His mother and father would be proud, and his brothers and sisters would be jealous and pout. It would be a night to remember.

Benny walked onto the stage, raised his trumpet to his mouth, and waited for his cue. Mr. Roybal raised his hand like a symphony conductor and let it fall dramatically. Benny inhaled and blew so loud that Manuel dropped his record, which rolled across the cafeteria floor until it hit a wall. Manuel raced after it, picked it up, and wiped it clean.

"Boy, I'm glad it didn't break," he said with a sigh.

That night Manuel had to do the dishes and a lot of homework, so he could only practice in the shower. In bed he prayed that he wouldn't mess up. He prayed that it wouldn't be like when he was a first-grader. For Science Week he had wired together a C battery and a bulb, and told everyone he had discovered how a flashlight worked. He was so pleased with himself that he practiced for hours pressing the wire to the battery, making the bulb wink a dim, orangish light. He showed it to so many kids in his neighborhood that when it was time to show his class how a flashlight worked, the battery was dead. He pressed the wire to the battery, but the bulb didn't respond. He pressed until his thumb hurt and some kids in the back started snickering.

But Manuel fell asleep confident that nothing would go wrong this time.

The next morning his father and mother beamed at him. They were proud that he was going to be in the talent show.

"I wish you would tell us what you're doing," his mother said. His father, a pharmacist who wore a blue smock with his name on a plastic rectangle, looked up from the newspaper and sided with his wife. "Yes, what are you doing in the talent show?"

"You'll see," Manuel said with his mouth full of Cheerios.

The day whizzed by, and so did his afternoon chores and dinner. Suddenly he was dressed in his best clothes and standing next to Benny backstage, listening to the commotion as the cafeteria filled with school kids and parents. The lights dimmed, and Mr. Roybal, sweaty in a tight suit and a necktie with a large knot, wet his lips and parted the stage curtains.

415

"**G**ood evening, everyone," the kids behind the curtain heard him say. "Good evening to you," some of the smart-alecky kids said back to him.

"Tonight we bring you the best John Burroughs Elementary has to offer, and I'm sure that you'll be both pleased and amazed that our little school houses so much talent. And now, without further ado, let's get on with the show." He turned and, with a swish of his hand, commanded, "Part the curtain." The curtains parted in jerks. A girl dressed as a toothbrush and a boy dressed as a dirty gray tooth walked onto the stage and sang:

> *Brush, brush, brush*
> *Floss, floss, floss*
> *Gargle the germs away—hey! hey! hey!*

After they finished singing, they turned to Mr. Roybal, who dropped his hand. The toothbrush dashed around the stage after the dirty tooth, which was laughing and having a great time until it slipped and nearly rolled off the stage.

Mr. Roybal jumped out and caught it just in time. "Are you OK?"

The dirty tooth answered, "Ask my dentist," which drew laughter and applause from the audience.

The violin duo played next, and except for one time when the girl got lost, they sounded fine. People applauded, and some even stood up. Then the first-grade girls maneuvered onto the stage while jumping rope. They were all smiles and bouncing ponytails as a hundred cameras flashed at once. Mothers "awhed" and fathers sat up proudly.

The karate kid was next. He did a few kicks, yells, and chops, and finally, when his father held up a board, punched it in two. The audience clapped and looked at each other, wide-eyed with respect. The boy bowed to the audience, and father and son ran off the stage.

Manuel remained behind the stage shivering with fear. He mouthed the words to "La Bamba" and swayed from left to right. Why did he raise his hand and volunteer? Why couldn't he have just sat there like the rest of the kids and not said anything? While the karate kid was on stage, Mr. Roybal, more sweaty than before, took Manuel's forty-five record and placed it on a new record player.

"You ready?" Mr. Roybal asked.

"Yeah . . ."

Mr. Roybal walked back on stage and announced that Manuel Gomez, a fifth-grader in Mrs. Knight's class, was going to pantomime Ritchie Valens's classic hit "La Bamba."

The cafeteria roared with applause. Manuel was nervous but loved the noisy crowd. He pictured his mother and father applauding loudly and his brothers and sisters also clapping, though not as energetically.

Manuel walked on stage and the song started immediately. Glassy-eyed from the shock of being in front of so many people, Manuel moved his lips and swayed in a made-up dance step. He couldn't see his parents, but he could see his brother Mario, who was a year younger, thumb-wrestling with a friend. Mario was wearing Manuel's favorite shirt; he would deal with Mario later. He saw some other kids get up and head for the drinking fountain, and a baby sitting in the middle of an aisle sucking her thumb and watching him intently.

hat am I doing here? thought Manuel. This is no fun at all. Everyone was just sitting there. Some people were moving to the beat, but most were just watching him, like they would a monkey at the zoo.

But when Manuel did a fancy dance step, there was a burst of applause and some girls screamed. Manuel tried another dance step. He heard more applause and screams and started getting into the groove as he shivered and snaked like Michael Jackson around the stage. But the record got stuck, and he had to sing

Para bailar la bamba
Para bailar la bamba
Para bailar la bamba
Para bailar la bamba

again and again.

Manuel couldn't believe his bad luck. The audience began to laugh and stand up in their chairs. Manuel remembered how the forty-five record had dropped from his hand and rolled across the cafeteria floor. It probably got scratched, he thought, and now it was stuck, and he was stuck dancing and moving his lips to the same words over and over. He had never been so embarrassed. He would have to ask his parents to move the family out of town.

After Mr. Roybal ripped the needle across the record, Manuel slowed his dance steps to a halt. He didn't know what to do except bow to the audience, which applauded wildly, and scoot off the stage, on the verge of tears. This was worse than the homemade flashlight. At least no one laughed then, they just snickered.

Manuel stood alone, trying hard to hold back the tears as Benny, center stage, played his trumpet. Manuel was jealous because he sounded great, then mad as he recalled that it was Benny's loud trumpet playing that made the forty-five record fly out of his hands. But when the entire cast lined up for a curtain call, Manuel received a burst of applause that was so loud it shook the walls of the cafeteria. Later, as he mingled with the kids and parents, everyone patted him on the shoulder and told him, "Way to go. You were really funny."

Funny? Manuel thought. Did he do something funny?

Funny. Crazy. Hilarious. These were the words people said to him. He was confused, but beyond caring. All he knew was that people were paying attention to him, and his brothers and sisters looked at him with a mixture of jealousy and awe. He was going to pull Mario aside and punch him in the arm for wearing his shirt, but he cooled it. He was enjoying the limelight. A teacher brought him cookies and punch, and the popular kids who had never before given him the time of day now clustered around him. Ricardo, the editor of the school bulletin, asked him how he made the needle stick.

"It just happened," Manuel said, crunching on a star-shaped cookie.

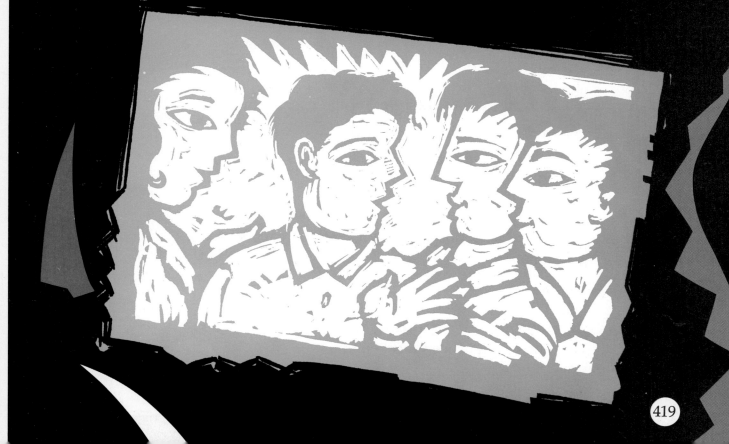

At home that night his father, eager to undo the buttons on his shirt and ease into his La-Z-Boy recliner, asked Manuel the same thing, how he managed to make the song stick on the words *"Para bailar la bamba."*

Manuel thought quickly and reached for scientific jargon he had read in magazines. "Easy, Dad. I used laser tracking with high optics and low functional decibels per channel." His proud but confused father told him to be quiet and go to bed.

"Ah, *que niños tan truchas,*[1]" he said as he walked to the kitchen for a glass of milk. "I don't know how you kids nowadays get so smart."

Manuel, feeling happy, went to his bedroom, undressed, and slipped into his pajamas. He looked in the mirror and began to pantomime "La Bamba," but stopped because he was tired of the song. He crawled into bed. The sheets were as cold as the moon that stood over the peach tree in their backyard.

He was relieved that the day was over. Next year, when they asked for volunteers for the talent show, he wouldn't raise his hand. Probably.

Should Manuel volunteer for the talent show next year? Explain why or why not.

Why is Manuel confused by the crowd's reaction to his performance?

What are some of the emotions that Manuel experiences? Describe the story event that causes each emotion.

WRITE Imagine that you performed in the talent show, too. Write a paragraph describing your act and the audience's reaction to it.

---

[1]what clever little rascals

Unforgettable Performances

In the selections, why is each public performance unforgettable for the person who gives it as well as for the audience?

WRITER'S WORKSHOP

Does the performance of Oliver Hyde or Manuel remind you of any performance you have witnessed or taken part in? Compare Oliver's or Manuel's performance to the one you're thinking about. Write a paragraph or two describing the similarities and the differences.

Writer's Choice

What do you think makes an experience unforgettable? Write what you think. Share your thoughts in some way.

CONNECTIONS

Multicultural Connection

Performing in Front of the Nation

Your family is watching the top-rated television news show in the nation. The team of newscasters on the show tell you not only what is happening but why it's happening.

Ed Bradley is a key member of that team. He's a special type of newscaster called a broadcast journalist. This means that he doesn't read stories written by other people but researches and writes his own. He flies all over the world to interview people and find out facts. He tells camera crews what he needs taped. After he creates a program from the facts and the tape, he goes on television to present the news.

Bradley's hard work, attention to detail, and fair presentations have won him the respect of his co-workers. He has won the Emmy, television's top award, three times.

Choose a broadcaster from a local or a national news program. Write a brief "TV Profile" describing that person's usual subject matter and style of reporting.

Social Studies Connection

The Week in Review

Collect the top newspaper stories about community events for one week. With a small group, use the facts from these to write a script for a news report that you and your classmates will perform. Have someone record your performance on videotape or on audiotape.

Science Connection

Performing Everywhere at Once

How is news broadcast across the world so fast? What part do satellites play? How are signals passed from place to place? Find out how our communication systems work. With a partner, create a diagram or a mural that shows the facts you learned.

UNIT FIVE
5
Lifelines

*In time of silver rain
The earth
Puts forth new life again.*
— *Langston Hughes*

Nature can be kind, but it can also be challenging. A Papago Indian girl faces the challenge of a raging flood in the Sonoran Desert. Environmentalists such as Harrison Ngau [nou] urge people to meet the challenge of befriending the earth. As you read the selections in this unit, think about what you can do to treat the earth with kindness.

THEMES

BOOKSHELF

SUGARING TIME

by Kathryn Lasky
photographs by Christopher G. Knight
Wade out into the deep snow with the Lacey family as they harvest their own maple syrup during the season they call "sugaring time."
Newbery Honor
Harcourt Brace Library Book

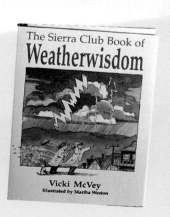

THE SIERRA CLUB BOOK OF WEATHERWISDOM

by Vicki McVey
Are you weatherwise? Can you spot the signs that foretell the weather in your area? Read about kids from all over the world who can, and learn how you can too.
Children's Choice,
Outstanding Science Trade Book for Children
Harcourt Brace Library Book

Volcano: The Eruption and Healing of Mount St. Helens

by Patricia Lauber

Fascinating photographs of the state of Washington in 1980 show the destructive power of a volcano and the slow return of life to the area.

Newbery Honor, ALA Notable Book, Outstanding Science Trade Book for Children

Walter Warthog

by Betty Leslie-Melville

A two-hundred-pound warthog takes up residence in a family's yard in Kenya and refuses to leave. The author shares her family's true experience.

Award-Winning Author

Salven Mi Selva/Save My Rainforest

by Monica Zak

Omar Castillo and his father set out on foot on a desperate journey to save the last rainforest in Mexico.

Award-Winning Author

THEME

Life in the Desert

When you think of a desert, do you think of a hot, dry, lifeless place? Would you be surprised to read about the desert as a place overflowing with life and activity? To its many inhabitants, including humans, that's exactly what it is.

CONTENTS

429

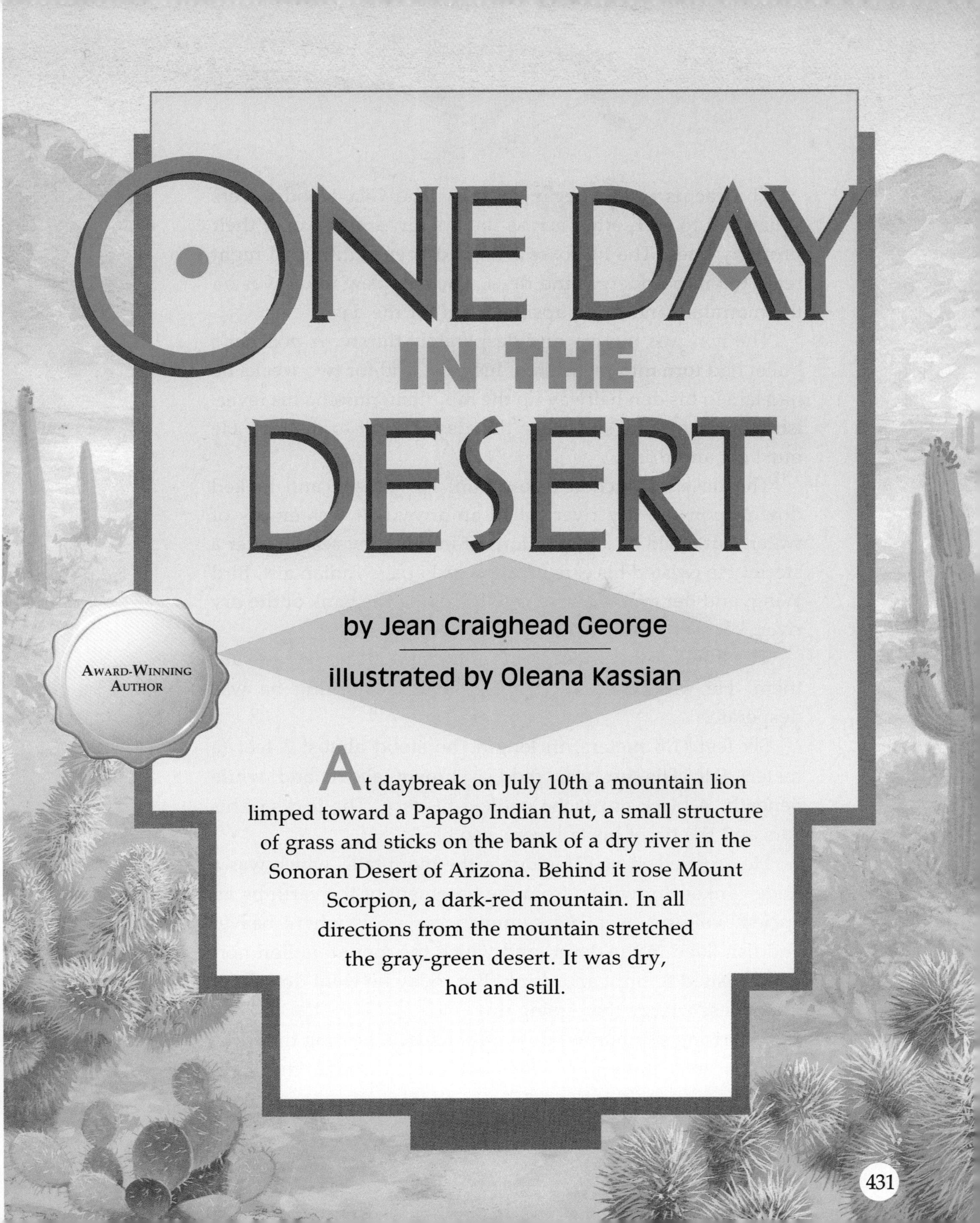

One Day in the Desert

by Jean Craighead George

illustrated by Oleana Kassian

Award-Winning Author

At daybreak on July 10th a mountain lion limped toward a Papago Indian hut, a small structure of grass and sticks on the bank of a dry river in the Sonoran Desert of Arizona. Behind it rose Mount Scorpion, a dark-red mountain. In all directions from the mountain stretched the gray-green desert. It was dry, hot and still.

The cactus wrens began to sing. The Gila woodpeckers squawked to each other across the hot air, arguing over their property lines. The kit foxes who had been hunting all night retreated into underground dens. The bats flew into caves on the mountain and hung upside down for the day.

The lion was hungry and desperately thirsty. A poacher's bullet had torn into the flesh of his paw, and for two weeks he had lain in his den halfway up the mountain nursing his feverish wound. As the sun arose this day, he got to his feet. He must eat and drink.

The desert stretched below him. He paused and looked down upon the dry river called an arroyo. It was empty of water, but could be a raging torrent in the rainy season after a storm. He twisted his ears forward. A Papago Indian girl, Bird Wing, and her mother were walking along the bank of the dry river. They entered the hut.

The lion smelled their scent on the air and limped toward them. He was afraid of people, but this morning he was desperate.

Six feet (1.8 meters) in length, he stood almost 3 feet (a meter) tall. His fur was reddish brown above and white beneath. A black mustache marked his face. The backs of his ears and the tip of his tail were also black.

He growled as he came down the mountain, which was a huge clinker thrown up from the basement of the earth by an ancient volcano. Near its summit were pools where beaver and fish lived in the desert and which the mountain lion normally visited to hunt and drink. But today he went down, for it took less energy than going up.

The rising sun burned down from space, heating the rocks and the soils until they were hot even through the well-

padded feet of the lion. He stood in the shade of a rock at 8 A.M. when the temperature reached 80° Fahrenheit (26.6° Celsius).

This day would be memorable. Bird Wing, her mother, the lion and many of the animals below Mount Scorpion would be affected by July 10th. Some would survive and some would not, for the desert is ruthless.

The Sonoran Desert is one of four deserts marked by distinctive plants that make up the great North American Desert, which extends from central Mexico to almost the Canadian border. The North American Desert covers more than 500,000 square miles (1,300,000 square kilometers).

All of the four deserts have one thing in common—little rain. Less than 10 inches (24 centimeters) a year fall on the greater parts of these deserts. The temperatures, however, vary from below freezing to the low 120s F. (about 50° C.).

Each one is slightly different. The Great Basin desert of Oregon, California, Idaho, Nevada, Utah and Wyoming—the most northern and the coldest—is largely covered with sagebrush, a plant that has adapted to the dry cold.

The Mojave Desert of California is the smallest and driest, with less than 4 inches (10 centimeters) of rain a year. The teddy-bear cactus called cholla (choy • ya), a cactus so spiny it seems to have fur, dominates this desert.

The third, the Chihuahuan (chee • wa • wan) Desert, lies largely in Mexico. Only 10 percent of it is in the United States, in New Mexico, Arizona and Texas. On this desert the yuccas and agaves, or century plants, have adapted and grow abundantly, lending a special look to the land.

The fourth and most magnificent is the Sonoran Desert of Mexico and Arizona. Unlike the other deserts, it has two rainy seasons—showers in March and deluges in July and August. The rains nourish magnificent plants that support a great variety of creatures. The outstanding plant in this desert is the giant saguaro cactus, a tall plant that resembles a telephone pole with upturned arms. All the cacti—the saguaro, barrel, teddy bear and prickly pear—are unique to North America. They have evolved nowhere else in the world.

The North American Desert is dry because it is robbed of rain by the Pacific coast mountains. The clouds coming in from the ocean strike the high cold peaks and dump most of their moisture on the western side of the mountains. Practically no rain reaches the eastern side, which is in what is called the "rain shadow" by scientists.

All deserts are lands of extremes: too hot, too dry, too wet. Yet they abound with living things that have adjusted to these excesses. To fight dryness, plants store water in their tissues or drop their leaves to prevent evaporation from their broad surfaces. They also grow spines, which do not use much water and which cast shadows on the plant to protect it from the blazing sun. They thicken stems and leaves to hold water.

The animals adapt by seeking out cool microclimates, small shelters out of the terrible heat. The microclimates are burrows in the ground where it is cool, crevices and caves in rocks, or the shade. Because of the dryness, the thin desert air does not hold heat. Shady spots can be 20° F. (11° C.) cooler than out in the sun.

A few animals adapt to the harsh conditions by manufacturing water from the starch in the seeds they eat. The perky kangaroo rat is one of these. Others move in the cool of the night.

The coyote hunts in the dark, as do the deer, ring-tailed "cat" (cacomistle), desert fox, raccoon and lion. The honeypot ant, on the other hand, has such a tough outer skeleton that it can walk in extremely hot sunshine.

On July 10th the wounded mountain lion was forced to hunt in the heat of the day. He could not wait for darkness. He made his way slowly down the trail toward the Papago Indian hut.

By 9 A.M. he was above the dwelling on a mountain ledge. The temperature climbed another degree. He sought the shade of a giant saguaro cactus and lay down to rest.

The scent of lion reached the nose of a coyote who was cooling off under the dark embankment of the dry river not far from the Papago Indian hut. He lifted his head, flicked his ears nervously and got to his feet. He ran swiftly into his burrow beneath the roots of the ancient saguaro cactus that grew beside the hut.

The huge cactus was over 100 years old, stood 75 feet (22.5 meters) tall and weighed more than 6 tons (5.5 metric tons). The last of its watermelon-red fruits were ripe and on the ground. Bird Wing and her mother were going to gather them and boil them in the water they had carried in buckets from the village. The fruit makes a sweet, nourishing syrup.

At 11 A.M. they stretched out on their mats in the hut. It was much too hot to work. The temperature had reached 112° F. (44.4° C.).

The old cactus was drying up in the heat. It drew on the last of the water in the reservoir inside its trunk and shrank ever so slightly, for it could expand and contract like an accordion.

The mountain lion's tongue was swollen from lack of moisture. He got to his feet again.

A roadrunner, a ground-dwelling bird with a spiny crest and a long neck and legs, saw the lion pass his shady spot in the grass. He sped down the mountain, over the riverbank and into the dry riverbed. He stopped under the embankment where the coyote had been. There he lifted his feathers to keep cool. Bird feathers are perhaps the best protection from both heat and cold, for they form dead air space, and dead air is one of the best insulations.

The roadrunner passed a family of seven peccaries, piglike animals with coarse coats, tusks and almost no tails. They stay alive in the dry desert by eating the water-storing prickly pear cactus, spines and all. They were now lying in the cool of the paloverde trees that grow in thickets. Like the pencil-straight ocotillo and almost all the desert leafy plants, the paloverdes drop their leaves when the desert is extremely hot and dry. On July 10th they began falling faster and faster.

The scent of the lion reached the old boar. He lifted his head and watched the great beast. The lion turned away from the peccary family and limped toward the Indian hut. All the pigs, big and little, watched him.

A warm moist wind that had been moving northwest across the Gulf of Mexico for a day and a night met a cold wind blowing east from the Pacific coast mountains. The hot and cold air collided not far from the Mexico-Arizona border and exploded into a chain of white clouds. The meeting formed a stiff wind. It picked up the desert dust and carried it toward Mount Scorpion.

As the lion limped across the embankment under which the roadrunner was hiding, the air around him began to fill with dust.

Near the coyote den dwelled a tarantula, a spider almost as big as a man's fist and covered with furlike hairs. She looked like a long-legged bear, and she was sitting near the top of her burrow, a shaft she had dug straight down into the ground. The hot desert air forced her to let go with all eight of her legs. She dropped to the bottom of her shaft, where the air was cooler. The spider survives the heat by digging underground and by hunting at night. The moist crickets and other insects she eats quench her thirst.

A headstand beetle felt the heat of the day and became uncomfortable. He stopped hunting in the grass and scurried into the entrance of the tarantula hole. He was not afraid of the spider, with her poison fangs that kill prey, but he was wary of her. Hearing the spider coming up her shaft to see who was there, the headstand beetle got ready to fend her off. He stood on his head, aimed his rear end and mixed chemicals in his abdomen. The tarantula rushed at him and lifted her fangs. The headstand beetle shot a blistering-hot stream of a quinonoid chemical at the spider. She writhed and dropped to the bottom of her den. The headstand beetle hid under the grass plant by the tarantula's door.

The temperature rose several more degrees.

At 12:30 P.M. a desert tortoise, who was protected from the heat by two unusually thick shells of bone, went on eating the fruit of a prickly pear cactus. He was never thirsty. The moisture from the plants he ate was stored in his enormous bladder, a reservoir of pure water that desert tortoises have devised over the ages to adapt themselves to the dry heat. The water cools the reptiles on the hottest days and refreshes them on the driest.

The temperature reached 117° F. (47.2° C.). At last the tortoise felt warm. He turned around and pushed up on his toes. On his short legs he walked to his burrow under the paloverde bushes where the peccaries hunched, their eyes focused on the lion.

Inside his burrow the tortoise came upon a cottontail rabbit who had taken refuge there out of the hot sun. The tortoise could not go on. The heat poured in, and to lower the temperature he plugged up the entrance with his back feet. On the ceiling above his head clung a spiny-tailed lizard and a Texas banded gecko, reptiles who usually like the heat. At 12:30 P.M. on July 10th they sought the protection of the tortoise's burrow.

The temperature rose one more degree. A cactus wren who had sung at dawn slipped into her nest in a teddy-bear cactus at the edge of the paloverde thicket. She opened her beak to release heat.

The peccaries heard soft sounds like rain falling. Hundreds of small lizards who usually hunted the leaves of the paloverde, even on the hottest days, could no longer endure the high temperature. They were dropping to the ground and seeking shelter under sticks and stones.

A kangaroo rat was in her labyrinth under the leafless, pencillike ocotillo plants. She awakened when the temperature reached 119° F. (47.3° C.). Her bedroom near the surface of the desert floor had become uncomfortably hot. Her body was drying out. She scurried along a tunnel, turned a corner and ran down a slope toward a room under the giant saguaro cactus. She paused at her pantry to eat seeds of the mesquite tree before retiring to the cool, deep chamber. While she slept, her internal system converted the starch of the seeds into water and revived her dry body.

The lion walked into the paloverde bushes. The peccaries squealed in fright and trotted out into the terrible sunshine. In a cloud of dust they sped into the dry riverbed and frightened the roadrunner. He ran out from under the overhang and flew into the saguaro forest on the far side of the dry river. The pigs hid under the embankment where the roadrunner had been.

The injured lion could not chase the peccaries. He lifted his head, smelled the sweet piglets and climbed up the Indian trail till he was at the hut. Bird Wing and her mother were sleeping. He stared at them and crouched. Slinking low, he moved to a bucket, drank long and gratefully, then lay down in the doorway of the hut.

The temperature climbed one more degree. The birds stopped singing. Even the cicadas, who love hot weather and drum louder and faster in the heat, could no longer endure the fiery temperature. They stopped making sounds with their feet and wings and sat still. The Gila woodpecker flew into his hole in the giant saguaro. Below him, in one of his old nests, sat the sparrow-sized elf owl. He opened his beak and lifted his feathers.

Bird Wing was awakened by thirst. She tipped one of the water buckets and drank deeply. The desert was so quiet she became alarmed.

Clouds were racing toward Mount Scorpion. They were black and purple. Constant flashes of lightning illuminated them from within. She crept to the back of the hut and lay down beside her mother. She closed her eyes.

At 1:20 P.M. the temperature reached 121° F. (49.4° C.).

This hour on July 10th was the hottest hour on record at the bottom of Mount Scorpion.

Even the well-insulated honeypot ants could not tolerate
the temperature. They ran toward the entrance of their
labyrinth near a pack rat nest by the hut. Some managed to get
underground in the caverns where sister ants hung from the
ceilings. Forager honeypot ants store the sweets from plants
they have gathered in the bellies of hanging ants, some of
which become as round as balloons and as big as marbles. The
last two foraging ants ran across the hot soil to get home. They
shriveled and died in seconds.

The peccaries under the embankment dug into the earth to
find coolness.

The clouds covered the sun.

Instantly, the temperature dropped four degrees.

The tortoise shoveled more dirt into the mouth of his
burrow.

The thunder boomed like Indian drums.

The kangaroo rat felt the earth tremble. She ran to her door, smelled rain on the air and scurried to a U-shaped tunnel. She went down it and up to a room at the top. There she tucked her nose into her groin to sleep.

The temperature dropped five more degrees. A rattlesnake came out of the pack rat's nest and slid back to his hunting spot at the rear of the hut. The cicadas sang again. The cactus wren looked out of the entrance of her ball nest in the teddy-bear cactus.

A thunderclap exploded sharply. Bird Wing awoke. She saw the lion stretched in the doorway. She took her mother's arm and shook her gently until she awoke. Signaling her to be quiet, she pointed to the mountain lion. Bird Wing's mother parted the grass at the rear of the hut and, after pushing Bird Wing out, backed out herself.

The rattlesnake buzzed a warning.

The sky darkened. Lightning danced from saguaro cactus to saguaro cactus. Bird Wing's mother looked at the clouds and the dry arroyo.

"We must get out of here," she said. "Follow me up the mountain." They scrambled over the rocks on hands and feet without looking back.

Huge raindrops splattered onto the dust. Bird Wing and her mother reached an overhanging rock on the mountain. Lightning flashed around them like white horsewhips.

The thunder cracked and boomed. Then water gushed out of the sky. The rain fell in such torrents that Bird Wing and her mother could not see the dry river, the hut or the old saguaro. They sat quietly, waiting and listening.

A flash of lightning shot out of a cloud and hit the old saguaro cactus. It smoked, split and fell to the ground. The elf owl flew into the downpour. His wings and body became so

wet, he soared down to the grass beneath the paloverde bushes. The woodpecker stayed where he was, bracing himself with his stiff tail.

The crash of the saguaro terrified the coyote. He darted out of his den under the tree and back to the dry riverbed. The peccaries dug deeper into the embankment. The roadrunner took to his feet and ran up the slope beyond the giant saguaro forest.

The rain became torrents, the torrents became waterfalls and the waterfalls cascaded out of the sky until all the moisture was wrung from the clouds. They drizzled and stopped giving rain. The storm clouds rumbled up the canyon above the dry riverbed.

The sun came out. Bird Wing and her mother did not move. They listened. The desert rocks dripped and the cacti crackled softly as they swelled with water. Cactus roots lie close to the surface, spreading out from the plants in all directions to absorb every possible drop of water. The roots send the water up into the trunks and barrels and pads to be stored.

A drumroll sounded up Scorpion Pass.

The peccaries heard it and darted out from under the embankment. They struggled up the bank and raced into the saguaro forest.

The lion got to his feet. He limped through the door.

The coyote rushed out of the dry riverbed. The wet elf owl hooked his beak around a twig of a paloverde and pulled himself upward toward higher limbs.

Water came bubbling and singing down the arroyo. It filled the riverbed from bank to bank, then rose like a great cement wall, a flash flood that filled the canyon. It swept over the embankment, over the hut, over the old saguaro cactus. It rose higher, thundered into the paloverdes and roared over the

rocks at the foot of the mountain. It boomed into the valley, spread out and disappeared into the dry earth.

The coyote was washed out from under the embankment. He tumbled head over heels, swam to the surface and climbed onto an uprooted mass of prickly pears. On this he sailed into the valley and was dropped safely onto the outwash plain when the water went into the ground. Stunned, he shook himself and looked around. Before him the half-drowned pack rat struggled. Recovering his wits, the coyote pounced upon him.

The lion was lifted up by the flood and thrown against a clump of ocotillo. He clung to it for a moment, then, too weak to struggle, slipped beneath the water.

The flash flood that had trickled, then roared, trickled and then was gone. The banks of the arroyo dripped. Bird Wing and her mother walked to the spot where their hut had been. There was no sign of house, pack rat nest, saguaro or lion.

"But for the lion, we would be dead," said Bird Wing. "We must thank him." She faced the mountain and closed her eyes for a moment. Her mother picked up an ocotillo stick and turned it over in her hand.

"We will rebuild our house up the mountain above the flood line," she said. Bird Wing nodded vigorously and gathered sticks, too.

The kangaroo rat sat in her room above the U trap that had stopped the water from reaching her. She waited until the floodwaters seeped into the ground. Then she began to repair her labyrinth.

The peccaries came out of the saguaro forest and rooted for insects among the billions of seeds that had been dumped on the land by the flood. The land was greening, the sky was blue. The roadrunner came back to the saguaro forest, ran down a young snake and ate it. The cactus wren and owl did not call. The rattlesnake did not rattle. They had not survived the wrath of the desert on this day, July 10th.

Bird Wing walked to the arroyo edge. The earth trembled at her feet. She looked down. Plugs of sand popped out of the wet bank like corks. In each hole sat a grinning spadefoot toad, creatures who must grow up in the water. Then what were they doing in the desert? Waiting for just this moment.

They hopped into the brilliant sunshine and leaped into the puddles in the arroyo. Quickly they mated, quickly they laid eggs and quickly they ate and dug backward into the sand with the spades on their feet. Far underground their skins secreted a sticky gelatin that would prevent them from drying up. In this manner they survived the hot waterless desert.

The warm sunlight of late afternoon heated the water in the puddles, speeding up the development of the toad eggs. They must hatch into pollywogs and change into toads before the blazing heat dried up the puddles.

At 7:33 P.M. soft blue and purple light swept over the beautiful desert. In the puddles pollywogs swam.

Would you like to live in this desert? Explain why or why not.

Describe the changes in weather in the Sonoran Desert on July 10th, from 8 A.M. to 7:33 P.M.

Do you think the author is correct when she says that the desert is ruthless? Explain your answer.

After the flood, why does Bird Wing say that she wants to thank the mountain lion?

WRITE   The author describes many different animals in this story. Choose one desert animal that interests you and write a name poem about it. Use each letter in the animal's name to start a line of the poem.

WORDS ABOUT THE AUTHOR:

Jean Craighead George

Jean George doesn't mind getting up at 5:30 on Sunday morning if she can share the wonders of nature. That is what she does when she leads nature walks in the town where she lives. She has been in love with nature since she was a child.

"All through my childhood, my parents had taken the three of us (I have identical twin brothers) into the forests along the Potomac River outside of Washington, D.C., where I was born," she remembers.

Jean George spent summers on a farm in Pennsylvania, where she learned a lot about nature. She learned about trees, flowers, birds, and insects. She camped on the sandy islands and went canoeing and fishing. She felt close to nature even though she grew up in a big city, and she has kept this feeling all her life.

Jean George's family helped get her love for nature started. Her father was an entomologist. He studied insects. Her twin brothers grew up to be ecologists. They study the ways plants and animals live in nature. Ms. George and her family often took care of wild animals right in their home. When Jean George won the Newbery Medal for *Julie of the Wolves*, she especially thanked her parents. She said they gave her "a love of nature and a deep respect for the earth and its precious cargo of life."

AWARD-WINNING AUTHOR

JACKRABBIT

from *Desert Voices*

by **Byrd Baylor**

illustrated
by **Peter Parnall**

ALA NOTABLE
BOOK

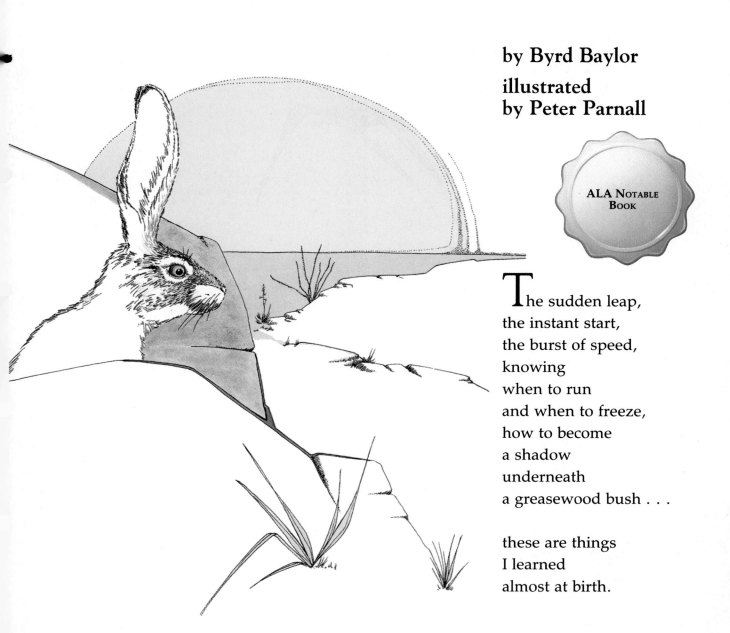

The sudden leap,
the instant start,
the burst of speed,
knowing
when to run
and when to freeze,
how to become
a shadow
underneath
a greasewood bush . . .

these are things
I learned
almost at birth.

Now
I lie
on the shadow-side
of a clump of grass.
My long ears bring me
every far-off footstep,
every twig that snaps,
every rustle in the weeds.

I watch
Coyote move
from bush to bush.

I wait.
He's almost here.

Now . . .

Now I go
like a zig-zag
lightning flash.
With my ears laid back,
I sail.

Jumping gullies
and bushes and rocks,
doubling back,
circling,
jumping high
to see where my enemy is,
warning rabbits
along the way,
I go.

I hardly touch
the ground.

And suddenly
I disappear.

Let Coyote stand there
sniffing
old jackrabbit trails.

Where I am now
is a
jackrabbit secret.

Life in the Desert

What difficulties and dangers do the desert animals in the selections face? What characteristics do they have in common that help them survive these dangers?

WRITER'S WORKSHOP

What makes a desert a desert? What are some deserts around the world? Choose a topic about deserts that interests you. Do research on your topic at a library. Take notes and use them to write a research report. You may want to include photographs, drawings, or charts in your report.

Writer's Choice
What do you think about life in the desert now that you have read "One Day in the Desert"? Write down your thoughts. Then share your ideas with others.

THEME

Seasons Within Seasons

There are some events that happen only at one certain place at one certain time of the year. Come along with a writer and a photographer as they experience these special events.

CONTENTS

MONARCHS

BY KATHRYN LASKY

Monarchs

KATHRYN LASKY

photographs by Christopher G. Knight

The Cubbyhole

In a bay off the coast of Maine there is an island with a cove on its northeast side. At the head of this cove is a deep notch between the rocks, like a cubbyhole, that is wind-safe and cozy. On one side of the notch a pine forest grows right down to the water's edge; on the other side the rocks give way to marsh grass growing thick and pale. Here the land dips to a swale sprigged with wildflowers and a tangle of sea roses, called rugosas. It then climbs steeply upward to a dirt road where a thick stand of milkweed grows.

A monarch butterfly has lighted on the leaf of a milkweed and has squeezed out a single egg, white and shiny, no bigger than the head of a pin. She flies off to another leaf, where she lays another egg. A single female can lay approximately four hundred eggs.

The little egg is very tough. A summer gale with pelting rain and scouring winds blows from the northeast and invades the usually wind-safe cove. Trees are ripped up and the marsh grass tosses wildly about, but the little egg stays on the leaf of the wind-bent milkweed plants.

Within a few days the egg hatches. The larva is so tiny—about one twenty-fifth of an inch long—it is barely visible to the naked eye. At one end of its grayish white body is a black dot perhaps one hundredth of an inch across. Amazingly, this is the head. And on this little head is a mouth one thousandth of an inch wide, and near this mouth is a pair of very short antennae that help the larva sense its way around a milkweed leaf. A pair of long black filaments near the front of the caterpillar and a shorter pair near the rear of its body are not antennae. They are used like small whips or clubs when the caterpillar twists its body about in defense against predators.

The tiny caterpillar also has eight pairs of legs. The front three pairs have small claws that help grab leaves for eating. The back five pairs, called prolegs, are stubbier and have hooks, or crotchets, which help the caterpillar cling and move along stems and leaves. When the caterpillar becomes a butterfly, the first three pairs of legs will become the butterfly's legs, while the prolegs will shrivel and disappear.

The larva's first meal is often its own egg case. Its next meal might be the hairlike filaments covering the surface of the milkweed leaf. Then it will begin on the leaf itself. All day and all night it munches, pausing only occasionally to rest. Milkweed is the only food that monarch caterpillars eat. For many other animals, especially birds, milkweed is poisonous. If they do not die from eating it, they get very sick. The poisons that accumulate in the bodies of the caterpillars, and later the butterflies, provide a natural defense against such predators as blue jays and other birds that might otherwise try to eat them.

After three days of almost nonstop eating, the little caterpillar has grown too big for its own skin. It stops and fastens itself to a leaf with a bit of silk produced from the spinneret just below its mouth. A shiver ripples through the caterpillar as it begins its first molt, or shedding of old skin. At this stage the old skin is as hard as a fingernail, and it splits down the middle of the caterpillar's back. The caterpillar will molt four or five times over the next few weeks, and with each molt it will grow bigger, adding more yellow and black stripes to its body.

After two weeks of eating, the caterpillar is now two inches long and is more than 2,700 times its original weight. If a six-pound human baby grew as fast as a caterpillar, it would weigh eight tons in twelve days. The caterpillar finally stops eating. For its next development stage it can travel to any twig or branch or stay on a milkweed plant. But wherever it goes, the caterpillar will climb straight up. Once it has decided on a spot, it produces more silk and weaves a button on the twig or branch it has chosen. Near the rear legs of the caterpillar is a tiny hook-shaped structure called a cremaster. The

caterpillar stabs the cremaster into the silk button and wriggles hard to see if it will hold. If it does, the caterpillar seems to relax and hangs from the silk button. Within minutes, the head curls up and the caterpillar looks like the letter J. For several hours it will stay this way, preparing for its final molt. Then the skin begins to split as the caterpillar twists and shivers, and as this last skin splits off, the bright bands of yellow and black dissolve into a milky green sheath called a chrysalis. Because the chrysalis seems to wrap itself around the form of the butterfly in the same way an infant is wrapped in swaddling clothes, this period of development is often called the pupal stage, from the Latin word *pupa* meaning "doll."

Within a short time the chrysalis hardens into a beautiful jade-green case studded with gold dots. It hangs like an exquisite magic lantern, inside which marvelous, seemingly magical changes are occurring. The body of the caterpillar melts away into a solution of transforming cells and tissues. Inside the chrysalis, the metamorphosis from caterpillar to butterfly takes approximately fifteen days.

New Wings Shimmer in the Sunlight

Clara Waterman is in a hurry to leave her store on North Haven Island in Penobscot Bay, Maine. But this morning the mail boat from the mainland has come and is turning right around for the return trip. All the supplies for the Waterman store have to be unloaded double-quick. At eighty-two Clara can beg off unloading thirty-pound crates of Georgia peaches and cases of soft drinks, but it means she has to stay on the cash register while the others unload the boat. Then everybody in town starts craving the big fat peaches as soon as they see them on the dock. Soon the line of customers at the Waterman store practically goes out the door.

Clara isn't going to be able to go home at noon as planned. She knew she should have brought the chrysalis down to the

store in the morning and set it right by the cash register. Now she'll probably miss it hatching out. She has seen hundreds of monarchs hatch out in her lifetime, and she never tires of it. For Clara there is only one thing better than seeing a butterfly emerge, and that is watching a child see it hatch. It's almost as

if two miracles are happening at the same time—the emerging butterfly and the wonder in the child's face.

The morning following the arrival of the peaches at the Waterman store, five children from another island come over to North Haven to talk to Clara about butterflies. She wants to

take them to the cubbyhole where the milkweed grows so they can look for caterpillars. Maybe there will even be some chrysalises they can take home to watch hatch.

Monarch chrysalises hatch just about anyplace. All summer long Clara brings home bunches of milkweed that are crawling with caterpillars. She props the branches in jars filled with water to keep the plants fresh and builds little shoebox terrariums to put the jars in. When the chrysalises hatch, Clara releases the butterflies into her yard. Sometimes she just puts the jars of milkweed on a table or a bookshelf. And caterpillars can travel! She remembers a summer years ago when she was a young girl. She went up to her closet to get out her best dress for a party and found a chrysalis hanging from the sash. When the children come to Clara's house, they are amazed to see where the caterpillars have crept to form their chrysalises.

"That one just flew off before sunset last night," Clara says, pointing straight up at the door frame as they walk into her kitchen. An empty chrysalis, dry and transparent, quivers in the noon breeze. The children spot another chrysalis that has not yet hatched on the handle of a pail in the sink.

And out on the porch a small darkened lantern hangs from the leaf of a potted milkweed plant. Inside this chrysalis is an orange glimmer like the flame of a flickering candle: the wings of the monarch. The chrysalis shakes and begins to split. Within minutes a new monarch has hatched. Wet and crumpled, it seems completely exhausted. But soon the monarch begins pumping fluid from its swollen body into its wings.

"Maybe it will fly away while we're here." Clara's voice swells with excitement. The children press around her. She explains that before the butterfly flies off, its feeding tube, or proboscis, must be assembled. The proboscis is a hollow tube through which the butterfly sucks nectar and water. When the butterfly first hatches, the two parts forming the proboscis are not yet interlocked, and until they are, the butterfly cannot feed. When the butterfly is not drinking nectar, the proboscis coils up under its head like a watch spring.

Gradually, over an hour's time, the once wrinkled and wet wings begin to spread, becoming bright and velvety. The children look closely. The edges of the wings are bordered in black with a double row of white spots. The body of the butterfly also has white spots. A web of black veins spreads across the orange wings, making them as bright as stained-glass windows with the sun shining through. This monarch is a female. If it were a male, it would have a single black dot on each hind wing.

The colors and patterns of a butterfly's wings are made by tens of thousands of microscopically small flat scales that overlap like shingles on a roof. If the scales are rubbed off, which can happen, the wing underneath is bare and colorless. The butterfly can still fly, however, even missing a few scales. On either side of the butterfly's head is a compound eye, which is actually many little eyes pressed into one. These little individual eyes have six sides and are called facets. The two compound eyes of the monarch are made up of thousands of these facets. So instead of seeing one image, a butterfly sees thousands of little images. Compound eyes are very good at detecting movement as well as perceiving a wide range of colors, which helps the butterfly find nectar-rich flowers.

"It's getting ready!" Clara's voice trembles with anticipation. The butterfly's wings shimmer in the noon sun, there is a quiver, and then silently it lifts into gentle fluttering flight.

What did you like or not like about this selection?

Describe the stages a monarch goes through from egg to butterfly.

Would you like to be in Clara Waterman's house to watch a monarch emerge? Explain why or why not.

WRITE   If you had the chance to study an animal or an insect closely, which one would you choose? Write a paragraph explaining your choice.

Words About the Author:
Kathryn Lasky

Writer Kathryn Lasky and her husband, photographer and filmmaker Christopher G. Knight, enjoy working as a team. They met when Lasky was running the sound equipment for one of Knight's films. After they married, the couple began combining their talents to create books for children.

Lasky and Knight have traveled near and far to capture, on film and in words, the images they turn into books. Both *Sugaring Time* (about tapping sugar maples) and *The Weaver's Gift* (about the weaving of sheep's fleece into soft blankets) take place in Vermont, not far from the couple's New England home. To write *Dinosaur Dig*, the author and photographer traveled to the Badlands of Montana.

People are an important element in Lasky's books. The many members of the Lacey family are the focus of *Sugaring Time*. Thinking about the Laceys' tradition of tapping sugar maples,

Lasky remarked, "It was a wonderful break for them, right near the end of winter; the sugaring time is like a little season unto itself." *Dinosaur Dig* depicts the excitement that six families share digging for dinosaur bones.

Lasky and Knight's research for *Monarchs* led them to more interesting places and people. They started out in Maine, where they watched the monarchs hatch from their chrysalises, and then followed the butterflies to California and to Mexico. Lasky got the idea for the book from an article in the *New York Times* about a town in California that decided to raise their own taxes so they could buy a grove where the monarchs rested during the winter. The people wanted to buy the grove because the owner of the property was planning to tear down the trees and build condominiums. "I was so impressed by this," Lasky said, "I decided I'd like to write a book about the monarchs. I'll never forget something the townspeople said—it has always stuck with me: 'You can't put a price on beauty, on how this beauty adds to our lives.'"

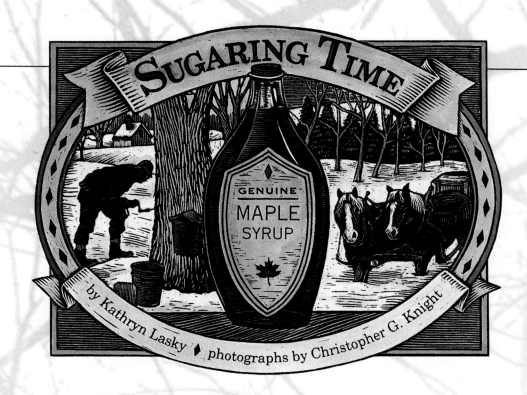

A TIME OUT OF TIME

There is a time between the seasons. It comes in March when winter seems tired and spring is only a hoped-for thing. The crystalline whiteness of February has vanished and there is not yet even the pale green stain in the trees that promises spring. It is a time out of time, when night, in central Vermont, can bring a fitful late winter storm that eases, the very next day, into sunshine and a melting wind from the southeast.

❖✳❖ ✳❖✳ ❖✳❖ ✳❖✳ ❖✳❖ ✳❖✳ ❖✳❖

Many people complain about this time of year. Snow cannot be counted on for sledding or skiing; cars get stuck in muddy roads; clothes are mud-caked and hard to clean; and the old folks' arthritis kicks up. Everyone, young and old, gets cranky about staying indoors.

But for a few people, this time is a season in its own right. For them it is *sugaring time,* when the sap begins to flow in the maple grove or sugarbush, as it is called. It is a time that contradicts all farming calendars that say crops are planted in the spring, cared for in the summer, and harvested in the fall. This crop, maple sap, is harvested in March, and that is part of the specialness of sugaring time. It is special, too, because young people have a reason to go outside, snow or no snow, mud or no mud, and older people have a reason to believe in the coming spring.

Alice and Don Lacey and their three children live on a farm that has a small sugarbush. They have been waiting almost two weeks for the sap to start running. Last year they had started to hang buckets by town meeting time in early March. But this year's town meeting has come and gone by more than a week and the snow is still almost as high as the bellies of their Belgian workhorses, Jumping Jack and Tommy. It covers the meadow leading up to the sugarbush in a wind-packed, crusty blanket.

The Laceys wonder if the sap will get a jump on them this year. Before they can begin sugaring, they will have to spend a day or more using their horses to break out the trails to the sugarbush. And they cannot start breaking out until the days turn warm enough to loosen up the snow so the horses can get through it. The sap might be running for some time before

❖✳❖ ✳❖✳ ❖✳❖ ✳❖✳ ❖✳❖ ✳❖✳ ❖✳❖

they can get to the stand of maples covering the hillside at the top of the meadow. But there is no other way to get there.

By the end of the second week in March, however, the weather begins to change. The nights are still cold, below freezing, but one midmorning the thermometer is above freezing and still climbing. Icicles that have hung like scepters since December suddenly begin dripping like popsicles in August.

"It really feels like sugaring weather," Alice says.

"Tomorrow?" "Tomorrow?" "Tomorrow?" Jonathan, Angie, and Jeremy all ask their mother at once.

"Maybe," she replies. "If this holds. If it's cold tonight and warm again tomorrow, we'll be able to start breaking out, and then by the next day hang some buckets."

❖✳❖   ✳❖✳   ❖✳❖   ✳❖✳   ❖✳❖   ✳❖✳   ❖✳❖

Tomorrow comes. It is warm but raining. Fog swirls through the valley and up into the meadow, covering the hills and mountaintops beyond. Everything is milky white. Snow-covered earth and sky melt together. Pines appear rootless, like ghost trees, their pointy tops wrapped in mist. It is a groundless world without edges or distances, a world that floats, private and cozy and detached, through the fog and clouds. There will be no breaking out today.

BREAKING OUT

Finally the day does come. A northwest wind blows the clouds and rain away, then quickly dies, and the sun shines until the mountaintops break through to a clear day. Snow is loosening up and the Laceys can almost hear the sap dripping in the sugarbush. Even a baby down in town was ready to get born and go! Don Lacey, who is a doctor, was up before the sun to deliver it.

Back home, Don harnesses up Tommy and Jumping Jack and walks behind them, urging them through the three-foot-deep snow. They are reluctant, even though there is no sled to pull on this first circuit. The snow is heavy, and their muscles are stiff.

Breaking out is the hardest part of sugaring. After three months of easy barn living with no loads to pull and not even a fly to swish away, the horses are winter lazy and stubborn. But the trails have to be broken if the trees are to be tapped and the sap gathered.

Don guides the horses toward the sugarhouse. Jonathan, who is eight, and Angie, six, follow on skis. The hoofprints that the horses leave are nearly a foot across and one and a

◆❊◆ ❊◆❊ ◆❊◆ ❊◆❊ ◆❊◆ ❊◆❊ ◆❊◆

half times as deep. With a sound like muffled thunder, their hoofs crush the snow.

This snow of early spring is called corn snow because the crystals are big and granular, like kernels of corn. But it is really more sugary in its texture, and when Jonathan skis it sounds as if he is skimming across the thick frosting of a wedding cake. He and Angie, on their skis, move faster than the horses across the snow, but at last the first loop to the sugarhouse and across the low ridge behind it is complete. Don turns the horses and circles back to the lower meadow. There, he and Alice hook the harnesses to a sturdy sled. They are going to cut out some runner marks on the trail.

◆❄◆ ❄◆❄ ◆❄◆ ❄◆❄ ◆❄◆ ❄◆❄ ◆❄◆

Max, a young neighbor, has his first sled ride on Alice's lap as she skillfully guides the horses through the ups and downs and twists and turns of the half-broken trail that leads through the sugar maze. The horses are even more obstinate, now that they are pulling the sled. They balk at a muddy trickle of a creek, they stop on the incline of a curve. They are like two stubborn babies—each weighing nearly a ton. But Alice is firm. She scolds and cajoles them through the heavy snow and gradually coaxes the winter laziness out of their bones. Two hours later the first trail is completely broken out. Tomorrow, they will go for the higher ones.

The next day is warmer still. The meadow is scored with dozens of small rivulets of melting snow, and the road and

❖✳❖   ✳❖✳   ❖✳❖   ✳❖✳   ❖✳❖   ✳❖✳   ❖✳❖

lower paths are muddy. Streams that have lain as still as black ribbons in the snow now rush, muddy and raucous, down the hills. The world slips and slides in the thick mud. Early this morning, a car slid into a ditch down the road, and another one followed while trying to get the first one out. Then a neighbor's dog got into the Laceys' sheep yard, barked, chased around, raised havoc, and scared the wits out of a pregnant ewe, who in her panic skidded headfirst into the creek. Alice came out when she heard the commotion and rescued the ewe. It is late morning by the time the horses are hitched up. But breaking out is easier this time and goes much faster.

TAPPING TIME

The big trails have been broken out. Another cold spell comes, giving the Laceys just enough time to get the tapholes drilled into the maple trees and the buckets hung before the sap starts rising again.

They load up the sled with buckets and lids, called hats, and spouts. In all, nearly two hundred holes will be drilled, two hundred spouts hammered into the holes, and two hundred buckets hung. Alice fetches the drill and bit. When the sled is stacked with buckets, spouts, and hats, there is room only for Alice and two small children, not medium-sized, but really small children, who would get stuck in the deep drifts of snow if they were not snug in the sled. So Jeremy and Max are packed aboard with the sugaring tools, while Don, Jonathan, and Angie strap on their skis.

The runners glide over the freshly broken trails. It is a cold, windless day. The sky is clear, and in the deep silence of the woods one bird can be heard singing. The trees stand

❖✱❖   ✱❖✱   ❖✱❖   ✱❖✱   ❖✱❖   ✱❖✱   ❖✱❖

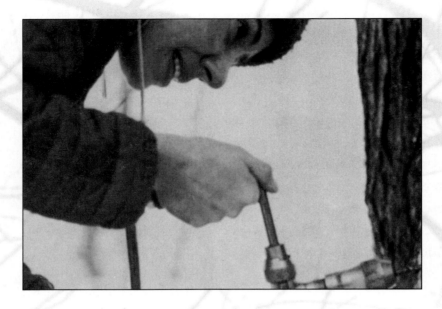

waiting, ready to give up some of the clear sap that circulates just beneath the bark. Alice and Don will drill carefully. Often, more than one hole is drilled in a tree, especially if it is a good running tree. But they will not go too deep or drill too many holes at a time in one tree. They mean to take only a little of each tree's sap, for that is its source of vitality, its nourishment, its life.

The sugar sap is made in the tree primarily for its own use, not for people's use. It helps the tree to live and grow. Sunlight and warmth start the sugar-making activity beneath the surface of the tree.

Some people, especially a long time ago, gashed maple trees with an ax or chopped big notches into their trunks. Like gaping wounds, these cuts would pour forth the sap, but they would never heal and within a few years the sugar maples would die.

❖✲❖   ✲❖✲   ❖✲❖   ✲❖✲   ❖✲❖   ✲❖✲   ❖✲❖

Alice and Don begin to drill. The bit, or pointed part of the drill, is just under one-half inch in diameter and the holes are no more than one and one-half inches deep. The holes are slanted upward into the tree to catch the sap, for although the saying is "Sap's rising!," the movement of the sap within the tree is downward as well as upward, around about, and every which way. Last year, Jonathan hammered in the spouts; this year he will do that again and help with the drilling, too.

Angie is now tall enough to reach up and put the hats on the buckets to keep out the rain and snow. Jeremy, three, and Max, four, still too small to walk a long way in the big drifts, will hand her the hats from the sled.

◆✳◆ ✳◆✳ ◆✳◆ ✳◆✳ ◆✳◆ ✳◆✳ ◆✳◆

❖✳❖ ✳❖✳ ❖✳❖ ✳❖✳ ❖✳❖ ✳❖✳ ❖✳❖

Seventy-five buckets have been hung by the end of this first day. Alice has steered the huge Belgians and her sledful of spouts and buckets and children through the twists and turns and dips and rises of the sugar maze without spilling a child or a hat.

"SAP'S RISING!"

The buckets have hung for over three days but the weather has not been the kind that makes for a real flow of sap. It

has been below freezing, day and night, with thick cloud cover. No sun, no warmth, no flow. Standing in the sugarbush, you can hear the creaking of maples as the cold wind blows in from Canada.

Finally, after a freezing cold night, the next morning is sunny. It is not the pale, thin, low-angle sunlight of November, but the direct, strengthening light of a sun that has passed the year's equator, the vernal equinox. It is the sun of longer days that feels warm on the cheeks, makes birds sing, and helps all things loosen up and stretch.

❖❖❖ ❖❖❖ ❖❖❖ ❖❖❖ ❖❖❖ ❖❖❖ ❖❖❖

The frost designs on Jonathan's bedroom window have melted before he has dressed this morning. Bright lances of sunlight do a crazy crisscross dance on Angie's covers if she wiggles her knees. Little Jeremy climbs up on a stool by his window and takes a quiet look at the sunlit world outside.

"Sap's rising!" Alice calls up. "It's going to flow today!"

And it will flow, because sunlight is the energy for the tree's sugar-making process. Last year, sunlight from the sky, carbon dioxide from the air, and chlorophyll in the green leaves worked together to make the sugar that nourishes the tree. All winter, the sugar has been stored in the bark and wood of roots and stems. Long before the first leaf is seen, watery sap carrying the sugar begins to stir under the bark, reviving the tree for a new cycle of growth.

❖❖❖ ❖❖❖ ❖❖❖ ❖❖❖ ❖❖❖ ❖❖❖ ❖❖❖

The sap flows all day, not in little drips or plinks, but in what Jonathan calls long "drrriiips." It is the sweet maple song of spring to Jonathan's and Angie's ears as they stand in the sugarbush. By tomorrow, they tell each other, the buckets will be full enough to gather. Angie and Jonathan lift the hats and peek into the buckets. The sparkling sap, clear and bright, runs like streams of Christmas tinsel. They each take a lick and wonder how so much crystal sweetness can come from a gnarled tree older than all their grandparents put together.

Would you like to visit and help the Laceys at sugaring time? Why or why not?

What is the right time in March to go sugaring?

Everyone works together at sugaring time. Explain the jobs each Lacey family member has.

In what ways do the Laceys protect their sugar maples when they tap them?

WRITE Sugaring time is an important season to the Laceys. What important seasonal thing happens in your area at about the same time every year? Write a short travel report to tell visitors what happens and where to go to see this special seasonal occurrence.

Seasons Within Seasons

What are the seasons within seasons in "Monarchs" and "Sugaring Time"? Why is it important to recognize these seasons?

Writer's Workshop

You learned how Clara Waterman collects monarch chrysalises and how the Laceys collect maple syrup. Find out how something else involving nature is done. Then write a how-to paragraph, giving the steps.

Writer's Choice

You have read that there are other types of seasons within the regular seasons of winter, spring, summer, and autumn. What do you think about this idea? Write your response. Then plan a way to share your writing.

T H E M E

Trees of Life

Some people think of trees as mere decorations. Some think of them as raw material for paper and lumber, or as bearers of fruit. The following selections show a few of the many ways in which people and trees depend upon each other.

C O N T E N T S

487

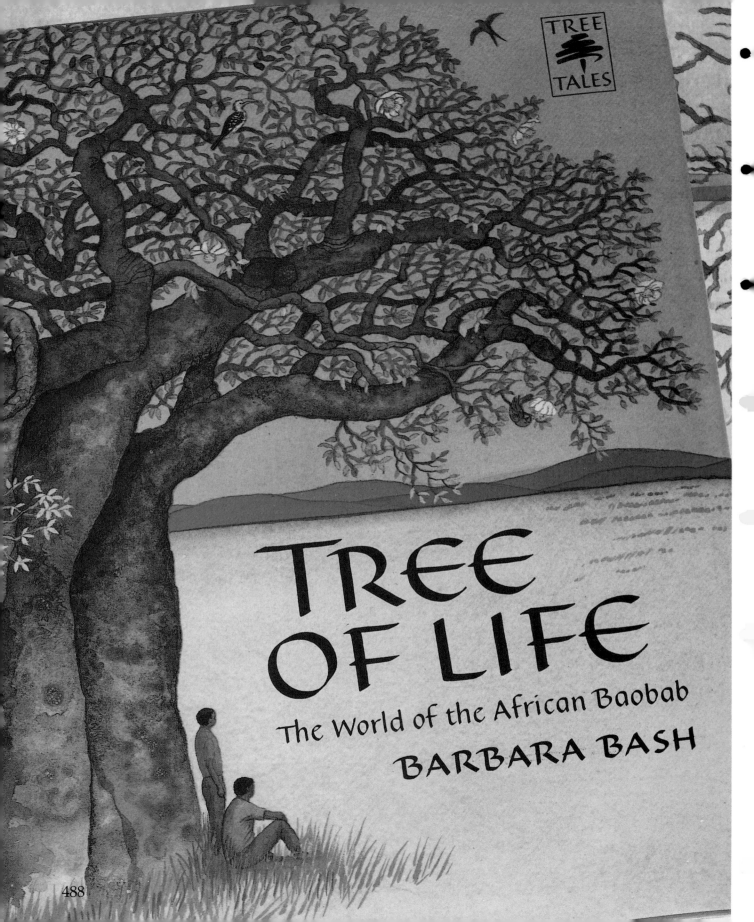

TREE
OF LIFE
The World of the African Baobab

BARBARA BASH

In the oldest times, as the !Kung Bushmen of Africa tell the story, the Great Spirit gave each animal a tree to plant. Hyena arrived late and was given the very last tree, the baobab. Being a careless creature, he planted it upside down—and that is why its branches look like gnarled roots.

The baobab grows on the dry savannahs of Africa. Reaching crookedly into the air, it stands silent and ancient. Many people believe there are no young baobabs—that they spring into being full grown. Perhaps this is because the young, slender trees look so different from the older ones. They begin to thicken and twist after forty years of growth and can eventually measure up to forty feet across and sixty feet high. With a life span of more than one thousand years, baobabs outlive nearly everything on earth.

For most of the year the baobab stands leafless and bare, but twice a year the rains come, and for a brief period the tree leafs out and blooms. Sometimes even before the rains begin, the baobab senses the coming moisture and sends out its soft new leaves and flower buds.

AWARD-WINNING AUTHOR/ ILLUSTRATOR

Soon birds arrive to make their nests in the baobab's hollows. The yellow-collared lovebird and the mosque swallow perch in the high branches. The old tree starts to hum with life.

At twilight, the large white flowers begin to open. Small furry creatures called bushbabies emerge from their hollows in the tree and smell the sweet nectar. They dart from branch to branch like little elves, pushing their faces into the flowers, lapping up the nectar, and carrying the sticky yellow pollen on to the next bloom. The soft leaves rustle as the bushbabies chirp and scurry about.

In the morning, the flowers that opened the night before have fallen to the ground, and a pair of eland comes to lap up the soft petals. A trio of impalas also munches the petals quietly, keeping a watchful eye on the horizon for signs of danger. No one seems to notice the tiny dik-dik that hides in the lush grass nearby. In the distance, a lone giraffe reaches for the baobab's tender leaves.

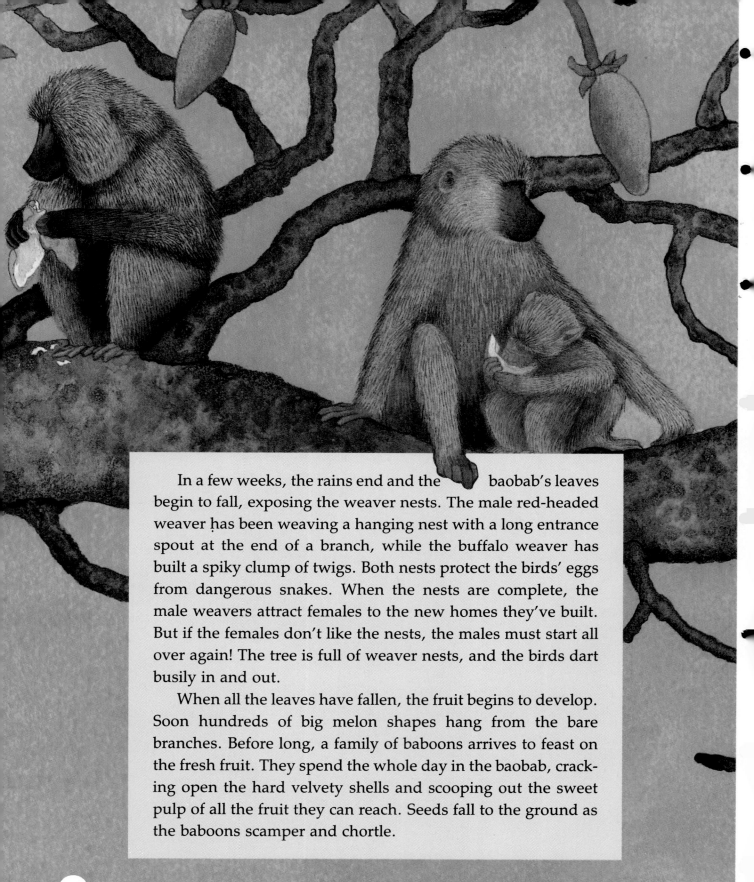

In a few weeks, the rains end and the baobab's leaves begin to fall, exposing the weaver nests. The male red-headed weaver has been weaving a hanging nest with a long entrance spout at the end of a branch, while the buffalo weaver has built a spiky clump of twigs. Both nests protect the birds' eggs from dangerous snakes. When the nests are complete, the male weavers attract females to the new homes they've built. But if the females don't like the nests, the males must start all over again! The tree is full of weaver nests, and the birds dart busily in and out.

When all the leaves have fallen, the fruit begins to develop. Soon hundreds of big melon shapes hang from the bare branches. Before long, a family of baboons arrives to feast on the fresh fruit. They spend the whole day in the baobab, cracking open the hard velvety shells and scooping out the sweet pulp of all the fruit they can reach. Seeds fall to the ground as the baboons scamper and chortle.

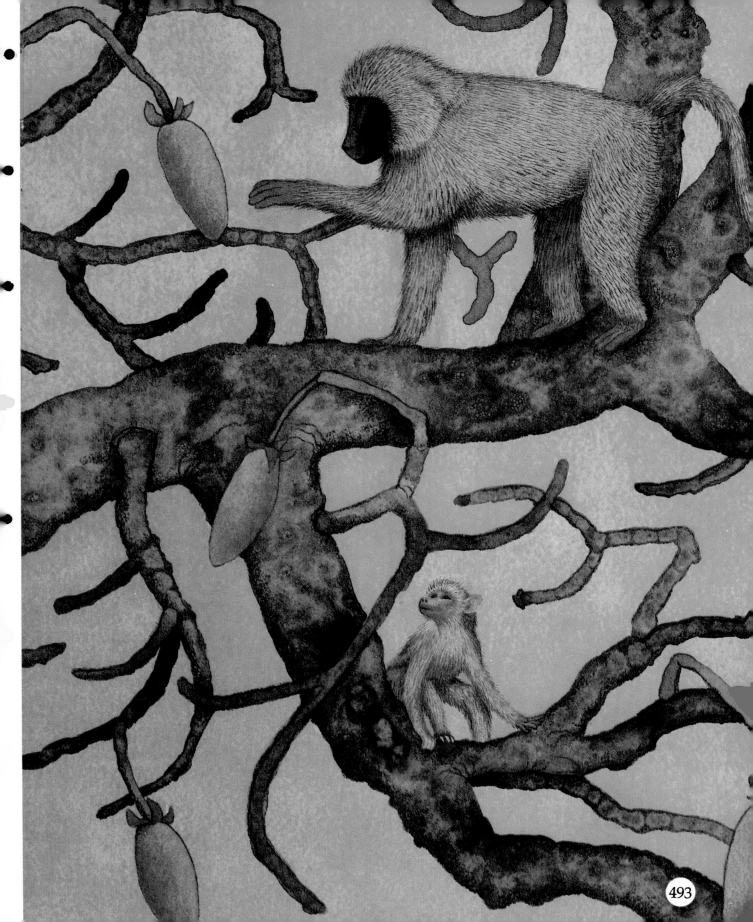

After the fruit is gone, the baobab is very still. A boomslang snake drapes its long body over a gnarled branch and waits. A praying mantis turns its head, its large eyes ever-watchful. A stick insect hides from the snake in plain sight, looking very much like a twig. A flap-eared chameleon is also camouflaged in the branches; it turns the color of its surroundings and does not move.

Sometimes the stillness is broken by the call of the honey guide bird—*aje-je-je-je*—and the voices of tribesmen who follow close behind. The bird dips and swoops, flashing its white tail feathers, until it gets close to a hive in the baobab. Then the honey guide perches quietly nearby and waits for the hunters to find the hive. The men climb the baobab, smoke out the bees, and scoop out the honey. But they always leave some beeswax behind, as thanks to the honey guide bird.

495

To the African people, the baobab is more than a source of honey. Its bark is stripped for baskets and rope; its fruit is made into candy and sweet drinks; and its roots and leaves are used as medicine. On the hot, dry savannah, the hollow trunks of ancient baobabs can also become water containers and even shelters.

At the end of the long, dry season, the thirsty elephants arrive and begin to eat the baobab bark, extracting juices from the soft fiber. With their enormous strength, the elephants strip away all the bark and pull down large chunks of wood, leaving gaping holes in the trunk. But the baobab heals its wounds, produces new bark, and keeps growing.

Finally, after many, many years, the old baobab dies. Perhaps too many elephants have chewed the wood and weakened its structure, or insects have broken down its inner core.

497

One day it collapses in on itself, a melted heap of ruins. Over time, only a soft mound of powdery fragments is left. The wind will blow these away until nothing of the baobab remains.

In the sky, the clouds begin to build for the coming rains. Near the dust of the dead tree, a baobab seed has sprouted. It is all alone on the wide savannah. Now the story of the baobab begins all over again.

Do you agree that the African baobab should be called the "tree of life"? Why or why not?

Why does the !Kung legend explain that the hyena planted the first baobab tree upside down?

Which animals help the baobab tree? How do they help?

Name some of the animals and people that depend on the baobab tree.

WRITE Imagine that you lived for one season in a tree house in your neighborhood. Write about that season in a brief journal entry describing events such as those in "Tree of Life."

499

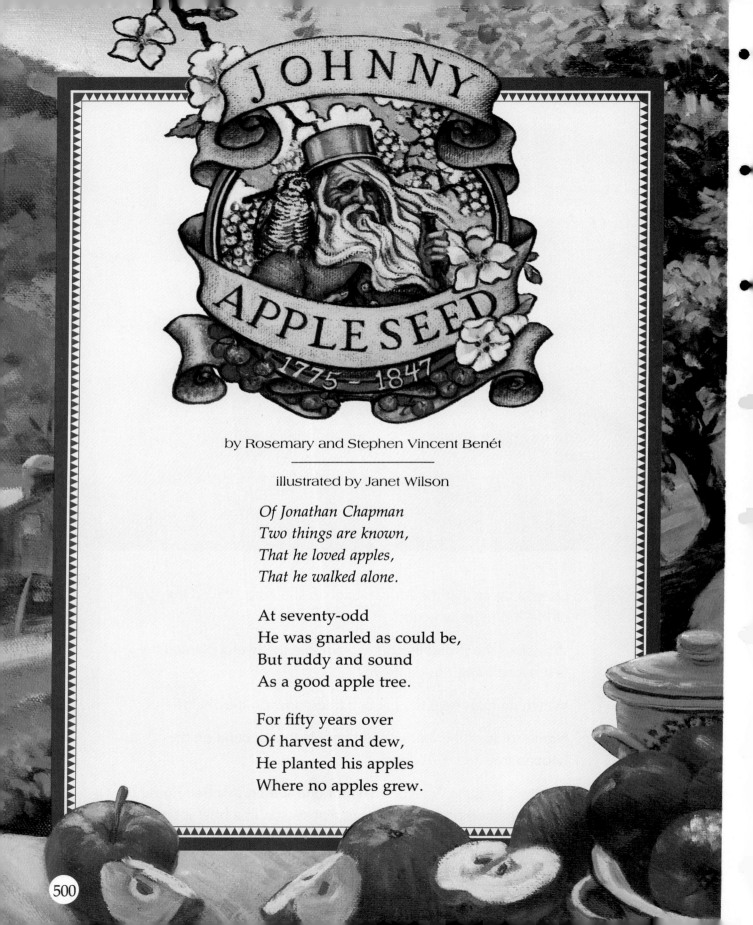

JOHNNY APPLE SEED

1775 – 1847

by Rosemary and Stephen Vincent Benét

illustrated by Janet Wilson

Of Jonathan Chapman
Two things are known,
That he loved apples,
That he walked alone.

At seventy-odd
He was gnarled as could be,
But ruddy and sound
As a good apple tree.

For fifty years over
Of harvest and dew,
He planted his apples
Where no apples grew.

The winds of the prairie
Might blow through his rags,
But he carried his seeds
In the best deerskin bags.

From old Ashtabula
To frontier Fort Wayne,
He planted and pruned
And he planted again.

He had not a hat
To encumber his head.
He wore a tin pan
On his white hair instead.

He nested with owl,
And with bear-cub and possum,
And knew all his orchards
Root, tendril and blossom.

A fine old man,
As ripe as a pippin,
His heart still light,
And his step still skipping.

Why did he do it?
We do not know.
He wished that apples
Might root and grow.

He has no statue.
He has no tomb.
He has his apple trees
Still in bloom.

Consider, consider,
Think well upon
The marvelous story
Of Appleseed John.

The Growin'of PAUL BUNYAN

by William J. Brooke   illustrated by Alex Murawski

CHILDREN'S CHOICE

ALA NOTABLE BOOK

THIS IS A STORY about how Paul Bunyan met up with Johnny Appleseed an' what come about because o' that meetin'. But it all got started because o' the problems Paul had with his boots one mornin'.

The hardest thing for ole Paul about gettin' started in the mornin' was puttin' on his boots. It wasn't so much the lacin' up that got him down (although when your bootlaces are exactly 8,621 feet an' four an' three quarters inches long, an' each one has to be special ordered from the Suwanee Steamship Cable Company in New York City, an' if because you're strong as ole Paul you tend to snap about two laces a week as a rule, then just tyin' your boots can be a bit of an irritation, too).

No, the hardest part o' puttin' on his boots was makin' sure he was the only one in 'em. Because, you see, they was so big an' warm that all the critters liked to homestead in 'em. So he'd have to shake 'em for nine or ten minutes just to get out the ordinary rattlesnakes an' polecats. Then he'd reach in an' feel around real careful for mountain lions an' wolf packs an' the occasional caribou migration. Fin'ly he'd wave his hand around real good to see if any hawks or eagles was huntin' game down around the instep. Then he could start the chore o' lacin'.

But ever' now an' then, no matter how careful he was, he'd miss a critter or two an' then he'd just have to put up with it. 'Cause once he had those laces all done up, it just wasn't worth the trouble to untie 'em all again.

So on this partic'lar day ole Paul is out o' sorts because of a moose that's got stuck down betwixt his toes. Paul's appetite is so spoiled he can't get down more than three hunnert pancakes an' about two an' a half hogs worth o' bacon afore he grabs up his ax an' takes off to soothe his ragged nerves in his usual way by shavin' a forest or two.

503

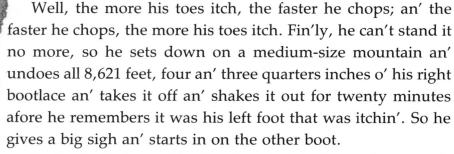

Well, the more his toes itch, the faster he chops; an' the faster he chops, the more his toes itch. Fin'ly, he can't stand it no more, so he sets down on a medium-size mountain an' undoes all 8,621 feet, four an' three quarters inches o' his right bootlace an' takes it off an' shakes it out for twenty minutes afore he remembers it was his left foot that was itchin'. So he gives a big sigh an' starts in on the other boot.

Fin'ly, both boots is off an' a slightly bruised moose is shakin' his head an' blinkin' his eyes an' staggerin' off betwixt the stumps. An' Paul has his first chance to take a deep breath an' have a look round. An' he's surprised, 'cause he can't see any trees anywheres, only stumps. So he gets up on a stump an' looks around an' he still can't see any standin' timber. He'd been so wrought up, he'd cleared all the way to the southern edge o' the big woods without noticin'.

Now this annoys Paul, 'cause he's too far from camp to get back for lunch, an' nothin' upsets him like missin' grub. An' when he's upset, the only thing to soothe him is choppin' trees, an' all the trees is down so that annoys him even worse.

There he sits, feelin' worse by the minute, with his stomach growlin' like a thunderstorm brewin' in the distance. An' then he notices somethin' way off at the horizon, out in the middle o' them dusty brown plains. All of a sudden there's somethin' green. As he watches, that green starts to spread in a line right across the middle of all that brown.

Now the only thing I ever heard tell of that was bigger than ole Paul hisself was ole Paul's curiosity. It was even bigger than his appetite. So quick as he can get his boots on, he's off to see what's happenin'. What he sees makes him stop dead in his tracks. 'Cause it's trees, apple trees growin' where nothin' but dirt ever growed before. A whole line of apple trees stretchin' in both directions as far as you can see.

It makes him feel so good he just has to take up his ax an' start choppin'. An' the more he chops, the better he feels. An' as he marches westward through all the flyin' splinters an' leaves an' applesauce, he sees that the trees is gettin' shorter until they're just saplin's, then green shoots, then just bare earth.

Paul stops short then an' leans on his ax handle to study the funny little man who turns around an' looks up at him. He's barefoot an' wears a gunnysack for clothes with a metal pot on his head for a hat. He looks up at Paul for a second, then he reaches in a big bulgy bag hangin' at his side an' takes out somethin' teeny-tiny, which he sticks in the ground. He gathers the dusty brown dirt around it an' pats it down. He stands up, an' out of a canvas waterbag he pours a little bit o' water on the spot. Then he just stands an' watches.

For a few seconds nothin' happens, then the tiniest littlest point o' green pokes out o' the dust an' sort o' twists around like it's lookin' for somethin'. All at once, it just stretches itself toward the sky an' pulls a saplin' up after it. An' it begins to branch an' to fill out an' its smooth green skin turns rough an' dark an' oozes sap. The branches creak an' groan an' stretch like a sleeper just wakin' up. Buds leaf out an' turn their damp green faces to the sun. An' the apples change from green to red an' swell like balloons full to bustin' with sweet cider.

The funny little man looks up an' smiles an' says, "My name's John Chapman, but folks call me Johnny Appleseed."

"Pleased to meet you," says Paul.

The little man points at his tree. "Mighty pretty sight, don't you think?"

"Sure is," says Paul, an' with a quick-as-a-wink flick o' his ax, he lays the tree out full length on the ground. "My name's Paul Bunyan."

The little man lifts his tin pot an' wipes his bald head while he stares at the tree lyin' there in the dirt. Then he squints up at Paul an' kneels down an' puts another seed in the ground. Paul smiles down at him while the tree grows up, then he lays it out by the first. The little man pops three seeds into the ground fast as can be. Paul lets 'em come up, then he lops all three with one easy stroke, backhand.

"You sure make 'em come up fast," says Paul, admirin'-like.

"It's a sort o' gift I was born with," says Johnny Appleseed. He looks at the five trees lyin' together. "You sure make 'em come down fast."

"It's a talent," says Paul, real humble. "I have to practice a lot."

They stand quiet awhile with Paul leanin' easy on his ax an' Johnny lookin' back along the line o' fallen trees to the horizon. He lifts his tin pot again an' rubs even harder at his head. Then he looks up at Paul an' says, "It seems like we got somethin' of a philosophical difference here."

Paul considers that. "We both like trees," he says real friendly.

"Yep," Johnny nods, "but I like 'em vertical an' you like 'em horizontal."

Paul agrees, but says he don't mind a man who holds a differin' opinion from his own, 'cause that's what makes America great. Johnny says, "Course you don't mind, 'cause when my opinion has finished differin' an' the dust settles, the trees is in the position you prefer. Anybody likes a fight that he always wins."

Paul allows he's sorry that Johnny's upset. "But loggin's what I do, an' a man's gotta do what he does. Besides, without my choppin' lumber, you couldn't build houses or stoke fires or pick your teeth."

"I don't live in a house an' I don't build fires an' when I want to clean my teeth I just eat an apple. Tell me, when all the trees are gone, what'll you cut down then?"

Paul laughs. "Why, there'll always be trees. Are you crazy or somethin'?"

"Yep," says Johnny, "crazy to be wastin' time an' lung power on you. I got to be off. I'm headin' for the Pacific Ocean an' I got a lot o' work to do on the way. So why don't you head north an' I'll head west an' our paths won't cross till they meet somewheres in China."

Paul feels a little hurt at this, but he starts off north, then stops to watch as Johnny takes off at a run, tossin' the seed out in front o' him, pressin' it down into the ground with his bare toes an' tricklin' a little water behind, all without breakin' stride. In a minute he's vanished at the head o' his long line of apple trees.

Now Paul has figured that Johnny hadn't really meant to offend him, but it was more in the nature of a challenge. An' Paul loves any kind of a challenge. So he sets down an' waits three days, figurin' he should give a fair head start to Johnny, who's a couple hunnert feet shorter'n he is. Then at dawn on the fourth day, he stands up an' stretches an' holds his ax out level a foot above the ground. When he starts to run, the trees drop down in a row as neat as the cross ties on a railroad line. In fact, when it came time to build the transcontinental railroad, they just laid the iron rails down on that long line o' apple trees an' saved theirselves many thousands o' dollars.

Anyways, Paul runs for two days an' two nights, an' when the sun's settin' on the third day, he sees water up ahead. There's Johnny Appleseed plantin' a last tree, then sittin' on a high bare bluff lookin' out over the Pacific Ocean. Paul finishes the last o' the trees an' swings the ax over his head with a whoop an' brings it down on the dirt, buryin' its head in the soil an' accident'ly creatin' the San Andreas Fault. He mops his brow an' sits down beside Johnny with his feet danglin' way down into the ocean.

Starin' out at the orange sun, Johnny asks, "Are they all gone?" Paul looks back over his shoulder an' allows as how they are. Paul waits for Johnny to say somethin' else, but he just keeps starin', so Paul says, "It took you six days to plant 'em and it took me only three days to chop 'em down. Pretty good, huh?"

Johnny looks up an' smiles sadly. "It's always easier to chop somethin' down than to make it grow." Then he goes back to starin'.

Now that rankles Paul. When he beats somebody fair an' square, he expects that someone to admit it like a man. "What's so hard about growin' a tree anyway?" he grumps. "You just stick it in the ground an' the seed does all the work."

Johnny reaches way down in the bottom o' his bag an' holds out a seed. "It's the last one," he says. "All the rest o' my dreams is so much kindlin' wood, so why don't you take this an' see if it's so easy to make it grow."

Paul hems an' haws, but he sees as how he has to make good on his word. So he takes the little bitty seed an' pushes it down in the ground with the tip o' one fingernail. He pats the soil around it real nice, like he seen Johnny do. Then he sits down to wait as the sun sets.

"I'm not as fast as you at this," Paul says, "but you've had more practice. An' I'm sure my tree will be just as good as any o' yours."

"Not if it dies o' thirst," says Johnny's voice out o' the dark.

Paul hasn't thought about that. So when the moon comes up, he heads back to a stream he passed about two hunnert miles back. But he don't have nothin' to carry water in, so he scoops up a double handful an' runs as fast as he can with the water slippin' betwixt his fingers. When he gets back, he's got about two drops left.

"Guess I'll have to get more water," he says, a mite winded.

"Don't matter," says Johnny's voice, "if the rabbits get the seed."

An' there in the moonlight, Paul sees all the little cottontails hoppin' around an' scratchin' at the ground. Not wishin' to hurt any of 'em, he picks 'em up, one at a time, an' moves 'em away, but they keep hoppin' back. So, seein' as how he still needs water, he grabs 'em all up an' runs back to the stream, sets the rabbits down, grabs up the water, runs back, flicks two more drops on the spot, pushes away the new batch o' rabbits movin' in, an' tries to catch his breath.

"Just a little more water an' a few less rabbits an' it'll be fine," Paul says between gasps.

Out o' the dark comes Johnny's voice. "Don't matter, if the frost gets it."

Paul feels the cold ground an' he feels the moisture freezin' on his hands. So he gets down on his knees an' he folds his hands around that little spot o' dirt an', gentle as he can, breathes his warm breath onto that tiny little seed. Time passes and the rabbits gather round to enjoy the warmth an' scratch their soft little backs up against those big callused hands. As the night wears on, Paul falls into a sleep, but his hands never stop cuppin' that little bit o' life.

Sometime long after moonset, the voice o' Johnny Appleseed comes driftin' soft out o' the dark an' says, "Nothin's enough if you don't care enough."

Paul wakes up with the sun. He sets up an' stretches an' for a minute he can't remember where he is. Then he looks down an' he gives a whoop. 'Cause he sees a little tiny bit o' green pokin' up through the grains o' dirt. "Hey, Johnny," he yells, "look at this!" But Johnny Appleseed is gone, slipped away in the night. Paul is upset for a minute, then he realizes he don't need to brag to anybody, that that little slip o' green is all the happiness he needs right now.

As the sun rises, he fetches more water an' shoos away the crows an' shields that shoot from the heat o' the sun. It grows taller an' straighter an' puts out buds an' unfurls its leaves. Paul carries in all the animals from the surroundin' countryside, coyotes an' sidewinders an' Gila monsters, an' sets 'em down in a circle to admire his tree growin' tall an' sturdy an' green.

Then Paul notices somethin'. He gets down on his hands an' knees an' looks close. It's a brown leaf. "That's not too serious," he thinks an' he shades it from the sun. Then he sees another brown leaf an' he runs back to get more water. When he gets back, the little saplin' is droopin' an' shrivelin'. He gets down an' breathes on it, but as he watches, the leaves drop off an' the twigs snap. "Help me, somebody," he cries out, "help me!" But there's no answer 'cept the rustlin' o' the critters as they slink away from him. An' while he looks down at the only thing he ever give birth to, it curls up an' dies.

For a second he just stands there, then he pounds his fists on the ground an' yells, "Johnny! Johnny! Why didn't you tell me how much it could hurt?"

He sets down an' he stares till the sun begins settin'. Then he jumps up an' says, "Only one thing's gonna make me feel better. I'm gonna cut me some timber! Maybe a whole forest if I can find one!" He reaches for his ax.

An' that's when he sees it. It stretches right up to the sky, with great green boughs covered with sweet-smellin' needles an' eagles nestin' in its heights. Johnny must have worked some o' his magic afore he left, 'cause when Paul struck it into the ground it wasn't nothin' but an ax. But now, in the light o' the settin' sun, it shines like a crimson column crowned in evergreen.

"I'll call it a redwood," says Paul, who knew now he'd never want an ax again as long as there was such a tree.

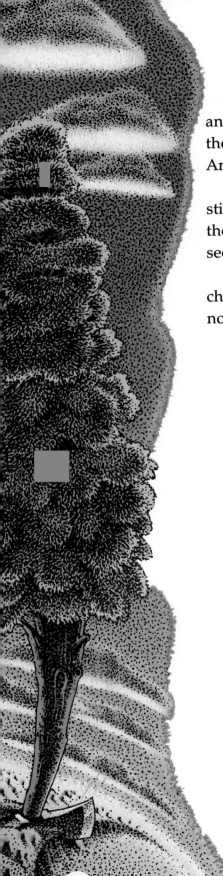

So he waited for the cones with the seeds to form an' drop, an' he planted them all over the great Northwest an' nurtured them an' watched a great woodland spring up in their shelter. An' he never felled a tree again as long as he lived.

For years he worked, an' there are those who say you can still catch a glimpse o' him behind the highest mountains in the deepest woods. An' they say he's always smilin' when you see him.

'Cause Paul learned hisself somethin': A little man who chops somethin' down is still just a little man; but there's nobody bigger than a man who learns to grow.

Is it fair that Johnny Appleseed doesn't tell Paul Bunyan how much a tree's death hurts? Give reasons for your answer.

In what way does Paul Bunyan grow in this story?

How does the author let you know that this is a legend and not a true story?

Paul Bunyan and Johnny Appleseed have very different opinions about trees. In what other ways are they different?

Why does Johnny Appleseed give his very last seed to Paul Bunyan?

WRITE   Which character in this story do you like better? Write an opinion paragraph explaining why you like that character. Use events in the story to support your opinion.

Trees of Life

For what reasons might the trees described in the selections be called "trees of life"?

Writer's Workshop

What other important message about protecting nature could a folktale deliver? With your classmates, brainstorm a list of living things that might be in danger. For example, a baobab might be threatened by an African woodcutter, or a wild bear might be in danger from Davy Crockett. Choose the one you would most like to save. Brainstorm ways in which a wise character might save it. Use your ideas to write a folktale.

Writer's Choice

Do you feel any differently about trees after reading the selections in the theme Trees of Life? Think of a way to express your feelings, and share your work with your classmates.

CONNECTIONS

MULTICULTURAL CONNECTION

Prizing Our World

Harrison Ngau [nou] grew up in the rain forests of Sarawak, a state in northern Borneo. He watched these forests being slowly destroyed by timber companies that sold the lumber worldwide. He knew that all rain forests are important to the health of our planet. He also knew that the rain forests of Borneo were home to the Irak and other native peoples.

To save the Irak culture as well as the forests, Ngau organized people to halt the logging in every way they could. For his efforts, Harrison Ngau was awarded the Goldman Environmental Prize in 1990. He quickly put his $60,000 prize money to work and financed a successful bid for a seat in his nation's parliament.

Ngau has shown that one person can do a lot to help our environment. Write a character sketch about someone you know who is making a difference in our world.

516

SOCIAL STUDIES CONNECTION

Saving the World Begins at Home

People all over the world are working to save the environment. What are your community's environmental problems? What groups are already trying to solve these problems? Create posters that tell how people can make a difference in your community.

MATH CONNECTION

Harrison Ngau won the Goldman Environmental Prize in 1990.

Calculating the Future

What percentage of the earth's surface is covered by rain forests? How fast are the forests being destroyed? Collect these and other statistics that show how our environment is changing. Use the information to compute the changes that may take place on our planet in the next ten years. Report your conclusions.

UNIT SIX

Flights

We have always been fascinated by the skies above us. This fascination goes back over 3,000 years, to the ancient astronomers of China, Babylonia, and Egypt. And our fascination has led us beyond mere looking. We actually travel into space for close-up views. Think about what fascinates you about the skies as you read the selections in this unit.

THEMES

BOOKSHELF

TO SPACE & BACK

by Sally Ride with Susan Okie

Spectacular photos and the words and thoughts of astronaut Sally Ride allow you to take a ride on the space shuttle *Challenger*.

ALA Notable Book, Outstanding Science Trade Book for Children

Harcourt Brace Library Book

SPACE CHALLENGER: THE STORY OF GUION BLUFORD

by Jim Haskins and Kathleen Benson

Aerospace engineer and astronaut Guy Bluford pursued his childhood love of flying machines to the limit, riding into space aboard the *Challenger*.

Outstanding Science Trade Book for Children

Harcourt Brace Library Book

SELF-PORTRAIT WITH WINGS

by Susan Green

Be careful what you wish for. Jennifer wishes that she could grow wings—never believing that her wish could come true!

BEFORE THE WRIGHT BROTHERS

by Don Berliner

Who were the people who planned, built, and used the flying machines of the nineteenth century? Find out in this collection of short biographies.

THE SECRET GROVE

by Barbara Cohen

Two boys grow up in a city divided by religious and ethnic hatreds. What will happen when they meet accidentally in the grove?

Award-Winning Author

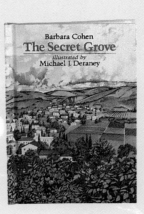

THEME

Through Space and Time

Is time always ticking away at the same pace, second by second? Or can time be condensed? Or expanded? Or even wrinkled?

CONTENTS

New Provid
A CHANGING CITYSCAPE

1910

New Providence is thriving. Cobblestone streets bustle with activity—Model T Fords, streetcars, and horse-drawn carts carrying meat, milk, and ice. There is no concert in the bandstand today, but a crowd has gathered in the square in front of the Town Hall and the Tenebo County Courthouse. A fountain has been built in commemoration of Chief Tenebo, a Native American from a local tribe. The statue is about to be unveiled. Around the base of the fountain is an inscription: GOOD CITIZENS ARE THE RICHES OF A CITY.

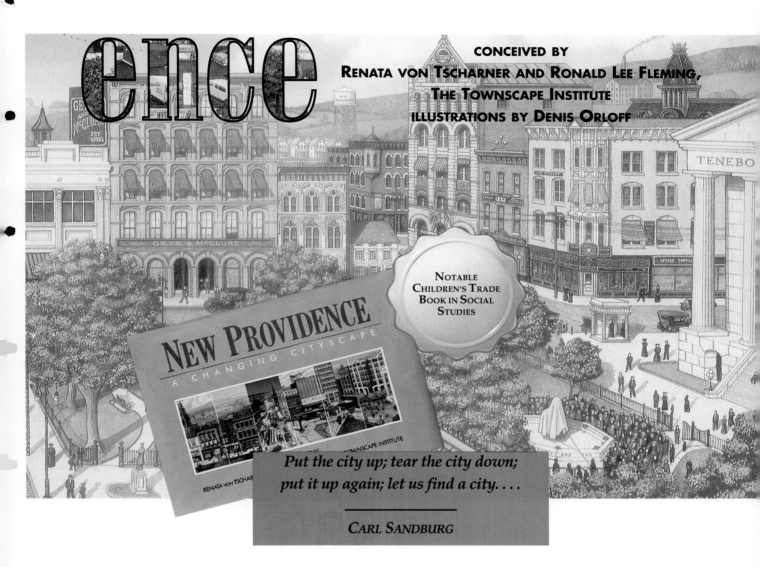

ence

CONCEIVED BY
RENATA VON TSCHARNER AND RONALD LEE FLEMING,
THE TOWNSCAPE INSTITUTE
ILLUSTRATIONS BY DENIS ORLOFF

NOTABLE
CHILDREN'S TRADE
BOOK IN SOCIAL
STUDIES

NEW PROVIDENCE
A CHANGING CITYSCAPE

Put the city up; tear the city down;
put it up again; let us find a city....

CARL SANDBURG

New Providence's good citizens—women in long skirts and men in hats—buy fruit at the sidewalk stand in front of the grocery and most of their clothing and household items at Getz & McClure's, the largest store in town. They shop for shoes and jewelry and office supplies and have supper at Gilman's or at the Butler House Cafe.

The rural hillsides surrounding the city are lush, with comfortable Victorian homes dotting the landscape and the Bloom mill and worker housing in the distance. The large red brick schoolhouse is attended by all school-age children in the region. A flock of birds flies peacefully overhead.

1935

As a mist rolls into New Providence, effects of the Great Depression are visible; the city has fallen on hard times. Gone is the bandstand from the courthouse square, where homeless men now huddle over trash can fires for warmth. A WPA sign publicizes the Works Progress Administration, a jobs program funded by the government. A line of jobless men waits for free bread outside the post office, and hoboes are taking a free ride out of the city on trains. Many buildings are in need of repair.

But even in times such as these, life goes on. A Charlie Chaplin movie is playing at the Strand Theater. A huge Coca-Cola advertisement goes up on the side of a building. A streetlight now controls automobile traffic. The Bloom mill—expanded before the stock market crash—is still in operation, the grocery has become a shoe store, and the dry goods store, a jeweler's. The Colonel Fleming House now accommodates three small businesses. Art Deco chrome and glass streamline some of the storefronts, contrasting with the older styles of the upper stories. A modern yellow apartment building squats on the hillside, while a biplane and a blimp cruise the skies.

1955

Apostwar prosperity settles over New Providence, although there are signs that downtown is deteriorating.

The night sky glows with neon, Christmas lights, and lighted billboards advertising bread, used cars, and cigarettes. Part of the courthouse square is now paved with asphalt to make room for more and larger cars. Buses have replaced streetcars. Franchises like Rexall's and Woolworth's have moved into town, and the Alpine Motel attracts traveling businessmen. Walt Disney's *Lady and the Tramp* is playing at the Strand.

The elegant Butler House is now a liquor store and a boarding
house for transients. Next to it, a Victorian cast-iron building is
being covered with prefabricated siding. Getz & McClure's has
already been sheathed with stark metal grillwork and a currently
popular style of lettering. Two of the small businesses in the Colonel
Fleming House are boarded up. Behind it, a bland new building has
been erected to house Monarch Insurance. The old slate roof of the
Town Hall has been replaced by asphalt shingles. A fire is raging at
the train station, while the citizens of New Providence go about
their holiday shopping.

1970

By 1970, downtown New Providence is an uninspired jumble of old and new. To attract people from thriving suburbia, part of Main Street has been converted into a pedestrian mall, dominated by a harsh concrete fountain. But there is less traffic than ever in the city center, and fewer people actually live there.

A number of people in town today are gathered outside the courthouse, taking part in a protest march against the Vietnam War. Across the newly sunken and cemented square, a mugging is in progress. Graffiti mars the area, as do more and more billboards—

530

advertising beer, cigarettes, whiskey, and an Army/Navy surplus store. The post office and several other buildings have been demolished and turned into parking lots, the Bloom mill is for rent, and the train station tower remains burnt out.

The Alpine Motel is now a Holiday Inn, a Fotomat has opened, and the Beatles' *Let It Be* is playing at the Strand. A day school has opened, complete with colorful murals and giant toadstools. The Colonel Fleming House seems about to be rescued by a preservation group. Victorian homes in the hills are disappearing to make room for highways, look-alike suburban housing, and another addition to the school. In the afternoon sky, a jet flies over the increasing number of powerlines strung across the horizon.

1980

Ten years later, there are signs that downtown New Providence is sadly in need of recovery—and also signs that help is on the way.

Chief Tenebo's statue has been vandalized; debris blows around its dry base and across the square. Graffiti is everywhere, street lamps are smashed, and a police box has appeared. The Colonel Fleming House has been moved across the street, but its placement does not look permanent. In its old location are a Cor-Ten steel sculpture and Monarch Insurance's new highrise, which bears no architectural relationship to the buildings around it.

But the streets seem more populated, and people are again living—even barbecuing—downtown in the new red brick infill structure next to McDonald's. The only billboard in town advertises health food and a cultural event. The old Strand Theater is being expanded into a Cultural Center. And although the Butler House has been all but abandoned, a sign shows that rehabilitation is being planned. A superhighway now cuts through the hillside, making downtown more accessible to summer holiday travelers. A large parking structure has been built, and well-tended plantings soften the mall.

1987

In the sunny afternoon sky a flock of birds heads back to its winter home. Below, people have returned to the city—living, shopping, working, playing. New Providence has never looked better. Sidewalk vendors sell their produce once more, and traffic again flows through handsomely paved streets. Buses are made to look like old-fashioned trolleys. Chief Tenebo has been restored, and the bandstand is back, a concert in full swing. Gone are graffiti, billboards, and harsh sculptures. Plants and fall flowers are everywhere—even the parking structure has been elegantly camouflaged.

It is wisdom to think the people are the city . . . .

CARL SANDBURG

All of the old building facades have been renovated, and the condition of most buildings is strikingly similar to what it was in 1910. The Town Hall's slate roof has been restored, and the air-raid siren is gone. Street furniture is comfortable and compatible with the architecture. The circular clock is back in front of the Butler House, now beautifully refurbished. An arcaded building where people live and work occupies the site of the controversial tower, serving as an entry into the restored train station, and an atrium full of plants softens the Monarch Insurance skyscraper. A Fitness Center has replaced the Feminist Health Center, and a film festival is in progress at the Strand Cultural Center.

The good citizens of New Providence have worked hard to make the city livable again—and true to its heritage.

New Providence, a small American city, will not be found on any map. It is the creation of a team of architectural historians and designers, and yet its fictional cityscape is truly authentic. The buildings, the signs, even the street furniture can be found somewhere in urban America. Almost every detail was discovered in old photographs and assembled by the design team at The Townscape Institute.

Baltimore, Maryland (McDonald's building and H_2O fountain); Binghamton, New York (courthouse lights); Boston, Massachusetts (church in center and 1970 concrete plaza); Brookline, Massachusetts (church); Cambridge, Massachusetts (signs); Chelsea, Massachusetts (storefront); Chicago, Illinois (metal awning on the Butler House); Cincinnati, Ohio (1987 City Identity System booth); Denver, Colorado (building across the street from courthouse in 1910); Eugene, Oregon (1970 modern concrete fountain); Flint, Michigan (1910 shoe sign and street awnings); Fresno, California (1970–80 sculptural clock tower); Garland, Utah (Bloom mill); Grand Rapids, Michigan (City Hall); Heber City, Utah (water tower); Junction City, Kansas (corner bank); Knoxville, Tennessee (billboard); Los Angeles, California (Getz & McClure building); Milwaukee, Wisconsin (suburban villas); Montclair, New Jersey (Colonel Fleming House); Montgomery, Alabama (Victorian cast-iron building); New York, New York (Butler House and train station); Portland, Oregon (fountain base); Richmond, Virginia (signs on Reiter's shoe store); Salem, Ohio (cornice on Main Street); San Diego, California (circular clock); Scottsdale, Arizona (parking structure with plantings); Staunton, Virginia (stained glass in McDonald's building); Syracuse, New York (layout of courthouse square); Topeka, Kansas (Alpine Motel sign); Townsend, Massachusetts (bandstand); Traverse City, Michigan (mansard roof on Butler House); Upper Sandusky, Ohio (horse fountain and pavilion); Waltham, Massachusetts (bench); Washington, D.C. (Masonic building); Westerville, Ohio (gas station); Wilkes-Barre, Pennsylvania (park outline); Wilmington, Delaware (1970 metal Main Street shelters); Winooski, Vermont (Main Street building).

Would you like to live in New Providence? Explain why or why not.

In what ways did New Providence change with the times?

How do you think the authors feel about the changes made in New Providence? Explain your answer.

Which would you say was a better year for New Providence—1910 or 1987? Explain why you think as you do.

WRITE Would you like to be involved in city planning? List some reasons why you would or wouldn't want to be a city planner.

A Wrinkle

Meg Murry's father disappeared several years ago while working on a top secret project. Did he somehow slip through a wrinkle in time? Meg, her friend Calvin, and her brother Charles Wallace are determined to find out. Aided by a trio of superhuman helpers named Mrs. Who, Mrs. Which, and Mrs. Whatsit, they investigate a series of strange places, including the capital city of Camazotz.

NEWBERY MEDAL

LEWIS CARROLL
SHELF AWARD

IN TIME

by Madeleine L'Engle

Illustrations by Kate Muellar

Below them the town was laid out in harsh angular patterns. The houses in the outskirts were all exactly alike, small square boxes painted gray. Each had a small, rectangular plot of lawn in front, with a straight line of dull-looking flowers edging the path to the door. Meg had a feeling that if she could count the flowers there would be exactly the same number for each house. In front of all the houses children were playing. Some were skipping rope, some were bouncing balls. Meg felt vaguely that something was wrong with their play. It seemed exactly like children playing around any housing development at home, and yet there was something different about it. She looked at Calvin, and saw that he, too, was puzzled.

"Look!" Charles Wallace said suddenly. "They're skipping and bouncing in rhythm! Everyone's doing it at exactly the same moment."

This was so. As the skipping rope hit the pavement, so did the ball. As the rope curved over the head of the jumping child, the child with the ball caught the ball. Down came the ropes. Down came the balls. Over and over again. Up. Down. All in rhythm. All identical. Like the houses. Like the paths. Like the flowers.

Then the doors of all the houses opened simultaneously, and out came women like a row of paper dolls. The print of their dresses was different, but they all gave the appearance of being the same. Each woman stood on the steps of her house. Each clapped. Each child with the ball caught the ball. Each child with the skipping rope folded the rope. Each child turned and walked into the house. The doors clicked shut behind them.

"How can they do it?" Meg asked wonderingly. "We couldn't do it that way if we tried. What does it mean?"

"Let's go back." Calvin's voice was urgent.

"Back?" Charles Wallace asked. "Where?"

"I don't know. Anywhere. Back to the hill. Back to Mrs. Whatsit and Mrs. Who and Mrs. Which. I don't like this."

"But they aren't there. Do you think they'd come to us if we turned back now?"

"I don't like it," Calvin said again.

"Come *on*." Impatience made Meg squeak. "You *know* we can't go back. Mrs. Whatsit *said* to go into the town." She started on down the street, and the two boys followed her. The houses, all identical, continued, as far as the eye could reach.

Then, all at once, they saw the same thing, and stopped to watch. In front of one of the houses stood a little boy with a ball, and he was bouncing it. But he bounced it rather badly and with no particular rhythm, sometimes dropping it and running after it with awkward, furtive leaps, sometimes throwing it up into the air and trying to catch it. The door of his house opened and out ran one of the mother figures. She looked wildly up and down the street, saw the children and put her hand to her mouth as though to stifle a scream, grabbed the little boy and rushed indoors with him. The ball dropped from his fingers and rolled out into the street.

Charles Wallace ran after it and picked it up, holding it out for Meg and Calvin to see. It seemed like a perfectly ordinary, brown rubber ball.

"Let's take it in to him and see what happens," Charles Wallace suggested.

Meg pulled at him. "Mrs. Whatsit said for us to go on into the town."

"Well, we *are* in the town, aren't we? The outskirts anyhow. I want to know more about this. I have a hunch it may help us later. You go on if you don't want to come with me."

"No," Calvin said firmly. "We're going to stay together. Mrs. Whatsit said we weren't to let them separate us. But I'm with you on this. Let's knock and see what happens."

They went up the path to the house, Meg reluctant, eager to get on into the town. "Let's hurry," she begged, "*please!* Don't you want to find Father?"

"Yes," Charles Wallace said, "but not blindly. How can we help him if we don't know what we're up against? And it's obvious we've been brought here to help him, not just to find

him." He walked briskly up the steps and knocked at the door. They waited. Nothing happened. Then Charles Wallace saw a bell, and this he rang. They could hear the bell buzzing in the house, and the sound of it echoed down the street. After a moment the mother figure opened the door. All up and down the street other doors opened, but only a crack, and eyes peered toward the three children and the woman looking fearfully out the door at them.

"What do you want?" she asked. "It isn't paper time yet; we've had milk time; we've had this month's Puller Prush Person; and I've given my Decency Donations regularly. All my papers are in order."

"I think your little boy dropped his ball," Charles Wallace said, holding it out.

The woman pushed the ball away. "Oh, no! The children in our section *never* drop balls! They're all perfectly trained. We haven't had an Aberration for three years."

All up and down the block, heads nodded in agreement.

Charles Wallace moved closer to the woman and looked past her into the house. Behind her in the shadows he could see the little boy, who must have been about his own age.

"You can't come in," the woman said. "You haven't shown me any papers. I don't have to let you in if you haven't any papers."

Charles Wallace held the ball out beyond the woman so that the little boy could see it. Quick as a flash the boy leaped forward and grabbed the ball from Charles Wallace's hand, then darted back into the shadows. The woman went very white, opened her mouth as though to say something, then slammed the door in their faces instead. All up and down the street doors slammed.

"What are they afraid of?" Charles Wallace asked. "What's the matter with them?"

"Don't *you* know?" Meg asked him. "Don't you know what all this is about, Charles?"

"Not yet," Charles Wallace said. "Not even an inkling. And I'm trying. But I didn't get through anywhere. Not even a chink. Let's go." He stumped down the steps.

After several blocks the houses gave way to apartment buildings; at least Meg felt sure that that was what they must be. They were fairly tall, rectangular buildings, absolutely plain, each window, each entrance exactly like every other. Then, coming toward them down the street, was a boy about Calvin's age riding a machine that was something like a combination of a bicycle and a motorcycle. It had the slimness and lightness of a bicycle, and yet as the foot pedals turned they seemed to generate an unseen source of power, so that the boy could pedal very slowly and yet move along the street quite swiftly. As he reached each entrance he thrust one hand into a bag he wore slung over his shoulder, pulled out a roll of papers, and tossed it into the entrance. It might have been Dennys or Sandy or any

one of hundreds of boys with a newspaper route in any one of hundreds of towns back home, and yet, as with the children playing ball and jumping rope, there was something wrong about it. The rhythm of the gesture never varied. The paper flew in identically the same arc at each doorway, landed in identically the same spot. It was impossible for anybody to throw with such consistent perfection.

Calvin whistled. "I wonder if they play baseball here?"

As the boy saw them he slowed down on his machine and stopped, his hand arrested as it was about to plunge into the paper bag. "What are you kids doing out on the street?" he demanded. "Only route boys are allowed out now, you know that."

"No, we don't know it," Charles Wallace said. "We're strangers here. How about telling us something about this place?"

"You mean you've had your entrance papers processed and everything?" the boy asked. "You must have if you're here," he answered himself. "And what are you doing here if you don't know about us?"

"You tell me," Charles Wallace said.

"Are you examiners?" the boy asked a little anxiously. "Everybody knows our city has the best Central Intelligence Center on the planet. Our production levels are the highest. Our factories never close; our machines never stop rolling. Added to this we have five poets, one musician, three artists, and six sculptors, all perfectly channeled."

"What are you quoting from?" Charles Wallace asked.

"The Manual, of course," the boy said. "We are the most oriented city on the planet. There has been no trouble of any kind for centuries. All Camazotz knows our record. That is why we are the capital city of Camazotz. That is why CENTRAL Central Intelligence is located here. That is why IT makes ITs home here." There was something about the way he said "IT" that made a shiver run up and down Meg's spine.

But Charles Wallace asked briskly, "Where is this Central Intelligence Center of yours?"

"CENTRAL Central," the boy corrected. "Just keep going and you can't miss it. You *are* strangers, aren't you! What are you doing here?"

"Are you supposed to ask questions?" Charles Wallace demanded severely.

The boy went white, just as the woman had. "I humbly beg your pardon. I must continue my route now or I will have to talk my timing into the explainer." And he shot off down the street on his machine.

Charles Wallace stared after him. "What is it?" he asked Meg and Calvin. "There was something funny about the way he talked, as though—well, as though he weren't really doing the talking. Know what I mean?"

Calvin nodded, thoughtfully. "Funny is right. Funny peculiar. Not only the way he talked, either. The whole thing smells."

"Come *on*." Meg pulled at them. How many times was it she had urged them on? "Let's go find Father. He'll be able to explain it all to us."

They walked on. After several more blocks they began to see
other people, grown-up people, not children, walking up and
down and across the streets. These people ignored the children
entirely, seeming to be completely intent on their own business.
Some of them went into the apartment buildings. Most of them
were heading in the same direction as the children. As these
people came to the main street from the side streets they would
swing around the corners with an odd, automatic stride, as
though they were so deep in their own problems and the route
was so familiar that they didn't have to pay any attention to
where they were going.

After a while the apartment buildings gave way to what
must have been office buildings, great stern structures with
enormous entrances. Men and women with brief cases poured
in and out.

Charles Wallace went up to one of the women, saying politely, "Excuse me, but could you please tell me—" But she hardly glanced at him as she continued on her way.

"Look." Meg pointed. Ahead of them, across a square, was the largest building they had ever seen, higher than the Empire State Building, and almost as long as it was high.

"This must be it," Charles Wallace said, "their CENTRAL Central Intelligence or whatever it is. Let's go on."

"But if Father's in some kind of trouble with this planet," Meg objected, "isn't that exactly where we *shouldn't* go?"

"Well, how do you propose finding him?" Charles Wallace demanded.

"I certainly wouldn't ask *there!*"

"I didn't say anything about asking. But we aren't going to have the faintest idea where or how to begin to look for him

until we find out something more about this place, and I have a
hunch that that's the place to start. If you have a better idea, Meg,
why of course just say so."

"Oh, get down off your high horse," Meg said crossly.
"Let's go to your old CENTRAL Central Intelligence and get
it over with."

"I think we ought to have passports or something," Calvin
suggested. "This is much more than leaving America to go to
Europe. And that boy and the woman both seemed to care so
much about having things in proper order. We certainly haven't
got any papers in proper order."

"If we needed passports or papers Mrs. Whatsit would have
told us so," Charles Wallace said.

Calvin put his hands on his hips and looked down at Charles
Wallace. "Now look here, old sport. I love those three old girls
just as much as you do, but I'm not sure they know *everything*."

"They know a lot more than we do."

"Granted. But you know Mrs. Whatsit talked about having been a star. I wouldn't think that being a star would give her much practice in knowing about people. When she tried to be a person she came pretty close to goofing it up. There was never anybody on land or sea like Mrs. Whatsit the way she got herself up."

"She was just having fun," Charles said. "If she'd wanted to look like you or Meg I'm sure she could have."

Calvin shook his head. "I'm not so sure. And these people seem to be *people*, if you know what I mean. They aren't like us, I grant you that, there's something very off-beat about them. But they're lots more like ordinary people than the ones on Uriel."

"Do you suppose they're robots?" Meg suggested.

Charles Wallace shook his head. "No. That boy who dropped the ball wasn't any robot. And I don't think the rest of them are, either. Let me listen for a minute."

They stood very still, side by side, in the shadow of one of the big office buildings. Six large doors kept swinging open, shut, open, shut, as people went in and out, in and out, looking straight ahead, straight ahead, paying no attention to the children whatsoever, whatsoever. Charles wore his listening, probing look. "They're not robots," he said suddenly and definitely. "I'm not sure *what* they are, but they're not robots. I can feel minds there. I can't get at them at all, but I can feel them sort of pulsing. Let me try a minute more."

The three of them stood there very quietly. The doors kept opening and shutting, opening and shutting, and the stiff people hurried in and out, in and out, walking jerkily like figures in an old silent movie. Then, abruptly, the stream of movement thinned. There were only a few people and these moved more rapidly, as if the film had been speeded up. One white-faced man in a dark suit looked directly at the children, said, "Oh, dear, I shall be late," and flickered into the building.

"He's like the white rabbit," Meg giggled nervously.

"I'm scared," Charles said. "I can't reach them at all. I'm completely shut out."

"We have to find Father—" Meg started again.

"Meg—" Charles Wallace's eyes were wide and frightened. "I'm not sure I'll even know Father. It's been so long, and I was only a baby—"

Meg's reassurance came quickly. "You'll know him! Of course you'll know him! The way you'd know me even without looking because I'm always there for you, you can always reach in—"

"Yes." Charles punched one small fist into an open palm with a gesture of great decision. "Let's go to CENTRAL Central Intelligence."

How did you feel as you read about the characters walking through the capital city of Camazotz?

How are the homes and the people of Camazotz similar to places and people anywhere else? How are they different?

What might be an Aberration in Camazotz?

Do you believe the children are in danger? What in the story makes you believe that?

WRITE   Do you think you would like to live in a place where people do everything exactly the same? Write a paragraph or two to explain your opinion.

Madeleine L'Engle

Madeleine L'Engle can't remember a time in her life in which she wasn't writing. As an only child, she enjoyed spending many hours alone, reading books and writing her own stories.

According to L'Engle, the main characters in her stories, male and female, are based on herself. The settings for her books are usually places she has visited. An exception is *A Wrinkle in Time*, in which three children traveling through space and time visit fantastic places beyond our world. *A Wrinkle in Time* was at first rejected by several editors who considered it to be too unusual for the general reading public. When the book was published, it was awarded the Newbery Medal "for the most distinguished contribution to American literature for children" in 1963.

L'Engle once said, "There are forces working in the world . . . for standardization, for the regimentation of us all, or what I like to call making muffins of us, muffins like every other muffin in the muffin tin." She believes that reading for pleasure can help children avoid such standardization and lead them to creativity.

L'Engle enjoys experimenting with all forms of writing—science fiction, suspense, young adult novels, poetry, playwriting, and nonfiction. But she is best known as a children's writer and has written her most difficult works for children because she believes "that children's minds are open to the excitement of new ideas and that they are able to understand what their parents have rejected or forgotten."

Through Space and Time

Do you think the city of New Providence could ever become like the capital city of Camazotz? Why or why not?

WRITER'S WORKSHOP

Two cities are described in the selections you read. The authors give details about the buildings, the landscapes, and the people who live there. The authors use specific language to express how they feel about the towns. Write a descriptive paragraph about the town you live in or one you have visited. Give details about the town you choose, and use specific, vivid words to let your audience know how you feel about it.

Writer's Choice   What do you think of the theme Through Space and Time now that you have read "New Providence: A Changing Cityscape" and "A Wrinkle in Time"? Plan a way to respond. Then carry out your plan.

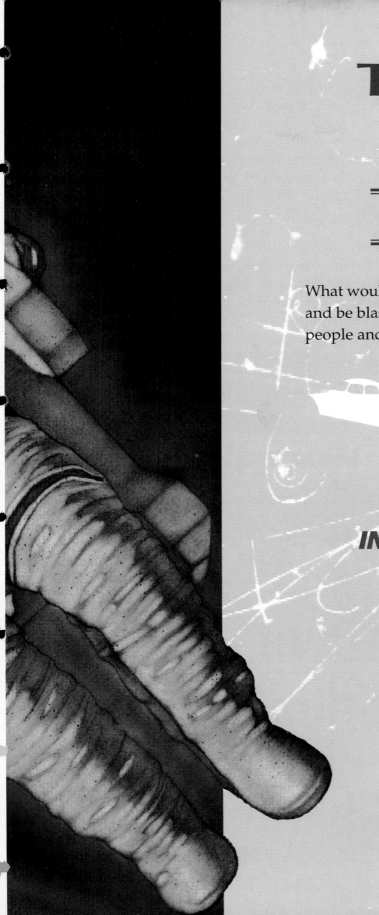

THEME

Space Flights

What would it be like to report to work in the morning and be blasted into space? Read about some fictional people and some real people who do just that.

CONTENTS

557

BUCK ROGERS

The idea of space travel was once so fantastic that it was confined to the comics pages. There, writers and illustrators could let their imaginations soar to describe what the future might hold. Were they right? Were they even close? You be the judge.

IN THE 25TH CENTURY

In 1929, writer Phil Nowlan and illustrator Dick Calkins began to chronicle the adventures of Buck Rogers, a man trapped in a cave who woke up 500 years into the future. Running until 1967, this comic strip entertained Americans well into the real space age.

558

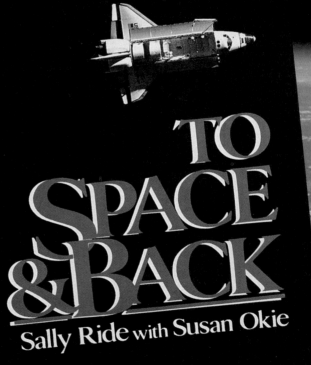

U.S. Astronaut Sally Ride
shares the adventure of outer space

ALA
NOTABLE BOOK
SLJ BEST BOOKS
OF THE YEAR

TO
SPACE
&BACK

Sally Ride with Susan Okie

SALLY K. RIDE

My first space flight was in June 1983, with four other astronauts: Bob Crippen, Rick Hauck, John Fabian, and Norm Thagard. We went up in the space shuttle, the world's first spaceplane, which carries all of today's astronauts into space. We blasted off from a launch pad in Florida; then we circled the Earth for seven days. As we went around and around the planet, we launched two satellites, studied the Earth, and learned about weightlessness. After a week in orbit we returned to Earth. Our adventure ended as the space shuttle glided back through the atmosphere to a smooth landing in California.

Crip, Rick, John, Norm, and I have each had a chance to visit space again. We have found time on every trip to relax, enjoy weightlessness, and admire the view of the Earth and the stars. And, like all astronauts, we have found time to take pictures. The pictures help us to capture the excitement of our trip into space and share the adventure with our friends when we get back.

Most of the photographs in this book were taken by astronauts on board the space shuttle. Some were taken on my flights, some on other space shuttle flights. They will show you what it's like to eat from a spoon floating in midair, to put on a spacesuit for a walk in space, and to gaze at the Earth's oceans far below.

When I was growing up, I was always fascinated by the planets, stars, and galaxies, but I never thought about becoming an astronaut. I studied math and science in high school, and then I spent my years in college learning physics—the study of the laws of nature and the universe. Just as I was finishing my education, NASA, the United States space agency, began looking for scientists

562

who wanted to become astronauts. Suddenly I knew that I wanted a chance to see the Earth and the stars from outer space. I sent my application to NASA, and after a series of tests and interviews, I was chosen to be an astronaut.

On January 28, 1986, this book was almost ready to go to the printer, when the unthinkable happened. The space shuttle *Challenger* exploded one minute after lift-off. After the accident I thought a lot about the book, and whether or not I wanted to change any part of it. I decided that nothing except the dedication and the words I write here should be changed.

I wrote this book because I wanted to answer some of the questions that young people ask of astronauts. Many of the questions are about feelings, and one that now may have added meaning is, "Is it scary?"

All adventures—especially into new territory—are scary, and there has always been an element of danger in space flight. I wanted to be an astronaut because I thought it would be a challenging opportunity. It was; it was also an experience that I shall never forget.

—*Sally Ride*

LAUNCH MORNING.

6 . . . 5 . . . 4 . . .

The alarm clock counts down.

3 . . . 2 . . . 1 . . .

Rring! 3:15 A.M. *Launch minus four hours.* Time to get up.

It's pitch black outside. In four hours a space shuttle launch will light up the sky.

Nine miles from the launch pad, in the astronaut crew quarters, we put on our flight suits, get some last-minute information, and eat a light breakfast.

Launch minus three hours. It's still dark. We leave the crew quarters, climb into the astronaut van, and head for the launch pad.

The space shuttle stands with its nose pointed toward the sky, attached to the big orange fuel tank and two white rockets that will lift it—and us—into space.

The spotlights shining on the space shuttle light the last part of our route. Although we're alone, we know that thousands of people are watching us now, during the final part of the countdown.

When we step out onto the pad, we're dwarfed by the thirty-story-high space shuttle. Our spaceplane looked peaceful from the road, but now we can hear it hissing and gurgling as though it's alive.

The long elevator ride up the launch tower takes us to a level near the nose of the space shuttle, 195 feet above the ground. Trying hard not to look down at the pad far below, we walk out onto an access arm and into the "white room." The white room, a small white chamber at the end of the movable walkway, fits right next to the space shuttle's hatch. The only other people on the launch pad—in fact, the only other people for miles—are the six technicians waiting for us in the white room. They help us put on our escape harnesses and launch helmets and help us climb through the hatch. Then they strap us into our seats.

Because the space shuttle is standing on its tail, we are lying on our backs as we face the nose. It's awkward to twist around to look out the windows. The commander has a good view of the launch tower, and the pilot has a good view of the Atlantic Ocean, but no one else can see much outside.

Launch minus one hour. We check to make sure that we are strapped in properly, that oxygen will flow into our helmets, that our radio communication with Mission Control is working, and that our pencils and our books—the procedure manuals and checklists we'll need during lift-off—are attached to something to keep them from shaking loose. Then we wait.

The technicians close the hatch and then head for safety three miles away. We're all alone on the launch pad.

Launch minus seven minutes. The walkway with the white room at the end slowly pulls away. Far below us the power units start whirring, sending a shudder through the shuttle. We close the visors on our helmets and begin to breathe from the oxygen supply. Then the space shuttle quivers again as its launch engines slowly move into position for blast-off.

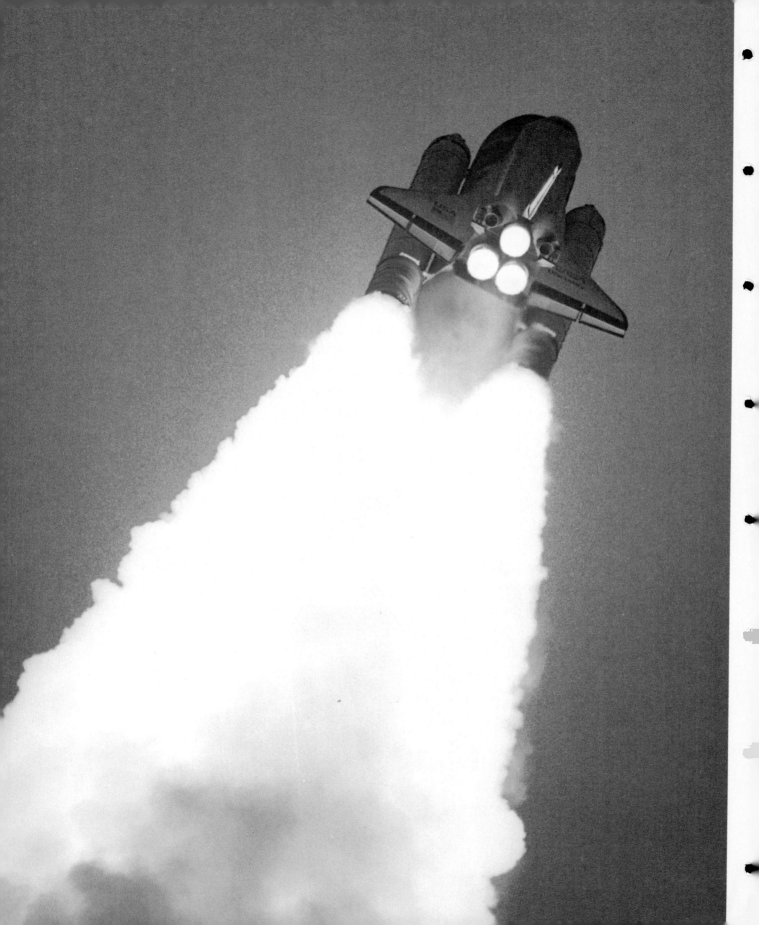

Launch minus 10 seconds . . . 9 . . . 8 . . . 7 . . . The three launch engines light. The shuttle shakes and strains at the bolts holding it to the launch pad. The computers check the engines. It isn't up to us anymore—the computers will decide whether we launch.

3 . . . 2 . . . 1 . . . The rockets light! The shuttle leaps off the launch pad in a cloud of steam and a trail of fire. Inside, the ride is rough and loud. Our heads are rattling around inside our helmets. We can barely hear the voices from Mission Control in our headsets above the thunder of the rockets and engines. For an instant I wonder if everything is working right. But there's no more time to wonder, and no time to be scared.

In only a few seconds we zoom past the clouds. Two minutes later the rockets burn out, and with a brilliant whitish-orange flash, they fall away from the shuttle as it streaks on toward space. Suddenly the ride becomes very, very smooth and quiet. The shuttle is still attached to the big tank, and the launch engines are pushing us out of Earth's atmosphere. The sky is black. All we can see of the trail of fire behind us is a faint, pulsating glow through the top window.

Launch plus six minutes. The force pushing us against the backs of our seats steadily increases. We can barely move because we're being held in place by a force of 3 g's—three times the force of gravity we feel on Earth. At first we don't mind it—we've all felt much more than that when we've done acrobatics in our jet training airplanes. But that lasted only a few seconds, and this seems to go on forever. After a couple of minutes of 3 g's, we're uncomfortable, straining to hold our books on our laps and craning our necks against the force to read the instruments. I find myself wishing we'd hurry up and get into orbit.

Launch plus eight and one-half minutes. The launch engines cut off. Suddenly the force is gone, and we lurch forward in our seats. During the next few minutes the empty fuel tank drops away and falls to Earth, and we are very busy getting the shuttle ready to enter orbit. But we're not too busy to notice that our books and pencils are floating in midair. We're in space!

The atmosphere thins gradually as we travel farther from Earth. At fifty miles up, we're above most of the air, and we're officially "in space." We aren't in orbit yet, though, and without additional push the shuttle would come crashing back to Earth.

We use the shuttle's smaller space engines to get us into our final, safe orbit about two hundred miles above Earth. In that orbit we are much higher than airplanes, which fly about six miles up, but much lower than weather satellites, which circle Earth more than twenty-two thousand miles up.

Once we are in orbit, our ride is very peaceful. The engines have shut down, and the only noise we hear is the hum of the fans that circulate our air. We are traveling at five miles a second, going around the Earth once every ninety minutes, but we don't feel the motion. We can't even tell we're moving unless we look out the window at Earth.

We stay much closer to home than the astronauts who flew space capsules to the moon in 1969. When those astronauts stood on the moon, they described the distant Earth as a big blue-and-white marble suspended in space. We are a long way from the moon, and we never get far enough from Earth to see the whole planet at once.

We still have a magnificent view. The sparkling blue oceans and bright orange deserts are glorious against the blackness of space. Even if we can't see the whole planet, we can see quite a distance. When we are over Los Angeles we can see as far as Oregon; when we are over Florida we can see New York.

We see mountain ranges reaching up to us and canyons falling away. We see huge dust storms blowing over deserts in Africa and smoke spewing from the craters of active volcanoes in Hawaii. We see enormous chunks of ice floating in the Antarctic Ocean and electrical storms raging over the Atlantic.

Sunrises and sunsets are spectacular from orbit. Since we see one sunrise and one sunset each time we go around the Earth, we can watch sixteen sunrises and sixteen sunsets every twenty-four hours. Our sightseeing doesn't stop while we are over the dark

side of the planet. We can see twinkling city lights, the reflection of the moon in the sea, and flashes of lightning from thunderstorms.

These natural features are not the only things we can see. We can also spot cities, airport runways, bridges, and other signs of civilization. When our orbit takes us over Florida, we are even able to see the launch pad at Cape Canaveral, where we crawled into the space shuttle just hours earlier.

Astronauts are sent into space to launch new satellites into orbit, to return orbiting satellites to Earth, to fix broken satellites, and to perform many different types of scientific experiments.

The space shuttle carries satellites into orbit in its cargo bay. Satellites may be as small as a basketball or as large as a bus. Most are designed to be released from the spaceplane; a few are retrieved before the shuttle returns to Earth, but generally they are left in orbit to do their jobs. Some relay television signals across the country, some point telescopes at distant stars, and some aim weather cameras back at Earth.

It is not an easy job to launch a satellite. Before a flight, astronauts practice every step over and over so that they will be able to release the satellite at exactly the right time, at exactly the right spot over the Earth, and with the shuttle pointing in exactly the right direction. During the countdown to the satellite launch, the crew works as a team—a very well trained team working very closely together. Each astronaut "plays a position" on the flight deck: two are seated (wearing seatbelts to avoid floating away from the computers at a critical moment), one is near the windows, and one is floating behind the seats near the satellite switches.

What kind of scientific experiments do we conduct in space? We observe the stars and the Earth from our position two hundred miles up. On some flights we carry telescopes outside in the cargo bay. Because our orbit is above the atmosphere, these telescopes get a clearer view of the sun, stars, planets, and galaxies than any telescope on Earth. On some flights we carry sensitive cameras to take pictures of the land, sea, and weather back on Earth. Information gathered at shuttle height can help scientists study storms, air pollution, and volcanic eruptions and learn more about the planet we live on.

Inside the space shuttle, astronauts perform experiments exploring ways to make new substances—medicines, metals, or crystals—in weightlessness. We also record data about our own bodies to help scientists understand the effects of weightlessness. Before astronauts can set out on a two-year trip to Mars, scientists must be able to predict what will happen to people who stay in space that long.

THE DAY BEFORE THE SHUTTLE RETURNS TO EARTH, astronauts have to put away all loose equipment. Cameras, food trays, and books will stay attached to the ceiling or walls with Velcro as long as they are weightless, but they would come crashing to the floor if we left them out during re-entry. We drift around collecting things and stowing them in drawers. An amazing number of lost pencils and books turn up floating behind wall and ceiling panels.

Immediately after launch we folded and put away all but two of our seats to give us more room inside. Now we have to reattach them to the floor so we can sit in them during re-entry. We must also find the suits, boots, helmets, and life vests that we haven't worn since launch and put them on again for landing. It is often hard to remember where we stored everything. Once I almost had to come back to Earth barefoot because I had forgotten where I had put my boots!

Four or five hours before landing, we begin to drink liquid—four or more big glasses each—and take salt pills to keep the liquid in our bodies. We have to do this because our bodies have gotten rid of some water during the flight to adjust to weightlessness. Now we are about to feel Earth's gravity again, and if we do not replace the lost fluid ahead of time, we will feel very thirsty and lightheaded—and maybe even pass out—as gravity pulls the fluid in our bodies toward our legs.

We also put on "g-suits," pants that can be inflated to keep the blood from pooling in our legs. If we begin to feel lightheaded as we re-enter the atmosphere, a sign that not enough blood is reaching the brain, we can inflate our g-suits.

Finally we strap ourselves into our seats, connect our helmets to the oxygen supply, and fire the shuttle's small space engines. This "de-orbit burn" slows the shuttle down and brings us back into Earth's atmosphere. Once the engines are fired to start re-entry, there is no turning back.

The space shuttle re-enters the atmosphere about thirty minutes later. It is moving very fast, and as it collides with molecules of gas in the air it becomes very hot—in places, over twenty-five hundred degrees Fahrenheit. Only the special heat tiles glued on the outside of the spaceplane keep it from melting. The tiles protect the shuttle so well that inside we do not even feel the heat. But we can tell that it is very hot outside, because all we can see through the windows is a bright, flickering orange glow from the hot air around us.

After we have traveled a short distance down into the atmosphere, we begin to hear the rushing of wind as we shoot through the thin air. We feel a little vibration, like what passengers might feel on a slightly bumpy airplane ride. Gravity slowly begins pulling us into our seats, and we start to feel heavier and heavier. Since we are used to weightless books, pencils, arms, and heads, all these things now seem very heavy to us. It's an effort even to lift a hand.

As the shuttle falls farther down into the atmosphere, it flies less and less like a spacecraft and more and more like an airplane. It gradually stops using its small space jets to maneuver and starts using the control surfaces on its tail and wings instead. These surfaces were useless in the vacuum of space, but they become more effective as the air thickens. When the shuttle is about as low as most airplanes fly, it is only a few miles from the runway and is traveling below the speed of sound. At this point it is flying like a glider—an airplane with no engines.

Until this stage of re-entry the computers have been flying the spaceplane, but now the commander takes control. We approach the runway much more steeply than we would in an ordinary airplane, and we feel almost as if we're flying straight down. We slide forward in our seats, held back only by our shoulder harnesses, as the shuttle dives toward the ground. The pilot lowers the landing gear when the spaceplane is only a few hundred feet above the ground. The landing gear slows us down, but we still land at about two hundred miles per hour—quite a bit faster than most airplanes. The rear wheels touch the runway first, so gently that inside we can't even be sure we've landed. Then the nose wheel comes down with a hard thump, and we know we're back on Earth.

The space shuttle rolls to a stop. As I unstrap myself from my seat and try to stand up, I am amazed at how heavy my whole body feels. My arms, my head, my neck—each part of me seems to be made of lead. It is hard to stand straight, it is hard to lift my legs to walk, and it is hard to carry my helmet and books. I start down the ladder from the flight deck to the mid-deck—the same ladder that was unnecessary just an hour ago—and I have to concentrate just to place my feet on the rungs. My muscles are nearly as strong as they were before the one-week space flight, but my brain expects everything to be light and easy to lift.

My heart, too, has gotten used to weightlessness. For several days, it has not had to pump blood up from my legs against gravity. Now it is working harder again, and for several minutes after we land it beats much faster than normal.

My sense of balance also needs to adjust to gravity. For a few minutes I feel dizzy every time I move my head. I have trouble keeping my balance or walking in a straight line for about fifteen minutes after landing.

We stay inside the spaceplane for a little while to give ourselves a chance to get over these strange sensations. We do knee bends and practice walking while the ground crew moves a boarding platform over to the shuttle and opens the hatch. Then a doctor comes on board to make sure everyone is in shape to get off. We are all still a little wobbly, but about thirty minutes after landing we are ready to climb out of the space shuttle and walk down the stairs to the runway.

Once my feet are on the ground, I look back and admire the space shuttle. I take a few moments to get used to being back on Earth and to say goodbye to the plane that took us to space and back.

What did you learn about a space shuttle launch and flight that you didn't know before?

When, do you think, are the most dangerous times for astronauts during shuttle flights?

Describe the changes that the astronauts' bodies go through upon their return to Earth.

How does Sally Ride feel about space flight? What in her story makes you believe that?

WRITE Would you want to blast off in the space shuttle? Write a paragraph explaining why you would or would not want to be part of a shuttle crew.

Space Flights

Think about how the selections provide contrast to one another. How does what we really know about space and space travel differ from what we enjoy imagining about them?

WRITER'S WORKSHOP

Many writers have been inspired to write about space or space exploration. Some write stories; some write poems. Think of a topic about space or space travel that is fascinating to you. Then write a poem that expresses your feelings about your topic.

Writer's Choice
You have read how space flights can be dangerous as well as thrilling. What do you think of space flights? Respond in some way to the theme. Share your writing with your classmates.

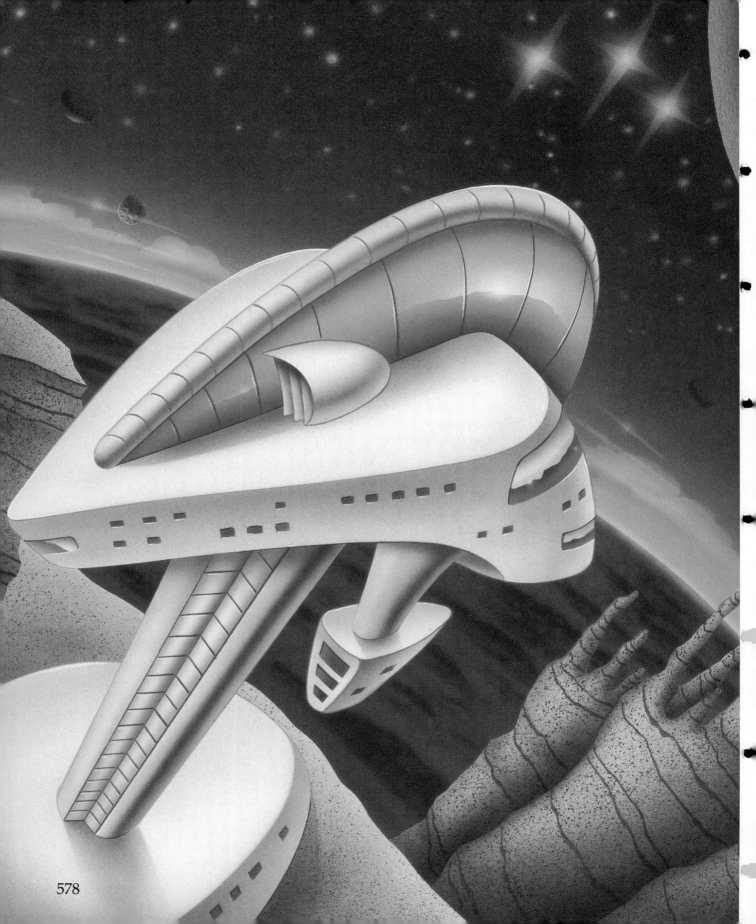

T H E M E

Beyond the Solar System

Many authors have written about people going on spaceships to colonize other planets. But what if a disaster destroyed our own planet? Would we have enough spaceships to take us away from here? Would we have any other place to go?

C O N T E N T S

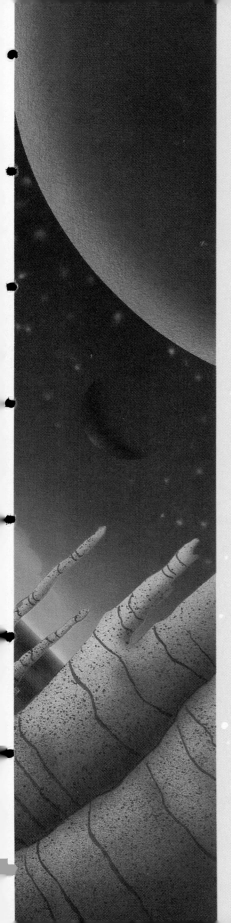

SECRETS

from
Space Songs

by Myra Cohn Livingston

Space keeps its secrets
hidden.

It does not tell.

Are black holes time machines?
Where do lost comets go?

Is Pluto moon or planet?

How many, how vast
unknown galaxies beyond us?

Do other creatures
dwell   on distant spheres?

Will we ever know?

Space is silent.

It seldom answers.

But we ask.

THE GREEN BOOK

JILL PATON WALSH

Will Pattie and her family survive on the planet Shine?

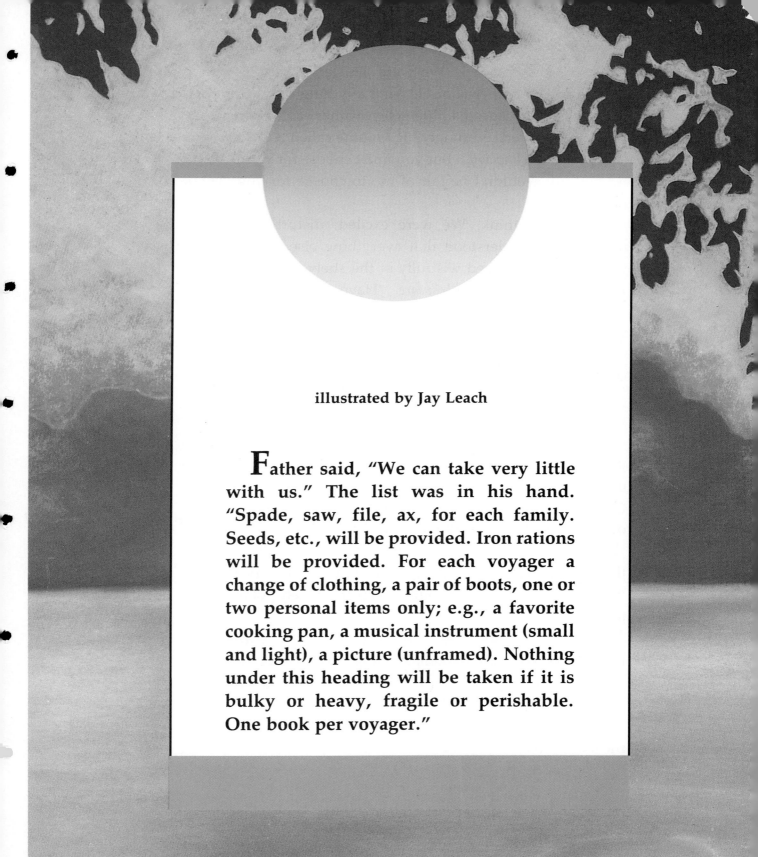

illustrated by Jay Leach

Father said, "We can take very little with us." The list was in his hand. "Spade, saw, file, ax, for each family. Seeds, etc., will be provided. Iron rations will be provided. For each voyager a change of clothing, a pair of boots, one or two personal items only; e.g., a favorite cooking pan, a musical instrument (small and light), a picture (unframed). Nothing under this heading will be taken if it is bulky or heavy, fragile or perishable. One book per voyager."

It was easy to pack. We were allowed so little, and we didn't have to bother about leaving anything tidy behind us. Only the books caused a little delay. Father said, "I must take this." He showed us an ugly big volume called *A Dictionary of Intermediate Technology*. "But you must choose for yourselves," he said. "It wouldn't be fair of me to choose for you. Think carefully."

We didn't think. We were excited, disturbed, and we hadn't really understood that everything else would be left behind. Father looked wistfully at the shelves. He picked up *The Oxford Complete Shakespeare*. "Have you all chosen your books?" he asked. "Yes," we told him. He put the Shakespeare back.

We had time to waste at the end. We ate everything we could find.

"I don't want to eat iron," Pattie said, but nobody knew what she meant.

Then Father got out the slide projector, and showed us pictures of holidays we had once had. We didn't think much of them.

"Have they all gone brownish with age, Dad?" said Joe, our brother, the eldest of us.

"No," said Father. "The pictures are all right. It's the light that has changed. It's been getting colder and bluer now for years . . . but when I was young it was this lovely golden color, just like this—look."

But what he showed us—a beach, with a blue sea, and the mother we couldn't remember lying on a towel, reading a book—looked a funny hue, as though someone had brushed it over with a layer of treacle.

Pattie was glad that Father wasn't going to be able to take the slide projector. It made him sad.

And the next day we all went away, Father and Joe, and Sarah, and Pattie, and lots of other families, and left the Earth far behind.

When this happened, we were all quite young, and Pattie was so young that later she couldn't remember being on the Earth at all, except those few last hours, and even the journey was mostly forgotten. She could remember the beginning of the journey, because it was so exciting. When we could undo our seat belts, and look out of the windows, the world looked like a Chinese paper lantern, with painted lands upon it, and all the people on the ship looked at it, and some of the grownups cried. Father didn't cry; he didn't look, either.

Joe went and talked to Father by and by, but Sarah and Pattie stood at a porthole all day long, and saw the world shrink and shrink and diminish down till it looked like a round cloudy glass marble that you could have rolled on the palm of your hand. Pattie was looking forward to going past the moon, but that was no fun at all, for the ship passed by the dark side and we saw nothing of it. And then we were flying in a wide black starry sky, where none of the stars had names.

At first there were voices from the world below, but not for long. The Disaster from which we were escaping happened much sooner than they had thought it would, and after two days the ship was flying in radio silence, alone, and navigating with a calculator program on the computer, and a map of magnetic fields.

The journey was very boring. It was so long. The spaceship was big enough to frighten us when we thought of it flying through the void. Joe kept telling Pattie not to worry. "Heavy things *don't* fall down in space," he told her. "There's nowhere for them to fall; no gravity."

"When I knock things over, they fall down, just like at home," Pattie said, doubtfully.

"That's just the ship's gravity machine, making it happen inside the ship," said Joe. "To make us feel normal."

But the ship was *small* enough to frighten us too, when we thought of spending years inside it. "We will still be here when I'm fourteen!" said Joe, as though he found that as hard to believe as Pattie found the lack of gravity.

"Better get used to it, then," said Sarah. We had pills to make us sleep a lot of the time, but the rules said everyone had to be awake some of each forty-eight hours. When people were awake, they played games, which were all on the ship's computer and could be played with the video screens. And one of the grownups had even brought along as his special luxury a funny hand set for playing chess which let you play it with another person instead of with the computer. When we weren't playing games, we could read the books we had brought. Joe asked Father why there were no books to read on the computer screens.

Father told us that all the new, well-equipped spaceships belonged to big wealthy countries. They had flown off to find distant, promising-looking planets. "We were the bottom of the barrel," he said, "the last few to go from an old and poorer country, and only an old ship available, and no time to outfit it properly. Our computer was intended for exploration journeys, not for colonization. It has no spare memory; it can barely manage our minimum needs. And there was so little fuel we couldn't get lift-off with anything extra on board—no useful livestock, like sheep or cows; just ourselves, and what the organizers thought we needed for survival. But we are lucky to be away at all, remember, and they allocated us a much nearer destination so that our old ship could get us somewhere."

There were some chickens in cages on the ship, with two very noisy cocks who had lost their sense of timing in the flight through darkness and crowed at all the wrong times when we were trying to sleep. And there were rabbits too; we could let them out and play with them. Rabbits are fun when you are very small and like furry things, but they aren't much fun, really. You can't teach them tricks. All they ever think about is munching. And when we got bored with rabbits, all we had was that one book each to go back to. Of course, we tried to read slowly. "Read each sentence at least twice, before you read another," the rule books said, under "Helpful Suggestions." But Sarah couldn't read that slowly. At home she read four or five books every week. She finished her book quickly and then wanted to borrow Pattie's.

Pattie wouldn't let her. So she swapped with Joe, and read his. He had brought *Robinson Crusoe*. Sarah didn't much like *Robinson Crusoe*.

"You'd better think about him, old girl," Joe said to her. "That island is just like where we're going, and we have to scratch a living on it, just like Crusoe."

Joe didn't like Sarah's book any better than she liked his. Hers was called *The Pony Club Rides Again*. Joe didn't like horses, and he couldn't resist telling Sarah that, after all, she would never see a horse again as long as she lived.

So then they both wanted to borrow Pattie's book. Pattie wouldn't lend it. "I haven't finished it myself yet," she kept saying. "It's not fair. You finished yours before you had to lend it."

In the end, Father made her give it to them. It was thin and neat, with dark green silky boards covered with gold tooling. The edges of the pages were gilded and shiny. It had a creamy silk ribbon to mark the place, and pretty brown and white flowered endpapers. And it was quite empty.

"There's nothing in it!" cried Sarah, staring.

"It's a commonplace book," said Joe.

"What's that?" asked Sarah.

"A sort of jotter, notebook thing, for thoughts you want to keep."

"And she's been pretending to read it for months!" said Sarah, beginning to giggle. They both laughed and laughed. Other people came by and asked what the joke was. Everyone laughed.

"Oh, Pattie, dear child," said Father when he heard about it. He didn't laugh, he looked a mixture between sad and cross.

"It was my choose," said Pattie very fiercely, taking her book back and holding it tight.

Father said, "She was too young. I should have chosen for her. But no use crying over spilt milk."

We did get used to being on the ship, in the end. A funny thing happened to the way people felt about it. At first, everyone had hated it, grumbled all the time about tiny cubicles, about no exercise, about nothing to do. They had quarreled a lot. Grownup quarreling isn't very nice. We were luckier than most families; we didn't seem to quarrel, though we got very cross and scratchy about things, just like other people. But time went by, and people settled down to playing games, and sleeping, and talking a little, and got used to it, and so when at last everyone had had four birthdays on the ship, and the journey had been going on for what seemed like forever and ever, and the Guide told us all there were only months to go now, people were worried instead of glad.

"We shall be lucky if we can walk more than three steps, we're so flabby," said Father, and people began to do pushups in their cabins, and line up for a turn on the cycle machine for exercising legs.

Joe began to ask a lot of questions. He didn't like the answers he got and he talked to Pattie and Sarah about it after lights-out in sleeping times. "They just don't know what this place is going to be like," he told them. "They *think* it should support life; they know there is plant growth on it, and they suppose that means we could grow wheat. But there may be wild animals, or any kind of monster people on it already, they don't know."

"Couldn't there possibly be wild ponies, Joe?" said Sarah.

"No, sis, I don't think so," said Joe, very kindly. "And if this place isn't any good, we can't go anywhere else. The fuel won't last."

* * * * *

A time came when we reached the light of a new sun. Bright golden light filled the spaceship from the starboard portholes. The cocks woke up and crowed as if for all the missing mornings on the whole long trip. The sun warmed the ship, and made it hard to sleep at sleeping time. And then the new planet loomed up on the starboard side. It looked unlike the Earth, said the grownups, who could remember what the Earth had looked like. It was redder and shinier; it had no cloud drifts around it. When it got near, it looked like maps in bright colors. It didn't look green. People spent all day looking anxiously through the portholes at it, trying to guess the meaning of what they could see. Just before touchdown, we could all see a land with mountains, craggy and rocky, and large lakes lying on the land surface everywhere; but as the ship came in to land, nightfall was racing us across the ground—a big black shadow, engulfing everything, moving faster than we were ourselves, its crescent edge going at a dizzy speed, and leaving us behind, so that we landed in total darkness. It was an auto-control landing anyway. It happened smoothly. The ship landed at a steep angle, but immediately straightened up by leveling its podlike legs. Then it switched off its own gravity and hummed quietly into run-down cycles.

When the gravity machine switched off, everyone felt lightheaded, and, indeed, light. The planet's own gravity was less than the ship had got us used to. Pattie found she could jump up and touch her cabin roof, and land without thudding enough to make anyone cross. Everyone felt full of energy, and eagerness to get out. But the Guide said the ship must be kept locked till daylight. So little was known, it would be dangerous to go out.

Arthur, the head of one of the families, said he would go and have a look, at his own risk, and then the Guide spoke to us very sternly.

"It's natural to feel excited," he said. "But this is not a holiday. We are a handpicked group; we are the minimum number that can possibly survive and multiply. Between us we have the skills we require. But the loss of a single member of our party will endanger the survival of us all. There is no such thing, Arthur, as 'your own risk.' Not any more. And may we all remember that."

We sat around, fidgeting, restless, talking together in lowered voices, waiting for dawn. None of the games interested us now. Pattie couldn't sleep, though Father made her lie down on her bunk. The feeling of suspense, the unfamiliar rhythm of the machines running themselves toward shutdown, the altered pitch of the voices around her kept her awake so late, so long, that when dawn broke at last she was fast asleep and did not see it.

But Sarah told her it had come like a dark curtain being swept aside in a single rapid movement; for a few minutes there was a deep indigo light, and after that, brilliance.

The Guide walked around the ship, looking out of each porthole in turn. All that he could see was rocks, white and gray, rather glittery crags, all very near the ship, blocking any distant view. They gave Arthur a breathing mask and put him through the inner door to the ship's main hatch, closing it behind him before he opened the outer door. He came back very quickly. "Come out," he said. "The air is good."

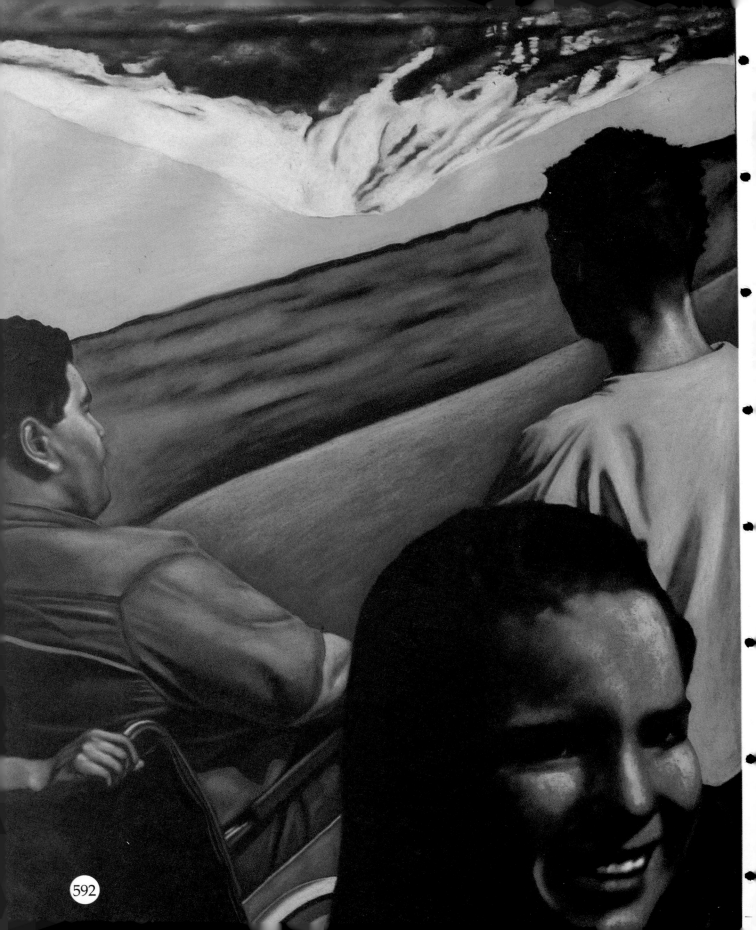

So we trooped down the ramp and found ourselves in the shadow of the ship, in a narrow gully between one rock face and another. It seemed to be a sort of hanging valley in a hill. A tiny runnel of flowing clear liquid threaded between rocks in the bottom of the dip, over a bed of silver-white sand and pebbles. Malcolm, the party's chemist, took a sample of the stream in a little specimen bottle, to test it.

Pattie was so sleepy after the night before that she could hardly walk, and Father picked her up and carried her, nodding with drowsiness, rather than leave her alone in the ship. She went in his arms, up the slope toward a gentle saddle between one side of the valley and the other, where all the others were walking. It was easy to walk, even up the slope; Pattie felt light and easy to carry. So up we all went to the rim of the hollow, and looked over.

Before us lay a wide and gentle plain sloping to the shores of a round wide lake some miles across. Beyond the lake, a very high mountain with perfectly symmetrical slopes rose into the sky, topped with snow. A mirror image of the lovely mountain hung inverted in the lake, quite still, for the surface was like glass, perfectly unruffled by even the slightest impulse of the air. The surface of the plain was gray and silver, shining like marcasite in places, in others with a pewter sheen. To the left and right of the plain, on gentle hills, were wide sweeps of woodland, with quite recognizable and normal trees, except that the leaves upon them were not green but shades of red, and shining, like the blaze of an amazing autumn. It was very beautiful, and perfectly silent, and perfectly still.

The children ran forward onto the open expanse of land before them, shouting. And at once we were limping, crying, and hopping back. We were still wearing the soft ship slippers we had been given to keep down the noise in the corridors of the spacecraft, and the pretty gray grass and flowers had cut through the thin leather at once, and cut our feet. The Guide ordered the crate of boots to be brought from the store and unpacked. Someone fetched ointment and bandages. Meanwhile, we stooped and picked the sharp plants, which broke easily in our fingers when gathered; they seemed to be made of glass, sharp and shining like jewels. But as soon as we all had boots on, we could walk over them safely, for the growth was crushed beneath the soles, as fragile and as crunchy to walk on as the frost-stiffened grass of winter on Earth.

We all walked over the crisp and sparkling frost plain, down toward the shores of the lake. It took an hour to reach it. The lake shore was a wide silver beach, made of soft bright sand, like grains of worn-down glass. And all the time we walked toward the lake, it did not move, or ruffle, even enough to shake the curtains of reflected mountain and reflected sky that hung in it. And though the air smelled good and sweet to breathe, it was windless, and as still as the air in a deep cave underground. Only the little rivulet that followed us across to the lake from the crag valley where the ship had lodged moved; it chuckled gently from stone to stone, and sparkled as brightly as the glass leaves and grass. When we got to the beach, Pattie went to look where it joined the lake, to see if it would make some splash or ripples for just a little way, but it seemed to slide beneath the surface at once and made only the faintest ripple ring, quickly dying in the brilliant mirror of the lake.

"I think we may be lucky," said the Guide. "I think this place is good."

People laughed, and some of the grownups kissed each other. The children ran to the edge of the lake and made it splash. Jason's mother ran along the beach, calling to the wading children not to drink from the lake until Malcolm had made sure it was water. Everyone was thirsty from walking, and the lake looked clear and good, but we all obediently drank from the flagons of recycled water from the ship.

"Right," said the Guide. "We shall begin the settlement program. And first we need to name the place we are about to build. The instructions suggest that the youngest person present should give the name. That can't include the real babies, obviously; Pattie or Jason—which is the youngest?"

Jason's mother and Pattie's father spoke together.

"It is Pattie, by a few days," said Father. "Well, Pattie, where are we?"

"We are at Shine, on the first day," said Pattie, solemnly.

"Good girl," said the Guide. "This place, then, is Shine. And now we must all work, and fast, for we do not know how long the days are here, or what dangers there may be." And he began to hand out jobs to each one in turn.

So people went back to the ship to unload the land truck, fill it with tents and food and sleeping bags, and bring them to the shore. Malcolm went to complete his tests for water. A work party was formed to unload the land hopper and put it together. The land hopper would glide or fly just above the ground, and let us explore quickly, and then it would run out of fuel and be of no more use. And the Guide had two men standing with guns ready, one each side of the camping ground, in case of wild beasts, or enemies.

"In science fiction, bullets go right through things and they come right on anyway, roaring, *urrrrrr*!" said Jason. "And we're in science fiction now, aren't we, so what good are guns?"

595

"We are in Shine," said Pattie. "And no monsters will come." Jason hadn't talked to her much on the flight; he was much shorter than she, and he thought she was older. But now he had found that, although she was taller, she was younger, and he got friendlier.

There was no job for either, so they watched Joe setting up a tally stick. It was a huge plastic post with rows and rows of holes in it, and black pegs to move in the holes.

"What's it for, Joe?" they asked.

"It's a calendar," said Joe. "We have to count the days here, or we'll lose track. All the things on the ship will run down and stop working—clocks, calculators, everything. So this thing just keeps a count—you move one hole for each day. You move the peg, and you remember when you are."

"A tree of days," said Pattie.

The grownups brought a stove from the ship, and a can of fuel, and set it up to cook supper on the beach, for the sand was soft and easy to sit and walk on, unlike the gray glass grass. A ring of tents went up around the stove. Malcolm decided that the little stream and the huge lake were both good water, fit to drink—and after the stale recycled water we had been drinking for so long, how fresh and clean and cool the lake water tasted! Everyone laughed again, and passed the cups from hand to hand, exclaiming.

The Guide said they must set a guard over the camp all night. "Any kind of living thing, harmless or savage, may be here," he said. The wilderness seemed so beautiful and so still it was hard to believe that, but they chose five of the men to take turns on watch.

And only just in time, for soon after the watch was chosen, the night came upon us. A curtain of deep lilac light swept across the lake, obscuring the sight of the mountain, and sinking almost at once to a deepening purple, then inky darkness. It got dark much quicker that it would have done on Earth—in less than half an hour. The darkness was complete for a moment or two; and then as our eyes got used to it, it was pierced by hundreds of bright and unknown stars—nameless constellations shining overhead. People began to spread their bedding in the tents, and to settle to sleep, and as they did so, a gust of air shook the tent walls, and there was a sighing sound of wind in the woods, and a lapping of water on the shore close by, unseen in the dark. And then the air was quite still again, and it began to rain, heavily and steadily, though the stars were still bright and clear above. When Pattie fell asleep she could hear Father and Malcolm talking together in low voices at the other end of the tent.

"There must be no dust at all in this atmosphere," said Malcolm. "That would scatter light and delay the dark. No wonder it feels so invigorating to breathe."

Father took his turn on watch, but nothing stirred all night, he said. The rain stopped in an hour or so, and not so much as a gust of air moved anywhere around. At the sudden return of daylight, all was well.

Would you want to set out on a four-year voyage to an unknown planet? Explain your answer.

Who are the people on the spaceship? Why are they making this journey to another planet?

Will people be allowed to do things their own way on the planet Shine? Why or why not?

What are the most important tasks facing the travelers once they land on their new planet?

WRITE   The children are allowed to take only one book apiece on the journey. Write a paragraph explaining what book you would take and why.

Words About the AUTHOR:

Jill Paton Walsh

Jill Paton Walsh grew up in London, England, during World War II. It was a time of danger, upset, and change for the whole world—especially for children. Ms. Walsh was born with Erb's palsy, which causes her right hand to be weak. When she was little, people thought she could not do many things and that she would have trouble learning easily in school. But young Jill found out she could do most things if she tried. In fact, when people thought she couldn't do something, it made her want to do that thing even more. Over the years, Ms. Walsh has learned there are only a few things she cannot do. She cannot lift heavy things from high shelves or be a

bell-ringer or put curlers in her hair. But these things are not important to her. What are important are all the things she is able to do despite her weak hand.

Ms. Walsh graduated from Great Britain's famous Oxford University. Then she got married and became a teacher. She quit teaching when her first baby was born, but soon she was bored. She got an old typewriter and began to write children's books. Why children's books? She says, "It never occurred to me to write any other kind." Even when she was a busy mother of three, she continued to write them because "you always have the time for what you really want to do."

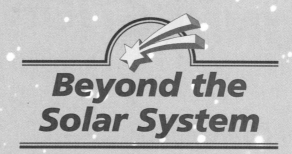

Beyond the Solar System

How did you picture outer space as described by Jill Paton Walsh in "The Green Book"? Compare your mental picture to the artist's illustration of outer space for "Secrets."

WRITER'S WORKSHOP

Many stories, movies, and television shows have outer space as their setting. They have unique characters and plots to go along with this setting. Think of your own unusual characters and plot for an outer-space setting. Then write a play in which your characters solve an exciting problem that they might encounter in space.

Writer's Choice
You have read about an imaginary trip to an imaginary planet beyond our solar system. Think about the new frontier beyond our solar system. Write down your thoughts, and come up with a way to share your response with your classmates.

CONNECTIONS

Multicultural Connection

Ancient Astronomers

Humans studied the heavens long before they believed it possible to explore them. Among the earliest and cleverest astronomers were those of ancient Egypt, in North Africa.

The Egyptians made maps of the night sky, identifying the paths of the moving stars. Their observations led them to create the most accurate of the early calendars. It had twelve months, each with thirty days, along with five extra days in each year. They also divided day and night into twelve equal parts of time and invented a very exact water clock.

Besides astronomy, these Egyptians excelled in engineering, medicine, agriculture, and many arts. They developed one of the greatest civilizations of the ancient world.

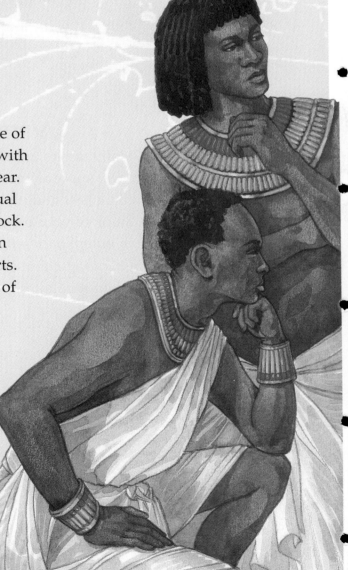

With your classmates, create a bulletin board display that shows the knowledge and the methods of early astronomers. Research such groups as the Anasazi, Aztec, Maya, Olmec, Pawnee, Tairona, Arabs, Babylonians, Chinese, Greeks, Romans, (east) Indians, and Khmer.

Social Studies Connection

Space Explorers

Since people first studied the sky long ago, we have gradually learned more about it. Research an astronomer, a pilot, an inventor, or an astronaut who helped add to our knowledge of the heavens. Share what you learn by writing a news story about this person.

Science Connection

Your Own Sky Chart

The winter nighttime sky is different from the summer nighttime sky. Find out how and why star positions change over a year. Look for interesting and unusual facts. In an oral report to your classmates, share what you have learned.

Astronaut   Aviator
Guy Bluford   Amelia Earhart

GLOSSARY

The **pronunciation** of each word in this glossary is shown by a phonetic respelling in brackets—for example, [ak'rə•bat'iks]. An accent mark (') follows the syllable with the most stress: [pes'kē]. A secondary, or lighter, accent mark (') follows a syllable with less stress: [i•vap'ə•rā'shən]. The key to other pronunciation symbols is below. You will find a shortened version of this key on alternate pages of the glossary.

Pronunciation Key*

a	add, map	m	move, seem	u	up, done
ā	ace, rate	n	nice, tin	û(r)	burn, term
â(r)	care, air	ng	ring, song	yo͞o	fuse, few
ä	palm, father	o	odd, hot	v	vain, eve
b	bat, rub	ō	open, so	w	win, away
ch	check, catch	ô	order, jaw	y	yet, yearn
d	dog, rod	oi	oil, boy	z	zest, muse
e	end, pet	ou	pout, now	zh	vision, pleasure
ē	equal, tree	o͝o	took, full	ə	the schwa, an
f	fit, half	o͞o	pool, food		unstressed vowel
g	go, log	p	pit, stop		representing the
h	hope, hate	r	run, poor		sound spelled
i	it, give	s	see, pass		a in *above*
ī	ice, write	sh	sure, rush		e in *sicken*
j	joy, ledge	t	talk, sit		i in *possible*
k	cool, take	th	thin, both		o in *melon*
l	look, rule	t̶h̶	this, bathe		u in *circus*

*The Pronunciation Key, adapted entries, and the Short Key that appear on the following pages are reprinted from *HBJ School Dictionary*. Copyright © 1990 by Harcourt Brace & Company. Reprinted by permission of Harcourt Brace & Company.

602

A

a·bate [ə·bāt'] *v.* **a·bat·ed,
a·bat·ing** To gradually
become less.

ab·er·ra·tion [ab'ə·rā'shən] *n.*
A departure from what is
right, correct, or natural: **A
four-leaf clover is an** *aberration* **of nature.**

a·brupt·ly [ə·brupt'lē] *adv.*
Suddenly: **Felix** *abruptly*
**stopped singing when he
forgot the words.**

a·bun·dant [ə·bun'dənt] *adj.*
Very plentiful: **Tomatoes
from the garden were so
abundant this year that we
couldn't eat them all.** *syn.*
ample

ac·ro·bat·ics [ak'rə·bat'iks] *n.*
Showy, skillful, and difficult
movements: **The monkeys
were swinging from branch
to branch and doing
acrobatics in the treetops.**
syn. gymnastics

a·dapt [ə·dapt'] *v.* **a·dapt·ed,
a·dapt·ing** To change to fit
certain conditions. *syns.* adjust,
conform

ad·just [ə·just'] *v.* **ad·just·ed,
ad·just·ing** To reposition or
reset something. *syns.* re-
arrange, regulate

al·le·giance [ə·lē'jəns] *n.* A
strong support of something:
**On some national holidays,
we sing patriotic songs to
show our pride in and our
allegiance to our country.**
syns. devotion, loyalty

al·lo·cate [al'ə·kāt'] *v.*
al·lo·cat·ed, al·lo·cat·ing To
set something apart for a special use: **Mr. Flores** *allocated* a
**part of his garden for beans
and a part for peppers and
tomatoes.**

am·a·teur [am'ə·choŏr *or*
am'ə·t(y)oŏr] *adj.* For enjoy-
ment rather than money; not
professional: **Joyce plays in an
amateur soccer league on
weekends.**

am·ble [am'bəl] *v.* **am·bled,
am·bling** To walk very slowly:
**The young puppy scurried
rapidly across the room, but its
mother merely *ambled*.** *syn.*
stroll

a·nat·o·my [ə·nat'ə·mē] *n.* The
structure of a person, a plant,
or an animal: **Doctors must
understand human *anatomy*
thoroughly.**

anx·ious·ly [angk'shəs·lē] *adv.*
In a worried way: **We waited
anxiously during my sister's
surgery.** *syn.* uneasily

ap·pro·pri·ate [ə·prō'prē·it] *adj.*
Right or proper; right to do at
a certain time: **It is *appropriate*
to send flowers when some-
one is sick.** *syn.* suitable

ar·ti·fi·cial [är'tə·fish'əl] *adj.*
Not made from nature: **Mr.
Fernandez bought an *artifi-
cial* Christmas tree for his
family last year.**

as·bes·tos [as·bes'təs] *n.* A min-
eral that will not burn or let heat
pass through it: **Before it was
found to be harmful to our
lungs, *asbestos* was used to
keep heat from escaping from
homes.**

amateur Athletes who
are paid for playing are
called *professionals*. Those
who take part in sports for
the sheer love of it, without payment, are known
as *amateurs*. Indeed, this
word means "lover." It
came into English by way
of French from the Latin
word *amare*, meaning "to
love."

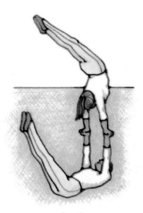

acrobatics

a	add	o͞o	took
ā	ace	o͞o	pool
â	care	u	up
ä	palm	û	burn
e	end	yo͞o	fuse
ē	equal	oi	oil
i	it	ou	pout
ī	ice	ng	ring
o	odd	th	thin
ō	open	th	this
ô	order	zh	vision

ə = { a in *above*   e in *sicken*
      i in *possible*
      o in *melon*   u in *circus* }

camouflage

cartwheel

chortle Sometimes writers like to coin, or invent, words. Once in a while, these words catch on with readers and become an everyday part of the language. In 1872, Lewis Carroll, the author of *Alice's Adventures in Wonderland,* coined the word *chortle.* Actually he took two words, *chuckle* and *snort,* and, as linguists say, "blended" them.

---

as·sure [ə·shoŏr′] *v.* **as·sured, as·sur·ing** To make someone feel certain or convinced. *syn.* guarantee

a·stray [ə·strā′] *adv.* Off the correct path; away from the mark.

at·mos·phere [at′məs·fir] *n.* The air around the earth.

au·thor·ize [ô′thə·rīz′] *v.* **au·thor·ized, au·thor·iz·ing** To give the right or permission to do something: **Mr. Wilson** *authorized* **Carmello to take attendance before every meeting.**

au·to·mat·i·cal·ly [ô′tə·mat′ik·lē] *adv.* Like a machine; without trying or thinking first: **Lindell** *automatically* **washes his face every morning before getting dressed.**

B

beam [bēm] *v.* **beamed, beam·ing** To smile happily: **When the teacher praised his poem, Cesar** *beamed* **with pride.** *syn.* grin

beck·on [bek′ən] *v.* **beck·oned, beck·on·ing** To call by motioning silently or by sending a signal.

brack·ish [brak′ish] *adj.* Somewhat salty: **Thomas tasted the** *brackish* **water on his lips.**

C

ca·jole [kə·jōl′] *v.* **ca·joled, ca·jol·ing** To coax, plead, or persuade: **I hope Alex** *cajoles* **Mark into joining us.**

---

cam·ou·flage [kam′ə·fläzh′] *v.* **cam·ou·flaged, cam·ou·flag·ing** To hide by changing one's looks to blend in with the surroundings: **The soldier** *camouflaged* **herself in the woods by putting green, leafy tree branches on her helmet.**

car·a·van [kar′ə·van′] *n.* A group of people traveling together.

car·bo·hy·drate [kär′bō·hī′drāt′] *n.* An important class of foods, supplying energy to the body: **People all over the world eat bread, which provides them with** *carbohydrates.*

ca·reen [kə·rēn′] *v.* **ca·reened, ca·reen·ing** To sway or lean over to one side: **The speeding car hit a curb and then** *careened* **on two wheels, throwing the passenger across the seat.**

cart·wheel [kärt′(h)wēl′] *n.* A sideways flip that is done by springing the body onto one hand and then the other, followed by the feet: **The gymnast turned three** *cartwheels* **and landed perfectly on his feet.**

cha·grined [shə·grind′] *adj.* Upset because of disappointment or failure: **After she dropped the ball, Maria looked** *chagrined.*

chauf·feur [shō′fər] *n.* A person employed as a driver: **The contest winner will be picked up by a** *chauffeur* **in a limousine.**

chor·tle [chôr′təl] *v.* To make a chuckling or snorting noise. *syn.* chuckle

cir·cu·late [sûr′kyə·lāt′] *v.* To move about or around: **I opened the window to let the air** *circulate*.

cit·i·zen [sit′ə·zən] *n.* A person whose legal home is in a certain place: **Elena and Ramon became U.S.** *citizens* **six years after they moved from Mexico.**

civ·il de·fense [siv′əl di·fens′] *n.* Program for protecting the public from attack or disaster, such as a flood or tornado.

col·lide [kə·līd′] *v.* **col·lid·ed, col·lid·ing** To come together with great force: **The car raced through a red stoplight and** *collided* **with a truck.** *syns.* crash, smash

col·o·ni·za·tion [kol′ə·nə·zā′shən] *n.* The act of setting up homes in a new place with the purpose of living there a long time: **Some people believe we should consider** *colonization* **of the moon.**

com·mo·tion [kə·mō′shən] *n.* Noisy confusion: **The** *commotion* **was caused by raccoons trying to get into the garbage cans.** *syns.* disturbance, uproar, agitation

com·pli·ment [kom′plə·mənt] *n.* Praise; nice words said about someone: **Lucia gave her brother a** *compliment* **for the careful way he had planned the party.** *syn.* flattery

com·pound [kom·pound′] *v.* **com·pound·ed, com·pound·ing** To make by mixing together.

com·pute [kəm·pyo͞ot′] *v.* **com·put·ed, com·put·ing** To figure mathematically. *syns.* calculate, reckon

con·ceal [kən·sēl′] *v.* To hide something.

con·jure [kon′jər *or* kun′jər] *v.* **con·jured, con·jur·ing** To seem to create by magic.

con·sis·tent [kən·sis′tənt] *adj.* Sticking to the same principles or ways of acting: **Julia's leadership with her playmates is** *consistent* **with her leadership with her classmates.**

con·tra·dict [kon′trə·dikt′] *v.* **con·tra·dict·ed, con·tra·dict·ing** To state the opposite of: **The defendant admits his guilt after an eyewitness** *contradicts* **his testimony.**

con·trap·tion [kən·trap′shən] *n. informal* An invention, such as a machine, that is odd and unusual: **Miguel built a** *contraption* **for watering his lawn from some wood, a hose, and a power lawn mower.**

cor·ri·dor [kôr′ə·dər] *n.* A long hallway or passageway with rooms opening onto it: **We walked down three** *corridors* **before we found our hotel room.**

cre·a·tiv·i·ty [krē′ā·tiv′ə·tē] *n.* The ability to make or invent things: *Creativity* **is a quality shared not only by artists and scientists but by anyone who is good at solving problems.** *syns.* originality, inventiveness

crim·i·nal [krim′ə·nəl] *adj.* Having to do with crime or those involved in crime.

crit·i·cal [krit′i·kəl] *adj.* Very important: **Completing every assignment is** *critical* **to your success.** *syns.* crucial, decisive

conceal

contraption If you created a device from assorted parts of different objects, you might refer to your invention as a *contraption*. Indeed, the word *contraption* is itself a kind of contraption: It is believed by some word experts to be a humorous blend of the words *contrive, trap,* and *invention*.

a	add	o͝o	took
ā	ace	o͞o	pool
â	care	u	up
ä	palm	û	burn
e	end	yo͞o	fuse
ē	equal	oi	oil
i	it	ou	pout
ī	ice	ng	ring
o	odd	th	thin
ō	open	ŧħ	this
ô	order	zh	vision

ə = { a in *above*   e in *sicken*
       i in *possible*
       o in *melon*   u in *circus*

605

debut　When a rookie baseball player steps up to the plate for the first time in the major leagues, we say that he is making his *debut*. This is an especially appropriate use of *debut* because the word first appeared in the world of sports. It came from an Old French word, *desbuter*, meaning "to play first" in a game or sports match.

dedication

cul·prit [kul′prit] *n.* A person guilty of a crime or misdeed: **Based on the evidence, the police arrested him as the** *culprit. syn.* offender

cu·ri·os·i·ty [kyŏŏr′ē·os′ə·tē] *n.* The feeling of wanting to know about something: **Emiko's great** *curiosity* **about our school led her to ask many questions about our courses and teachers.**

cur·ric·u·lum [kə·rik′yə·ləm] *n.* The classes that a school requires or offers: **Math, reading, and science are part of the fifth-grade** *curriculum* **in our school.**

D

de·but [dā·byŏŏ′ *or* dā′byŏŏ′] *n.* A first appearance or performance before an audience.

de·cline [di·klīn′] *v.* **de·clined, de·clin·ing** To steadily become less: **Attendance at the football games has** *declined* **in the past year because the admission prices have risen.** *syn.* shrink

ded·i·ca·tion [ded′ə·kā′shən] *n.* 1 Devotion to something: **The doctor received an award for her** *dedication* **to her patients.** 2 A personal note in a book in which the author thanks or remembers someone: **The author's** *dedication* **to her father was on the third page of her new book.**

de·fi·ant [di·fī′ənt] *adj.* Opposing or resisting power or authority: **The angry criminal stood before the judge with a** *defiant* **look on his face.**

des·per·ate [des′pər·it] *adj.* With great need; very anxious: **Marie was** *desperate* **to get home because she was afraid she had left the iron plugged in.** *syn.* frantic

de·te·ri·o·rate [di·tir′ē·ə·rāt′] *v.* **de·te·ri·o·rat·ed, de·te·ri·o·rat·ing** To become worse or less valuable: **The new owners were alarmed to discover that the old house was** *deteriorating* **at a rapid pace.**

de·ter·mined [di·tûr′mind] *adj.* Feeling very strongly about making sure that something is done: **Allison was** *determined* **to finish building the model, even if it meant she had to work all night.** *syns.* committed, resolute

dig·ni·ty [dig′nə·tē] *n.* The quality of being respected and respecting oneself: **The winners of the trophies received the applause with pride and** *dignity. syns.* worth, pride

di·lem·ma [di·lem′ə] *n.* A situation in which a person must make a difficult choice: **The boys' difficult** *dilemma* **was whether to tell what they saw and risk punishment or to keep quiet and let a crime go unpunished.**

di·min·ish [di·min′ish] *v.* To become smaller or look smaller: **We watched the kite** *diminish* **as it went higher.**

dis·charge [dis′chärj *or* dis·chärj′] *n.* Something that is released or sent out from its source.

dis·cour·aged [dis·kûr′ijd] *adj.* Having lost courage or confidence: **Angela looked *discouraged* because her experiment would not work.**

dis·grun·tled [dis·grun′təld] *adj.* Resentful, discontented: **The *disgruntled* fans started to leave before the game was over.** *syn.* dissatisfied

dis·mayed [dis·mād′] *adj.* Feeling alarm and confusion: **The audience was *dismayed* when a stage light caught fire.** *syn.* uneasy

dra·mat·i·cal·ly [drə·mat′ik·lē] *adv.* In a sudden or alarming way: **The principal's voice boomed *dramatically* from the public address system.**

drape [drāp] *v.* draped, drap·ing To cover with a piece of cloth: **The statue was *draped* so that no one would see it before the party.**

drear·y [drir′ē] *adj.* Causing sadness: **The house with its sagging roof and broken porch was a *dreary* sight in the rain.** *syn.* gloomy

dumb·found [dum′found′] *v.* dumb·found·ed, dumb·found·ing To make silent from surprise; to shock.

dwarf [dwôrf] *v.* dwarfed, dwarf·ing To make something look small by comparison: **My baby sister is *dwarfed* by the trees she is playing under.**

E

e·lab·o·rate [i·lab′ər·it] *adj.* Complicated; carefully planned out; detailed: **The suspect told an *elaborate* story about where he was and what he was doing at the time of the crime.** *syn.* complex

e·lec·tri·cal [i·lek′tri·kəl] *adj.* Having to do with electricity, a form of energy used for light and heat. *syn.* electric

em·bank·ment [im·bangk′mənt] *n.* A wall used to hold back water: **Mr. Payo walked down the steep *embankment* toward the river.**

em·brace [im·brās′] *v.* em·braced, em·brac·ing To hug; to accept something completely: **Carlos *embraced* his stepfather's way of doing things because it was usually better.**

en·er·get·ic [en′ər·jet′ik] *adj.* Lively; not easily tired: **The most *energetic* dancer was Stephanie, who didn't stop once.**

en·gulf [in·gulf′] *v.* en·gulfed, en·gulf·ing To cover completely; to close over.

en·light·en·ing [in·līt′(ə)n·ing] *adj.* Educating, informative: **After Ms. Estrella's *enlightening* talk, we felt we had learned a great deal about whales.** *syn.* instructive

en·to·mol·o·gist [en′tə·mol′ə·jist] *n.* A scientist who studies insects: **The *entomologist* identified the insect as an earwig.**

drape

entomologist You may already know that the word ending *-logist* means "a person who studies." You probably don't know that the ancient Greek word for "insect" was *entomon*. If you put the parts together, you now know that an *entomologist* is someone who studies insects.

a	add	o͝o	took
ā	ace	o͞o	pool
â	care	u	up
ä	palm	û	burn
e	end	yo͞o	fuse
ē	equal	oi	oil
i	it	ou	pout
ī	ice	ng	ring
o	odd	th	thin
ō	open	t͟h	this
ô	order	zh	vision

ə = { a in *above*   e in *sicken*
      i in *possible*
      o in *melon*   u in *circus* }

etiquette Knowing proper *etiquette* could be the ticket for a "commoner" to mix with "polite society"—and with good reason! In French, the literal meaning of *etiquette* is "ticket."

exhibits

e·rect [i·rekt'] *v.* **e·rect·ed, e·rect·ing** To build or construct: **The students** *erected* **a pyramid made from cardboard boxes.**

et·i·quette [et'ə·kət] *n.* Rules that one should follow for polite behavior: *Etiquette* **requires that you write a thank-you note to someone who sends you a gift.** *syn.* manners

e·vap·o·ra·tion [i·vap'ə·rā'shən] *n.* The loss of water into the air: **In science class we compared the rate of** *evaporation* **from pans of water during humid and dry days.**

e·ven·tu·al·ly [i·ven'choo·əl·ē] *adv.* After the passing of some time: **The drive home from Grandmother's was very long, but we knew that we would** *eventually* **get there.** *syn.* ultimately

ev·i·dence [ev'ə·dəns] *n.* One or more facts or items that can be used as proof.

e·volve [i·volv'] *v.* **e·volved, e·volv·ing** To come into being: **Over the years, the quiet little town** *evolved* **into a big, busy city.** *syn.* develop

ex·hib·it [ig·zib'it] *n.* An item on display: **The museum has** *exhibits* **of Civil War uniforms.**

ex·pan·sion [ik·span'shən] *n.* The increase in the size of something: **The** *expansion* **of his business meant that he had to hire more employees.**

ex·pose [ik·spōz'] *v.* **ex·posed, ex·pos·ing** To make something easy to see: **The boy lifted up the heavy rock,** *exposing* **an active colony of ants underneath.** *syns.* reveal, uncover

ex·tinct [ik·stingkt'] *adj.* No longer existing or living: **If dinosaurs were not** *extinct,* **we would be able to study them in the wild and perhaps keep some in zoos.**

ex·trav·a·gant [ik·strav'ə·gənt] *adj.* Beyond reason or proper limits: **They spent an** *extravagant* **amount of money on a merry-go-round and performing clowns for the child's birthday party.**

F

fa·nat·ic [fə·nat'ik] *n.* A person whose interest in something is greater than normal: **Bonita loved baseball so much that she was not just a fan, but a** *fanatic.*

fas·ci·nate [fas'ə·nāt'] *v.* **fas·ci·nat·ed, fas·ci·nat·ing** To attract and hold interest: **She was so** *fascinated* **by the bird building its nest that she couldn't stop watching it.**

fa·tigue [fə·tēg'] *n.* A tired condition resulting from hard work, effort, or strain: **After two miles of walking,** *fatigue* **overtook me and I had to stop to rest.** *syn.* weariness

feist·y [fī′stē] *adj. informal* Very active or spirited.

flail [flāl] *v.* **flailed, flail·ing** To move wildly as if beating something: **Charles was** *flailing* **around in the water so violently that the people on the beach thought he was drowning.** *syn.* thrash

flax [flaks] *n.* A slender plant with blue flowers, used to make linen cloth: **Whenever we visit the farm, we see** *flax* **growing in the meadow.**

flick·er [flik′ər] *v.* **flick·ered, flick·er·ing** To change unsteadily from bright to dim light: **The light was** *flickering* **during the thunderstorm.**

for·lorn [fôr·lôrn′] *adj.* Sad or pitiful because alone or neglected: **The tall weeds made the house look old and** *forlorn.*

fran·tic·al·ly [fran′tik·lē′] *adv.* In a manner wild with fear, worry, pain, or rage: **The boy searched** *frantically* **for a way out of the tunnel.**

free·style [frē′stīl′] *n.* A contest in which any style of swimming may be used: **Gus's parents were proud because he won a medal for the** *freestyle* **race at the swimming meet.**

fret·ful [fret′fəl] *adj.* Restless and unhappy or seeming to be: **The music sounded** *fretful,* **like screeching birds.** *syn.* irritable

fruit·less [frōōt′lis] *adj.* Without any success; useless: **Teresa knew it would be** *fruitless* **to try pushing the fallen tree, so she took a different path.**

frus·tra·tion [frus·trā′shən] *n.* A feeling of anger or disappointment at not being able or allowed to do something: **Antonia's** *frustration* **increased when she could not finish the test.**

fun·nel [fun′əl] *n.* An open cone, wide at the top with a smaller end: **Mrs. Francisco used a** *funnel* **to pour cereal into a jar.**

fur·tive [fûr′tiv] *adj.* Done in secret: **The child took a** *furtive* **peek through the curtains.** *syn.* stealthy

funnel

G

gap·ing [gāp′ing] *adj.* Wide open: **The explosion left a** *gaping* **hole in the wall.**

gasp [gasp] *v.* **gasped, gasp·ing** To pant breathlessly. *syns.* puff, wheeze

gin·ger·ly [jin′jər·lē] *adv.* In a careful or reluctant manner: **I** *gingerly* **lifted the priceless vase.** *syn.* cautiously

gnarled [närld] *adj.* Twisted or knotted. *syn.* tangled

goad [gōd] *v.* **goad·ed, goad·ing** To use some object to make an animal move: **Luz was** *goading* **the horse with a small stick so that it would run faster.**

graf·fi·ti [grə·fē′tē] *n. pl.* Words illegally written or painted in public places: **The** *graffiti* **on the buildings and fences made the city look very ugly.**

gnarled

a	add	o͝o	took
ā	ace	o͞o	pool
â	care	u	up
ä	palm	û	burn
e	end	yo͞o	fuse
ē	equal	oi	oil
i	it	ou	pout
ī	ice	ng	ring
o	odd	th	thin
ō	open	th	this
ô	order	zh	vision

ə = { a in *above*   e in *sicken*
i in *possible*
o in *melon*   u in *circus* }

609

gunnysack When you say *gunnysack*, you are repeating yourself. *Goni* is the word for "sack" in Hindi, a language of northern India. So a *gunnysack* is really a "sack sack."

horizontal

grap·ple [grap′əl] *v.* **grap·pled, grap·pling** To grab and struggle. *syns.* wrestle, contend

grove [grōv] *n.* A group of trees.

guile [gīl] *n.* Cleverness; the ability to trick others: **The spy used *guile* to win the trust of the official and trick her into giving him the plans.** *syn.* slyness

gun·ny·sack [gun′ē·sak′] *n.* A sack made out of heavy cloth.

H

hail·stone [hāl′stōn′] *n.* A small, round pellet of frozen rain.

hav·oc [hav′ək] *n.* Widespread destruction of life and property: **The hurricane roared across three states, leaving *havoc* in its wake.** *syns.* ruin, devastation

hoarse [hôrs] *adj.* Sounding husky or rough.

home·ly [hōm′lē] *adj.* Plain looking: **His *homely* face suddenly looked beautiful as he rocked the child to sleep.**

home·stead [hōm′sted′] *v.* To make a place one's home: **Pioneers of the West had to *homestead* land to earn the right to own it.** *syn.* occupy

hor·i·zon·tal [hôr′ə·zon′təl] *adj.* Level from side to side, the way the horizon looks: **Book shelves are *horizontal*.**

hy·giene [hī′jēn′] *n.* Practices that keep people clean and healthy: **Good dental *hygiene*, like toothbrushing, helps prevent cavities.**

I

i·den·ti·cal [ī·den′ti·kəl] *adj.* The very same: **The twin sisters wore clothes that were *identical* in every way.**

ig·no·rant [ig′nər·ənt] *adj.* Not knowing something: **The students were *ignorant* of the history of their state until they studied it in school.** *syn.* unaware

il·lu·mi·nate [i·lōō′mə·nāt′] *v.* **il·lu·mi·nat·ed, il·lu·mi·nat·ing** To fill with light: **We lit several candles, which *illuminated* the room.**

im·pro·vise [im′prə·vīz′] *v.* **im·pro·vised, im·pro·vis·ing** To make up at the time of performance; to make from whatever material is available: **The campers used large, flat rocks to *improvise* a table.**

in·crim·i·nat·ing [in·krim′ə·nāt′ing] *adj.* Showing proof of guilt: **The burglary tools found in the trunk of his car were considered *incriminating* evidence by the jury.**

in·di·cate [in′də·kāt′] *v.* To show or describe: **The directions *indicate* which way we should turn.**

in·dig·nant [in·dig′nənt] *adj.* Angry because of something that is not right, just, or fair: **Ricardo became *indignant* when his older brother wouldn't let him play the game.**

in·flu·en·tial [in′floo·en′shəl] *adj.* Important; able to change people's thoughts on something: **Albert Einstein was an *influential* scientist because his work changed the way people think about the universe.**

in·her·it [in·her′it] *v.* To receive something, usually from a parent or relative, after that person dies: **When his aunt dies, Sergio will *inherit* her house.**

in·i·ti·a·tive [in·ish′(ē·)ə·tiv] *n.* The ability to start something or take the first step: **Mr. Díaz has the *initiative* necessary to become a good salesman.**

in·suf·fi·cient [in′sə·fish′ənt] *adj.* Not enough: **We could not make tacos because we had *insufficient* amounts of tomatoes and cheese.** *syn.* inadequate

in·tel·lec·tu·al·ly [in′tə·lek′choo·əl·ē] *adv.* In a way that uses or shows the reasoning powers of the mind: **Computer programming can be *intellectually* satisfying work.**

in·tim·i·date [in·tim′ə·dāt′] *v.* To make someone afraid: **Lorenzo looks tough, but he is too nice to *intimidate* anyone.**

in·ven·tive·ness [in·ven′tiv·nis] *n.* Skill at creating things: **Luisa's *inventiveness* helped her win first prize in her class's Build-a-Better-Mousetrap contest.** *syns.* creativity, originality

ir·re·sis·ti·bly [ir′i·zis′tə·blē] *adv.* In a way that cannot be overcome or opposed: **Although I was unsure of what might be in the room, my curiosity drew me *irresistibly* toward the door.** *syn.* magnetically

ir·ri·ta·tion [ir′ə·tā′shən] *n.* Something that makes a person mildly angry: **At the picnic, the bee buzzing around our food was an *irritation*.** *syn.* annoyance

J

jave·lin [jav′(ə·)lin] *n.* A spear that is thrown for distance as an athletic event: **My father won an athletic scholarship for throwing the *javelin*.**

K

keen·ing [kēn′ing] *adj.* Sharp; mournful: **The *keening* howl of the coyote made shivers run down my spine.**

L

lab·y·rinth [lab′ə·rinth] *n.* A place that has a complicated layout, like a maze: **The princess in the fairy tale could not find her way out of the forest because it was a *labyrinth* of many paths.**

labyrinth When *Labyrinth* is spelled with a capital "L," it refers to the maze in Greek mythology where the Minotaur, a mythical monster, was imprisoned.

javelin

a	add	o͝o	took
ā	ace	o͞o	pool
â	care	u	up
ä	palm	û	burn
e	end	yo͞o	fuse
ē	equal	oi	oil
i	it	ou	pout
ī	ice	ng	ring
o	odd	th	thin
ō	open	th	this
ô	order	zh	vision

ə = a in *above* e in *sicken*
i in *possible*
o in *melon* u in *circus*

limelight The chemical calcium oxide was discovered in 1808. This material, often called lime, shone with a bright white light when heated. This quality made it useful for lighting plays and shows in dark theaters. Even in the age of electrical lighting, people who are the center of public attention are "in the limelight."

lopsided

mandolin

laugh·ing·stock [laf′ing·stok′] *n.* A person or thing that is the object of ridicule: **Lorraine had turned in her homework late so many times that she was afraid she would be the** *laughingstock* **of her class.**

lime·light [līm′līt′] *n.* The attention or notice of other people. *syn.* spotlight

lop·sid·ed [lop′sī′did] *adj.* Hanging over to one side; uneven: **The cake was lower on one side, so it looked** *lopsided.*

lux·u·ry [luk′shər·ē] *n.* An item that adds to pleasure and comfort but is not necessary: **The Dillman family decided to cut back on buying** *luxuries,* **so they decided not to get a video camera.**

M

ma·chet·e [mə·shet′ē *or* mə·shet′] *n.* A long, curved knife used for cutting tall vegetation.

man·do·lin [man′də·lin *or* man′də·lin′] *n.* A musical instrument with eight to ten strings.

ma·neu·ver [mə·n(y)ōō′vər] *v.* **ma·neu·vered, ma·neu·ver·ing** To move in a skillful way: **Elbowing her way through the crowd, the photographer** *maneuvered* **herself to a position near the stage.**

mar·vel [mär′vəl] *n.* Something that is remarkable or exciting: **The white tiger was a** *marvel* **to the patrons of the circus.** *syns.* sensation, wonder

mas·sive·ly [mas′iv·lē] *adv.* Hugely; with much size and weight: **The house,** *massively* **enlarged by the two new wings, now seemed to sprawl across the whole hilltop.**

me·chan·i·cal [mə·kan′i·kəl] *adj.* Having to do with machines.

meg·a·phone [meg′ə·fōn′] *n.* A cone or electric device that makes the voice sound louder when it is spoken into.

met·a·mor·pho·sis [met′ə·môr′fə·sis] *n.* A change from one form, shape, or substance into another: **In science class, we watched the** *metamorphosis* **of a tadpole into a frog.**

me·te·or·ol·o·gist [mē′tē·ə·rol′ə·jist] *n.* A person who studies the weather.

mim·ic [mim′ik] *v.* **mim·icked, mim·ick·ing** To imitate: **The parrot** *mimicked* **every word I said.**

min·gle [ming′gəl] *v.* **min·gled, min·gling** To join or mix together: **At the party Oscar** *mingled* **with the other guests, but he still felt out of place.** *syn.* associate

mis·er·a·ble [miz′ər·ə·bəl] *adj.* 1 Causing unhappiness. 2 Shameful: **The** *miserable* **conditions at the jail caused problems among the prisoners.**

mis·giv·ing [mis·giv′ing] *n.* A feeling of worry: **Michael had** *misgivings* **about the picnic because dark storm clouds were gathering.** *syn.* qualm

mo·bile [mō′bēl] *n.* A sculpture with objects attached that moves lightly as air passes it: **Rosa made a** *mobile* **out of wood and paper and hung it over her sister's crib.**

mol·e·cule [mol′ə·kyool′] *n.* A tiny particle: **Scientists tell us that** *molecules* **and atoms are the basic building blocks of everything in the world.**

mor·sel [môr′səl] *n.* A little piece of food: **Kay loved the cake, and she ate every tiny** *morsel* **on her plate.** *syn.* bit

mourn·ful·ly [môrn′fəl·ē] *adv.* In a sad manner. *syn.* sorrowfully

muf·fled [muf′əld] *adj.* Having a deadened sound: **Even though the twins laughed into their pillows, Mother could hear their** *muffled* **giggles through the door.**

mus·ket [mus′kit] *n.* An old type of gun with a long barrel, similar to a rifle: **Each soldier in the volunteer army brought his own** *musket.*

mys·ti·fied [mis′tə·fīd] *adj.* Puzzled or not able to figure something out: **Rick was** *mystified* **by the strange sound and decided to find out exactly where it was coming from.**

N

nau·seous [nô′shəs *or* nô′zē·əs] *adj.* Sick to the stomach.

nav·i·gate [nav′ə·gāt′] *v.* **nav·i·gat·ed, nav·i·gat·ing** To control or decide in which direction something will go: **Bernardo was** *navigating* **the boat, and I was rowing.**

near·sight·ed [nir′sī′tid] *adj.* Able to see only things close by: *Nearsighted* **people often need glasses so they can see what is written on signs.** *syn.* myopic

nes·tle [nes′əl] *v.* **nes·tled, nes·tling** To sit very close to someone else: **All five children** *nestled* **together on the small couch.** *syns.* cuddle, snuggle

neu·tral [n(y)oo′trəl] *n.* Someone who is not on either side during a war: **During the American Revolution the** *neutrals* **refused to take the side of either the colonists or the British.**

non·cha·lant [non′shə·länt′] *adj.* Showing a jaunty coolness: **Paulo seemed** *nonchalant* **about winning the tennis match, but we knew he was excited.** *syns.* unexcited, unconcerned

O

ob·sti·nate [ob′stə·nit] *adj.* Stubbornly holding to one's opinions or purposes: **The** *obstinate* **child refused to eat his carrots.** *syn.* unyielding

ob·vi·ous [ob′vē·əs] *adj.* Easily noticed or understood: **The rainstorm makes it** *obvious* **that we can't play outside today.**

musket

nauseous Have you ever been seasick? The ancient Greeks associated this feeling with sea voyages and named it *nausia* from *naus,* their word for "ship." Some dictionaries state that *nauseous* strictly means "causing sickness," not "being sick." However, other dictionaries do accept the latter meaning as standard.

a	add	oo	took
ā	ace	oo	pool
â	care	u	up
ä	palm	û	burn
e	end	yoo	fuse
ē	equal	oi	oil
i	it	ou	pout
ī	ice	ng	ring
o	odd	th	thin
ō	open	th	this
ô	order	zh	vision

ə = { a in *above* e in *sicken* i in *possible* o in *melon* u in *circus* }

pendulum

parlor The room in your house called the *living room* was once known as the *parlor*. This word is related to the French word *parler*, meaning "to speak." A *parlor*, then, was a room in which people gathered to talk with each other.

off·hand·ed [ôf'han'did] *adj.* Without a lot of care or planning: **Because Tom told us about the play in an *offhanded* way, we didn't think he cared if we came.** *syn.* casual

op·po·nent [ə·pō'nənt] *n.* A person or group that takes the opposite position, as in sports. *syn.* rival

or·i·gin [ôr'ə·jin] *n.* The first use or the beginning: **Our class learned about the *origin* of the use of silver by Native American artists.**

or·nate·ly [or·nāt'lē] *adv.* In a way that involves much decoration: **Renaldo gave Lydia a package *ornately* wrapped with gold paper and silver ribbons.**

out·skirts [out'skûrts'] *n. pl.* The outer edges or areas far from the center of a city: **We drove to the *outskirts* of town to picnic by a quiet lake.**

P

pan·to·mime [pan'tə·mīm'] *n.* A play in which actors use only gestures with no speech. *v.* To express in gestures alone.

parch·ment [pärch'mənt] *n.* A scraped and dried piece of animal skin used to write or paint upon.

par·lor [pär'lər] *n.* A room that is usually used for talking or entertaining.

par·tic·i·pa·tion [pär·tis'ə·pā'shən] *n.* The act of getting involved with others: *Participation* in team sports can be fun.

pe·cul·iar [pi·kyōōl'yər] *adj.* Oddly different from the usual: **My dog has a *peculiar* habit of eating cat food.**

pe·des·tri·an [pə·des'trē·ən] *n.* A person who walks: **A *pedestrian* must obey traffic signals too!**

pelt·ing [pel'ting] *adj.* Striking over and over: **Seeking cover from the *pelting* rain, the kitten ran under the porch.**

pen·du·lum [pen'jōō·ləm *or* pen'də·ləm] *n.* A weight that hangs down and swings evenly from side to side: **A large clock with a *pendulum* is usually called a grandfather clock.**

per·ish·a·ble [per'ish·ə·bəl] *adj.* Likely to spoil.

per·ma·nent [pûr'mən·ənt] *adj.* Meant to last without changing: **This time, Robert's cure was *permanent*, and the illness did not come back.** *syn.* enduring

per·mis·sion [pər·mish'ən] *n.* An act by one person that allows someone else to do something: **Ashley asked for her mother's *permission* to go to the dance.** *syns.* approval, consent

per·sist [pər·sist'] *v.* **per·sist·ed, per·sist·ing** To keep doing something; insist: **Lome *persisted* in bouncing the ball on the floor, even after I asked him not to.** *syn.* continue

pes·ky [pes'kē] *adj. informal* Annoying; being like a pest.

phy·si·cian [fi·zish'ən] *n.* A medical doctor: **Our family *physician* prescribed penicillin when I had a sore throat and a fever.**

plum·met [plum′it] *v.*
plum·met·ed, plum·met·ing
To fall quickly: **The heavy
rock** *plummeted* **to the bottom
of the pond.**

pounce [pouns] *v.* **pounced,
pounc·ing** To jump onto something: **The cat** *pounced* **happily
on the ball of yarn.** *syn.* leap

pred·a·tor [pred′ə·tər] *n.* A person or animal that lives by
preying on others: **A porcupine uses its quills as a
defense against** *predators.*

pre·fer [pri·fûr′] *v.* **pre·ferred,
pre·fer·ring** To like one thing
better than another: **Mrs.
McCormick** *preferred* **working
in her vegetable garden to
seeing a movie.**

pre·his·tor·ic [prē′his·tôr′ik]
adj. From the time before historical records were kept:
**Since they left no written
records, the only way to learn
about** *prehistoric* **humans is to
study their drawings and the
things they made.** *syn.* ancient

pre·miere [pri·mir′] *n.* The first
showing or display: **We're
going to the** *premiere* **of
Ellen's new play.**

pres·er·va·tion
[prez′ər·vā′shən] *n.* The act of
keeping from danger or harm:
**Juan helped raise money for
the** *preservation* **of the city's
oldest schoolhouse.**

prick·le [prik′əl] *v.* **prick·led,
prick·ling** To tingle or sting.
syn. tingle

priv·i·lege [priv′ə·lij] *n.* A special benefit, favor, or advantage:
**News reporters often enjoy the
privileges of meeting interesting people and traveling to far-
away places.**

pro·ce·dure [prə·sē′jər] *n.* The
specific way in which something is done: **To learn how to
work this machine, you have
to follow the** *procedure*
described in the manual.

prom·i·nent [prom′ə·nənt] *adj.*
Important; well-known: **The
mayor is the most** *prominent*
woman in our town.

pros·per·i·ty [pros·per′ə·tē] *n.*
A condition that includes
material wealth and success:
**The new mayor promised to
help the townspeople open
businesses that would bring
prosperity to their city.**

pros·per·ous [pros′pər·əs] *adj.*
Doing well: **The Joneses are a
happy,** *prosperous* **family
with good jobs, healthy children, and a big garden full of
vegetables.** *syn.* successful

pro·tein [prō′tēn′ *or* prō′tē·ən]
n. One of several substances
that are a necessary part of our
diet: **Meat, fish, dairy prod-
ucts, nuts, and beans can
supply needed** *protein* **in
our diet.**

premiere

rankle When someone's
insulting remark *rankles*
inside you, you might
imagine that a little
dragon is gnawing at you.
The Latin word for
"dragon" was *draco.* A
"little dragon" was called
dracunculus.

R

ran·kle [rang′kəl] *v.* To make
someone annoyed and mad:
**Losing the game by forfeit
still** *rankles* **Yoshio and
makes him feel angry whenever he thinks about it.**

rau·cous [rô′kəs] *adj.* Rough
in sound: **The** *raucous* **sounds
of football practice broke
through the half-open classroom windows.** *syns.* hoarse,
harsh

a	add	o͝o	took
ā	ace	o͞o	pool
â	care	u	up
ä	palm	û	burn
e	end	yo͞o	fuse
ē	equal	oi	oil
i	it	ou	pout
ī	ice	ng	ring
o	odd	th	thin
ō	open	t̶h	this
ô	order	zh	vision

ə = {a in *above*, e in *sicken*, i in *possible*, o in *melon*, u in *circus*}

re·as·sur·ance [rē′·ə·shoŏr′·əns] *n.* Freedom from doubt or fear: **Sonya was nervous about giving her speech, and she looked to her teacher for** *reassurance. syn.* confidence

re·con·struct [rē′kən·strukt′] *v.* To put something together or make it again: **After the barn blew down in the storm, we worked to** *reconstruct* **it.** *syn.* rebuild

re·en·act [rē′in·akt′] *v.* To act out again; to perform as if for the first time: **Mr. Jackson's seventh-grade class will** *reenact* **several scenes from American history for the school assembly.**

ref·uge [ref′yoōj] *n.* A place to hide: **When the bears came into the camp, the family ran to the car because it was a safe** *refuge.*

re·lieve [ri·lēv′] *v.* **re·lieved, re·liev·ing** To free from worry, pain, or unhappiness. *syn.* ease

re·luc·tant [ri·luk′tənt] *adj.* Unwilling: **Phillip was so warm and comfortable by the fire that he was** *reluctant* **to go outside into the cold.**

ren·o·vate [ren′ə·vāt] *v.* **ren·o·vat·ed, ren·o·vat·ing** To make as good as new: **These buildings looked old and shabby before they were** *renovated. syn.* repair

rep·re·sent [rep′ri·zent′] *v.* To act or speak for someone or something; to stand for something.

res·er·voir [rez′ər·vwär′ *or* rez′ər·vwôr′] *n.* A place where water is stored.

rest·less [rest′lis] *adj.* Not relaxed; eager to do something else: **Anna felt bored and** *restless* **having to sit still during the long movie.**

re·sume [ri·zoōm′] *v.* To start again after stopping: **My father's cooking class** *resumes* **after two weeks of vacation.**

re·treat [ri·trēt′] *v.* To turn around and go back to where one came from. *syn.* withdraw

rit·u·al [rich′oō·əl] *n.* A set action or series of actions: **Andy went through a** *ritual* **of pulling up his socks and tugging on his shirt every time he shot a free throw.**

rook·ie [roŏk′ē] *n.* A first-year player in sports; a beginner.

S

sar·cas·tic·al·ly [sär·kas′tik·lē] *adv.* In a mocking or taunting way: **Tracy is so clumsy that her family has** *sarcastically* **nicknamed her "Miss Graceful."**

sa·van·nah [sə·van′ə] *n.* A grassy plain that has very few trees.

scoot [skoōt] *v. informal* **scoot·ed, scoot·ing 1** To move quickly. **2** To slide something, especially while seated.

scur·ry [skûr′ē] *v.* To move about quickly. *syn.* scamper

sem·i·cir·cu·lar [sem′ē·sûr′kyə·lər] *adj.* Shaped like a half-circle: **Tiffany draws** *semicircular* **lines that look like smiles.**

savannah It was Arawak people, speaking Taino, who greeted Christopher Columbus when he landed in the West Indies. The Arawak are no more, but their language gave us the word *zabana,* which has survived as *savannah.*

reservoir

set·tle·ment [set′(ə)l·mənt] *n.* A new place for people to live: **When the pioneers first reached the valley, they built a** *settlement.*

shin·dig [shin′dig′] *n. slang* A party with noise and dancing.

shrewd·ly [shrōōd′lē] *adv.* In a practical way: **Edward** *shrewdly* **talked his sister, who was dieting, into trading her large piece of pie for his smaller one.** *syn.* slyly

shriv·el [shriv′əl] *v.* **shriv·eled, shriv·el·ing** To contract into wrinkles; shrink and dry up: **I forgot to water the plant, so its leaves have begun to** *shrivel* **and fall off.**

shud·der [shud′ər] *n.* A quick, light shaking motion; shiver: **The cold air made a** *shudder* **run through my body.**

si·mul·ta·ne·ous·ly [sī′məl·tā′nē·əs·lē] *adv.* Happening, done, or existing at the same time: **Everyone in the audience jumped** *simultaneously* **when the villain burst onstage.**

slan·der [slan′dər] *n.* A cruel, false, and sometimes illegal spoken public statement made about a person: **Anyone who publicly says something untrue about another person is guilty of** *slander.*

sleigh [slā] *n.* A carriage with runners instead of wheels that is pulled by a horse over ice or snow: **After the last snowfall, Mr. Cowley let us hitch up the horses and ride in both** *sleighs.*

smoth·er [smuth′ər] *v.* **smoth·ered, smoth·er·ing** To hide or suppress: **She** *smothered* **a laugh with her handkerchief.**

so·ber·ing [sō′bər·ing] *adj.* Serious; causing to be suddenly aware and able to think clearly.

sol·emn·ly [sol′əm·lē] *adv.* Quietly and seriously: **Mr. Jenkins** *solemnly* **read the names of the people who had been injured.**

star·board [stär′bərd] *adj.* The right-hand side of a ship as one faces the bow: **We looked for sharks and whales over the** *starboard* **railing.**

stat·ic [stat′ik] *n.* A rough sound that comes from a radio or television set that is not receiving properly.

stow [stō] *v.* **stowed, stow·ing** To store; put away.

stu·pen·dous [st(y)ōō·pen′dəs] *adj.* Wonderful. *syn.* fabulous

sub·mit [səb·mit′] *v.* To say or to put something forward for someone else's reaction; to suggest in a formal way.

sue [sōō] *v.* To ask a court to solve a problem legally.

suf·fra·gist [suf′rə·jist] *n.* A person who thinks that the right to vote should be extended to others.

sum·mit [sum′it] *n.* The top of a mountain. *syn.* peak

sup·port [sə·pôrt′] *v.* To provide food and clothing and other necessities: **Mrs. Swoboda will** *support* **the family while her husband looks for a new job.**

shindig The only thing word experts agree on is that *shindig* comes from Ireland. The word may have come from a game called *shindy,* a wild kind of hockey played on a field with balls and curved sticks. Or *shindig* may go back to the Irish word *sinteag,* which means "a skip" or "a jump."

sleigh

a	add	o͝o	took
ā	ace	o͞o	pool
â	care	u	up
ä	palm	û	burn
e	end	yo͞o	fuse
ē	equal	oi	oil
i	it	ou	pout
ī	ice	ng	ring
o	odd	th	thin
ō	open	th	this
ô	order	zh	vision

ə = a in *above*   e in *sicken*
    i in *possible*
    o in *melon*   u in *circus*

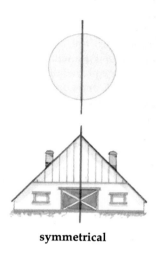

symmetrical

unanimously   If you and your classmates voted *unanimously* on an issue, you would all be in agreement, or of one mind. *Unanimous* comes from the Latin words *unus,* meaning "one," and *animus,* meaning "soul or mind."

tumble

sur·feit [sûr′fit] *n.* Too much of something. *syn.* over-abundance

swag·ger [swag′ər] *v.* **swag·gered, swag·ger·ing** To walk in a boastful and proud way. *syn.* strut

sym·met·ri·cal [si·met′ri·kəl] *adj.* Alike on both sides.

T

ta·per [tā′pər] *v.* To fade; to decrease in amount or size.

tech·nol·o·gy [tek·nol′ə·jē] *n.* A way to use science to produce useful things: **Computers and cars both make use of modern *technology*.**

temp·ta·tion [tem·tā′shən] *n.* An instant urge or desire: **The *temptation* to eat the cookies may be too much to resist.**

ter·rain [tə·rān′] *n.* The features of an area of land: **The race was run on rough *terrain* of steep hills and rocky valleys.**

ter·rar·i·um [tə·râr′ē·əm] *n.* A transparent container in which small land animals or plants are kept: **Our group built a *terrarium* for hermit crabs.**

tes·ti·mo·ny [tes′tə·mō′nē] *n.* The answers that must be given truthfully to a lawyer's questions in court.

tour·na·ment [tŏor′nə·mənt *or* tûr′nə·mənt] *n.* A set number of contests that includes many teams or players and produces one winner overall.

trai·tor [trā′tər] *n.* A person who goes against his or her family, friends, or country to join the opposite side during a war. *syn.* betrayer

trans·form [trans·fôrm′] *v.* **trans·formed, trans·form·ing** To change the form or appearance of: **The caterpillar is now *transforming* itself into a butterfly.**

trans·mis·sion [trans·mish′ən] *n.* The sending of pictures or sounds through the air, as by radio or television.

trans·par·ent [trans·pâr′ənt] *adj.* Easily seen through: **The wings on this butterfly look as if they are *transparent*.** *syn.* clear

tum·ble [tum′bəl] *v.* **tum·bled, tum·bling** To turn over and over: **The puppies were rolling and *tumbling* on the carpet.**

tur·bu·lence [tûr′byə·ləns] *n.* Wind currents that move very quickly.

U

ul·ti·mate·ly [ul′tə·mit·lē] *adv.* Finally; at the end: **We will *ultimately* arrive in California after we stop in Arizona for a rest.**

u·nan·i·mous·ly [yŏō·nan′ə·məs·lē] *adv.* With all voters voting the same way: **Sasheen was *unanimously* elected class president when all the students voted for her.**

un·in·spired [un′in·spīrd′] *adj.* Showing no originality: **The committee rejected the building plans as boring and** *uninspired.* *syn.* unimaginative

un·veil [un·vāl′] *v.* **un·veiled, un·veil·ing** To remove the covering from: **The new statue will be** *unveiled* **today.** *syn.* reveal

V

vague [vāg] *adj.* Not clearly understood.

ve·ran·da [və·ran′də] *n.* A long, open, outdoor porch along the outside of a building: **The addition of a** *veranda* **made the small house more comfortable.**

ver·ti·cal [vûr′ti·kəl] *adj.* Straight up and down.

vig·or·ous·ly [vig′ər·əs·lē] *adv.* Very fast or with great energy: **The chief** *vigorously* **waved his arms to get our attention.** *syns.* energetically, rapidly

vi·o·lent·ly [vī′ə·lənt·lē] *adv.* Harshly; with destructive force.

vis·u·al·ize [vizh′o͞o·əl·īz′] *v.* To imagine; to see something in the mind.

volt [vōlt] *n.* A measure of electricity.

W

wal·low [wol′ō] *v.* To tumble or roll with slow and lazy movements: **My cat likes to** *wallow* **in the warm sand.**

war·i·ly [wâr′ə·lē′] *adv.* In a watchful and suspicious way: **Kevin watched** *warily* **as the magician put his watch into the hat.** *syns.* carefully, cautiously

weight·less·ness [wāt′lis·nəs] *n.* Having little or no weight: **A helium-filled balloon's** *weightlessness* **will allow it to float away if you do not hold it.**

wind·break [wind′brāk′] *n.* Anything that blocks the force of the wind, such as a wall or a line of trees.

wist·ful·ly [wist′fəl·ē] *adv.* Wishing for something.

wretch·ed [rech′id] *adj.* Very unhappy: **My ankle ached so badly that I had a** *wretched* **day at school.** *syns.* miserable, poor

vague If the details of that story you just read are *vague,* maybe your mind was wandering as you turned the pages. *Vague,* in fact, is closely connected to the Latin word *vagari,* meaning "to wander." We call people who wander around aimlessly *vagabonds* and *vagrants.*

windbreak

a	add	o͞o	took
ā	ace	o͞o	pool
â	care	u	up
ä	palm	û	burn
e	end	yo͞o	fuse
ē	equal	oi	oil
i	it	ou	pout
ī	ice	ng	ring
o	odd	th	thin
ō	open	t͟h	this
ô	order	zh	vision

ə = ⎧ a in *above*   e in *sicken*
⎨ i in *possible*
⎩ o in *melon*   u in *circus*

INDEX OF
TITLES AND AUTHORS

Page numbers in light print refer to biographical information.

Acknowledgments continued

HarperCollins Publishers: "The Growin' of Paul Bunyan" from *A Telling of the Tales* by William J. Brooke. Text copyright © 1990 by William J. Brooke. "Fireflies" from *Joyful Noise* by Paul Fleischman, illustrated by Eric Beddows. Text copyright © 1988 by Paul Fleischman; illustrations copyright © 1988 by Eric Beddows. *One Day in the Desert* by Jean Craighead George. Text copyright © 1983 by Jean Craighead George. Text and cover illustration from *In the Year of the Boar and Jackie Robinson* by Bette Bao Lord, cover illustration by Marc Simont. Text copyright © 1984 by Bette Bao Lord; cover illustration copyright © 1984 by Marc Simont. *Sarah, Plain and Tall* by Patricia MacLachlan. Text and cover illustration copyright © 1985 by Patricia MacLachlan. Cover illustration by Ruth Sanderson from *The Facts and Fictions of Minna Pratt* by Patricia MacLachlan. Illustration © 1988 by Ruth Sanderson. From *Flower Moon Snow: A Book of Haiku* by Kazue Mizumura. Copyright © 1977 by Kazue Mizumura. Text and cover illustration from *Night of the Twisters* by Ivy Ruckman, cover illustration by Jim Spence. Text copyright © 1984 by Ivy Ruckman; cover illustration © 1984 by Jim Spence.

Holiday House: "My Horse, Fly Like a Bird" and illustrations from *Dancing Teepees: Poems of American Indian Youth*, selected by Virginia Driving Hawk Sneve, illustrated by Stephen Gammell. Text copyright © 1989 by Virginia Driving Hawk Sneve; illustrations copyright © 1989 by Stephen Gammell. Cover illustration from *Ferret In the Bedroom, Lizards In the Fridge* by Bill Wallace. Copyright © 1986 by Bill Wallace.

Houghton Mifflin Company: From *The Sign of the Beaver* by Elizabeth George Speare, cover illustration by Robert Andrew Parker. Text copyright © 1983 by Elizabeth George Speare; cover illustration copyright © by Robert Andrew Parker.

Richard Kennedy: "Oliver Hyde's Dishcloth Concert" from *Richard Kennedy: Collected Stories* by Richard Kennedy. Text copyright © 1987 by Richard Kennedy.

Alfred A. Knopf, Inc.: *Like Jake and Me* by Mavis Jukes, illustrated by Lloyd Bloom. Text copyright © 1984 by Mavis Jukes; illustrations copyright © 1984 by Lloyd Bloom. From *Flying Machine* by Andrew Nahum. Copyright © 1990 by Dorling Kindersley Limited, London. From pp. 61–72 in *The Kid in the Red Jacket* by Barbara Park, cover illustration by Rob Sauber. Text copyright © 1987 by Barbara Park; cover illustration copyright © 1987 by Rob Sauber.

Lerner Publications Company: Cover illustration from *Before the Wright Brothers* by Don Berliner. Copyright © 1990 by Lerner Publications Company.

Little, Brown and Company: Cover illustration by Ted Lewin from *Self-Portrait with Wings* by Susan Green. Copyright © 1989 by Susan Green.

Little, Brown and Company, in conjunction with Sierra Club Books: From *Tree of Life: The World of the African Baobab* by Barbara Bash. Copyright © 1989 by Barbara Bash. Cover illustration by Martha Weston from *The Sierra Club Book of Weatherwisdom* by Vicki McVey. Illustration copyright © 1991 by Martha Weston.

Lothrop, Lee & Shepard Books, a division of William Morrow & Company, Inc.: From *To Space & Back* by Sally Ride and Susan Okie. Text and cover photograph copyright © 1986 by Sally Ride and Susan Okie.

Macmillan Publishing Company: From *Sugaring Time* by Kathryn Lasky, photographs by Christopher G. Knight. Text copyright © 1983 by Kathryn Lasky; photographs copyright © 1983 by Christopher G. Knight. From *The House of Dies Drear* by Virginia Hamilton, cover illustration by Eros Keith. Text copyright © 1968 by Virginia Hamilton; illustration copyright © 1968 by Eros Keith.

McIntosh and Otis, Inc. and Union of American Hebrew Congregation: Cover illustration by Michael J. Deraney from *The Secret Grove* by Barbara Cohen. Illustration copyright © 1985 by Michael J. Deraney. Published by Union of American Hebrew Congregation.

Joseph T. Mendola Ltd., on behalf of Steve Brennan: Cover illustration by Steve Brennan from *A Gathering of Days* by Joan W. Blos. Illustration copyright © 1990 by Steve Brennan.

The Metropolitan Museum of Art: The trademark of The Metropolitan Museum of Art. The Renaissance M is a registered trademark of The Metropolitan Museum of Art.

Morrow Junior Books, a division of William Morrow & Company, Inc.: From *Storms* by Seymour Simon. Text copyright © 1989 by Seymour Simon. Cover photograph courtesy of the National Center for Atmospheric Research. Cover illustration by Paul O. Zelinsky from *Dear Mr. Henshaw* by Beverly Cleary. Copyright © 1983 by Beverly Cleary.

Philomel Books, a division of The Putnam & Grosset Group: Cover illustration by Mitsumasa Anno from *Anno's Hat Tricks* by Akihiro Nozaki. Illustration copyright © 1984 by Kuso-Kubo and Akihiro Nozaki.

Jerry Pinkney: Cover illustration by Jerry Pinkney from *Pride of Puerto Rico: The Life of Roberto Clemente* by Paul Robert Walker.

Poetry: "Kansas Boy" by Ruth Lechlitner. Text copyright 1931 by The Modern Poetry Association. Originally published in *Poetry*.

Marian Reiner: "Elizabeth Blackwell" from *Independent Voices* by Eve Merriam. Text copyright © 1968 by Eve Merriam.

Marian Reiner, on behalf of Myra Cohn Livingston: "Secrets" from *Space Songs* by Myra Cohn Livingston. Text copyright © 1988 by Myra Cohn Livingston.

Melodye Rosales: Cover illustration by Melodye Rosales from *Beetles, Lightly Toasted* by Phyllis Reynolds Naylor. Illustration copyright © 1987 by Melodye Rosales.

Scholastic Inc.: From *You Be the Jury* by Marvin Miller. Text copyright © 1987 by Marvin Miller.

Charles Scribner's Sons, an imprint of Macmillan Publishing Company: "Jackrabbit" from *Desert Voices* by Byrd Baylor, illustrated by Peter Parnall. Text copyright © 1981 by Byrd Baylor; illustrations copyright © 1981 by Peter Parnall.

Smithsonian Institution Press: "Sun, Moon, Stars" from *Twenty-seventh Annual Report of the Bureau of American Ethnology 1905–06*, Smithsonian Institution, 1911.

Rosemary A. Thurber: *Many Moons* by James Thurber. Text copyright 1943 by James Thurber; text copyright renewed 1970 by Rosemary Thurber.

Viking Penguin, a division of Penguin Books USA Inc.: From *A Long Way to Go* by Zibby Oneal. Text copyright © 1990 by Zibby Oneal.

Volcano Press, Inc.: Cover illustration by Bengt-Arne Runnerström from *Save My Rainforest* by Monica Zak, English version by Nancy Schimmel. Originally published in Sweden under the title *Rädda Min Djungel* by Bokförlaget Opal, 1989.

Neil Waldman: Cover illustration by Neil Waldman from *Hatchet* by Gary Paulsen. Illustration copyright © 1987 by Bradbury Press.

Walker Books Limited: Cover illustration by Iain McCaig from *Boat Girl* by Bernard Ashley. Illustration © 1990 by Iain McCaig.

Photograph Credits
KEY: (t) top, (b) bottom, (l) left, (r) right, (c) center.

UNIT 1
130–131, HBJ/Dan Peha

UNIT 3
338, Harry Landgon Photography/Office of March Fong Eu; 339, State Bar of Arizona; 339, used by permission, *Mel Bay's American History Songbook*, © 1992, Mel Bay Publications, Inc., Pacific, Missouri, all rights reserved

UNIT 4
422 (b), CBS; 422–423(t), TRW, Inc.; 423(c), HBJ Photo; 423(b), HBJ/Erik Arnesen

UNIT 5
424–425, 426–427, 429, 453, 455, 485, 487, 515, 516–517 (bkgrds.) Earth Scenes/© Francis Lepine; 516, The Goldman Environmental Foundation; 517, © Luiz C. Marigo/Peter Arnold, Inc.

UNIT 6
518–519, 520–521, 557, 577 (bkgrds.) *Atomic Particle Tracks in Bubble Chamber*/Fermilab Visual Media Services, Fermi National Accelerator Laboratory, Batavia, IL; 579, 599 (bkgrds.), 601(t), NASA; 601(b), Historical Pictures Service

Illustration Credits
KEY: (t) top, (b) bottom, (l) left, (r) right, (c) center.

Theme Opening Art
Janice Castiglione, 396–397; Vince Chiaramonte, 302–303, 556–557; Renee Daily, 240–241; Chris Ellison, 280–281, 486–487; Deborah Haeffele, 370–371; Jennifer Hewitson, 428–429; Gay Holland, 88–89; John Kane, 170–171, 578–579; Kristin Kest, 344–345; Ruben Ramos, 136–137; Roni Shepherd, 196–197; Andrea Tachiera, 454–455; Russell Thurston, 522–523; Cristina Ventoso, 56–57; Darryl L. Warfield, 20–21

Connections Art
Rondi Collette, 601(t); Renee Daily, 600–601(b); Mouli Marur, 422–423, 516–517(b); Steve Shock, 234–235, 338–339; Dean Williams, 130–131

Unit Opener and Bookshelf Border Art (4/c)
Tony Caldwell, 4–5, 16–17; Pat and Robin DeWitt, 426–427, 516–517(t); Mary Jones, 10–11, 340–341, 342–343

Selection Art
Barbara Bash, 488–499; Eric Beddows, 346–347; Lloyd Bloom, 348–359; Dick Calkins, 558–559; Harvey Chan, 74–86, 186–194; Lambert Davis, 324–336; David Diaz, 410–420; Katy Farmer, 360–368; Michael Garland, 22–37; Sheldon Greenberg, 288–300; Amy Hill, 38–51; Ronald Himmler, 164–168; Irmeli Holmberg, 90–125; Thomas Hudson, 58–73; Oleana Kassian, 430–447; Jay Leach, 582–597; Gary Lippencott, 260–278; Davy Liu, 128; Jack Malloy, 306–323; Kazue Mizumura, 372–373; Kate Mueller, 538–553; Alex Murowski, 502–514; Michelle Nidenoff, 260–261; Peter Parnall, 449–452; Jerry Pinkney, 138–140; Mark Reidy, 202–231; Marcia Sewall, 398–409; Marc Simont, 374–393; Jeffery Terreson, 150–163; Rick Tom, 242–256; Janet Wilson, 500–501